Sir John Henry Lefroy, John L. Smith, Nathaniel Boteler

The History of the Bermudaes or Summer Islands

Sir John Henry Lefroy, John L. Smith, Nathaniel Boteler

The History of the Bermudaes or Summer Islands

ISBN/EAN: 9783744732574

Printed in Europe, USA, Canada, Australia, Japan

Cover: Foto ©ninafisch / pixelio.de

More available books at **www.hansebooks.com**

THE

HISTORYE OF THE BERMUDAES

OR

SUMMER ISLANDS.

EDITED,

From a MS. in the Sloane Collection, British Museum,

BY

GENERAL SIR J. HENRY LEFROY, R.A.,

C.B., K.C.M.G., F.R.S., Etc.;

FORMERLY GOVERNOR OF THE BERMUDAS;
AUTHOR OF "MEMORIALS OF THE DISCOVERY AND EARLY SETTLEMENT OF THE
BERMUDAS OR SOMERS ISLANDS".

LONDON:
PRINTED FOR THE HAKLUYT SOCIETY.

MDCCCLXXXII.

The Hakluyt Society.

REPORT FOR 1882.

SINCE the last Report was submitted to the Members of the Hakluyt Society, the Council has been able to issue two volumes, which, with the three volumes now in the press, will meet the just demands of subscribers up to the end of the present year.

The following volumes were issued to members during the year 1881:—

THE VOYAGES OF WILLIAM BAFFIN, 1612-1622. Edited, with Notes and an Introduction, by Clements R. Markham, C.B., F.R.S.

THE NARRATIVE OF THE PORTUGUESE EMBASSY TO ABYSSINIA, BY FATHER FRANCISCO ALVAREZ. Translated and Edited by Lord Stanley of Alderley.

And the three following volumes are in the printer's hands:—

A HISTORY OF BERMUDA (MS. in the British Museum, *Sloane* 750). Edited by Lieut.-General Sir J. Henry Lefroy, K.C.M.G., C.B.

Voyages of John Huigen van Linschoten to the East Indies. Edited by Arthur Burnell, Esq., C.I.E., Ph.D.

Manuscript Diary of Richard Cock, Chief of the English Factory in Japan, 1615-1622. Edited by E. M. Thompson, Esq.

Besides the volumes actually in the press, four others have been undertaken by Editors.

It is satisfactory to find that the Society maintains the average number of its Members, and indeed shows a considerable increase in the last ten years. There are now 234.

The practical usefulness of the Society's volumes is always a source of gratification to Members, and special instances of their value have, on several occasions, been noticed in previous Reports. This year it has been brought under the notice of the Council that the volumes relating to South America have proved of very considerable assistance to Dr. Hayes of Boston, in the preparation of an exhaustive article on "The Alpaca and its Congeners", published in the *Bulletin* of the American Association of Wool Manufacturers for 1881.

The following three Members retire from the Council:—
  Admiral Sir Richard Collinson, K.C.B.;
  E. A. Bond, Esq.;
  Augustus W. Franks, Esq., F.R.S.;
and the following gentlemen are proposed for election:—
  Captain Lindesay Brine, R.N.;
  B. F. Stevens, Esq.;
  J. Wise, Esq., M.D.

Statement of the Accounts of the Society from June 1880 to Feb. 1882.

Dr.		£	s.	d.	Cr.		£	s.	d.
Balance at the Bankers, June 1880	...	729	1	11	Mr. Richards for Printing ...	...	584	11	0
Received by the Bankers from June 1880 to Feb. 1882	...	398	3	0	Transcription ...	...	35	5	2
					Typographic Etching Company		28	8	0
					Mr. Weller for Maps ...	...	42	9	0
					Cheque Book ...	...	0	2	6
							£690	15	8
					Balance at Bankers, March 1882		436	9	3
		£1127	4	11			£1127	4	11

COUNCIL

OF

THE HAKLUYT SOCIETY.

COLONEL H. YULE, C.B., PRESIDENT.
ADMIRAL C. R. DRINKWATER BETHUNE, C.B. } VICE-PRESIDENTS.
MAJOR-GENERAL SIR HENRY RAWLINSON, K.C.B. }
W. A. TYSSEN AMHERST, ESQ., M.P.
REV. DR. G. P. BADGER, D.C.L.
J. BARROW, ESQ., F.R.S.
WALTER DE GRAY BIRCH, ESQ., F.S.A.
CAPTAIN LINDESAY BRINE, R.N.
E. H. BUNBURY, ESQ.
THE EARL OF DUCIE, F.R.S.
CAPTAIN HANKEY, R.N.
GENERAL SIR J. HENRY LEFROY, C.B., K.C.M.G.
R. H. MAJOR, ESQ., F.S.A.
REAR-ADMIRAL MAYNE, C.B.
E. DELMAR MORGAN, ESQ.
ADMIRAL SIR ERASMUS OMMANNEY, C.B., F.R.S.
LORD ARTHUR RUSSELL, M.P.
THE LORD STANLEY, OF ALDERLEY.
B. F. STEVENS, ESQ.
EDWARD THOMAS, ESQ., F.R.S.
LIEUT.-GEN. SIR HENRY THUILLIER, C.S.I., F.R.S.
J. WISE, ESQ., M.D.

C. R. MARKHAM, ESQ., C.B., F.R.S., HONORARY SECRETARY.

DEDICATION.

TO THE

HON. JOHN HARVEY DARRELL, C.M.G.,

LONG THE ATTORNEY-GENERAL AND NOW AN EX-CHIEF JUSTICE OF THE BERMUDAS.

My dear Mr. Darrell,

I avail myself of a privilege of authorship not yet entirely obsolete, to dedicate this volume to you as pre-eminently the representative not only of the ancient English stock of our oldest Plantation, and the guardian of its best traditions, but also of all that it has produced of eminence and distinction in the present century. The hope that one whom I so highly respect would appreciate this further contribution to the history of his native country, has been no small inducement to me to undertake the task now brought to a conclusion.

With sincerest regard and esteem,

I am, yours,

J. H. LEFROY.

June 1, 1882.

ILLUSTRATIONS.

PORTRAIT OF CAPTAIN JOHN SMITH		*To face Title*
MAP OF BERMUDA, 1623		,, 1
PORTRAIT OF SIR GEORGE SOMMERS		,, 11
VIGNETTE OF SIR GEORGE SOMMERS' LOADSTONE		,, 305

INTRODUCTION.

THE volume, now for the first time printed, forms part of the Sloane MSS. in the British Museum, No. 750, and consists in the original of 363 pages of closely written foolscap, exclusive of some documents bound up with it, but written in a different hand. There is no Title-page or date, and no clue to its authorship from beginning to end, except what is supported by a very sparing introduction of the personal pronoun, and by an amount of internal evidence which leaves no doubt in the Editor's mind that we have here an unpublished work of Captain John Smith, the historian of Virginia—the individual of whom it has been said, with much justice, that "he has for nearly three centuries maintained the unparalleled honour of being the most distinguished member of the most numerous family (patronymically speaking) of all the tribes of men".[1] Well established as Smith's reputation is, however it rests rather on the intrinsic interest of the subjects on which he wrote, and the debt of gratitude we owe to him as the editor, compiler, and preserver of the narratives of other men, than on the quantity of his

[1] Allibone's *Dictionary of English Literature, etc.*, 1870, *s.v.* Smith, John.

own writings, any addition to which must be acceptable to his admirers. In effect, the present work needs no recommendation, for though the theatre of the events described was a small one, and the Bermudas have not, and could not possibly have, maintained the prominent place before the world which they occupied on their first plantation, the graphic style of his narrative, and the vivid picture he gives of the social conditions of life in his day, must always have attractions for those who delight to throw themselves into the past, and to contrast its habits, its ideas, and its aspirations, with what succeeding centuries have brought forth.

The MS. terminates abruptly with the trial of one Thomas Harriott of Southampton Tribe, at the Assizes of 1622, and the appointment of Mr. John Yates, to be Captain of Southampton Fort, and there is added, in a different hand, this important note.

"And here it was the will of God to take out of this world the writer of this Historye, hee intendinge a further progress, in it. But as I have heard from the last mentioned Gouernour's mouth,[1] the Companye of Adventurers in Englande, accordinge to theire wonted cavallinge manner with preceedinge Gouernours, played fast and loose with him as with the rest, and though hee stayed his full tyme at the Somers Islands, and tooke much care and paines, not only in the orderinge the strenthcninge of the chiefe forts, plantinge of necessaryes, and doeinge what possibly could be done in the Infancy of this plantation, butt alsoe in establishinge honest and convenient Lawes for the

---

[1] The "last mentioned Gouernour" is Captain Nathaniel Butler, appointed 1619, and superseded about November 1622. See my *Memorials of Bermuda*, i, p. 271.

INTRODUCTION.

good of the place, yett, he hath returned with very little profitt or thanks more from that ungrateful Company then those that were before him."

From the great prominence given to Captain Nathaniel Butler's sayings and doings in this History, and from a note at the end of a chapter in the Fifth Book of Smith's *History of Virginia*, " collected out of their Records by N. B., and the relations of Mr. Pollard and diuers others", it might be hastily concluded that Butler was the author of the work ; but the above extract clearly implies the contrary. He may have furnished Smith with the collections in question, or they may have been furnished by the Rev. Nathaniel Bernard, one of the first ministers, whose initials are the same; but Butler long survived Smith. He was Governor of (old) Providence Island,[2] 1638-1641, and appears to be the individual who was committed to Newgate by the Council of State for dispersing treasonable and scandalous books, in June 1649.[1]

He omitted to inform the writer of the note quoted, that although "he stayed his full time on the Island", perhaps, or within a few days of it, he quitted it very irregularly and contrary to his instructions, before the arrival of his successor, and being the nominee of the Court party, with which the commercial element of the Company was at feud, he fared as one or the other got the upper hand. In 1622, the commercial party, led by Sir Edwyn Sandys, was in the ascendant.

[1] *Cal. Dom. Papers*, 1649-50, p. 208.
[2] Sta. Catalina of some modern charts.

The baptismal register of Captain John Smith is preserved at Willoughby, Lincoln. "John, the son of George Smith, was baptized the sixth day of January 1579." That is to say, as we now compute, 6th January 1580. He died on 21st June 1631, aged about fifty-one years and a half, rather unexpectedly, being still actively engaged on literary labour. He had published in that year his *Advertisements; or, Pathway of Experience to erect a Plantation*[1], in which he refers to a *History of the Sea* on which he was engaged in terms rather implying a conscious failure of strength. "It is hard to conceive whether those inhumanes" (tyrants and persecutors) "exceed the beast of the forrest, the birds of the aire, the fishes of the sea, either in numbers, greatnesse, swiftnesse, fiercenesse or cruelty, whose actions and varieties, with such memorable observations as I have collected, you shall find with admiration in my *History of the Sea*, if God be pleased I live to finish it." His last Will, dated the same year, has been printed by Mr. Charles Deane, in the Proceedings of the Massachussetts Historical Society for 1867. We can scarcely suppose that the present unfinished work, expressly entitled a *History of Bermuda*, was any part of the intended *History of the Sea*, but there is no difficulty in the supposition that he had both works on hand.

[1] *Advertisements for the unexperienced Planters of* New England *or anywhere; or the Pathway of experience to erect a* Plantation, *with the yearely proceedings of this Country in Fishing and Planting since the yeare* 1614, *to the yeare* 1630, *and their present estate, etc.* By Captain John Smith, sometimes Governour of Virginia, and Admirall of New England. London, 1631. p. 26.

The fulness of detail, and the great prominence given to particulars which lost all their importance as soon as men's minds began to be absorbed in the great political and religious struggles of the reign of Charles I, preclude the idea that it was written much after 1631. The prominent place given in it to Butler marks his influence in the composition, but that personage left England in August or September 1619, and the writer was at home, and a member of the Virginia Company, when Sir Edwyn Sandys was Treasurer (1619-20), for, he says (p. 248) he was " noe less passionate than when I heard him, being Treasurour of the Virginia Company, for one only yeare, to tearme the whole Company uniuste".[1]

This is the fact as regards Smith, who returned from New England in 1617, and appears not to have left it again. He was certainly at home when the news arrived of the massacre of the settlers in Virginia, by the Indians, 27th March 1622, as he offered himself to the Council of Virginia to go out and avenge it. Butler, on the contrary, left England for the Somers Islands, as just observed, about August 1619, and cannot have returned before 1623, for he left Bermuda in October 1622 and went first to America.[2] But there is even stronger confirmation

[1] Sir Edwin Sandys was elected Governor, April 28th, 1619.

[2] " Much about this time arrived a small barke of Barnestable, which had been at the Summer Iles, and in her Captain Nathaniel Butler, who hauing beene Gouernor there three yeares, and his commission expired, he tooke the opportunity of this ship to see Virginia. At James Towne he was kindly entertained by Sir Francis Wyat, the Gouernor. After he had rested there fourteene

of Smith's authorship in the minute coincidences of this work with his account of Bermuda in Book V of his *Generall History of Virginia*, first published in 1624, which are so numerous as to show beyond a doubt that it was written subsequently to that publication, and based on the same materials, an amplification, in fact, of the same narrative, with such fuller particulars and occasional corrections as were likely to come into his hands. In Smith's lifetime no one could have done this but himself.

Smith never was in Bermuda, he derived all his information from his opportunities as a member of the Virginia Company, and from correspondence, or personal narratives of returned planters. This was his habitual way. And the following list of authorities he quotes, will show how extensive his documentary materials were.

A List of Authorities quoted by Captain JOHN SMITH, *in his "History of Virginia" (edit. 1626).* B *signifies a reference to Bermuda.*

	PAGE		PAGE
Abbott, Jeffrey . . .	83	Baker, Dan. . . .	223
Anonymous correspondent, 1614	117	Boothe, Serjeant . . Box, William . . .	121 108
Argall, Sam. . . .	125	Brierton, John, 1602 .	18
Bagnall, Anth. . . .	66	Cantrill, Will. . . .	121

daies, he fell vp with his ship to the river of Chickahamania, where meeting Captaine William Powell, ioyning together such forces as they had, to the number of eighty, they set upon the Chickahamanians, that fearefully fled, suffering the English to spoile all they had, not daring to resist them. Thus he returned to James Towne, where he staied a month, at Kecoughtan as much more, and so returned for England." He was at Kecoughtan in February 1623. *Generall History of Virginia*, Book iv, p. 159.

INTRODUCTION. vii

	PAGE		PAGE
Council of Virginia	109	Pots, Rich.	94
Dale, Sir T.	116	Powell, Nath.	66, 121
Davies, Jno.	95	Robinson, Edw.	202
Evens, Jno. (B)	174	Rolfe, J.	116, 125, 127
Fenton, R.	50	Rosier, James, 1605	20
G. P.	94	Russell, Walter	59
Gurganey, Edw.	121	Salterne, Rob., 1603	18
Hamor, Mr. Ralph	110, 116	Shelly, Henry, (B)	174
Harlow, Capt. Edw.	204	Simmons, W., D.D., W.S.	106
Harrington, Edw.	50	Smith, John	21, 39, 227, 244
Heriot, Thos., 1585	12	Sparkes, Thos. (B)	191
Iordan, Master[1] (B)	174	Studley, Thos. (the first Cape	
I.S.	50-248	Merchant in Virginia)	50, 54
Layne, Ralph	9	Tankard, W.,	94
La Ware, Lord, 1611	110	Todkill, Anas	54, 59, 66, 83
May, Henry, (B)	173	Whitbourne, Capt. Chas.	244
N. B. (B)	190	White, Jno., 1589	16
Momford, Thos.	59	Virginia Council, Letters	
Phittiplace, W.	83	of -	109, 139, 140
Pollard, Mr. (B)	190	Wyffin, Rich.	83, 96
Pory, John	141		

The initials *W.C.* written in pencil with a bracket, thus, "] W.C." occur nine or ten times in the MS.; they are those of the Author of the "Epistle Dedicatorie" to the *Discovery of the Barmvdas, now called the Sommer Ilands*, 1613, addressed to Sir Thomas Smith; which is identical in text with the *Discovery of the Barmudas otherwise called the Ile of Devils, etc.*, by Sil. Jourdan, 1610. He is supposed to have been Dr. William Crashaw, D.D. (Neill, p. 54) and there is nothing very improbable in the idea that the MS. may have been overlooked by him. On the other hand, they may be simply the notations of some forgotten copyist.

[1] Probably Sylvester Jourdan, page to Sir Thomas Gates.

Smith's literary success bore no proportion to his diligence. The Prospectus of his *History of Virginia* concludes with these words:

"These observations are all I have for the expense of a thousand pound, and the losse of eighteene yeeres of time, beside all the travels, dangers, miseries and incumberances for my countries good, I have endured *gratis*, and had I not discouered and liued in the most of these parts, I could not possibly have collected the substantiall trueth from such an infinite number of variable Relations that would make a volume of at least a thousand sheetes, and this is composed of less than eighty sheetes, besides the three Maps, which will stand me neere in an hundred pounds, which some I cannot dishursse, nor shall the Stationers have the coppy for nothing. Therefore I humbly entreat your Honour[1] either to adventure, or giue me what you please towards the impression, and I will be both accountable and thankfull; not doubting but that the Story will give you satisfaction, and stirre up a doubly new life in the adventurers, when they shall see plainely the causes of all those defailements and how they may be amended."[2]

Elsewhere he says: "Though I had divulged, to my great labour, cost, and losse, more than seven thousand bookes and maps, and moved the particular companies in London, as also noblemen, gentlemen and merchants, for a Plantation, all availed no more than to hew rocks with oister-shels, so fresh were the

---

[1] No individual: the patron canvassed.
[2] *See* Prospectus of "The *General History of Virginia, the Somer Iles, and New England*, with the names of the Adventurers, and the Adventures, from their first beginning 1584, to this present 1623, giving an Index or Table of contents." Broadsides, 1623-49, Library of Society of Antiquaries, pp. 4.

living abuses of *Virginia* and the Summer Iles in their memories."[1]

Posterity has, however, been more kind. I subjoin an eloquent tribute to his memory, borrowed from a source where we should perhaps have little expected to find it.

" The little book of Antoninus (Marcus Aurelius Antoninus, A.D. 121-180) has been the companion of some great men. Machiavelli's *Art of War*, and *Marcus Antoninus*, were the two books which were used, when he was a young man, by Captain John Smith, and he could not have found two writers better fitted to form the character of a soldier and a man. Smith is almost unknown and forgotten in England, his native country, but not in America, where he saved the young Colony of Virginia. He was great in his heroic mind and his deeds of arms, but still greater in the nobleness of his character. For a man's greatness lies not in wealth and station, as the vulgar believe, nor yet in his intellectual capacity, which is often associated with the meanest moral character, the most abject servility to those in high places, and arrogance to the poor and lowly : but a man's true greatness lies in the consciousness of an honest purpose in life, founded on a just estimate of himself and everything else, on frequent self-examination, and a steady obedience to the rule which he knows to be right, without troubling himself, as the Emperor says he should not, about what others may think or say, or whether they do, or do not do that which he thinks and says and does."[2]

Not less gratifying to Smith's admirers is the genuine appreciation of Alexis de Tocqueville, himself pre-eminently qualified to value the breadth of

[1] Smith, *Advertisements, etc.*, sub 1618-19-20.
[2] *The Thoughts of the Emperor Marcus Aurelius Antoninus*, translated by George Long, M.A., 1875. Bohn.

view, the large prescience, and the manliness of tone, which characterize his writings, and atone for his unpolished style.

"Le premier de tous les historiens de la Virginie est son fondateur, le Capitaine Jean Smith. Le Capitaine Smith nous a laissé un volume in 4º intitulé : *The general History of Virginia and New England, by Captain John Smith, sometime Governor in those countryes and Admiral of New England*, imprimé à Londres en 1627. (Ce volume se trouve à la Bibliothèque royale). L'ouvrage de Smith est orné de cartes et de gravures très curieuses, qui datent du temps où il a été imprimé. Le récit de l'historien s'étend depuis l'année 1584 jusqu'en 1626. Le livre de Smith est estimé et mérite de l'être. L'auteur est un des plus célèbres aventuriers qui aient paru dans le siècle plein d'aventures à la fin duquel il a vécu : le livre lui-même respire cette ardeur de découvertes, cet esprit d'entreprise qui caracterisaient les hommes d'alors ; on y retrouve ces moeurs chevaleresques qu'on mêlait au négoce, et qu'on faisait servir à l'acquisition des richesses.

"Mais ce qui est surtout remarquable dans le Capitaine Smith, c'est qu'il mêle aux vertus de ses contemporains des qualités qui sont restées étrangères à la plupart d'entre eux; son style est simple et net, ses récits ont tous le cachet de la vérité, ses descriptions ne sont point ornées.

"Cet auteur jette sur l'état des Indiens à l'époque de la découverte de l'Amérique du Nord des lumières précieuses."[1]

I have retained the orthography of the original, which is sometimes sufficiently quaint, partly for convenience of comparison with those parts of Smith's *History of Virginia* which, he expressly tells us were "writ with his owne hand," chiefly Books II and VI.

[1] *De la Démocratie en Amérique ; par A. de Tocqueville*, Paris, 1864. Tome i, p. 298. (note F.)

The resemblance in the spelling perhaps does not go for much, but it will be apparent at once on turning to that work. The resemblance in the tone, when he is referring to the factions that divided the Virginia Company, and marred their great enterprise, to the greed and shortsightedness of the trading element, and to the aspirations of the Colonists for a larger measure of self-government, is even more striking, and very characteristic of the bold adventurer, and valiant soldier, whose name I venture, with considerable confidence, to connect with this volume.

I have abstained from many references to my previous work, the *Memorials of Bermuda*; but may remark generally that the present History, while travelling over much of the same ground, as far as it goes, supplies some defects of that work, especially as to the Assizes of 1621-1622.[1]

I am greatly indebted to Miss Bellamy of Plymouth, for permission to engrave for this volume an original and unpublished portrait of Admiral Sir George Sommers, which she has inherited from her ancestor, Dr. Bellamy, M.D., who was connected with the Sommers family.[2] The darkened condition of the picture made it impossible to obtain a photograph, but a faithful copy has been produced by an

---

[1] *Memorials of the Discovery and Early Settlement of the Bermudas or Somers Islands*, 1515-1685. 2 vols. Longmans, 1877-79.

[2] The name is spelt by Smith, in his *History of Virginia*, generally 'Somers', sometimes 'Summers', in this work 'Sommers'. In the parish register of Lyme Regis, and in *Strachy's Narrative*, generally, 'Summers.' The modern official form is 'Somers.'

excellent amateur artist, Lieut.-Colonel B. A. Branfil, late 86th Regiment, whom I have to thank for taking much trouble to do justice, in this likeness, to one of England's greatest naval worthies.

J. H. LEFROY.

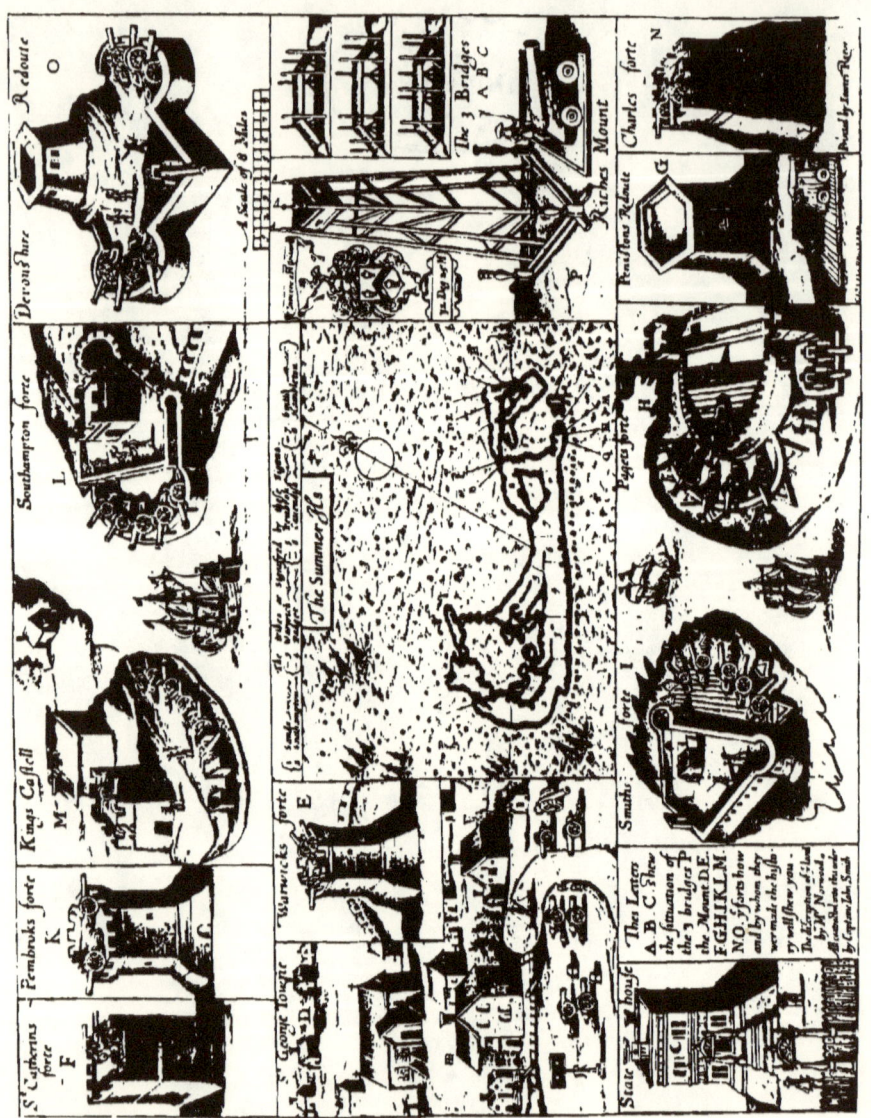

THE HISTORYE OF THE BERMUDAES OR SUMMER ISLANDS.

Lib. I.—a.d. 1609.

Before we present you with the relation of matters of fact, it is fitt to offer to your vewe the stage wheron they wer acted. For (it is well sayd) as geography without historye seemeth a carkasse without motion, so history without geography wandreth as a vagrant without certaine habitation.[1]

The ilands of the Bermudaes, therfore, lieing in a huge maine ocean, and two hundred leauges from any continent, not farr from the mouth of the bay of Mexico, are situated in 32 degrees and 25 minutes of northerlye latitude, and are distant from England to the west south-west 3300 miles or there abouts, being in an equall eleuation with that of the Holy Land, and in perticuler very nere with the very citty of Jerusalem, which is a clime of ye sweetest and most pleasinge temper of all others, especially when the naturall heates are somewhat moderated by accidents of coolenesse, as here is by an open and maine ocean.[2] They consist of diuers small broken ilands severed one from another by narrowe breaches and inletts of sea, wherby are made many necessary sandy bayes for the anchorage of botes; two commodious and large soundes for the vse of fishinge, and two

---

[1] *Verbatim* from the beginning of the Fifth Book of the *Generall Historie of Virginia, New England, and the Summer Islands*, 1624, p. 169.

[2] This comparison with the Holy Land is an afterthought, not found in the *History of Virginia*.

excellent harbours. Lieing thus together they become in forme not much vnlike a reaper's sickle, being in their whole longitude from east to west not aboue twentye miles English; in the latitude (wher most extended) not fully two and a halfe; the surface and outwarde posture of the whole lieing altogether vneuen, and distributed into smale hills and dales. As for the soyle, the inner-most part of it is of two sortes, either a whitish soft rock, not much different from our English marle, or a craggie hard rock whereof lime is made, the vppermost a light sandy mould, of coulour in some places whitish, in some redd, and in others brown, the which by a naturall production affords great varietye of symples; many tall and goodly cœders, infinite store of palmitoes, numbers of mulberrie trees, wild oliues, very many, with diuers others of unknowen both name and vertue, wherby (as yet) they become not only namelesse, but lost to many vsefull employments, which time and industry noe doubte will one day discouer; and already certaine of them, since the comeinge in of the newe guests, haue gotten them appellations from their apparent effects, as the prittle peare, the which growes like a shrub by the ground, with broad thick leaves, all ouer armed, with long and sharpe dangerous thornes, the fruict being in forme not much vnlike a smale peare, greene on the onside, but inwardly reddish and full of juice, with grains not much vulike a pomegranate; as likewise the poysonous weed, being in shape but little different from our English yuie; but being touched causeth reddnesse, itchinge, and lastly blysters, the which, howsoever, after a while they passe away of themselues without further harme; yet because for the time they are somewhat painefull, and in aspect dangerous, it hath gotten to itselfe an ill name, although questionlesse of noe very ill nature.[1]

[1] The plant referred to is *Rhus toxicodendron*, still commonly called the poison ivy.

Now, besides thes naturall productions of the earth, prouidence and paines haue since the plantation offred diuers other seedes and plants which the soyle hath greedily embrased and cherished. Hence, at the present, are their a great aboundance of figge-trees, numbers of plantans, plenty of pome-granates, many vines, orange and lemon trees, wild olives, very many and great store of mulberrie trees, goodly tobacco, and store of corne (I mean Indian corne, for the Christian proues not as yet had, by ouer vnkindnesse of the ground runnes all to grasse), besides many other proffitable rootes, as an infinite quantitie of white, redd, and orange-couloured potatoes, sugar canes, indicoe, per-snipps, exceedeinge great radishes, the Americane bread-roote, cassuda, the Indian pompion, water-melons, musk-melons, and the delicate pine-apple: briefly, whatsoever els may (in this kind) be expected for the satisfaction either of necessitye or delight.

Neither hath the ayre for her part bin wantinge, with due supplies of many sortes of foules; as the graye and greene plouer; some ducks, and mallards, red-pshancks, sea-wigeons, graye bitturnes, cormorants, the white and graye herne, great store of sparrowes and robins (which haue lately bin destroyed by the catts), woodpeckers, very many crowes (who for a while overboldly wonderinge at the newe sight of men) many of them findinge the cost of their curiositie, the rest are now flowne away, and seldome seene, only some few are sometimes found in the most solitary partes, from whence, notwithstandinge they are generally obṣerued to take their flight to se, about the sunnes settinge, allwayes directinge their course to the north-west; whence many (not improbably) conjecture that some vnknowen iland lieth out that waye; nott farr of here are also, sometimes of the yeare, faulcons, and farfalcons, osprayes, and a smale kind of hawke, in shape and plume like a sparrow-hawke, but larger winged, and hoofers for her praye, like a cay-

strell, but thes being but seldome found, are (iustly) thought
to be only passengers. But aboue all thes, most deseruinge
obseruation and respect are thoes two sortes of birdes, the
one (from the tune of his voice), the other (from the effect),
called the cahowe[1] and egge-bird;[2] of the which thes last,
arriueinge with the first of the spring, vpon the first of
May, a day constantly kept, falls a layeinge infinite store
of egges, vpon certaine smale sandy ilands reserued for
them; and so continue all that monethe, being all the while
so tame and fearelesse that they suffer themselues, with
much adoe, to be thrust of their egges, the which, notwithstandinge they laye and sitt vpon promiscuously: so that
many thousandes of egges (being as bigge as hen's egges)
are yearely eaten, and many more would be, but that by
stricte inhibition, they are preserved. For the cahowe (for
so soundes his voice), it is a night bird, and all the daye
long lies hidd in holes of the rocks, whence both themselues
and their young are in great numbers extracted with ease,
and proue (especially the young) so pleaseinge in a dish, as
ashamed I am to tell, how many dosen of them haue bin
deuoured by some one of our northern stomacks, euen at
one only meale. Some few other kindes of foule ther are
also, which are unknowen in our partes; as the tropick
birde, which is as large as a pullett, in coulour white, with
one only very long feather in the tayle, and hath its name
(as I think) by reason it is neuer seene, either to the northward or southward, far distant from one of the two tropicks.
Another smale birde ther is, the which, by some ale-hanters
of London sent ouer hether, hath bin termed the pimplicoe,[3] for so they imagine (and a little resemblance putts
them in mind of a place so dearely beloued), her note
articulates; and this also, for the most part, is a bird of the

---

[1] Cahow. *Puffinus obscurus*, dusky shearwater.
[2] Egg-bird; probably a tern.
[3] *Pimplicoe*. Pimlico, a well-known place of resort near Hogsden,

night, and whensoeuer she sings is too true a prophett of
black and foule weather. And thes are the natiues of the
ayre; to which haue bin added, by the late inhabitants,
great store of turkeys, and aboundance of cocks and hens,
which euery daye growe wilde; numbers of tame chicks,
and some fewe geese and house-pigeons; but thes last two
like not so well, for by some disagreeinge foode they kill
themselues. As for the beasts of the field—cowes and
bulls, ther are which prosper exceedingly; hogges (wherof
some fewe wilde) in great numbers; Indian and English
goates likewise, but of noe great hope, for (like the pigeons)
they also are found dead and dieinge in euery corner; and,
lastly, there are a late great increase of tame conyes, the
which, being reserued in certaine empaled places about the
houses, are ther fedd with the potatoe slipps, and other
simples natiue of the place, the which they eate very
greedely; they fare well withall.[1] Concerning vermin, and
noysome creatures, many ther are not, only ratts and catts
(and you will think it strange thes two should stand to-

famous for cakes and ale; probably named from its first pro-
prietor.
         Lorewit. " Gallants, men and women
And of all sorts, tag-rag, been seen to flock here
In threaves, these ten weeks, as to a second Hogsden
In days of *Pimlico* and Eye bright."
                               The Alchemist, 1610, Act v, sc. i.
Sir Lionel. " I have sent my daughter this morning as far
          As *Pimlico*, to fetch a draught of Derby ale, that it
          May fetch a colour in her cheeks."
                                   Tu Quoque, 1614.
    A place of entertainment of the same description near Chelsea bor-
rowed the name, and bequeathed it to the district.
    Captain Savile Reid, R.E., conjectures the bird to have been the
Virginian Partridge, *Ortyx Virginiana*, the male of which has a
peculiar call.
    [1] This great increase of conies is of date subsequent to 1624, perhaps
attested by the name Coney Island. Rabbits are kept now, but not in
numbers to affect the bill of fare.

gether) are too common; the moscitoes and flies also are
somewhat over busie, with a certain Indian bugge called,
by a Spanish appellation, a caca-roche,[1] the which, creepeinge
into chestes and boxes, eate and defile with their dung (and
thence their Spanish name) all they meet with; as doe likewise the litle aunt, which are in the summer time in infinite
numbers; wormes in the earth, and mould also, ther are
but too many (but of them we shall saye somewhat more
by and by), as likewise the grass-hopper, and a certaine
sommer-singinge great flie, the sure token of the established springe (and in that respect as the English night-
ingale and cukoe), whose loud note very much resemblinge
the whirle of a spindle, hath caused herselfe thereby to be
called the good-huswife.[2] For venemous creatures ther are
none at all knowen; the serpent, snake, adder, toade, nor
any of those kindes wer euer seene there; certaine spiders,
indeed, of a very large size, are found hangeinge vpon the
trees; but insteade of beinge dangerous, or any way
harmefull (as in other places), they are here of a most
pleasinge and beautifull aspect, all over, as it were, deckt
with siluer, gold, and perle; and their webbs (woven in
the sommer vpon trees) are found to be perfect silck, and
that as well in respect of substance as coulour, and so
stronge they are generally, that birds bigger, and by much
stronger than sparrowes, are often taken and snarled in
them as in netts.

But aboue all the rest of the elements the sea is found
most aboundantly liberall to thes islands; hence haue they
as much excellent fish and of a much varietye most easily
taken as any place in the world; the most of which being
vnknowen to our more northerly partes, haue lately gotten
them names, either from their shapes or conditions, as the

[1] Evidently the origin of Cockroach, which is not from Cock, *pace*
Mr. Stormonth.
[2] *Fidicina tibicen*, now called *Scissors-grinder*.

large rock fish, from his like hewe, and hauntinge amoung the rockes; the fatte hogge fish, from his swine-like shape and snoute (for this is not the old knowen hogge fishe with prickles on his back); the delicate amber fish, from his tast and smell; angell fish; cony fish, the smale yellowe taylo, from that naturall paintcinge; the great grouper, from his odde and strange gruntinge; with many other kindes, some of them knowen to the Americans only, as the porguise, the cavallo, the garrfish; the rest in common to them with other continents, as they are in parallel with them, as the whale, the sharke, the pilote fish, the sea-breame, the oyster, the lobster; and, for the amphybians, the tortoise, with diuers other tedeous to reherse.[1] And thus haue you briefly epitomized mother natures beneficence towards this spott of earth. Neither wer it ingenuitie in me to conceale the perticulers wherin she shewes herselfe inclinable to the step dame, especially since they are so fewe and gentle as may, indeed, rather seeme fitte and necessarye antidotes to proserue against idlenesse and for the quickenning of industry, than any true cause of great trouble, much lesse dispayere, and of thes ther are only two, the windes and the wormes (for as for their not haueinge streames of fresh water, the streightnesse of the place and the situation therof, can in no possibilitie allowe it), and yet are they in most places very sufficiently supplied with wells, not aboue a fadome deepe, whereinto through the sandy redd soyle the sea-water being vented, and, as it wer, strayned through leauinge its saltnesse behinde, becomes very fresh, sauorye, and holsome.[2] For the windes, for two moneths space in the autume, and as many in the spring, they blowe with extraordinary boystrousnesse, and therby do greatly offend

[1] *Verbatim* from the *Generall Historie*, from " But above all . . . . ."
[2] This is not an unnatural mistake of the writers. The fact is correctly stated, the explanation is that rain water percolated through the soil rests on the surface of the sea water.

the houses on the land, the ships in the harbours, and oft times blast the winter crops of corne (for the ilands haue two haruests yearely), tearinge the tobacco and other plants. The wormes (which many times, especially vpon frequent easterne gales, are found in wonderous number) do sodenly douore both corne, tobacco, and almost euery greene thinge. And thus conditioned rest thes small ilands, in the midst of a huge maine ocean, whose violence is borne of and broken in their north east side by infinite numbers of vncertaine rocks being shallowely hidd for three leagues out at sea. As to the southwarde of them is found a continued ledge of the same mettall within halfe league of the shore, serueinge to the same purpose on that side, the which betwixt them (leauinge noe open approach to any part of the shore which vessels of any burthen, saue onely through thoes two channells which gently and peaceably conueye the benefitt of the sea through the straight and narrowe mouthes of the two harbours into the large bosome of the firme and rocky earth) proue therby so terrible and sure a fortification against all inuasiue attempts that waye, as by haueinge some art added vnto them at the harbours mouthes since the plantation, they cause the whole peece to become as fully impregnable, and as easily to be defended against any ennemye as (I think) any one in that nature of Christiandome. As for the health and generall salubritye of the place, I doubt not to affirme but that ther is not a part of the world that can excell it, fewe equall it. I deny not but that at the first entrance of newe commers most of them for a while are troubled with a gentle flux, and some ther are that neuer recouer it, but (by its groweinge into extremitye) purge out their lives with all; but this generally worcks thus only vpon such diseased bodyes as consist only of corruption, wherby it seemes that the qualotye of the ayre is either to cure or kill quickly. For the serenitie, it may as truely be sayd of these ilands as euer it was of the Rhoodes,[1] that ther is noe one day through-out the yeare but that in some houre therof the sunne lookes clearely and smilingly out vpon them; stinckinge and infectioues micts are neuer seen, nor the coffe and reumatic unknowen. For their temperature, it is admirable, noe colde ther is beyonde an English Aprill, nor heate much greater than a hott July in France. And thus haveing presented you with the furniture and trimme of this little theatre, not poetically and in fiction, but in truth and realitye, we will nowe proceede to the narration of such representations as have bin acted vpon it since the discouery and plantation.

It was not long after Columbus his fatall discovery of America and particularly of the West-Indies, but that the Spaniards, who had as luckely embrased this offer, as the Portugalls, and our Henry the 7th, improvidently neglected it, in their voiages to and againe from thes partes, fell within the sight, and some of them (to their cost) vpon the rocks and sholes of thes shores : which the first, a Spanish shipp called La Bermuda, wrecked vpon them and by the losse of her selfe, bequeathed her name to the (vntill then) namelesse Ilands:[2] whether her people saved themselves by

[1] I am indebted to Mr. E. H. Bunbury, the learned author of the *History of Ancient Geography*, for tracing this allusion :—
"Nunquam ita cœlum nubilum est, ut in sole Rhodos non sit."—*Solinus*, c. xi, § 31.
"Nullus unquam dies tam magna turbulentaque tempestate fuerit, quin aliquo tempore ejus diei solem homines viderent."—Cicero, *Orat. in Verrem*, v. c, 10.
Cicero is referring to Syracuse, but the same was evidently said of both places; Solinus merely paraphasing it. Rhodes was dedicated to the Helios, "the Spotless God", from remote antiquity. See Pindar, *Olyp.*, vii, 54. Translated by T. C. Baring, M.A., M.P., 1875.

[2] Smith (or the writer) here repeats the common English belief of his day; on the other hand, it is much more probable that Herrera, whose *Historia General*, published in Spanish in 1601, is not likely to have

their botes and recovered the shore, and so afterwards shypped themselves for the Continent in some small pinnaces raysed out of her ruines; or whether they perrished in the sea, or died vpon the land, I have not heard: but by all probabilitie as she was one of the first discoverers, so from out of her thoes hoggs were first delivered up thither, which since have multiplied into good encrease. Howsoever, most apparently it is, that either then or since, these ilands have bin for some time trode upon by that nation; witnesse certaine crosses left erected vpon rocks and promontories. Some .pecces of their coyne found scattred vnder trees, and the like signs of their being here. Vpon which grounds, ioyned with some intelligences (as they saye) out of Spayne it selfe, a report hath bin raysed of a great treasure, that should be hidd ther abouts, which hath caused divers greedy searches; which all of them hitherto have proved vaine and effect-lesse. And truely this place hath alwayes bin very adverse to the approaches of the Spainards, whence it is in an anger by them styled the Ilande of Devills, and by ther marriners therfore to this daye shunned and avoyded as much or more than their Vtopian purgatory.

Besides thes, I find also that one Henry Maye, an Englishman, was ill welcomed hether by the roks (by reason it may be that he came in a French bottome which wracked vpon them) but he himselfe and most of his company wer spared; and so scaped home, to tell the tydeinges both of his owne fortune and the fortune of the place. And thus farr of such pilgrims, who in their peregrinations,

been known to him, would be correctly informed. Herrera says, " This island was called Bermuda, or La Garza, because the captain who discovered it was called Juan Bermudez, and his vessel La Garza" (*Herrera*, Dec. iv, lib. ii, cap. vi). I have shown in my *Memorials of Bermuda* that this must have been earlier than 1511, and therefore before the visit of Oievdo in 1515. Herrera had access to Spanish records, which until the treasures of Simancas are catalogued, must remain unknown to us.

SIR GEORGE SOMERS

from the original Picture in possession of Miss Bellamy.

being cast upon this mayden earth, fled from her embraces, and with all the speed they could retired themselves. Hereafter we treate of thoes who by the like accidents, comeing to have a sight and knowledge of her perfections, have accepted the offer, and taken her to wife (as it wer) by a willinge and ioyfull residence. And this was in the yeare 1609, when the Virginian Company at London perceiveinge that by the slack and lame supplyes of former times (which alwayes came droopeingly on) that plantation went rather backwards than forwards (being a worck, to speake truth, which to bring it to perfection requires the power and purse of a monarch) resolved to fall somewhat more lively and substantially to the bussinesse; they therefore rigged and set out for that voiage eight sayle of shipps, whose cheife commandours wer, Sir Thomas Gates, for the land-service; Sir George Sommers and Captaine Newport for the sea. This fleete puttinge out from England, kept fayrely together from the 15th of May vntil the 23rd of July, when (being gotten up much about the heighte of the Açores or Westerne Ilands) ther sodenly arose so terrible and strong a tempest of wind and weather as forced them to a dispersion and every one to shift for themselves. In which storme the Admirall, called the Seaventure, wherein most of the commandours were, being a shipp of three hundred tunnes, lost sight of the rest, and by the violence and extremitye of the weather was carryed farr to the south-ward, at what time springinge a leake and so maine a one as that she had nine foote depth of water in her hold, she became everye houre ready to founder in the sea, all her men being vtterly spent with want of rest, and continuall bayleinge and pumpeinge. Being in this hard plight and almost come to vtter dispayre, Sir George Sommers who satt bound vpon the halfe deck condeinge the shipp[1] to her most ease from the

[1] *Sic* in MS. Qy. conning? In the *History*, etc., it is " couing the ship".

blowes of the billowe, vnexpectedly discouers and cryes out
Land: this sodaine welcome news hurryeth all men aboue
hatches to looke out and see, what they could scarce belieue,
so that improuidently forsakeinge that taske which imported
them noe lesse than their liues, they gaue such aduantage to
their greedy enemye, the salt water, which mainely entred
at the large breach of their wooden castle, as that in gapeinge
after life, they had well nigh swallowed their death: but
being vrged and brought back againe to their former defence, by the better settled discretion of their commaundours,
they thereby kept themselves aboue water with very much
adoe, the crazeie shyp being the whilst hastned to her full
speed by the spreadinge of all her canuas before a fresh and
lusty gale of wind, and thus drew they nere the shore, to
the great comfort of the ignorant passengers; but with the
skillfull and understandinge marrinour (who by this time
was come to a perfect knowledge of the place and the dangers of it), restinge as much horror and dispayre as euer
before; yet findinge noe better euasion and resoluinge to
see a quick end, they determined if it was possible to thrust
in the shipp upon a smale sandy bay, which lay fayrest to
their eye, but before they came nere it by three leagues,
they struck upon a rock the which they rubbed over, and
then presently vpon another, from whence also (expectinge
from euery blowe a death), they wer violently carried betwixt two rocks and ther stuck fast. The shyp being thus
luckely lodged, and licing upright as if she had bin on the
stocks, behold sodenly the wind giues waye to a calme, and
the billowes, which els by ouer-rakeing of her would haue
shivered her in peeces, becomes peaceable and quiet, so that
with great conueniencye and ease they unshypped all their
goods, victualls, and persons into their botes, and with extreame ioye, almost to amazednesse, arrived all of them in
safetye on the shore, without losse of anythinge, saue the
shyp only.

Being thus gotten on drye-land, with their furnitvre and prouision, euery man presently begins to playe a seuerall part, for the good of the whole: some looked out for fish which euen offered themselues to their hands: others to catch birdes and foules, who likewise with their multitudes and tamenesse wearied the catcher with being caught; the rest contriued cabbins to keepe themselues from weather, which was a taske as easily performed as the other by reason of the store of palmitoe leaues, most proper for that turne, and the nerenesse of woode. The whilst the wisest and most prouident among them bestowed a curious search for fresh water, the which also, haueing digged but a smale depth into the bowells of the earth, at the very first essaye, flowed out upon them, to good satisfaction. And thus rested they the first night, dureing the which wer first found (by such whose turnes fell out to watch whilst others slept) the wilde natiue hoggs of the Ilands; who sentinge thes newe commers, and especially some tame liue swine, that they had preserved and landed with them, came presently to see in the darck what newes they had brought with them, by which meanes, the next daye, an eager chase began for the takeing of thes wild game, and therby many of them killed and many more discouvered: so that by reason of the pleasure of the place, and their present ease and plenty the most of the company began to growe into such a content and carelessnesse, that not only they seemed to forgett all former perills, but even to neglect the cares due to a future returne and remoue; only the commandours and some fewe of the chiefe, that discerned the danger on the one side and the losse of reputation on the other, meditated upon it; and therefore contriueinge their shyp-bote into the form of a pinnace, with a deck, a good mast and sayle, some compases, and very well victualled; certaine to the number of fourteen of their most resolute men, aduentured to make a voiage of aduisse to Virginia, and so from thence to bring a shyp, for the conveycinge of them thether. But of this, neither bote nor men wer euer heard of.

After ten monethes abode and expectance of them, therefore, by the rest of the company, in the newe discouered ilands, the commandours toke a resolution to make that good of themselues which they dispayred to find from others: and so being furnished by the ilands, they framed two smale pinnaces of ceedar, which, being finished, and aboundantly supplied with poudered porck, liue turtles, salted birdes, and fish, which the place afforded them of her owne natures, they at last, all of them, shypped themselues for Virginia: only two of the company (seeming to be in loue with the ease and pleasure of the place) hideinge themselues in the woodes vpon the time of departure, and by noe means to be found (as it wer to keepe possession of the place for the rest that wer afterwarde to come), wer left behinde: their names wer Christopher Carter, and Robert Walters: but, how-soeuer, this was the publicke apprehension of their staye: the secret was, that the sea and land-commandours, being alienated one from another (a qualetye ouer common to the English), and falne into jealousies), ther was produced, not only a separation of the company (even in this extremitie, euen in this streight place), but an affection of disgraceinge one another, and crossinge their designes, so that thes two men, cleauing notoriously to Sir Geo. Sommers his side, and improuidently haueing slipt in some actions that gaue aduantages against themselues to the other parties, they were eagerly sought out to receiue sharpe rewardes; neither could Sir George otherwise preuent it, than by giueing them this direction of stayeinge secretly behind, makeing them a faithfull promise that he would speedily returne to their releife, the which (as you shall see hereafter) he sone made good vnto them: an accident questionlesse, not without any especiall hand from Heauen; yt so in the interim, the place and the worth of it might the better be discerned, and a returne nourished. It was not long before thes two pinnaces thus fraughted arrived safely in Virginia, wher they found the colony in much distresse of victuall; so that the ouer-plus of their sommer ilands store relieued many, and saued some liues.

But Sir George Sommers meditating a returne into thes ilands, as well by reason of his promise to thoes two left behind, as vpon an affection he carryed to the place it selfe, under a pretence of fetchinge newe releife from thence for the languishinge Virginia colony, in a short time made a seconde voiage thether, wher he found his two friends both aliue and lustye, and from them receiued farther light of the commodities of the soyle, the which, ioyned with his first inclination, so inflamed him as it is well knowen (and wittnesse that part of Sands his Tribe, called by him Sommers-seate[1]), that he resolued vpon a plantation, though it wer but by the purse and meanes of himselfe and his freinds. When labouringe in thes desires, it pleased God to ease him of them, and all others, by takeing him out of this world to his mercye; and dieing upon the iland of St. George's, and at that very place wher the cheife towne and residence of the gouernours is since erected and established, his heart and bowels wer ther buried, a great crosse of wood being pitched ouer his graue, which remained ther vntil, about eight yeares after, Captain Butler being chosen and sent ouer gouernour of the ilands, comeing to the knowledge and sight of it, and mislikeinge the smale respect showed to the memory of soe true and noble a deseruour, of his own cost caused a smale monumental tombe to be framed ouer it, the fabrick whereof rather expressed his present meanes, and the meanes of the place, then either the deceased's deserts, or his owne desires.

[1] Now Somerset.

As for the rest of his corps, it was carried into England secretly putt vp into a ceder chest, and so putt abord the shyp, for otherwise it had not bin possible to haue wonne the superstitious marriners to the receipt of it within bord, who (as all knowe) hold the portage of dead bodyes extreamely, prodigiously, omminous.

Sir George Sommers thus dieing, howsoeuer his last charge to the captaine of the shyp, and some other of the cheife was to returne into Virginia with their relieue, yet the greatest part, which is generally the vnworthy, feareinge to be stayed ther, and (as noe where contented) longing to be at home againe, forced the rest (who, perhaps, were not so thoroughly resolued as became them) to shape their course for England; so that once again thes ilands had bin left desolate, had it not bin for one of those two formerly left behind, named Christopher Carter (who, for the fact only deserues to be personally mentioned), who being verely perswaded that Sir George Sommers had taken some order with his friends in England, and had made some preparations for a plantation, he would by noe meanes be induced to a returne with the rest, but vowed a longer staye, although it wer by himselfe alone, the which vnvsuall resolution moued them all, but especially it wrought vpon the humours of two (one of which had bin Sir George's seruant), so that at last they offered themselues to be the compagnions of his fortunes, the which, being tollerated by the rest, and accepted of by him: the ship departes, and leaues thes three behind.

Not long it was before the home-minded company had their wished desire by a safe footeing in England (for the westerne voiages, howsoeuer they are generally long and tedious outward, yet, for the most part, in the returne are fauorable and quick), noe soner are they ther, but euery man tells abroad, and euery wher rumours his trauailes and aduentures; and as trauailours wer they heard and not belieued, only some of the most temperate and discreet (vnderstandeinge the benefit of the place, and weighinge the importancye), wisely made choice of more charitable cares to powre their intelligences into, so that therby diners of eminencye and ranck (especially of the Virginian Company, who rightly apprehended the aydefull vicinitie of the place to that colony of thers), began not only to hearken to the reportes, but at last to propound a course of experiment, and so resolued vpon a generall purse (which could not be much senceable of it) to send ouer thether for the discouery some voluntary men, who wer to be entised with hope of gaine; and to be conducted by some such commandour, as was fittest for the present, and as would serue them vpon generall tearmes and hopes. After two yeares' consultation, therefore, they rigged up a smale shyp called the *Plough*, and manuing her with about fiftie passengers of all sortes, they made choice of one Mr. Moore (by his trade a carpenter, but an excelliuge master of his art), to be their commandour; a man certainly who, had he but bin educated answerably to the capacitye of his mind and speritt, would haue expressed himselfe very worthely, since, when clogged with the impediments of an vnrulye company, and want of authoritye to beare him out (for as yet the king's letters patents wer not procured for the enableinge of their commission) he hath, notwithstandinge, left behind him in thoes partes many testimonyes, both of his sufficiencye and honesty. But, for a while, we will leaue him and his company at sea, to see how our triumviri left in the Sommer Ilands bestowed themselues in the mean time, dureing their solitary abode ther.

The shyp that brought them in, being thus out of the harbour and past ken: thes three (for the time the only lordes of the ilands) began their common wealth for a

while with equall and brotherly regencye: and first of all
they fell to clearing of some ground, plantinge of corne
and settinge of pompions, as their groundworck; next for
connenicncye, they began to cutt downe timber, saweing
of bordes and plannocks to make them cabbins, then a
feelinge superfluitye and wealth, they make a priuye
search into euery nooke and corner of the craggie rocks
for whatsoouer of value the open armed ocean had for a
long time conuayed thether and secretly horded up, so
that at length (answerable to their wish and paines) they
chaunced vpon the goodlyest and greatest peece of Amber-
Grece that the world is knowen euer yet to have had
in one lumpe; and nowe are they become rich folke; and
so to be proude, and from being proude to be ambitious,
and from that into a contempt one for another, and a
desire of super-eminencye: so that lastly (being only three
forlorne men in a narrowe desolate place, three thousand
miles from their natiue country and to their knowledge
in noe likly-hoode of euer recoueringe of it) they fell into
a most hott and violent contention for superioritye and commande; so that quickly they came from wordes to blowes;
beinge sometime by the eares and at cuffs, about the
dressing of their victualls, in which fitt one of them being
scufflinge with his fellowe is bitten by his owne dogg, as
if the dombe beast (like Balaams asse) would reproue the
madnesse of his master. One while, would they begin a fierce
combatt in their bote at fishinge, and with their oares
strike one another ouer board; another while chalendges are
deliuered for the feilde, ther to trye it out with their swordes,
likely enough to a sharpe entertainment, but that allwayes
in this case the third man became a stickler (as affectinge
rather to liue among enemies, for so wer they nowe, than
by loseing them to liue all alone) and kept away their
weapons. And thus in this desolate place and miserable
fashion liued thes three poore men, for the space of full two

yeares without hearcing the least newes from England, so that their cloathes were all worne and falne away from their backs, and their hopes of forrainge reliefe as naked as their bodyes. At last they begane a little to recouer their witts, and concludeinge a tripartite peace of their matachina[1] warre, they resolved to frame as bigge and conuenient a bote as they wer possibly able, and therin to make a desperate attempt for New-found-land, and so with the fishinge fleete to gett to their country; but noe soner wer they entred into this apprehension, but they descried a sayle, standinge for the ilands, when halfe ouer ioyed, (though neither knoweinge what she was, nor what she would) they determine themselves happy in her howsoeuer, and hastinnge thus to meet with her, to the accomplishment of their wish, she is found to be English, being the *Plough*, that manned with Mr. Moore and his Company, lustely furrowed the maine towardes the shore; and sone after entringe the harbour of St. Georges, to a mutuall ioye, ther came to an anchor. And thus at length, we haue lead you to the point of a plantation, so that hence-forward we must speake of a kinde of settled gouernment, and formall constitution.

[1] *Matachina*. In the *General History of Virginia*, "Matachin war".

".   .   .   . But that I'm patient,
And not a choleric old testy fool
Like your father, I'd dance a matachin with you."
   The Elder Brother, by Fletcher, 1637.

The expression is used by Smith contemptuously. It was a sort of military morris dance. " Such a dance was that well known in France and Italy by the name of the dance of fools, or *Matachins*. . . . They carried in their hands a sword and buckler, with which they made a clashing noise, and performed various quick and sprightly evolutions."—Douce's *Illustr. of Shakespear*, ii, 435.

Lib. II.—*Mr. Moore the first Gouernour*, 1612-1615.

Thes newe guests being thus come in and findinge their three resident countrymen, not only aliue and lustye, but well stored with diuers sortes of prouisions; as an acre of good corne ripe and ready for the gatherour: numbers of pompions, Indian beanes, many tortoises ready taken; and good store of hogge-flesh salted and made into flitches of bacon, wer exceedeinge cheared, and putt in life: and so presently fell to landinge both of goods and persons in a smale iland upon the south side of the harbours chanell, the which at this time carryeth the name of Smithes iland, in honnour of Sir Thomas Smith, who was then, as he is yet, the gouernour of the company in England.[1]

It was not long after their landinge (either by chaunce and in iest, as some saye, or rather, as I conceiue by the sequell, upon some priuate intelligence), but that Mr. Moore the gouernour takeinge one of three insulers aside (being of the most masterfull speritt among them, and so had proued himselfe), began to enquire of him what amber greece, perle, and other commodities he and his fellowes had found, dureinge theire two yeares habitation: when the fellowe (as well witty as masterfull, and noe lesse couetous than witty), with a soudaine confidence made answer, that for his owne part he had found none of any of thes, mary what his consorts had done he knew not: yet in time and by occasion he doubted not to gett it out from them, if any such thing wer, and then would he not fayle to discouer it, and this he spake to winne time, and meanes to conferre with the other two, doubtinge least otherwise, if the

---

[1] This observation, which is repeated below, determines the date of the commencement of the MS. to be not later than April 1619, when Sir T. Smith tendered a compulsory resignation. We shall find the author writing further on when his successor's, Sir Edwyn Sandy's, year of office was also a thing of the past.

gouernour should take them separately vnprouided, they
might be found in some different tales, or some slipps
that were ynough to reueale all: but being by thes fayre
words dismissed with encouragements and many promises,
away he goes sodainly and in all haste to his mates: and
noe soner finds them but (quite contrary to his protestations) he not only disswaded them from a discouery but
coniured them by all meanes possible to a concealement:
assureinge them, that otherwise (for so it was euidently the
gouernours hastie and eager inquisition) they should totally
be depriued of their riche purchase of amber greece and all
that they had; wheras, if they would followe his directions,
he doubted not but to conuaye both it and themselues
into England by the return of the shyp then in harbour,
and therby to remaine for euer after made men. This
was easily (as you may belieue) consented vnto, so that
thincking euery houre an age vntill it was brought into
action, they found it necessary (for the closer conueyence)
to acquaint with their horde one Dauis, the master of the
shyp, and one Mr. Edwin Kendall (a gentleman that had
shyp't himselfe for the uoyage upon southerly hopes), tellinge them, how that haueinge gotten into their handes a
great quantitie of amber-greece, to the waight of about nine
score pounds, they wer willinge and readye to make them
partners in their fortune, prouided, that they would afford
them their assistance for the freeing of it from the gouernors vigilant eye, by the secret carrying of it abord, and
proue true sharers to them, when they came home. This
was the bayte that thes gaped after: so that without farther
ceremony, the offer is accepted, the match absolutely concluded on, the plott layd, and the time and place sett downe
for the receiuing and conueyance of it into the shyp: but
whilst they attended the appointed houre to giue life to their
entontions, one of the three insulers (the very same man who
as you heard occasioned the other two to stay behind at the

departure of Sir George Sommers his shyp) whether fearcing some disastrous euent, or mistrustinge false measure when they came into England, or being of a more tender conscience than the rest, priuily conueyed himselfe to the gouernor, and reueales the whole bussinesse.

This intelligence almost equally distracts the gouernor betweene hope and doubt: on the one side he seeth a waye to wealth to the good satisfaction of the company at home; on the other he findes difficultye in the attaineinge of it, and danger by dis-vnion of his people, and apparent want of fayth in some of them, and thoes of the principall; yet being resolued not to lose so fayre a prize for want of aduenture-inge, he first of all reueales himselfe to Kendall, and with much temperance reproues his disloyaltye: but being answered with stoutnesse and contempt he causeth him to be emprisonned, together with the same fellowe whom he first questioned about it: the next Sabaoth, the master of the shyp also comeinge ashore he roundly expresseth himselfe to him, and chargeth him with indirect and dishonest courses: protestinge that vnlesse he speedely desisted and rectefied himselfe, he would bestowe both himselfe and his shyp, sure ynough for their forth comminge. The wary master, for the present replies but litle and waites upon the gouernour to the church: but being in the midst of deuine seruice, he riseth up, and at his goeinge forth commands his seamen to followe him: who obeyeing, they goe altogether sodainely abord his shipp, wher he encourageth them to stand to him like men; and tells them, that his meaneinge is to free Kendall and the other from imprissonment; to ceaze upon the amber-greece, and so to be gone. The gouernour hearcinge of this resolution determineth also to stande vpon his guarde, and with his land-men to repulse force with force, so that a generall expectance of an vn-ciuill ciuill warre possesseth euery man: as if the deuill, the author and father of diuision, enraged with a likely-hoode of a christian plantation, plotted the supplanting of it, by playeing his first master-peece this way: but this threateninge gust passed ouer more calmely than was looked for; for Dauis, through want either of a dareing speritt, or a good cause, or both, shruuck in his head, and the next day, in a deiected fashion (as the custome of such delinquents is) mediated and supplicated for a reconcilement: the which the good nature of the gouernour easily yeelded vnto: so that a peace on all sides is concluded, and Kendall also released out of prison: only the other remaineth under command as being a fellowe much suspected, and therefore ill affected by the gouernour: and therefore so held restrained for the most part of his gouernment: and thus, also, the most part of the amber-greece was recouered; some peeces only ther wer, the which haueinge falne into Kendalls fingringe wer (either by the ignorance or conniuence of the gouernour) by him stolne ouer into England; and with which he made his voiage, although not without molestation of the company, who afterwards came to an inckliuge of it.

This disturbinge brabble thus passed ouer, and the shyp that brought him in cleared of the harbour, and carryinge away with her Kendall and some other of the discontents, the gouernour, who had remoued his seate from Smith's Iland to St. Georges, for the commoditie and nerenesse of the fresh water; after he had fitted up some smale cabbins of Palmitoe leaues for himselfe, his wife, and some fewe others, in that vally wher nowe standes the prime towne of the ilands, he began to applye himselfe to performe some what of fortification at the harbours mouthes; and choose to settle his first worck vpon the point of a smale iland lieing on the north-side of that channel that leadeth into St. Georges harbour, wher he cutts out a plattforme, and planted some ordinance to good purpose. This iland was since tearmed Penistones Island, and the fort, which hath bin also altered (as we shall heare) by Captaine Tucker, is now called Pagetts Fort, in honnor of the Lord Pagett, whoe is one of the company.[1]

The Gouernour being thus busied (and as the necessitie of the time required), keepeing his men hard to their work, the minister that came ouer with him, who was a Scottishman, and named Keath, whether it wer by the secret prouocation of some idle drones of the company, that grew weary of their taskes; or that, in his owne nature, he delighted to be in a snarleinge opposition with euery one in place ouer him, or that he affected popularitie, and thought by this course to effect it; this clergie man, I saye, contrary to his coate and profession, begins to bussell vp himselfe, and to fall into tearmes with the gouernour, and at last proceeded so far, as publickly in the pulpit (the which too many of them abuse to the ventinge of their private spleens) he vpbrayed him with seueritie, naye crueltye, tellinge him in plain tearmes (but yet in Scripture phrase) that he did grinde the face of the poore, and oppresse his Christian brethren with Pharaoths taxes, vseing very many mutinous and turbulent wordes to that purpose, that might, in all likelyhoode, enrage the auchtors, and stirre upe the people against the innocent man. To cleare himselfe, therefore, from thes vncharitable and woundeing imputations, callinge all the company together, he sent for the sayd minister, and before them all repeated the charge and accusations that by him had been publickly, from so respectfull a place, throwne vpon him, wishinge them all freely to deliuer themselues, whether thoes vrged suggestions wer due to him or noe; whervpon, by a very vniuersall crye, was affirmed the contrary; in so much, that Keathe himselfe (findeinge, as it should seeme, that he had missed his mark, or, perhaps, feeleinge some kind of remorse), kneeleinge down before them all, openly confessed

[1] Fort Cunningham now occupies nearly the same spot. The change of name is to be regretted.

that he had done him wrong, and most humbly craued to
be forgiuen; but the gouernour, hastelye riseinge out of his
chayer, with the teares euen tricklynge downe his cheekes,
takeing him vp in his armes and rayseinge him vp, sayd,
I doe not expect this kneeleinge at your haudes, Mr. Keath,
nor for any such askeinge of forgiuenesse of me, pray to
God for it, learne to amend, and hereafter vse the reuerend
place you hold with more modesty and charitie.[1] At the
same time, also, or not long after, and perhaps from the
same occasion, diuers other discontents manifested themselues; and expostulations began boldly to be made by
some about their beinge so hard kept at work; but the
gouernour, in good time, apprehendinge the ill that might
issue from such a fountain, sodainely caused two of the
cheafe (being the mouthes of the rest) to be made prisonners; and although he well knewe that his comission extended not so far, nor ment he to transcend it, yet, to
make a shewe, and breede terrour, he caused twelve men to
be empannelled vpon them, who (because, as they sayd
themselues, they could not tell what to make of it) referred
it wholy to the gouernour himselfe; whervpon, giueinge it
out with great earnestnesse (to the great terror of the
poore followes, in so much as one of them fell into a fitt
of a dead palsie with all) that they should both be hanged,
the whole company, in very humble and dutifull fashion,
begged their liues (which he neuer ment to take), and so at
last, with a great deale of seeminge much adoe, after some
weekes of emprisonment, they wer both of them sett at
libertie, and proved very true labourers, and respectfull
men ever after.[2] These cracks being thus semented, the

[1] See the Editor's *Memorials of Bermuda*, i, p. 706, for notices of this clergyman.

[2] Moore's Instructions are silent as to the extent of his jurisdiction; the settlers were under the protection of English law, and he certainly had no power of capital punishment, but had probably, by a tacit under-standing, and the necessity of the case, the powers of justice of the peace.

Gouernour falls a fresh to his worcks, and continuall cheares up his men with good wordes, and promises of paye, out of England; so that, hauinge made the plattforme at Pagetts Fort somewhat seruiceable for matter of offence, weighinge two pieces of artillerye, with much adoe, out of the ruines of the *Sea-venture*, he planted one of them vpon a little iland opposite to Pagetts Fort, and the other he mounted upon a rock which commanded the mouth of the west harbour, called the Gurnetts Head, ther to make a shewe for the time, and to serue in some smale steed, vntill he could prouide better. After this he prepares timber, and rayseth the mould of a framed church; but noe sooner was it pinned together, but that (partly by reason of negligence in some entrusted worckmen, but especially through the ouer-bleake fitcinge it vpon a hill, by the next great wind it was ouerthrowne; so that that attempt being giuen ouer, in steed thereof was erected a church of Palmitoe leaues, and with the ruynes of the other the gouernour framed a pretye hansome house contriued into the fashion of a crosse, the which, by the convenient disposition therof, sufficiently expressed him an artist in that kind, as being nowe in his true element. And this frame serueth aptly vnto this day for the entertainment of the gouernours in succession; and in this house the gouernour carefully layd up that large lumpe of amber-greece, which (as you heard) he had discouered at his first landinge, the which, not long after, together with the house and all that was in it, was in great danger to haue bin burned to ashes, had not the governours wife herselfe (her husband being at the same time abroad els wher), and some one or two more, nimbly bestirred themselues. And thus bestowed, was the first part of the gouernours first yeare.

But in the interim, the company in England haueing receiued a sure intelligence, by the returne of the *Plough*, of the estate and condition of the ilands, with the safe arriuall of their people ther, and especially the cheareinge relation of the amber-greece, quickly resolued vpon a speedy secondinge supply for that colonye; and to this they wer the speedier induced, by reason of some distrusts they tooke of the Spaniards soudaine supplantinge of it in its birth (as not likely to endure patiently such a thorne in his West Indies sides), but especially for the fetchinge awaye of the amber-greece, the which they could neuer beleaue to be their owne, vntill they had it vnder their owne lock and key; and, to say truth, this curious care was not altogether vnnecessary: for the fore-mentioned Dauis and Kendall (haueinge receiued from the aduenturers, as they well deserued, some disgusts, but noe contentment) secretly proiected to make a voyage thether once more, and by one meanes or other, although it wer euen by the murther of their countrimen ther (as one of their associates afterwards confessed), to possesse themselues of the amber-greece; to which purpose they priuily hired a smale barck in the west-country; but as they were thoroughly prouiding themselues, and euen ready to sett forth, the two prime men, Kendall and Dauis, fell foule, and were almost together by the ears about the shareinge of the prize which was yett farre ynough from them; like the poore man who would needes sell the beasts-skin before he had the beast: so that whilst they were standeinge vpon thes tearmes, the adventurers came to the knowledge of their entended voiage, and thervpon presently procured a purseueant to be sent for Dauis, who, hearing of it, conuayed himselfe into Ire-land, and hath not since bin seene in England, and Kendall also retired himselfe out of the waye.

The adventurers being thus rid of this feare, goe on liuely with ther resolued supply: and to that end they hire and sett forth a smale shyp called the *Elisabeth*, the which, haueing thirtie passengers in her, and a good supply, arriued in the ilands in the depth of winter, and about nine months after the gouernours first landinge.[1] At her comeinge in, she found the gouernour busied about the rayseinge of a foure-square frame of timber vpon a high hill ouertoppeinge the towne of St. Georges to the westwards, to serue for the discouery of shippinge vpon the coast; the which worcke the gouernour accounted for his masterpeece, and was earnestly affected to haue it carry his owne name, and to be called Moores mount, although (as we shall see hereafter) it proued not long-liued, being turned vp by the rootes with a huricanoe, or whirlewind. This shyp, the *Elisabeth*, was especially sent to fetch home the whole quantitie of amber-greece; but the gouernour wisely apprehending that it was that chiefly which was the *Adamant* that drew on supplies from England, which he feared would, after the partinge, be greatly neglected, by noe meanes would be induced to part with more than a third of it, pretendinge that it was much indiscretion to aduenture all in one bottome, and altogether contrary to the fashion of merchants: but this act was generally ill apprehended by the aduenturers (who endure not to haue their orders controuerted, especially in the point of haueinge); and it was in part an occasion of some farther breaches, which not long after ensued betweene them and the gouernour; and thus thys shyp, after a smale staye in harbour, cleareth her selfe of the ilands, and makeing her waye homeward by Virginia (whether she was also homeward bound), not long after arriued safely in England.

But before she had made her voiage, the company at home, resolueinge vpon a thorough-plantation, had rigged up and sent out the *Martha*, with about sixty passengers more, who, in June, an. 1613, came to an anchor in the harbour of St. Georges: the gouernour, at her comeinge, being in employment with his best men in rayseinge some fortifications at the Gurnetts Head. Vpon her was also

[1] This will have been about March 1613.

shypped one Bartlett, a miscarryed merchant, employed by the adueuturers to suruaye the ilands, and to prie into the gouernours actions; but the gouernour (who, certainely, for a man of his coate, was apprehensive ynough), in a short time made a discouerye vpon him; and, findinge the jealousies of the companye, found it necessary for himselfe to stand vpon his gard, and yet outwardly kept himselfe vpon fayre tearmes with Bartlett dureinge his abode with him; who, haueinge practised his eyesight to noe great aduantage, after five weekes stay, returned with the shyp that brought him; the which had also laded vpon her the second third part of the amber-greece; for, with the whole, the gouernour, vpon his first grounds, would by noe meanes (though much solicited by Bartlett) be brought to part with all at one time. The *Martha* thus gone, the gouernour haueinge made up a certaine fashion of fortification, and planted some ordinance at the Gurnetts Head, to serue for the present, he remoues the most of his men from thence, and begins to fall to worck, in a smale iland lieing on the south-side of the harbours mouth of St. Georges, where, with much adoe, he makes a kind of platforme, planteth some ordinance upon it, and erecteth a redoubt; the which, how it was altered and perfected, we shall see when we come to that time. He also layeth the foundation of a large redoubt vpon a hill to the east of St. George's towne, the which he afterwards brought to good perfection, beinge at the present called Warwick Fort, and haueinge three peeces of ordinance mounted upon it, serveth both to play out towards the harbour, and to garde the fresh water belouginge to the towne. Much about the same time also, he began the first triall of tobacco, which he planted in St. Georges Iland, and which, proueinge very fayre in the growth, was the most part of it spoyled, by want of knowledge and skill in pruneinge, cureinge, and makeinge of it up. The totall somme of persons that the colony consisted of at that present, ammountcinge to the number of one hundred. But in the interim, the adnenturers in England abhorrcinge the delays that the Gouernour vsed in sendeinge home the totall of the amber-greece, the which they had nowe a second newes of (perhaps with some vnsound aggrauations) by the *Martha,* and more and more fallinge into distastes of him and his actions, with in three weeks after her arriuall, they cause the *Elizabeth* to be sent out the second time,[1] who brought with her fortie persons to be residents, and an especiall charge and iniunction to the Gouernour for the sending away of the residue of the amber-greece, the which pressure he (being noe longer able to auoyde) yeelded vnto, and so with in a while after, with her wished fraught she cleares herselfe of the ilands, and, accordinge to appointment, makes her returne by Virginia, and so home. In her wer first brought into thes partes certaine potatoe rootes sent from England, the which being planted and flourishinge very well, wer by negligence almost lost; at last, by a lucky hand, again reuiued from two cast awaye rootes; they have since encreased into infinite store, and serue at the present for a maine releife to the inhabitants.[2] In her also came ouer a certain Frenchman, hired in England by the aduenturers to deliuer his censure of the natiue mulberrye trees, which are in great aboundance in the ilands, as whether they wer the right kind for the foode of the silcke-worme; who, haucinge taken a slight vewe of them, returned an answer of dislike, as that they wer altogether improper for that effect; but of this you shall heare more here after.[3]

Within one moneth after the *Elisabeths* departure, two

[1] About September 1613.

[2] These potatoe roots, sent from England, can only have been the common potatoe, *Solanum tuberosum,* introduced towards the end of the previous century, and not yet even known in Holland.

[3] The tree was probably *Conocarpus racemosa,* called sea-mulberry.

sayles wer discouered from the Gurnetts head, wher wer
only at that time eight or ten men ; at whose approoch some
what nere it was discerned that one of them was towed by
her skiff; and with all that they both continually vsed their
lead and sounded for the chanell. A bote therfore (accordinge to the vse, but with some more caution than ordinary
by reason of the pregnancye of the suspicion) was sent out
to vewe them, the which keepeing her wind, and being come
within call, haled the skiff, but being only answered from
the shyp, that they should come abord, and perceiuing that
one only man gaue them that answer, and that answer only,
they durst approach noe nearer, but in all hast made back
againe. Presently vpon it, comes the gouernour from the
towne with about ten men more ; and approueinge the intelligence giuen in by the bote, he concludeth that they wer
enemies and resolueth vpon a braue defence: whervpon,
after prayer to God and a speach of encouragement to his
men (to which he was noted to be much disposed, and conueniently able) he manned out the bote once againe, with an
entention to take the shyps skiff, that came soundinge still
before her: but feareinge that his owne bote might proue to
weake for her he presently sent out a second to relieue her,
if need wer. By this time the first bote once againe hales
the skiff, which retireinge towards the shyp, giues noe
answer. Herevpon the gouernours botes also make a stand;
so that the formost shyp being gott up somewhat nere, the
gouernour himselfe (who was a very good gunner) makes
a shott at randome, and findinge that he could reach her,
he makes a second shott at her, the which (as it is sayd to
haue bin confessed by some that wer in her) passed through
and through her. Howsoeuer, certaine it is that vpon that
shott, both the shyps, cuttinge their maine-sayles, cast about
and made quite awaye, and thus ended that fraye.

Wherein certainely ther was euidently discernable a great
deale of denine prouidence for the good of the poore planta-

tion; for ther wer not at that time abouc twenty persons at the Gurnetts head, and many of thoes very weake and feeble with want of foode: ther wer then only foure peeces mounted, the which though they wer all of them laden, yet was ther not aboue three quarters of a barrell of powder besides, and one only shott. Upon the very expectance of the entrance of these shyps, and in the hurrey of the preparation for a defence, the only barrell of powder that they had was improuidently tumbled vnder the mussell of one of the ordinance, the which being one of thoes two that wer dis-charged, the powder notwithstandinge, which lay thus vnder her, fired not certaine cartredges slightly made of paper and filled with powder, being brought vp to be vsed vpon occasion, a negligent fellowe left his lighted match vpon one of them all the whilst they wer at prayer, the cole whereof, though it continually touched the paper, yet kindled noethinge. Thes direct demonstrations of heauenly assistance exceedeinge wrought vpon most of them, and especially it moued the gouernour, who (as I find him generally) was noe lesse pious then painefull; so that callinge his men together like a good christian and a soldier he publickly gaue thancks to God for this his so protecting a preseruation. What thes two shyps ment, it is not certainely knowen. I deny not, but that I haue heard it as a report from Spaine it selfe, that they wer only merchand men, who being in distresse of water, and fallinge vpon the ilands by chaunce (not imagineinge them to be inhabited), resolued to make in with the shore, and seeke for some refreshments: but as they drewe nere they kenned the fortes, and yet iudgeinge that either they might be receiued as friends, or durst not be resisted as enemies, they continued their approaches, vntil findeinge the ordinance to speake more loud and hottly than they expected (for the Spaniard although a good soldier generally, yet abhorres to march vpon the cannon) they presently retraicted, and, as you haue hearde, tooke their leaue. But howsoeuer it wer, as the gouernour did discreetly in his flowrish of defence, on the one side, so on the other, it was God's great mercye, that it tooke so well; since certaine it is, that (by being so ill prouided) if they had proued enemies, they might haue done much; and findinge so much, what there vpon they would haue proued, who knowes.

This feare being thus blowen ouer, the gouernour begins to have the sence of a greater, which was the extremitye of famine; for by his continuall keepeinge of all his men together in one place, which was at St. George's iland, from whence they wer not to part vpon paine of death, the which he did, to haue them the better and speedier in a readynesse to answer all such soudaine alarmes and occasions, as he euery day expected (and was continually quickned with-all from England), he fell into two maine inconueniences; the one (as you heard) the want of bread, by followeinge his worcks so closely, as he neglected to plant a sufficientye of corne; the other, the oner cleareing of St. George's iland, which was the place of their residence, by cuttinge downe the palmitoe trees, to have their heades for foode, a cheife releife of the people at that time, but such a disableinge of the place for tobacco (which is as yet the staple commoditie), as that not only to this day, but for many yeares to come it must needes feele the weight of that stroke: neither was it possible for the gouernour to cure or preuent this ill, by any prohibition, because the belly hath noe eares. The gouernor and colony languishinge in this distresses, the one of hunger, the other discontent, behold a frigate makes to the shore, the which being discouered to be manned with English is wellcomed and pilated into the harbour, and (in a good houre) found to be cheifely laden with Spanish meale: her commandour was named Daniell Elfrye, who serueinge vnder one Fisher, that was sent out vpon a discouery into

the river of the Amazones;[1] as they went, this Spainish frigate
comeinge in their waye their catchinge fingers layd fast
hold on her, and this Elfrye (being in good trust with Fisher)
was putt into her as master, who takeinge his opportunitie,
requited him so well as sone after he gaue him the slyp and
then shaped his course hether; wher he arriued so luckely,
as by haueinge his meale shared among the hungry colony
much content for the present is recouered, by the gouernour, and many that wer in very hard distresse fedd and
reloued. The newe guests restinge here and takeinge their
partes of it, vntill not long after they were shyped away for
England. But howsoeuer this runne away frigate brought
with her a timely and acceptable sacrifice of her meale; yet
the companions of her meale, numbers of ratts (which wer
the first that the ilands euer sawe), being receiued with-all
and on a soudaine multiplyinge themselues by an infinite
encrease (for ther is noe place in the world so proper for
them), within the space of one only yeare they became so
terrible to the poore inhabitants, as that (like one of Pharaoths plagues) the whole plantation was almost vtterly sub-
uerted therby; and so farr gone it was at last, that it proued
Captaine Tucker's masterpeece all his time (which was not
long after) to deuise trapps and stratagems to conquer and
destroye them, though indeed all of them proued to noe purpose (as you shall see hereafter) vntill afterwards, one
moneth of cold and wett weather did the deed.

About two moneths after the first arriual of this frigate
arriued the *Blessinge* from England,[2] fraughted with one

[1] Probably the Captain Edward Fisher who accompanied Robert
Harcourt to the Amazons in the *Rose*, of eighty tons, 1608, in which
voyage Harcourt took possession, by Turfe and Twigge, in the name of
our sovereign lord, King James, "of the whole Continent of Guiana,
lying betwixt the Riuers of Amazones and Oronoque, not beeing actually possessed, and inhabited by any other Prince or State: wherewith
the Indians seemed to be well content and pleased."—Relation of a
voyage to Guiana performed by Robert Harcourt. *Purchas.* iv, p. 1267.

[2] About March 1614.

hundred passengers for the ilands; two dayes after her comes in the *Starre*, and in her one hundred and eightie more; among which wer diuers gentlemen and men of fashion; as one Mr. Lower, sent ouer (as was sayd) to be marshall; and one Mr. Barrett, takeinge vpon him to be an inginier; in her also came ouer one Mr. Felgate, an old soldier, who hath ouer since, for the most part, bin resident here, and hath done many painefull seruices for the good of the plantation, being at the present liuetenant of the gouernours company. All thes people, with their necessaryes, were speedely landed and vewed by the gouernour, who haueinge taken their names, and considered of their condition, distributed and fitted euery one to his employement and labour; for some of them he sent to the Gurnetts head, to make that plattforme and rayse thoes battlements, that to this daye lie out vpon the mouth of the harbour; the which, haueinge finished in some reasonable manner, was called the Kings-Castle; others wer employed about the mountinge of such ordinance as wer sent ouer by the newe come shyps; the most of the rest were disposed of to the finishinge of St. Katheraines Fort, to the makeinge of fire-worcks, fellinge of trees, hauoing of stones, and to the prepareinge of materialls fitt for those turnes. The gouernour also (to make an essaye of his newe come officers) caused Lower to drill and exercise his men, and conferred with Barrett about newe worcks of fortification; but from both of them (either in deed or seemingly), received so smale satisfaction, as that openly manifestinge his distaste of their insufficiencyes, and continually puttinge vpon them witty disgraces (whether deseruedly or noe, it is variously deliuered), he made them sone find that neither presumptious weaknesse can long lie hid from an apprehensive experience; nor an imposed seruice proue at any time wellcome to a iealous master; so that being almost noe sooner arriued, than cloyed and euen loathinge their employments, they retired themselves from whence they came by the same shyp (the most of them) that brought them in.

Within fourteen dayes after the arriuall of thes last forementioned shyps, the shyp called the *Margeret*, with two pinnaces,[1] whereof the one was named the *Thomas*, the other the *Edwin*, entred the harbour of St. Georges, and in them 160 newe residents more; with thes came Bartlett the second time, with a secret commission (as some thought) to succeede the gouernour; but without question, with an especiall charge to the gouernour to cause the ilands to be layd out into tribes and shares (as they are nowe), and so to haue the people planted vpon them accordingly, the which worck he was to be an eye-witnesse of, and by all meanes possible a setter-forward. But the gouernour (partly because he found that by this course his men must needes be drawen away from him, and so worcks be left vndone which he was ambitions to finish; but especially by reason that in veweing the forme and instructions sett downe by the company for the distribution of the tribes and shares, he saw noe mention made of himselfe, nor of any such quantitie of land as the Court had promised him at his setting out) resolued by all meanes to disturbe the sayd order, tellinge Bartlett plainely that the daye of plantation was yet to early, to allowe any such dispersion of the people from the partes of defence; neither could it but be a course of much hazard and improuidence; and that it was visible ynough vnto him how as yet the halfe of that which was necessary was not performed; as also that forraign attempts wer not wantinge, wittnesse the two Spanish shyps; the company of adnenturers must pardon him, therefore, if in this point he declined from this their iniunction and command; for he had the advantage of them by ocular experience, and the lives of himselfe and his men

[1] About April 1614.

laye at the stake, the aduenturers indeed might lose some expence of coyne; but he and his wer to make it good, upon the expence of bloud.

Bartlett being able to drawe from him noe other answer but this, grew at last somewhat rough and violent; insomuch as he brought up more choler from the gouernour than euer the climate had thetherto purged; in which heate and passion he gave him this distempered answer, that if he expected and stayed for more, he must cutt it out with his sword. But Bartlett, whose errand was to no such purpose, perceiueinge that ther might well ensue some danger but noe good by a farther opposition, determined to forsake both it and the ilands, and back againe by returne with the shyp for England; and the rather he formed this resolution timely and requisite, for that euery daye the generallitie of the people, especially the old planters, whether encouraged or conniued at by the gouernour it is not knowen, threw their discontents in his face, and at last came up so roundly to him, as they forbore not to tell him plainely, that if he came amongst them any more, with his newe tricks, vnlesse he brought with him their old paye, which they pretended due to them from the merchands, they would share it out upon him, though it wer but in thougs of his skinne. Thus skared, awaye goeth he with the shyp, and with him the master of the *Edwin*, as great a discontent as himselfe.

As for the originall cause and secrett of sendinge of the two pinnaces vnto the ilands, various wer the opinions that wer receiued and mainteyned about it, accordinge as the humours wer, that they wer fedd with-all; for the gouernour (by this time growen as jealous of the company as they sone after of him) would needes apprehend it, that it was only a plott for the entiseinge of him vpon so fayre an occasion to some vnwarrantable employment of them vpon the West Indies, that therby they might take him at an

adnantage, and so paye him with his owne monye : but this
seemes not only an vncharitable censure, but an improbable
one also; for the trick could not counteruayle the charge of
it. Others conceiued it that the aduenturers had both a
secret desire and an ententiue meaninge, that they should
be employed by the colony that waye; marry they affected
to carry the bussines, so as it might be in their owne choice
either to auouch or disauouch the action, accordinge to the
speed of it, and as they found cause. For mine owne part,
I should rather thinck that the true entention of their
fittinge of them up, and sendinge them vnto the plantation,
was for the secureinge of it against all casuall accidents of
famine; that by them, vpon all occasions, might be carryed a
lawfull traide in corne with the natiues of the sauuage ilands,
who are not aboue fourteen dayes sayle from them,[1] from
whence they might be conueniently supplied with hogges,
goates, together with many kindes of plantes and fruicts,
the which a newe plantation could not but for a long while
stand in need of: and euen to this daye such a meane as
this (howsoeuer the place is since very well improued)
cannot chuse but be very extraordinaryly wellcome and of
great securitie and comfort; and as an inducement leadeinge me to this coniecture, I may alledge that speach
which is sayd to haue proceeded from a forward prime man,
and a stiff talker in their courts in England, who being,
with the rest, informed of the great wants and mysery that
the colonye endured at that time, and being one of thoes
that wer petitioned for releife, why (quoth he) will thes
fellowes neuer be weaned, haue we not sent them two
hansome pinnaces to helpe themselues? I graunt, indeed,
that this sayinge maye endure a double construction, and
be equally taken both wayes; yet being as fully (if not
more) fauorable for me as for any of the rest, I am will-

[1] The Lucayas or Bahamas appear, at this time, to be generally intended by the Savage Islands, but sometimes the Virgin Islands.

ingly contented to receiue it the most charitable waye.
But howsoeuer the secret of it was certaine, it is that the
gouernour, whether vpon the strength of his owne beleife,
or some other by respects, could neuer be induced to haue
the least thought of employeinge of them, either this waye
or any other, so that within a while after they became
vnseruicable.

The harbours being thus cleared of all shyps, saue the
two pinnaces, the gouernour being well stored with people,
falls againe to his fortinge : and haueinge done with Pagetts
Fort, he rayseth a fashionable redoubt in Coopers Iland,
and calls it Pembroke Fort. He buildeth also a certaine
slope bridge at the Townes-warfe, for the easie shoreinge
of goodes, the which (by want of due ground-worck) is
shortly after broken to peeces by the windes and waues.
He bestoweth some time, also, in contriueinge of fire-
worcks, and the frameinge of certaine slight engines of
timber, and the like deuises, the most part wherof proued
of smale effect, and as smale continuance. And thus
passed he ouer the second yeare of his time, and nowe was
well stept into the third ; when the company in England,
haueing receiued, by Bartlett, euery thinge at the worst
hand, and therby fallen into an absolute disgust and suspicious loathinge of all his proceedeinges ther, they not
only spake sharpely and bitterly against his peeuishnesse
and presumption (for those wer the best titles they could
nowe afford his actions) in their open courts ; but so sea-
sonned their generall and perticuler letters, which they
from henceforth wrote vnto him, with sharpe and biteinge
sauce, as the afflicted man (and in some sort certainely
wronged) hath bin heard to saye, with teares tricklinge
downe his cheekes, that they vexed him to the very soul ;
and, in good truth, how could it be otherwise (especially
if that be true, which an eminent and leadinge sperit
among them is reported to have spoken in publick, that he

hoped the king would send for him home shortly, and hang him) for the woundes of a freind, from whom not only applause, but reward is expected, strike deeper, and make a farr greater impression than the mainest blowes of an open enemye, from whence noething but malice and mischeife is looked for.

Dureing this hard measure from England, the gouernour (who had not yet the full sense of his ill) began to find the prouerbe true, that one mischeif neuer comes without a second; for, haueinge kept his whole number of people so close at worck, as that he allowed noe employment for the settinge of corne, but for his sustentation that waye relied wholy vpon his store out of England; and a speedy supply which (it is sayd) Bartlett, at his departure, had confidontly and faythfully promised him; began within a while to haue his prouisions shorten vpon him; and so short at last, that scarce any thinge at all was left; at what time (still lookeinge out in vaine for a shyp) he at length became constrained in plaine tearmes to tell the people, that consideringe the case they wer in, in compassion of them he neither could nor would hold them any longer at their worck: he aduised them, therefore, to practice their best endeuours, and to prouide for themselues, by fishinge, birdinge, and such like, promiseing to euery one his best assistance, only, for the safetye of the fortes and the secureinge of the harbours mouthes, he would reserue some fewe of his best men, and especially the carpenters, bricklayers, and masons, to goe on (though but slowly) with the begun worcks, alloweing of them somewhat (by pincheinge himselfe and famely) wherwith they might keepe themselues in some strength; and with this (for a chearcing and incouragement) he did also dayly and diligently labour himselfe. But thes shyfts seruing but for a while, so that the disease (like a palliated cure) sone after brake out worse than euer before; it was for the last refuge resolued (all hope of

English releife being now quite taken away) that the *Edwin* should be rigged up and sent for England, to carry newes to the aduenturers of the great distresses they were falne into, and to craue a speedy supply. This being nimbly performed, and a master appointed her out of the ilands, she cleares her selfe of the harbour, and goes her waye. Vpon her at the same time also (hopeinge it might giue some kind of allay to the sowrenesse of her errand) was shipped a small quantitie of tobacco, which some fewe handes for a triall had nursed and bred up to a tollorable perfection.[1]

Whilst this Pinnace was on her way for England, scarcetie and famine euery day more and more preuayleinge vpon the sickly colony, caused the gouernour to look well about him; in the beginning of the newe yeare, therefore (1615), 150 persons, of the most ancient, sick, and weake, wer sent into Coopers Iland, ther to be relieued by the comeinge in of the sea birds, especially the Cahowes, wher, by this halfe hunger-starued company, they are found in infinite numbers, and with all so tame and amazed they are, that vpon the least howeteinge or noyce, they would fall downe, and light vpon their shoulders as they went, and leggs as they satt, suffering themselues to be caught faster than they could be killed.

Here likewise they had admirable aboundance of fish; but as the vse of Heauens blessinges with good men causeth them to breake out into thancksgivinge and a holy respect of the deuine prouidence, so the abuse of them by intemperate gluttons and beastly swine, turnes it into excesse, and raueninge; wittnesse the generall carriage and behauiour of this company, who being thus arriued and gott up to a libertie aud choice of eateing as much as they would, how monstrous was it to see, how greedily euery thing was swallowed downe; how incredible to

[1] Towards the close of 1614. Tobacco was gathered in October.

speake, how many dosen of thoes poore silly creatures, that euen offered themselues to the slaughter, wer tumbled downe into their bottomelesse mawes : whervpon (as the sore effect of so ranck a cause, the birds with all being exceedeingly fatt) then sodenly followed a generall surfettinge, much sicknesse, and many of their deathes : the which comeinge to the Gouernours knowledge, (conceiueing that a chaungeing of the ayre, and especially an abstinence frō so fatt a feedoinge might be a meanes of recouery) he speedely causeth them all to be instantly conueyed from thence to a place called at this day Port-royall, wher he allowed them a bote, and a gang of men to fish for them : but this gang (as most of the rest yet are to this daye) groweing lazey, carelesse, and negligent in this important employment, such an extreame want and miserie came vpon themselues and the whole company, that all of them grewo sodainely feeble and lamentably sickley, in so much that many through famine died. At which time also this ill effect followed, that certaine cowes with a bull sent out of England by the aduenturers, and pastured in that part of Sands, his tribe, called then and nowe Sommers-seate, wer by this improuident and rauenous company all of them killed and devoured ; the Gouernour sufferinge them to thinck that he belieued their report of it, which was, that in hott weathcr they ranne into the sea, to coole themselues, and so wer drowned.

But vpon this, botes are presently sent downe to conuaye them all to the towne, but ther being scarce halfe botes ynough, the women and children wer carried by sea, the men trauayled by land : only some fewe ther wer who makeinge choice and earnest suite to be left behind, conueyed themselues into the woddes and ther sustayned themselues with wilcks (which is a kind of shell-fish like a snaylo) and land-crabbs ; among the rest one of them, singlinge himselfe from all others and liueinge all alone for diuers monethes, without so much as the sight of any reasonable creature, so well nursed vp himselfe with that only foode, as being, after the arrivall of a shyp, sought after and with much adoe discoucred, he was at last found, though with neuer a ragge to his back yet with good store of fatt on his belly. The people being once againe for the most part all of them at the towne, the Gouernour takes exceedeinge care for their releife, and trimminge up all his botes, manns them with the best and ablest of his men, and so putts them to continuall fishinge for the rest; in so much that ordinarily 150 and sometimes 200 great fishes are brought home in a daye: at last the hookes and lines groweing scarce, he causeth the smithes to make hookes of old rustye swordes; and cuttinge a cable belonging to the pinnace called the *Thomas*, setts the people on worck to make lines, and oft times would he rise himselfe at midnight, call vp his fishermen and sett them out to sea: with which course and by which meanes for two or three monethes wer the people in some conuenient fashion kept and maintayned.

By this time the *Edwin* (sent out as you have heard to call for releife) hath made her voiage into England: by whose lamentable discouery of the diseases of the Colony fresh exclamations are raysed against the Gouernour; accuseinge his wilfulnesse and self conceite, which wrought him to a continuall contempt (as they sayd) of their allsufficient directions, as the originall cause of all these distempers: notwithstandinge, findinge themselues euery way engaged, both in purse and credit, they resolue by all meanes to make good what they had begun: yet not determineinge upon the chaunge at that time of a Gouernour, either because though (as they thought) they found themselues ill serued, they yet knewe not how to be bettered; or that they made some doubt whether their commands for his returne (so straunge and vncharitable wer their iealous apprehensions) would be obeyed or noe: and ther-

fore thought it fittest to attend some farther opportunities.
Howsoeuer the good shyp the *Welcome* is presently and
in all haste sent out for that voiage, and franghted altogether with English corne, and not long after safely arriues
whether she was bound, and by her longed for fraught
proues herselfe the wellcome as well in deed as name.
Noo sooner was she come in, but the Gouernour commands
from her a quantitie of some barrells of meale, the which
the next day is (with straunge ioye) deliuered and recciued
by the people, who for many mouethes before had seen noe
bread: the rest of the prouisions he causeth also presently
to be vnshypped and commits them to the charge of the
Clearck of the Publick Store. This done, and the company reasonably well quietted, findinge his tearme and
limited time of gouernment expired; and that the burthen
of it was likely rather to encrease than otherwise by the
dayly accesse of newe commers, and assureinge himselfe,
besides, that the aduenturers had forborne to send for him
home more vpon the respects of themselues, than any good
of his, he resolued to leaue the Ilands and make home with
this shyp: but before his departure, weighinge and ponder-
inge within himselfe what forme and order to leave the
Gouernment in, which he nowe ment to forsake, he at last
resolued to settle it upon the shouldiers of six persons which
he made choice of, whose names (for charitye sake) I will
forbear to mention, for their deedes sake, that I am nowe
to remember[1]; the which six (callinge in vnto them the assistance of certaine others whom he also nominated for that
turne) wer euery one of them in their moneths to take his
course at the helme: the which act of his as it was the last
publicke one that euer he did here, so certainely it was the

---

[1] This suppression is curious, Smith having published their names in
his *History*. They were Captain *Miles Kendall*, Captain *John Mansfield*,
Thomas Knight, *Charles Caldecot*, *Edward Waters*, and *Christopher
Carter.—Gen. Hist.*, lib. v.

very worst (in that kind) that euer he committed dureinge
the whole time of his abode: for howsoeuer it is most true
(and his owne experiences could not chuse but tell him
as much) that not any one of thes thus putt in authoritie
wer fitt for the place or capable of the employment; neither
wer then any better here at that time to be found, yet the
maine fayle and error of his iudgement was in bringinge up
so many vnsufficient and dangerous ones together and at
once into the circle of command. For who knowes not
but that five theeues are better to be endured than ten,
three tyrants than six, one maddman than two.

The affayres of thes Ilands, and the disposition of them,
being thus constituted, within a while after awaye goeth
the old Gouernour with the shyp, and nowe begines the
rule or rather mis-rule of the six: the which before we
aduenture upon we will bring Mr. Moore into England, and
shewe you, in breife, the entertainement the Company gaue
him at his comeinge home, and so once for all, make an end
with him: who although it was not long after his departure
before he safely arrived in England with the *Welcome*; yet
not knoweinge what wellcome he should haue giuen him,
either by particular creditors (by whom by some vnfortunate
losses he was much engaged), or by the Company of aduenturers, in whose seruice he found that he had spent three
yeares to a mutuall discontent and distast, he noe soner
was gotte to London but retires himselfe into a very priuate
and poore lodgeinge in Millford Lane, the which vpon this
were gott the name of the Bermudoes,[1] from whence the next

[1] "*Overdo.* Look into any angle of the Town, the Streights, or the
Bermuda's, where the quarrelling lesson is read, and how do they enter-
tain the time, but with bottle, ale, and tobacco?..."—*Bartholomew Fair*,
by Ben Jonson, 1614.

"......These men ever want; their very trade
Is borrowing; that but stopt, they do invade
All as their prize, turn pirates, here at land
Have their Bermudas, and their Streights i' the Strand.

daye he sends the certainetie of his arriuall to Sir Thomas Smithe, who then was (and yet is) the Gouernour of the Company; lettinge him knowe the cause of his not presentinge himselfe vnto him in person, the which being secured of, he would willingly and speedely perform. Thes newes somewhat startled the adventurers, as well in respect of their being much deceiued in the point of his comeinge home, as in the regard of the danger and ill ease they suspected the Ilands might be left in, by this his so soudaine an vnexpected a leaueing of them. Diuers of them, therefore, quickly repayred vnto him; from whome receiueinge satisfaction in euery particular to their good content (for such shewe they made) they left him comforted with good wordes, and promises of procureinge for him a protection from his creditors, that so he might freely and safely resort to their Courtes, giue up his account, and have his *quietus est* and promised rewarde: and indeed, it was not long before his sayd protection was made good vnto him, so that without danger in that respect, he shortly after came amongst them; when, after some varietie of chideinge, and litle lesse (by some of the meanest of them) than vnciuill and base of vpbraydeinges, he at last receiued his salary of eight shares of land, and so was dismissed with showe of fauour and friendshyp.[1] And nowe we must returne (though even loath I am to fall vpon such

Man out their boats to the Temple, and not shift
Now, but command; make tribute what was gift."

Epistle to Sir Edward Sackvile, afterwards Earl of Dorset, about 1625, *id.*

"The Streights consisted of a nest of obscure courts, alleys, and avenues, running between the bottom of St. Martin's Lane and Chandos Street."—W. Gifford's *Ben Jonson*, note in *loc. cit.*

Millford Lane still exists.

[1] These were in Southampton Tribe, by the schedules in Smith's *History*, and six of them are identified by Norwood, in his Survey of 1663 (*Memorials*, etc., ii, p. 703, where the name is erroneously written "Morar" or "Moorer" instead of Moore).

confusions) to treate of our halfe dosen of Gouernours left behind in the Sommer Ilands.

Lib. III.—*The Rule of the Six Gouernours.*—1615-1616.

The first publick attempt they tooke in hand was the castinge of lotts, to see who first should begin the playe, the which by good fortune fell upon one of the ciuillest; who though, hereby, he had the advantage and start of the rest in the haveinge of a full store, yet he vsed it in a farre better temper than any of them would have done, and therby left somewhat for his companions in the reare to shewe their ill-husbandry and reeleinge expence. Toward the end of this man's first moneth a proiect was sett abroad, and greedely swallowed, for the sendinge out of a smale barck to fiddle vpon the West Indies: wherevpon the frigate before mentioned, brought in by Elfrye, was sodainely rigged up, and being manned with thirty-two men (whereof three of them were three of the gouernours, full of conceite and iollitie,[1] she cleares herselfe of the Ilands and makes awaye). But this poore vessell (whether through ill weather, or want of marriners, or both) insteade of the West Indies falls vpon the Ilands of the Canaries, wher she hitts vpon a poore Portugall and takes her, the which being manned with ten of her owne people is sone after in a storme separated from her, and the nexte day after found by a French rouer and by him carried awaye; so that the frigate, out of hope of the recouerye of her prize, makes a second time for the Indies, wher she noe soner arriued but is foundred in the sea; but her men, recoueringe a desolate iland in their bote, wer after some moneths of stay ther fetched off by an English pyrate, who conuayed them

[1] These three were Chard, Knight, and Waters.

in to their country. And thus ended the first act beginninge in the first moneth of the playe of the six gouernours.

When the second man for the second moneth (who had only so much more witt than his fellowes as to helpe him to be so much the more vitious) presently began his worck, with a generall giueinge of leaue to playe, so that nowe the brauest and tallest fellowe was he that could drinck deepest,[1] bowle best with saker shott in the gouernours garden, and winne most lobllolly.[2] Yet withall (to shewe he had somewhat in him) scorneinge so much as once to doubt, or in the least manner to question, the golden returne of his frigate, being sent out by such hands and heads as himselfe and his companions, he plodded vpon some deepe reachinge trick, for the keepeinge of it when it came ; and to this extent, three or foure of them, slappeing their soundeinge pates together, deuised and framed a certaine petition contriued as from the people in generall vnto the worthy triumuirate of Gouernours (for the other three as you haue heard wer gone in the pinnace), wherin they wer most humbly and earnestly besought and supplicated, that by noe meanes they would resigne or deliuer up the wholesome regiment they nowe had in their hands, to any person or persons whatsoeuer, although sent with all the authoritie and accomplishment that possibly might be from England, vntill six moneths after the arriuall of the said frigate. The which petition, after much hammeringe vpon, examination, correction, puttinge in and puttinge out, wrightinge ouer and ouer and finall contruement, was committed to the fingers of a sure carde, and so euer ready to be carried into the maine in state, for the collection of handes ; when (be-

---

[1] Smith was himself conspicuous for temperance, as well as for bravery, and his contempt for the vice of drunkenness is one of the internal evidences of his authorship of this work.

[2] A sort of porridge made of Indian corn.

hold the chaunce) one of their ministers named Mr. Lewes
Hughes, who aboue all men they desired to keepe in ignorance, came to an incklinge of it, and findinge the irregular-
itie and vnwarrantablenesse of the action, sodenly resolues
(his resolutions being for the most part soudaine) by all
meanes possible to disturbe it; and the rather, by reason
that neither the person for that monethes Gouernment, who
had bin the prime deuisor and propounder of the trick, nor
the carriage and fashion of his fellowe clergie man, a well
approuer thereof (being the same Keath that we had occasion
to speake of in Mr. Moore's time), wer any waye acceptable
vnto him. His first attempt vpon it, therfore, began by
taking an opportunity to rush in vpon them when they wer
euen at the point of an issue, and in the readeinge and so
fare-well-takeinge of the petition, nowe goeinge for the
maine; whervpon findeinge themselues discouered, and that
it was necessary to sett a good face vpon the matter, they
held on the readeinge of it out to his teethe. The which
beinge done and the societie breakeinge up, the minister
makeinge choice of one of them (who was indeed a fellowe
that euer held it as a being true to him selfe to be false to
all others), demanded of him, who was the penner of the
sayd petition? He (who himselfe was guiltye of the fact) de-
murely answered that in truth the Gouernour had sent and
sent for him selfe to that purpose, and still by waye of excuse (as mislikeinge the course) he had pleaded ignorance,
vntil at last, being vrged and in a manner noe better than
compelled vnto it by the Gouernour, who also gaue him his
directions, he had sett it downe in the forme he had nowe
heard. Being not able to gett out more from him, awaye goes
the minister to the scribe who was newely in hand with the
fayre coppyeinge of it out, and to him he gaue so vehement
a caution against his medlinge with so infectious a bussinesse, as the poore fearefull man becomes so terrified vpon
it as he presently giues him up the petition. Haueing thus

E

gotten what he came for, back againe goes he to the Gouernour, and tells him plainely and roughly what he had done; addeinge withall, that he had done more than he could answer, in that fashion, to stirre up the people by a trick of a petition framed by him selfe to a resistaunce and noe better than a mutinye against a legitimate Gouernour, shortly to be expected from England. But the Gouernour (being a man who rather had a mind to make himselfe somebody by bold actions, than a sperit to execute them), although he chafed and swelled terribly, yet gaue him noe other answer for the instant but that he sayd not true, to tearme the petition his act, since it was the generall voice and desire of the people, which he neither could nor would refuse to heare; and withall awaye he flings from him to his companions, and to them relates the presumptuous behauiour (for so at last he dares call it) of the minister: whervpon bigg lookes and soure faces are very generally throwen vpon the honest pooreman, who notwithstandinge (as not being to be diuerted that way) marcheth on confidently to the vtter dashinge and confoundinge of their petitionary stretageme.

The next Sunday, therefore, out of the pullpitt (though not so fitt a place for that turne), in the presence, and to the fronts of the contrary partie, he breaks up and desects before a full auditory, the unlawefullenesse and danger of the propounded course; he coniures and importunes them to renounce and forsake it, and the better to quiett and bring them to it, he reades certaine letters, cunningly written vnto him, from the Governor of the Company in England, a good while before, wherin was expressed the sorrowe that the undertakers receiued by the apprehension of their suffrings and misery: assuringe them that they wer not sent ouer to liue like slaues, but as freemen: and that if matters had bin discreetly carried and true information giuen vnto the Company, ther had long ere then a remedy and redresse bin procured; "You see, therefore, my masters (sayth he) that all former discontents are likely very shortly to be redressed; be perswaded, therefore, to a discret patience and manly temper; least otherwise, by a precipitated and misguided resolution, vntimely and vnluckely entred vpon, you houte and gaster awaye[1] that fayre flock of satisfactions and contents which is euer ready to fall vpon you and alight on your heades." This oration is noe soner ended by the minister, but vp starts the monethly Gouernour, and (as it is sayd) with a pale looke and tremblinge iointes, he summoneth the company to a staye and the heareinge of his answer; when, first of all, directinge his speach to the preacher, he tareth and reproacheth him for the readeinge of the foresayde letters; he telleth him that they had bin long ynough fedd with windye and wordye pro.nises; and that as it was more than timely that some of them had bin long ere then made reall and good vnto them, so it was more than petty that they should be any longer deluded and abused with the like. It was an impudence also in himselfe to tearme that petition rebellious and mutinous, which was not only honest and lawfull, but euen (passinge under the severest censures) charitable, equall, and most necessarye. Then turneinge himselfe to the people: "You see, Sirs (quoth he) how open-mouthed this man is nowe, because no longer since than yesterday he tooke his full vewe of this petition, and could not reproue it. By speakeinge against it nowe, therefore, you may see what he is." The minister being thus netled stands up againe, and begins to venter vpon an extempore replye, especially determineinge to bend his speech to the confutation of that point wherin he was charged of approveinge the petition one day, and reproucing it the next, as also to discouer to the people the subtletye and cunninge of their vsurpeinge Gouernour, who being the

[1] Hoot and frighten away. "Gasted by the noise I made, full suddenly he fled."—*King Lear*, ii, 1.

principall, if not the only actor in this dangerous plott, and
contriueinge it only to serve his owne turne, yet went about,
by freeinge of himselfe to laye the whole burthen on them.
But the Gouernour not endureinge the least touch vpon that
stringe, in a rage (with a couple of his twang) departs the
church, the rest behind remaineinge in a plaine diuision
among themselves: some of them beginninge to consider of
the minister's laying forth of the case, and especially harp-
inge vpon the danger, and the burthen of the danger likely
to fall vpon them; so that they seemed, by keeping themselves quiett and hanginge downe of their heades, either to
repent, or to be well in the waye vnto it. Others ther wer
lesse discreet, certainly perhaps haueing lesse also to lose,
who, haueing but little forecast and lesse honesty, with
threateninge lookes and insolent cryes, manifested a promp-
titude to anything but what became them. Among the
rest, one of thes gets vp vpon a forme, and sweares it out
that for his part, come of it what would, he had rather be
hanged and hanged againe, than liue any longer a slaue to
the gripeing and couctous merchands. Another black rough
hewed fellowe followes the preacher out of the church, and
falls into such a fierce and eager expostulation with him
bout the bussinesse, as the poore man is glad to ridd himselfe out of his company with all the haste he can, for feare
of a foule cuffinge with a filthye payre of fists.

The minister gettinge cleare of this beateinge, with much
adoe procures to be conuaide to the king's castle, wher, at
that time, was resident one of the three Gouernours, and
the very same who was to be next in succession (*Mansfield,
Ed.*); to him he relates the passage of the whole bussinesse,
vehemently craueing his assistance, wherin he protested
that as he was nowe their hope, so should he in soe doeing
proue their helpe against a maine distemper and dangerous
infection. This done, and recciuinge some promises that
gaue some reuinement backe againe, he getts to the towne.

Noe soner was he returned, but that the Gouernour *in esse* (misdoubtinge least some distraction might be wrought in his successor by the minister) makes to him to the castle, wher he quickly winnes him (for he had a tonnge glibb ynough, especially to an ill end) to a relaps from his promises; for he told him how the sayd minister had not only saucely inveighed against the regencye of Gouernours, disgraceinge them openly before the people, wherin himselfe must needs bear a part, but that also in perticuler he had in diuers speaches misused both himselfe and his wife. This report, especially the last clause of it, so fastned vpon the man, none of the wisest (such being the fittest subiects for credulitye to worck upon, especially to the worst part), that he sodainely resolues vpon the givinge of his ioint assistance against the minister; and to that purpose (not haueinge the patience to stay for the knowledge of the truth) they both of them together instantly em-bote themselves for the towne: and the easie man was noe soner ther, but in a fury he betakes himselfe to seeke out the preacher, whom he finds alone in his chamber; wher hottly he falls vpon him concerneinge his disparagement of the Gouernours, but all on a fire he was about the perticuler concerneing himselfe and his wife. But the minister (wisely declineing from his naturall speritt, for he saw ther was noe remedy), with the coole ashes of suffrance and the allay of protestations to the contrary, so moderates and tempers him, that once againe he is recouered, and so well satisfied as he professeth himselfe for euer after to stande at least an indifferent man and a newter. And in this moode they goe both together to the Gouernour.

When the Gouernour (constant ynough to his owne courses, and madded with the lenitie of his partnour, being with all prouoked by fresh exprobations from the minister), breakinge out to extremitie of passion, fumes vpon him, and sweares that it wer a good deed to clap him neck and heeles together; the which, for his coate sake only, he forebore to doe; and therefore commanded him, vpon his allegience, to appeare personally the next day in the church, before himselfe and the people, to answere his misdemenours. The next day they are all assembled in the church, and the Gouernour in his seate also, expectinge the appearance of the minister; and not long it was before he comes in among them, and takes up his seate also; from whence (not attendinge the assembly) he himselfe giues the onsett, exhortes the company to take heede of the warninge lyon broken loose among them: tells them that the deuill had gotten stroung footeinge already, and that it behoufed them to looke vnto it betimes; wishinge them, therfore, to praye heartely to God for grace, to be deliuered from his temptations before they wer absolutely and fully possessed. The Gouernour findinge himselfe, in steade of arraingeinge, to be as it wer arraigned, and wher he looked to be a iudge, to be himselfe brought (as he thought) to the barr, not able any longer to endure the affront, he stands up and offers to enter vpon his resolued of iudiciary course; when, sodainely, a huge gust of wind and weather (the which the one side almost cride out for a miracle, the other slighted as an accident vulgar and common in thoes ilands) so ruffles in the leauege (leafy) church, and confounds and disturbs the whole assembly with extreame raine and noice, that therby the bussines is forceably broken of for the instant, and the progression appointed to be in the afternoone in the Gouernours Hall. Being a second time assembled, in the hall, and the minister brought to the barre, a jury of twelve men is empannelled and sworne to passe vpon the poore man, their charge, giuen vnto them by the Gouernours owne mouth, was to enquire about contempt of the Gouernours authoritie, practised and acted by the prisoner at the barre, by his tearmeinge of the petition aforesayd a rebellious and mutinous petition, as also by his addeing farther vnto his contempt, a sedetious and dangerous speach, in callinge the said Gouernour himselfe Machiauell, and sayeing that this was one of his Machiauileian tricks. This charge being thus deliuered, and the jury (without expectance of further proofe) being ready to goe out together to fetch in their verdict, the minister calls vnto them to staye, and aduiseth them, first, to consider and heare his replye. "Concerneinge the petition (sayeth he), it is true, indeed, that I tearmed it rebellious and mutinous, the which I doe thus and thus proue vnto you." "Beare wittnesse," cryes out the Gouernour, "you may nowe iudge him by his owne mouth." "Beare witnesse, and spare not," cryes out the minister; "but with all, beare wittnesse that he calls it an honest and conscionable petition: and wheras it hath bin suggested vnto you that I should tearme this your Gouernour Machiauell, you can all wittnesse with me (for whatsoeuer I spake in thes kind was before you all) that it is most false. True it is, that vpon his open iustification of this ungracious petition, and his enticeinge of the people to proceede in it, I desired and entreated them to consider thoroughly of his cunning and subtletye; and did, indeed, alledge Machiauell as the father of such tricks; but as for the nameing or tearmeinge of him a Machiauell, it came neuer out of my mouth; let me see one wittnesse besides himselfe (who is a partye) that will affirme it." Upon this the jury goes together, and are scarce out before they come in againe; so that presently, with out so much as being once demanded whether they wer agreed, they giue in their verdict; and the hastie Gouernour proceedes to sentence, although one of the jurors, with an audible voice, is heard to saye thes wordes, "This is the foremans verdict only, not ours": the which verdict was, that the minister was guilty of a heinous contempt, both towards the Gouernours authoritie and person. The sentence followed, deliuered by the Gouernors owne mouth, and was that he should be committed to prison; and the other minister, named Keath, to be sent for out of the maine, to serue in his roome. Upon the deliuery of which sentence, one of the Gouernours assistaunce, and diuers others of the company, makeinge a confused noice, at last speake it out aloud, that they wer starued ynough in their bodyes already, and it was neither reason nor conscience to starue their soules too. Why (replies the Gouernour), Mr. Keath shall preach to us in his steade; the other answer that he was noe minister; and, besides, that that when he tooke vpon him to preach, he did it so lamely as they could receiue noe edification by it; and that, therfore, they came to heare him rather vpon constrainct than otherwise.[1] Whereupon the Gouernour concludes, with this kingly or rather popelike catastrophy: "Why then (quoth he) we will make him a minister, and then you shall see he will please you": and so breakes up the Court; but yet with all, findinge that some distast began to be taken at his courses, and not knoweinge how stroung the contrary partye might proue, for that time he slacks the execution of the former sentence against the minister, and suffers him to goe abroad at large.

But not long after (his malice not sufferinge him to let either the man or matter so to rest) he contriues a deuilish plott, for the settinge of the two ministers in extremitie together by the eares : the which quickly worckinge its effect, Keath in the company of the Gouernour in succession comes sodainely to the towne; wher he is noe soner arriued but that (to giue satisfaction to the Gouernour, and to crosse his opposite) he takes openly vpon him to maintaine the course and forme both of the fore-sayd petition; to which end (very vntowardly and idely) he quotes the people of Israells reuolt from their King Rehoboam, when he would not be induced to case them of their grieuances, as also their puttinge to death of Attaliah, and the makeinge of

[1] This is evidence that Keath or Keith was not in Episcopal orders.

Joash king. Vpon this, the two ministers fall instantly into so hott an argumentation and disputes (the Gouernour laughinge at them both in his sleeue the whilst) that ere long publick and pulpitt inuectiues are practised on both sides, besides many other most bitter passages in house and home meetinges; and some actions passing betwixt which wer litle lesse than blowes, in so much that the Scottish minister Keath (findeinge his strength by the Gouernours secret fauour and supportance, and rather affectinge to trust to that than the strength either of his armes or cause) presents an humble petition vnto the Gouernour for justice against the Welsh minister Lewes.[1] And thus hath the malitious man his desire: so that the very next day, the poore Mr. Lewes is a second time haled to the barr, and hath this twelue God-fathers empanelled vpon him; who are nowe to enquire concerneinge certaine abuses, by him offred to the person of his fellowe minister, that reuerend man Mr. Keath, as in perticuler for tearmeinge of him a sower of sedition, an heretick, and had violently thrust him out of his chamber; to which pointes Mr. Lewes made the best answer he could for himselfe, and so sufficient (it seemed) they seemed to the jury, as that only taxeinge him for the last and leaste, he became therby free from all capitall inflictions, and so escaped that snare, to the noe smale discontent of him that layed it for him.

But by this time growes this Gouernours first moneth to an end (for why should I blott my paper, and abuse my reader, with the rehearsalls of so many fooleries, cousanages,[2] and barbarismes, by some cruell strappadoeinge executions vpon poore and deiected delinquents that his aquavita-moneth, produced ouer and aboue), and nowe stepps in his successor, who, whether it wer in mistake of the violences of his predecessor, in respect he knew that they wer for the

[1] Lewis Hughes. Smith frequently drops his surname also in his *Generall History*, which is one of many internal evidences that this work is by the same author.   [2] Query cozenages.

most part maliciously contriued and prosecuted, or that, in his owne nature he affected to sitt still, eate, and especially drinck, at his ease and to his full, the which he found (followeinge the others stepps) he could not so delicately doe; whichsoeuer I saye of thes it was that wrought vpon him, notoriously knowen it is, that for the most part, a still, calme, quiet and drousie moneth he held; in which most pleaseinge and beloued path his destinated successor also most brauely marched in; so that for their two times of regencye (and thoes wer two whole monethes) saue that the constant sunne made it clearely daye, a man might haue taken them for a perpetuall night; not a hoe, axe, sawe, pickaxe, or shouell was so much as once heard in their streates; not an oare scene, or heard, or dash in their harbours, vnless some times, and at some certaine and sett seasons, when their stoute stomachs compelled them vnto it: only (that you might knowe, when they wer awake) the shrill clang of a peuter pott beete an alarm sometimes, the which for the most part, was so resolutely and deepely answered, as that before the end of the desperate fraye, either the one was vtterly spent, or the other confounded and ouer-throwne; and thus employed, bestowed, finished wer the two sweet monethes of these two sweet youthes.

For the moneth followeinge (in his cue) vp starts vpon the stage the second time that man of mickle might the minister-maker, and marrer: he in whose dayes (oh! happy dayes) comes in the *Edwin* from England, fraughted with a generall supply, and especially well prouided with liquours; whose master, an old acquaintance of the Gouernours, is exceedeingly wellcomed by him: yet rather (I must tell you) for his liquorish supply than old acquaintance. This shyp is sodainely, therfore, vnladen, and her longed for fraught committed to a clerck of the store, newly created for that purpose, beinge a man euery waye after the Gouernours owne heart. Durcing her stay also (misdoubtinge some telltaleinge letters by her returne) this Gouernour secretly mediateth a reconcilement with the minister he had formerly so vexed, the which also by his interposition of the sayd master of the bark he easily obteyneth of the casye man : and withall dureing the short time of her abode in the harbour he so absolutely disposeth of all thinges after the directions and iniunctions sent him from the adventurors, and seemes so altered and conuerted a man, as that euen letters of commendation and hope are procured in his behalfe from that very hand which he so much distrusted, and so the edge of that weapon turned, and the blowe not only diuerted but strikeinge for him.

The *Edwin* stayes not long here, for haueinge done that she came for, and findinge noe home-fraught (for from no worck, no care, noe gouernment, what could be had but priuations, that is to saye noethinges) she sodainely quitts the ilands, and being thoroughly emptied of all her liquours, so makes her way homeward. Vpon her also (whether it wer to make fayre weather for himselfe and his brethren, or for himselfe only) one of the three gouernours would needes shyp himselfe, so that two only of the six are left behind. This bark is no soner gone, and so the feare of tale telleinge departed with her, but that most naturally and greedely, the late conuerted Gouernour (become now in effect the only one) returns to his vomitt, to his vomitt indeed ; for haueing made a Scoggins dole of all her supply,[1] the liquor and best necessaryes being shared betwixt himselfe and his fauorites (and they only the drinckers only), in the meane time the weake and sick people, women with child and such like (who for the most part neuer came nearer to it than the hearesaye, although for them it was both most proper and most entended), fell quickly into many distresses and miserable wants; whilst the Gouernour and his gourmandizeing

[1] Scoggins' dole. I have sought in vain for an explanation of this singular expression.

minions, dayly and hourely wallowed in their swineish excesses. Incredible it wer to write what iniurious tricks, distempers, wroungs, confusions, ridiculous behauiour, disgraces, contempts, and euen shames both to their creation as they wer men, and to their place, as they tooke vpon them to be magistrates, wer hourely and continually bred up and practised by them dureinge their few moneths of lordinge it; and to augment the misery, many other accidentall ills also concurred; as very vnseasonable weather; mightie windes, and frequent huricanoes: so that at one time eight botes wer lost, and some lines withall (a blowe at that age of the plantation as deepe and dangerous to it as the ruine of the 88-fleete to the Spaniard). The fortes also wer generally defective, and not so much as one bote left at the towne to manne them vpon any occasion: so that at last, not only the people very generally (especially those of the soberest sort) but euen some of thoes who by Mr. Moore's directions (in nature of a commission) wer appointed as assistants in that six-fold Gouernment, began to be impatiently weary, and in loathinge of so abominable and worse than heathenish a life. It was therfore priuately resolved among some fewe of them (the minister, Mr. Lewes, being head of the partye) that the present gouernment should formally be called into question, and reduced vnto that prime forme, left by Mr. Moore, of haueinge six gouernours, in their severall moneths, and twelve assistants; noe affayres and bussinesse of what nature soeuer being to be determined and decided without the consent of three of the sayd gouernours and six of the assistants; and to this order the sayd six gouernours and twelve assistants had formerly sett their hands, it being also the very same thatt was afterward allowed and confirmed by the letters of the aduenturers from England. But whilst these new confederates wer in contriueinge how to drawe the assistants together with most secrecye and conveniencye to a consultation and

so a resolution, it fell out that one of the partye, beinge
a forward man, had a warrant serued vpon him from the
Gouernour, that commanded the deliuery of a certaine dogg;
this command, the ouer hastie and precipitated man refuseth
to obey, publickly pretendinge for himselfe a vsurpation in
the Gouernour; and withall he obserues that the hand of
the Gouernour in succession, fixed to the warrant, was coun-
terfeited and falsse: whervpon, the day followeinge, the
minister repayres to the sayd Gouernour in succession (being
then in the Maine) and enformes him of the bussinesse and
in the perticuler of the falsefieinge of his hand; he also acquainted him with the intention for the renewement of
Mr. Moore's order in the forme of Gouernment; tellinge
him that the execution of it was already in action by the refusall of a submission to a warrant sent from the vsurpour;
as for himselfe in his owne person the distastes and exceptions against him wer far lesse, and likely ynough it was
that he might be continued in his command and accepted of
for one of the six, prouided he did betimes ioyne himselfe to
so good and stroung a side, and so summon the assistants
to a meeteinge to that purpose, the which (to saue him a
labour) he himselfe would do for him against the next
Saterdaye, and the rendeuous to be at the very towne itselfe.
But to this the plaine (not to saye dull) speritted man (who
neuer did much of his owne head, and yet for the most
part chose alwayes worse heads than his owne to be his
guides) gave noe answer; but that that sett daye he spake
of for the meeteinge was somewhat at the sonest, "for
wheras (quoth he) you have appointed it vpon Saterday
next, I have some occasions that will not let me be at the
towne vntill Monday after": the which speach, whether it
proceeded from his vnder or ouer-apprehension of the danger
it may very well be questioned; but howsoeuer, it rather
quickned than slacked the diligence of the minister; so that
findinge it necessary to relye rather vpon themselues than

such a broken reede, himselfe with one more of the assistants make instantly for the towne, ther to be ready against the limited daye of meetcinge; wher they assure themselues to find more of their partye, and especially of the assistants.

But in the interim, the gouernour ther, by the ouer-open and improuident carriage of the businoss, had gotte not only an incklinge, but a plaine and thorough knowledge of the whole conspiracye; so that callinge his deare Bacchanalian crue to counsell vpon it, it is conceiued and concluded, both for wisdome and necessitie, to stand vpon their garde, and to that end the people of the towne are for diuers days held together: the drumme beats, the coulours are flieing; shott and powder prepared, and the smale shott fixed; and (for the last refuge) it is valiantly and stoutly resolued on, that some barrells of powder being conueyed into the fort that commands the towne, and is at the present called Warwick Fort, vpon findinge themselues ouerprest with multitudes, though all the munition was in their hands, they should retire theither, and from thence playe vpon them with the ordinance, and so talke with them far ynough of. In the thickest of which resolutions and executions the poore minister and his companion, little dreameinge of any such reuelations or preparations, come quietly with a full wind saylcinge vp to the towne, and land vpon the warfe. Noe soner are they on shore, but their lodgeinge is prouided for them by the gouernour, vnder the command of the marshall, and a warrant presently conueyed into the maine for the apprehension of a third man of the societye, whom the gouernour especially feared, and therfore hated; who, by vertue therof is quickly brought up to the towne, and vnder pretence and coulour of extorteinge from him some farther important confessions, throughly tortured; wer vpon a generall expectance of the conclusion (by some delaye of proseqution against the delinquents) followeth vpon it, and varietie of other opinions and censures flie about and enlarge themselues in their flight.

But the gouernour haueinge obteyned his cheife drift, which was by the breakeinge of this course to hold on his owne with out interruption, and not holdinge it safe to call vp more speritts at once then he could charme downe againe, and keep out of the circle, by litle and litle began to make shewe of the assawageinge of his fury and reuenge, and to suffer himselfe (as urged forsooth by his innate disposition and delicate good nature) a second time to be reconciled to the minister, and for his sake with his prison-fellowe also; who, for their partes likewise, by this time wer willinge and desirous of any reasonable composition; only the third man (as haueinge endured that which would not suffer him to be endured abroad) was remoued prisonner at large to Coopers Iland, wher he remained in custody of the captain of that fort vntill the arriuall of Captain Tucker, which was not long after. And thus was this bundle of bussinesse both pierced and pieced.[1]

Some fewe monethes after (the gouernours bowle being returned to its old byasse) ther fell out an accident, which though it lighted vpon the persons of certaine poore and private men, yet, in respect of its raritie, and litle lesse than miraculousnesse (that withall, also, I may a litle refresh my reader with some varietie, especially wher the fare hath bin so ill cooked, as by thes six gouernours) I am resolued to bestowe vpon it as well a large as true description.

Vpon a Fridaye morneinge, in a March (the moneth aboue all others apt to produce such effects), and the yeare 1615, one Andrewe Hilliard, with six more able and strounge bodied men, in a bote of two or three tunnes, went out to sea to fish; and so eager they wer on the voiage, that neither a break-fast is made before they went, nor any

[1] Captain Tucker arrived in May 1616. The actual application of physical torture to this prisoner, by the rack or thumbscrew, seems clearly hinted at.

other victualls carried along with them, saue only a fewe palmitoe berries. The wind was fayre of the shore, a smale constant gale from a cleare skie, which seemed to promise a continuance of it; and so it did vntill they wer come to their fishinge place, which was about some foure leauges of to sea: wer they had noe soner cast killock, but the wind begins somewhat to blowe; and at an instant, so ouer growne it was, that their killock roape broke,[1] when, being not able, neither with sayle nor oare, to make any way to the shore, the violence of the weather at last so preualed, as they quite lost sight of land, when, dispayreinge of all recouery, and vtterly tired with roweinge, they committed themselues to Gods mercye, and throweinge some few fish (most improuidently) into the sea that they had taken at their beginninge to fish, they let the bote driue whether she would. In this case and manner they remained from Friday vntill Sunday, with a continuall and exceedeinge tempest lieinge vpon them. On Sunday morneinge, the storme being somewhat abated, they hoysed sayle and made (as they guessed) towards the ilands. Towards night it grew stark calme; so that (being too weake, both in body and minde, to use their oares) they left their boate vpon drift all that night. Vpon Munday, by peepe of day, Hilliarde (for nowe all his companions wer past strength, either to helpe him or themselues), before a smale gale of wind, spreade his sayles againe; and on Tuesday one of them died, and was throwen ouer bord by Hilliard. On Wednesdaye died three more; on Thirsdaye another; and on Thirsday, at night, the sixth man. All these, saue the last, wer by Hilliard buried in the sea; for, being nowe growen ouer weake himselfe, he was forced to lett this last carkasse lie by him in the bote, because he was not able to throwe it ouer bord, being nowe left desolate and all alone.

This wreatched poore man (for what is wreatchednesse in

---

[1] Killock rope. The rope attached to the killock, the heavy stone used as an anchor.

this worlde, if his was not), being left in this case with
only one dead corps by him, who, in spight of his nose,
would keepe him company; being of an extraordinary
stroung constitution, and yet sustaineinge extreame com-
punctions, putt vpon him both by feare and famine, at last
resolued to make some vse of his stinckinge bedfellowe, to
serue his rageinge appetite; whervpon he dissects the carkasse, and with much adoe, throwinge the intrayles into
the water, he spreads the body abroad, tilted open with a
stick, and so lets it lie, as a cesterne to receiue some lucky
raine water; and this God sent him presently after, so that
in one smale shower he recouered about foure spoonefulls,
to his unexpressable refreshment; he also preserued some
of the bloud in a shoe, to the quantitie of halfe a pinte,
which he did very spareingly drincke of to moysten his
mouth. He did also cutt of some of the flesh out of one of
the thighes, and did eate thereof two scuerall dayes, to the
quantitie and waight in the whole of about a pound. On
Munday, which was the eleventh day from his loseinge
sight of the land, two flieinge fishes (by Gods prouidence,
certainely, since a sparrowe falls not on the ground with
out it) fell into his boate; and the one of which he tooke,
and cuttinge of the head sucked the warme icusie bloud
therof, to his great comfort. About an houre after (to his
incomparably farr greater comfort, you will not doubt), he
once again discrieth the land, from the which (as you haue
heard) he had bin separated cleuen whole dayes and nights,
and in which time he had buried in the bottome of the sea
all his compannions, and was thus gotten home all alone,
sustained and kept aliue for the most part with their flesh
and bloud. About some foure houres with in night, after
his first recouery of the sight of land (neither knoweinge
nor careing what or wher it was so he could but gett to it),
he was cast upon the rocks nere vnto a place called Port-
royall in Southampton Tribes, wher his bote was presently

F

splitt to peeces, but himselfe (though extremely weake) made shyft to clamber up so steepe and high a rock as would haue troubled the ablest man in the ilands to haue done that by day which he did by night.

Being thus astride on the rock, the tumblinge sea had gotten such possession on his braynes, that for a while it was before his giddy head would suffer him to venter upon the forsakeinge of it. At last, towards the morneinge, he crawles ashore, and then, to his accomplished joy, he discernes wher he is, and trauayles halfe a daye with out any other refreshment than water, in the drinckinge wherof, wisely and temperately for a man of his coate, he stints himselfe to a wilck-shell full only at a time (for otherwise, certainely, he had drunk his death); in which case he attaines a friends house of his, wher sodenly entringe upon them, he is for a good while taken for a ghoast. At last (well looked vpon) acknowledged and receiued with ioye; his story (after some houres recouerye of strength to tell it) heard out with admiration; and himselfe, not long after, conuayed to the towne, wher the gouernour takes so much time of truce from doeinge noethinge sane drinck hard, as to see him, then to wonder at him, and once againe to cause him to tell ouer his legend; the which being finished, he letts him depart to liue as poorely as euer he did before, and returnes himselfe, also, to his old tricks and beloued occupation, as you shall nowe heare.[1]

For the two gouernours (wherof one of them stoode for very litle better than a cypher), being cleared from all impediments (the opposite faction being dasht, as you haue heard), began to haue a sence of their owne ouerlastinge, especially in the point of liquour; so that nowe haueinge noe more headye drincks in their store at the towne and being tyred with their loblolly bowleinge, they grew starck weary with doeing noethinge, and scorneinge to be thus kept sober

[1] It is added in the *General History* that Andrew Hilliard, the hero of these adventures, was living in the year 1622.

in spight of their teethes, diligent and well nosed intelligencers are presently employed to make discoueries of close hords and secret mines of bottells in the maine; whervpon some fewe being serued open, and aduertisements sent up therafter to the emptie flaggons of the towne, a progresse (vnder most important pretences) is presently resolued vpon by the Gouernour into thoes partes, and the jests sorted and layed out, accordinge to the most admired and delicate situation of the Aquavita. With three or foure choyce and selected men, therfore, captaines, lieutenants, and old soldiers, all of the bacchanalian band, amaine flies the Gouernour into the Maine; a flagg is carryed before him in signe of state; a messenger is sent before to proclaime his approach. To to tell you what antick naked masks of both sexes; what fisshinge, fireworcks, are euerywher prepared to entertaine him; what extreame ridiculous and contemptible actions ensue vpon it; wer scarce either credible or clenly to talke of; especially considereinge that the ententiue man himselfe, and his drie societie (ameinge mainly at the end of the bussinesse he came for) in respect therof neglected all other ceremoniall complements; so that deepely diueinge into the bottome of euery concealement, they leaue not, vntill in all places they haue suckt out the uery dreggs therof; and so haueinge made a finall and through discouery, returne by the same way they came, to the towne, to the great applause and alacritie of the whole Court.

The Gouernour being thus returned to his setled house, not long after, euen as he was sittinge by the fire and takeinge a whiff of tobacco, one of the prime baylies of the tribes (who although noe resident courtier), yet not altogether out of the societie at that time) by rushinge in vpon him shakeinge his pocketts and cryinge out "Good newes", snatched (as it wer) the fire out of his mouthe; so that sodainely startinge up out of his chayre: " What newes, man, (saythe he) is ther any rosa-solis come to towne." "Noe sir",

F 2

answers the baylie, "but next that the best in the world"; and fluttcringe his pocketts againe, who thervpon giue a clang with a fewe dollers that wer in them; "the treasour is found at the Flemish wrack, the treasour is found: we are all made men, made men." Madd men indeed.

But herevpon (this as they would have it, being so greedely swallowed, as they almost wer choked withall, and the Gouernour himselfe euen ready to crack with swellinge) a bote with a choyce gang is posted awaye to lade herselfe up to the brimes with Spanish dollers and Portugall crusadoes: among the which merry gang I must nott forgett a charitable smith, who being told by one of the company (betweene iest and earnest) that in respect he was one of the cheife of the gouernours fauorites and a good bowler, it could not be but that his share in this purchase would amount to noe lesse than the makeinge of him a gentleman, if not with an improuement of a ladyship for his wife, "And then (quoth he) you will not knowe vs poore men." "Yes, yfaith", answers the blacksmith, "whatsoeuer becomes of me in this kind, I will whilst I am here make fishe-hookes for the poore people rather than they shall starue." Neither doth the Gouernour himselfe forbeare to proclaime what he would doe with this huge treasure, when it was brought to him. "We will first of all (sayeth he) paye ourselues to a doite of all that the aduenturers doe owe vs; then we will farther lick our fingers as we shall see cause, and so leaue the remainder to them." But awaye (euen ready to kill themselues with roweinge) goeth this gang vpon their golden errand: when, arriueinge at the hopefull place, instead of the heapes they looke for, behold some smale aspersions of dollers (to the totall value of about some twenty poundes sterlinge) are found; some of them gathered by the neighbouringe people before their arriuall, the rest with extreame diligence raked together by themselues; being a remnant, noe question, of some greater store, the which being washt out of some wreake not farr of, was beaten vpon that shore. But this, after the collection of it from all hands, and a long search in vaine for more (as being loath euen to creditt their owne eyes which nowe serued them cheifly to the frustrateing of their farther hopes), they at length returned with what they had to the gapeinge Gouernour at the towne, who recciveinge of them the account of their employement, and withall the fruict it had produced, was glad to make much and be contented with the gleaneinge instead of the huge haruest he promised to himselfe; the which, because it proued not sufficient to discharge the great arreages and debts challenged by the people from the aduenturers, like the wise stewart, he layd it by to serue to feede himselfe against the time he looked and feared to be putt out of his stewardshyp; vpon which, from that time forward, he began euery day more and more to ruminate, and indeed not without cause.

For the company of aduenturers in England, haueinge recciued newes by the *Edwin's* safe arriuall of the rouells and the perpetuall Christmas kept in their Sommer Ilands, found it more than necessary to make them breake up house: so that truely vnderstandinge that the originall of those gamboleinge times proceeded from the miserable insufficiencye of the commandors ther, they resolued to make presently an election of a newe gouernour, and with all speed to send him awaye: when being in the deepest of their cares, how to serue their turnes best this waye, Mr. Tucker, the prime searcher of Grauesend, by meanes of certaine of the custome farmers, who wer of the Company, made sute for the acceptance of Mr. Daniell Tucker, his brother, who was lately come ouer to him from Virginia, wher he had bin for diuers yeares Cape-merchant:[1] the which (by reason of the neere

[1] This term, Cape merchant, occurs frequently in connection with the affairs of the Virginia Company, but its precise origin I have not been able to discover. He was a subordinate person; factor, supercargo, or agent. Thus, in 1617, Captain Argall, when acting as Deputy-Governor

correspondencye, and mutuall traffique between the farmers and the searchers) was so affectionately pursued and sollicited for him, that the aduenturers were brought to a consent, and the rather, as conceiueinge that by his being in Virginia, and his sight of the conduction of the affayres ther, could not chuse, but much enable him for that charge. At the next great quarter court therfore, the sayd Mr. Daniell Tucker is, by a generall erection of hands, chosen Gouernour: and within a while, after haueing his commission signed, and therby made a captaine, being throughly instructed and reasonably well prouided, he is shypped awaye in the good shyp called the *George*, and so makes onwards of his voiage; in her company was also consorted the *Edwin*, diuers times fore-mentioned; and upon them shypped besides diuers other passengers to be residents in those ilands.

It was not long before thes shyps thus fraughted arriue upon the coast of the Sommer ilands: from whence being discouered, word is by and by carryed to the Gouernour: who at the first being somewhat daunted, sodainely recouers by sufferinge himselfe to be assured (his flatteringe hopes allwayes leadeinge him to belieue as he would haue it) that of thes two discouered sayles, the smaller was the frigate that he had (as you haue heard) sent out to the West Indies, the other some riche prize that she had taken.

of Virginia in the absence of Sir Thomas Dale, "held himselfe disparaged in that the Company thought their Cape merchant a fit man to deliver their letters into his hands" (*Neill*, pp. 115-18). They write to the Council of the Colony 1621: " With great difficulty we have erected a private magazine, men being most unwilling to be drawn to subscriptions that may end in smoke. If you expect for the future any such place, it must be your principall care the Cape merchant be not constrained to vent his commodities att any sett price, and in particular not to be enforced to take tobacco at any certain rate" (*id.*, p. 226). The phrase has perhaps some connection with early settlements near Cape Henry. It does not appear to have had long currency. The writer refers below to a vainglorious project of Tucker in 1618, to charter a vessel for Virginia: " He conceived it would proue an action of reputation, if he who had bin a Cape merchant in Virginia, should nowe sett out a vessell vnto there as a Cape Governour."

Whervpon the gang are commanded to make out to wellcome them and to bring back the good newes of their great fortune. But before the nowe growen rustic rowers could be gotten together, and gett to them, the *Edwin* (being a barke of very good sayle) recouers the harbour of the King's castle, wher being found by the towne bote she is boarded, and tells them (the litle looked and lesse wished for) truth of the bussinesse; as that they both of them came directlie from England, and that the shyp (yet) abroad, had brought a newe Gouernour in her; and diuers other passengers of sort, some wherof were for subordinate officers, and the rest for priuate inhabitants, and to be planters in the ilands.

The bote returneinge thus heauily laden, vnburthens herselfe into the gouernours ears; who, at an instant, findinge all his hopes thus blowne up, lookes pale, growes malincholy, and, in plaine tearmes, appeares directly deiected; but his blusteringe councellours (who, indeed, wer ladds that durst proiect any thinge, so that the execution of it wer absent), with bigge lookes and loude oathes, bring him into a litle holdinge up his head; so that at last, with a huge much adoe, they clap and hale hime into a course, the which (passeing on in but so far as he did) would perhaps haue cost an honester man the makeing of a wrie mouth; for they told him that it could not be, but that the colonye and plantation in generall was so taken and wonne with a loue of his gouernment and clemencye, that if he would but hold up his finger, they would venter all they had to goe through stich with him, though it wer into the deepest cane in the ilands, and yet ther are terrible straunge ones, and some of them as rare peeces of naturall worckman-shyp, as I am perswaded the world hath). They coniure him, therefore (for a while at least), to stand vpon his strength, and brauely to giue this newe commer to vnderstande that vnlesse he brought with him either mony, or some other answerable content, the people (who in vaine had sweat thcmselues drye ynough already, haueing their reward spunne out vnto them in hopes only) wer fully resolued that they would accept of noe straung and newe Gouernour whatsoeuer; noe, though he came commissioned with ten thousand martiall lawes; but would keepe and hold him they had, being a man both well knowen vnto them, and as well beloued. This course, after some warme objections, and very many but what its the Gouernour at last settles himselfe vpon; trusty messengers are ther vpon presently posted into the Maine, to grope the mind of the multitude; and frequent meetinges had, in a desolate cabbin, somewhat remoued from the towne, for the fashionninge up and lickinge of this monstrous bearewhelpe; amidst the midst of which contriuements, the ship the *George*, with the newe Gouernour, moores herselfe in the harbour also of the Kings-castle: and Mr. Lewes, the minister (fatall to the faction), comes to a discouery of the plott, and resolues, with all expedition, to aduertize the new Gouernour of it; and to that end secretly prepares a bote to carry him abord the shyp, from whence also is sent a message from the newe Gouernour ther to him at the towne, to lett him vnder stande of his being ther, and his being there, what he was.

To the one (some heate being receiued out of the Maine, though it proued afterward but as a St. Anthonies fire), it was presently answered, that he should heare more from them shortly: for the other, a command is layd vpon him not to stirre from the towne; the which he refuseinge to obey, and entringe a bote to act the disobedience, certaine muskettiers are sent out, who, from the shore, threaten to deliuer a volly of shott upon him vnlesse he returne, who (not trustinge to their cortesie) performes what they extort, and so is stayed. The next morrowe (to make good the work), a barberous heraught (herald) (for ouer and aboue his manners, he was a barber), infinitely worse cloathed than he that Lewes of France sent to our Edward of England, is found out and sent to the shyp, to deliuer this message peremptorily to the newe Gouernour, that with out mony and content, noe consent or acceptance. To this the newe Gouernour replies, throughly and stoutly, that he bore Kinge James his authoritie with him, which should proue sufficient and auayleable ynough to curbe all such rebellious persons, as durst make that errand good; and with that short reward commands him to be gone; who, at his returne, relateinge what he had found, the great mans resolution is againe so be-shaken, as he thincks it the best course to be quiett, and to vse suspension vntill he sees farther: and, by waye of a beginning to it, himselfe, with the minister Keath, and some two or three of his consorts, restort abroad to that purpose, wher they are fashionably recciued by the newe Gouernour (who would take noe notice of any thinge); and so, without any farther discourse, dismissed back to the towne, wher they are noe souer ashore but againe another fitt takes them, and newe deuises are broached, the euent of which vents you shall nowe also heare.

For the newe Gouernour presently, after the departure of these ladds of the towne, enters into counsell, and resolues vpon a speedie goeing thether himselfe, for findinge the humourous heate of their braynes very well allayed, he thincks it noe discretion, by the least delay to giue time to a relaps, by some newe distillations: the next daye, therfore, is appointed for that purpose; at what time, accompanied with his owne shyp-company, and some of the best sort of the maine, being euen ready to sett his foote into the bote, ther comes one in panting haste from the Kingscastle, and tells him that ther are certaine botes and men sent from the towne with directions and command to ceese vpon that peece. The Gouernour being somewhat stirred with this intelligence, commands the master of the shyp, the pilote, and two or three of the best of the maine men, to take some force with them, and to make good that important place. Thes being gott to the castle, finde noe manner of resistance, nor the least shewe of it; so that leauing some of their people ther, and giueinge in charge to the gunner, that he should neither suffer any man to land vpon them, nor any of his to quitt the place, but to stand vpon their garde vntill he heard farther, they presently make back themselues to the shyp and informe the Gouernour, that all things wer quiett and sure: true, indeed, that some three or foure of the towne, commanded by an old soldier, had bin ther that morneing; but stayd not, returneinge instantly to the place whence they came.

The Gouernour being thus assured, prepares (although disswaded by some) to make his waye for the towne; and the same afternoone is sett downe for it: in the meane space, the man at the towne, hauinge receiued knowledge from thoes that (as you haue heard) were at the Castle that morneinge, and sent by him to ioyne with some other of his partie that vpon promise he expected; that noe creature appeared ther for him, nor any good possibly to be done, and besides that the newe Gouernour was certainly vpon his waye to the towne, very well accompanied, with manye reuolted maine-men in his troupe; grewe vpon the newes so quite appalled, calme and cast downe (his feare nowe preuaylcinge ouer his ambition), that from thence forward he absolutely (yet secretly) resolues to giue ouer all further aspireinges, and to yeeld to the time. By this time the Gouernour with his company are descried from the towne's warfe, wher vpon (by command of the old, nowe a newe man) a garde is prepared for him to passe through, and himselfe attends to receiue him at his landeinge. Sone after he attaines the shore, and is mett and saluted to the shoe, from whence he goeth directly and instantly to the church which was hard by; but by the waye thether hath the better hand taken of him by the quondam man (an error which, if he tooke notice of, was so much the greater by his enduro-ance). Being entred the church, and a sermon ended, the old Gouernour begins a speach concerneing grieuances, and some (I cannot tell what) amends makeinge for them; but being cutt of by the newe, and a few good words scattred among them, he at last (though not without some druncken mutterings) causeth his commission to be read out, and so is receiued and accepted of for their Gouernour. And nowe, being to fall vpon somewhat more serious and fashionable times, it is exacted that our stile also proue more sober and graue; for it is a decorum requirable and becomeinge all historians to fitt their phrase to their matter, for otherwise it shewes as vnseemely and mishapen as to apparell a dwarfe in one of the garde's coates.

Lib. IV.—*Captaine Tucker, the 3rd Gouernor.*—1616-1619.

The newe Gouernour being thus settled, Anno 1616, and so to begin his regencye and the forme of it, not findinge any beaten path troden out vnto him by his predecessors the six Gouernors; nor being acquainted, or so much as knoweinge any other president besides that of Virginia, tho which he had both seene and felt dureing his time of Cape merchantshyp ther, he nimbly and readyly resolued (as a course also that best sorted with his owne disposition) wholy to pursue thoes stepps, and the rather because he found the people generally both abborreinge all exacted labour, as also in a manner disdaineinge and loatheinge to be com-manded by him, so that he conceiued noe better course could be taken either to force them to worck or to worck his owne reuenge, than by that stricktness and rigour which he had discerned to produce some such effect in that other colonye.

Sodainelye, therefore, he fell to dispose and enioine the

[1] See p. 69 for explanation of the phrase "Cape merchant".

people of the generallitie, which were resident with him at St. George's (being at that time about 150 persons) to seuerall kinds of labours, as some to cleare ground and sett corne, others to fall timber, hale trees, square and sawe them, the rest to plant vines and other fruicts brought with him out of England; and these labourours had certaine seuerall onerseers sett ouer them in the nature of task-masters, and wer by breake of day to repayre to the towne's warfe at the sound of the drumme, and from thence to be disposed to their places of employment, and ther to worck vntill nine of the clock in the morneinge; and in the afternoone, from three vntill sunnes sett. Neither had they any other allowance at that time for all this than meate, drinck, and clothes, with a certaine paye of base-mony (deliuered vnto the Gouernour by the Company), the which haueing a hogge stampt upon it on the one side (in memory it should seeme of the great number of wild swine found vpon the Ilands at their first discouery) was, in a scoff, tearmed by the people hogge mony.[1]

[1] Specimens of this coinage are extant, but extremely rare. The writer is fortunate enough to possess the examples figured below. Only two other specimens are known in England, and there are none in the British Museum.—See *Numismatic Chronicle*, 1876-1878.

This course thus fastened vpon and squared after the Virginian rule, and in perticular imitatinge diuers orders digested by Sir Thomas Dale, while he was marshall ther, a coppy wherof he had brought with him and often consulted with,[2] he began from them to looke into his English instructions giuen him by the Company; whervpon (by one Norwood, a surveyor, sent ouer for that and some other purposes in Mr. Moore's time) he began to lay out the eight tribes in the Maine, which were to consist of fiftie shares to a tribe, and five-and-twenty acres to a share. He also began at the same time to place some colony men on some of his especiall friends' shares. He swore also certaine of the cheife men of the tribes to be baylies of every tribe; and appointed as many men as he was able for all supplied shares. This done, haueinge caused the shyps that came with him to be vnladen, and their ladeinge to be layd up in the publick store; he from thence distributed it to his worckmen in generall. Some newe botes likewise began to be builded, and the pinnace called the *Thomas*, which laye vpon the rocks, was brought to the town, where (by the Gouernour's feare and command) she was haled vp into the dock and ther laye chayned, wher her rotten ribbs are to be discerned vnto this day. In the beginninge also of the second moneth of his gouernment, he directed warrants to the baylies of the tribes for the holdinge of a generall assize at St. George's on the fourteneth of the same moneth; presently after which summons he visited the King's castle at the Gurnett's Head, and appointed one Mr. Stoke, that came ouer with him (being his ancient acquaintance in Virginia, as was also his wife), to be the prime commander ther, and the title of Liuetenant of the Castle, being

---

[2] Sir Thomas Dale was Governor of Virginia May-August 1611. His orders will be found in a tract by W. Strachey, "For the Colony in Virginea Britannia, Lawes Diuine, Morall, and Martiall, etc. London, 1612." (*Peter Force's Tracts*, 1844, vol. iii.)

the same man, who at this day, by a speciall commission from the Company, holdeth the same command as captaine, which certainely is a charge and place that requireth a very able, sufficient, sober, and trustie person.[3]

Much about which time the pinnace called the *Edwin*, which came out of England with the Gouernor, is sent out for the Ilands of the West Indies (some of which, called the Sauuage and Virgin Ilands, being not aboue eight or ten dayes' sayle distant) by direction from the Company in England, to trade with the natiues for catell, corne, plants, and other commodities necessarye for a plantation, a course of great importancye, and which, had it been followed and pursued, would certainely have produced fayrer and more hopefull effects for the good and growth of that solitary colonye, than all the supplies or magazin shyps from England either haue or will doe thes twenty yeares, the which, notwithstandeinge, hath not only bin since vtterly discontinued but (from some secret reasons hereafter to be touched) strictly forbidden, and all concourse and receit of any such vpon great penalties inhibited.

Presently, after this pinnace's departure, began the assize at St. George's, wher (fewe matters of note being handled besides) ther was arraigned and condemned by a jury of twelue men (but in a disorderly form, mixt betwixt martiall lawe and the lawes of England) which defaced them both, one John Wood, a poore but desperate and open-mouthed Frenchman, who, in his cupps, haneinge saucely and arrogantly spoken to the Gouernor, was herevpon attached; and being endicted of mutiny and rebellion, vpon his triall was cast; and so being sentenced by one deputed to that purpose (for the Gouernor himselfe, findinge his insufficiencyes that way, neuer satt iudge in his owne person) was publicly

[3] Stokes held this command down to 1627, when the Assembly deposed him. See the " Petition of the People" (*Memorials of Bermuda*, i, 421).

hanged within two dayes after, choyce being made of the person of that poore man to lett the rest knowe that both his authoritie extended to life, and that they should all of them take heed how they prouoked him hereafter; and indeed from that time forward it was obserued that he ouerfast declined to such a height of seueritie towards all men as wanted but very litle of crueltye and tyranny; so that he hath bin seene, in one morneinge before breakefast to cudgell with his owne hands not fewer than fortie of his poore workmen euen for very smale and slight neglects, in so much as that it grewe at last to be a receiued generall obseruation amongst them, that when in a morneinge his hatt stoode on the one side, and such a couloured sute of cloathes was worne, ther was noe comeinge nere him all that whole daye after.

But this impatiencye and ouer-rigour of the Gouernour produced, within a short time after, an effect not much lesse than a miracle; for fine plaine and simple fellowes, whose names wer Richard Saunders, Thomas Harrison, William Godwin, Henry Puitt, and one James Barker (the only gentleman among them, being one of old Judge Barkers sonnes, and cunningly sent ouer by some of his friends or rather kindred, and as straungely by them procured to be kept here), thes fiue I saye, wherof Saunders was questionlesse the prime man, and only marriner, being in extreme discontent, and resolueinge to vndergoe all hazards rather then to live vnder so hard a condition, which they esteemed noe lesse than a meere slauery, confederated themselues and determined to make an escape out of the ilands at what prize soeuer. The course therfore being plotted by Saunders, William Godwin, being a shypcarpenter, and Thomas Harrison a joyner, repayred to the Gouernour, and with pleaseinge insinuatious tell him, that if it might stand with his goode likeingo to furnish them only with some bords, tarre and rozin, and some other smale necessaries, they wer resolued, of themselues, to build, in Sands his tribe, being a farr fitter and conuenienter place than the towne, both for launceinge and fittinge of her, and being priuate also could offer them noe distractions, a stoute bote with close hatches, of some two tunnes in burthen, to goe out to sea in all weathers to fish: the which haueinge absolutely finished, they would bring up to the towne, to rest ther at his seruice and dispose. The Gouernour (halfe proude that he had thus brought (as he conceiued) his men to so good a passe, as in this manner to offer themselues to so necessary a worck, instantly with all willingnesse furnished them with whatsoeuer they could desire, and with the best wordes his disposition could afford, encourageth them to their task: who being quickened and lightned by so luckye a beginninge, goe lustily on in their bussinesse; so that in a short time the bote is brought to perfection; of whose stoutnesse, and what excellent fishinge seruice she should doe for the Gouernour, they bragge of to all that come neare them.

By this time the shyp that brought the Gouernour is vpon her departure, and readye to take her leaue: and he himselfe very busie about the discharge of her, and in taking order for her ladeinge, which was only billetts and loggs of cædar: but yet he is not vnmindefull of his newe bote at Sommer-seate, but dayly sends to vrge expedition, determineinge, as it should seeme, at his next goeinge to the shyp, to be rowed thether in her in state, and so to haue newes carried to the adventurers of the manyfold atcheifments by him performed in so short a time. About some three dayes therfore before the prefixed time of cleareinge of the sayd shyp, he sends away a lustie gang to conduct the longed for newe bote to the towne, who arriueinge at the place wher she was builded, and where they looked to haue found her and her builders, missinge both of the one and the tother, they make enquirie by some nere neighbours to the dock, what was become of them, who told them that they had putt out to sea the eueninge before their comeinge, giueing it out that their entention was to try the newe botes sayleinge, since which time they had neither heard nor seen them; but they verely beleiued that they were gone to Port Royall, ther to bestowe the Sunday at a sermon, or els departed for the towne. With this intelligence the gang make back againe; when informeinge the Gouernour how they had sped, and what newes they had learned of his newe bote, he sodainely begins to fall into a furious muse, and a deepe doubt, wher she should bestowe herselfe; but not long it was, before he was putt past his dumps; for certaine letters being discouered in the cabin of one of thoes departed in the bote, one of them, being directed to the Gouernour himselfe, was in all haste carried to him; and being as hastely openned, the contents therof wer found to this effect: that "in respect of the tyranny and crueltie that he, the Gouernour, continually practised vpon all men, and in particuler vpon themselues, together with the smale hope they found of the least redresse and recouerye for this their hard condition, they fiue had bin forced to putt themselues vpon the extreame and noe lesse than desperate hazard of freeing themselues from him and his rule, by adventureinge to make for their country of England in so smale and ill prouided a vessell, as his newe hoped for bote was; in which attempt, if they sped otherwise than well (as it was much to be mistrusted) their liues and bloud should be required at his hands." Other letters of thers likewise ther wer seene, directed to diuers of their friends, and in perticuler to Mr. Lewes, the minister, of whom one of them haueinge borrowed a fayre sunne diall, with the pointes of the compasse in it, and carrying it away with them (for it was borrowed to that end), he wrote to him, by waye of excuse, that as he in his sermons, speakeinge of the paye that the merchants owed them, would continually perswade them to patience, and tell them, that if the sayd merchants payed them not, God would: so he for his part, must be bold to quote his owne wordes vnto him, concerncinge his compasse diall, which he confest he had somewhat vnmanerly taken from him; that he hoped one day to giue him a due content for it, but if not, God would. Such leysure found this poore fellowe to be merry with the minister, euen when, in the eye of reason, he was marchinge to a certaine ruine.

The Gouernour haueing thus attained the full knowledge of this escape, and bold aducnture of thes fiue persons, holdinge them all but as dead men, in an extreame fury was openly heard to saye that if euer he caught any one of them with in his possessions againe, he would saue them a labour of drowcninge themselues with a hanginge; and that this they should be sure of, though they had Sir Thomas Smiths and the companyes letters to the contrary hanginge about their necks. But litle cared thes fiue passengers, by this time far ynough out of his reach, for either his threatnings or fury: the stormes of the ocean wer nowe their only feares; the which, notwithstandinge, resoluinge to venter vpon, being reasonably well stored with victualls, hauing a good newe sayle for their mast, and an excellent (though smale) newe bote vnder them, they committed themselues to sea, and shaped their course (as nere as their smale skill would serue them) for England; being a voiage, as all marriners knowe, of about three thousand and fiue hundrede miles, haueinge a huge and vast sea to trauerse, and full many a dangerous and horrible tempest to expect; yet, for three weekes space, so fauored they wer, that they felt noethinge of what they had cause to feare; at last a blusterous gale, bloweing in their teeth at north-east, putts them in all extremitie for diuers dayes together, then becomeinge more gentle, awaye they passe prosperously on

againe for some eight or ten dayes more, at what time,
being discouered by a French rover, they are chassed and
taken; to whom, relatinge their fortunes and extent, they
are notwithstandinge inhumanely and barberously robbed
of all their tobacco and much of their victualls, and so cast
of againe, to pursue their first resolutions, though vpon
much worse tearmes than when they mett with them:
being thus losed from thes barbarians they hold on their
northerly course for England; so that after seuen weekes
departure from the Sommer Ilands, in their bote of about
two tunnes in burthen, their victualls being falne to the
lowest ebbe, and the very knees of their smale vessell more
then halfo of them hewed awaye by themselues, vpon necessitie of fire-wood, they at last, to their infinite joye, discouered land, and fell with it; wher arriueinge, it is found
to be Ireland, and the part of it where the Erle of Tomond
hath his residence, who, being informed with this their
strange adventure and miraculous escape, entertained them
very christianly and nobly, and for a monument hangs vp
their bote in his castles hall, wher I thinck it remaineth to
this daye.[4] As for the persons, haueinge remained some
monethes ther, wher they first arrived, at last, one after
another, they gott into England, wher, fallinge to demand
their supposed part of due from the Company, and to complaine and accuse the Gouernour in the Sommer-Ilands,
they found that neither of the cources tooke effect; so that
at length, wearied with attendance and hopelesse of any
good, in extreame angry discontent they betooke themselues to their severall wayes, and (for aught I knowe) are
all of them still alive, to professe as much as I haue nowe

---

[4] "Donogh or Donatus O'Brien, the great Earl of Thomond, fourth of
that title, was at this time President of Munster. His principal residence being in the County Clare, there, and at the mouth of the Shan-
non, in all probability, did these daring men effect their landing."—See
the *Peerage of Ireland*, by J. Lodge and M. Archdall, vol. ii, 1789.

written. True it is that here-vpon some of the petie men of the aduenturers (as willing to catch at all occasions of snarleinge at any man that they employe) wrote snappishly and tantingly to the Gouernour, but this vpon euery falsse and vaine hearesaye is to this day (and perhaps euer will be) found to be the fashion and fooleinge of most of the meanest; and they doe it for the most part without all respect or examination of either his guilt or innocence, worth or basenesse; a tolloration and sufferance that certainely within a short time (vnlesse sodainely redressed) will not suffer any honest and deserueinge man to subiect himselfe to so both an unproffitable and vnregarded, as well as vnrewarded a seruice; wherby the whole plantation is not vnlikely within a short time to be shaken and vtterly ruined.

Within three dayes after the first notice of the stealeinge away of thes fore-sayd men, the shyp called the *George*, that brought in the Gouernour, departed out of the harbour of the King's-Castle, after almost three moneths staye, her out ladeinge (as before sayd) being only cæder; for at that time the tobacco-traffique was not come to the least perfection. Presently after her farewell, the Gouernour (not yett at rest from his late cholor), to reuenge himselfe vpon his runne-awayes, sends down his liuetenant to cease vpon all such goods, corne, and whatsoeuer els as belonged vnto all or any of thes fiue, all which he appropriated vnto himselfe.

Aboute one weeke after this the *Edwin* makes her returne out of the West-Indies, whether (as you haue heard) she was sent for plants; of which she came furnished with diuers sortes, as plantans, suger-canes, figges, pines, and the like, all of which wer presently replanted, and are since encreased into great numbers, especially the plantans and figges, very infinitely: she brought with her also one Indian and a Negroe (the first thes Ilands euer had), the rest of her ladeinge was lignum-vitæ, with which she made a saueinge voiage.

The Gouernour being thus busied in settinge of his plants and makeinge fences with rowes of figge-trees, and in rayleing them in, to preserue them from the hogges; as also in carrying a Pale ouer-mark the Iland of St. Georges, from west to east, therin to keepe seuered such cattell as had bin sent out of England, some of which belonged to the generall Company, but most of them to the Erle of Warwick; and in the performance of such husband-like bussinesse, for which indeed he seemed very fitt, and deserued commendation. The aduenturers at home (who had promised him at his departure a speedy supply) wer as attentiue also in makeinge goode their words vnto him, to which end they hired and sett out a smale bark (but an excellent sayler) called the *Hope-well*, and made master ouer her one Powell, a good marriner, and very well traded in all the West Indies, whose open and professed commission was first to shore his passengers and goods in the Sommer-Ilands, and then to pass on to the Virgin and Sauuage Ilands lieing to the southwest, and within eight dayes sayle of them [Bahamas, *Ed.*], and ther to trade with the natiue Indians for cattell, as goates and the like, and so to transport them to the colony. But this bark being on her waye, and gotten up to the Western Ilands, called also the Azores, meetes with a Portugall shyp comeinge from Brasil, laden with suger and some passengers of fashion; so that hauing a master practised in thoes courses, and whose fingers so itched at all he mett, that he could not chuse but fall a rubbeinge when he mett them: with his nimble sayler he giues chase to the Brasil man, and in a short time both fetcheth her vp and takes her; so that remoueinge most of her people into his owne shyp, and manninge his prize with some of his owne men, awaye sayles he his owne course, together with his newe gotten goods; this haueing done, and but then perhaps beginninge to thinck what he had done, not knoweing how the fact would be receiued at home, nor how he might be vsed at the Sommer Ilands, when he came ther, he resolues to make directly for the West-Indies, and ther to take time to thinck of it; and not long it was before he attained that coast, wher, fallinge into the company of a roueing Frenchman (one euery way as cuninge as himselfe, but more trecherous), a great league of kindnesse is sone made vp betwixt them. Vpon confidence wherof, Powell and some of the cheife of his company, being inuited abord the French shyp, is easily entised, and in the midst of his cupps, both himselfe and his company inhospitably and treacherously made prisoners; whervpon word is sent out by a bote well manned with French to the Brazilian prize, that vnlesse she quickly and quietly rendred her selfe and all she had in her to their dispose, her captain and all his emprisonned company should paye for it with their liues at the maine-yard-arme; with which dismall message being scared (as well knoweinge the vilanous resolution of thes French in the like cases, and withall tenderly respecting the liues of their captaine and the rest), the sayd prize is presently deliuered vp in to their hands; vpon which the prisonners, being sett at libertie and landed vpon the next shore, away goes this rascally Frenchman in triumph with his base and cowardly gotten goods.

Powell and his company being thus prize-lesse ashore, is fetched off by the bote of his owne shyp, the *Hope-well*, wher, being aboard, and findinge his prouissions every waye growen scant, and hopelesse vtterly of recoueringe his stolne away prize, (stormeinge, stampeinge, and sweareinge reuenge) he at last resolueth, in the emptie case he was, to make back for his first harbour in the Sommer Ilands; so that (first settinge on shore his Portugall prisonners vpon the Maine of the West Indies) he weyeth anchor and maketh thetherward, wher, not long after, he safely arriued, and fiudeth the Gouernour about his husbandry, as also newly beginninge a framed house for the minister at St. Georges, to whom he himselfe declareth the whole passage of his fortunes, feareinge, perhaps, least otherwise they might be worse told by some second, which the Gouernour, by his outward wellcome seemed well ynough to approue.

The most part of the followeinge moneth was employed as formerly in matter of husbandrye, with which the Gouernour so wholy was taken vp, as that it gaue occasion to some of the snarleinge meaner sort of the aduenturers in England (such of them especially as had receiued some personall discontents) to write vnto him in their scuruie priuate letters that he was fitter to be a gardiner than a Gouernour. Among other things of note acted by him at the same time, he caused a pond to be digged a litle distance from the fresh water well that serueth the towne; but hauing brought it to the depth of two foote, it began to be considered that if it should be carried deeper, it might preiudice the well and spoyle the water, whervpon that worck ceased; in the same moneth he held his second generall Assize at St. Georges, as irregularly as the first, wherin not any matter of note was handled, only a proclamation (or rather article, as it was then tearmed) was published (but ouerlate) against the spoyle and hauock of the cahowes, and other birds, which already wer almost all of them killed and scared awaye very improuidently by fire, diggeinge, stoneinge, and all kind of murtheringes. The Gouernour went, presently after this, to take a vewe of a certaine rock lieing in flauncker with the Kings-castle,[5] the which, by an order of court from England, was appointed to be fortified; but findinge a great difficultie in the attempt, both by reason of the badd landinge vpon the place for ordinance, and his owne pouertie of knowledge in thoes affayres, it was quite

[5] Now Southampton Fort.

giuen ouer, and not meddled with all, all his time; but in lieu therof, some 8 or 10 men are appointed to cutt out a plattforme at Pagett's Fort, the which (as the worck itselfe sheweth to this daye, and euer will doe in despight of all amends) proued so vnfashionable, vncapable, and ill layd out, that it is absolutely the most vnceruiceable and vnsightlest peece in that kind of the whole ilands; and yet by situation and for vse, requireinge as much or more protection than any other whatsoeuer.

You heard euen nowe of the comeinge in of Powell and of his fortune; but hauinge not performed in the Sauuage Ilands what he stoode obliged in vnto the Company, concerneinge the traffique for cattell ther, he is nowe employed a second time thether by the Gouernour, vnder coulour and pretence of the same service; who also furnished him with all thinges necessary and manned him out with thirteene or fourteene of his owne colony people, most of them being prime men and of cheife account, of whose voiage and returne we shall speake hereafter. In the meantime, the Company at home (who had bin fully possest and putt in great hope of much good to be done in thes partes by fishinge for the whale, by reason that dureinge the moneths of January, February, and March, great numbers of thoes kinds of fishes are seene vpon the coast) fell vpon a resolution to make an experiment that waye; whervpon they caused a tall shyp called the *Neptune* to be prouided, and furnished her with skillfull men, and all other thinges necessary for such a voiage; but before she could arrive at her destinated port, the Gouernour ther (who at his comeinge in had brought with him also diuers tooles, instruments, and shalopes, with some persons fitt and proper for that employment) determined to breake the yce for them, and to deserue somewhat by aduentureinge first; so that settinge vp three newe shalopes, whose peeces wer shypped with him out of England, and manning them with seuen or eight men apeece, he caused the company to sett forward to that bussines; but the effect of this attempt answered not his hopes, for whether it wer by reason of the extraordinary swift swimming and stoute mettall of this kind of whale (for it is the trunck whale,[6] and is knowen by experience to haue store of sparme), or the condition of the place, the sea being ther in some places very deepe, or that by reason of the rocks the hawsers could not be kept cleare, or what other mischiefe or mischance so euer it was, certaine it is that after many trialls, hazards, adventures, and continuall rayleinges vpon poore mistris Fortune, not so much as one peece of a whale could euer be recouered, though diuers of them were often strook and wounded; vpon which ill luck the Gouernour for that time layd aside this sea-seruice and fell again to the land.

In the beginneinge therefore of the newe yeare, being the second of his gouernment, he held his third Assize after the old manner; wher diuers inflictions being layd vpon sundry delinquents, as whippeinge for suspicion of incontinencye publick askeinge of forgiuenesse for matters of slaunder and such like; three persons among the rest wer condemned to die, the first for stealeinge of a paire shoes; the second was a woman, who, vpon heareinge the report of the execution of the Frenchman, that the Gouernour (as you haue heard) caused to be hanged within three weekes after his first arriuall, in a feminine passion, burst out into thes wordes: that if she had bin a man, and had knowen it before hand, he should not so quietly haue bin so hardly vsed; the which speeches being, almost a yeare after they wer spoken, reported to the Gouernour, he thervpon caused her to be attached, endicted, and arraigned vpon mutiny and rebellion; and so being cast by a fearefull jury, was condemned and sentenced to be hanged; but thes two, the Gouernour in his great mercye (for in thoes very words I find it recorded) suspended from the execution of the sentence, and

[6] Trunk whale. This designation appears to be forgotten.

so they remained aliue (and yet are) condemned persons vnto this daye. But the third man (whose name was Paul Deane) scaped not so well, for being endicted for the stealeinge of a peece of cheese, he was arraigned and condemned, and thervpon craueinge the benefitt of his booke (the prize of the stolne goodes being valued at twenty pence), it was answered him by the Gouernours owne mouth (very vnwarrantably) that he would allowe noe booke in a plantation; so that thervpon being sentenced, he was hanged the next daye;[1] and it was secretly muttered, as if the Goueruour had owed him some secrett spleene, and the rather because at his arringement, when the stolen cheese was at the first valued vnder twelue pence, he caused it (in a fury) to be prized at twenty pence; as also, that he had bin often heard to saye to this poore fellowe, vpon euery slight occasion, that he looked like a knave, and that if euer he tooke him in the least manner trippeinge, it should cost him a hanginge; as if he ment to hang for ill lookes. At this Assize also, the first order was sett downe for a presse and leuye of men out of the tribes, for the mountinge of the ordinance in Pagetts Fort, and the repayreinge of the decayed platformes in the Kings-castle; whose labour and sweat was for the most part lost and mispent through want of knowledge, good direction, and iudgement in matters of that nature.

Sone after the conclusion of this assize came a hott alarme from Sands his tribe, of a fierce assault made by the ratts vpon their newe sett corne, who scratched it out of the ground in the night as fast as they put it in in the day; thes race of ratts being (as you have heard) first brought in by the runne away frigate from the West Indies, in Mr. Moores time, began presently so sylently and sodainely to encrease (ther being noe place of the world more apt to nourish them, partly by reason of the sweet temper of the aire, but especially through the

[1] See *Memorials of Bermuda*, i, p. 129, for the official record of the atrocity, which occurred in March 1618.

generall shelter and couert that it affords them) that they
then became felt before they wer feared, and yet not so
duely feared as befitted; so that litle or noethinge being
done against them at that time, and lesse in the lazie
dayes of the six Gouernours, they wor by this time gotten
to so ranck a head that swimeinge in huge troupes from
iland to iland (for fishes haue bin taken three leauges of at
sea with whole ratts in ther bellyes), they eate up the
whole country before them, whersoeuer they went, vtterly
deuoureinge all the corne they mett with all in au instant;
so that, in despight of all the catts sent from out of England, and the layeinges of poyson, the Gouernours often
fireinge of the whole ilands, to the huge wast aud spoyle of
much excellent cæder timber, or whatsoeuer els could be
deuised against them, they euery day more and more so
multiplied and growe vpon the poore amazed people, as
that it very litle wanted that the whole place had once
againe bin vtterly and quite left voide of her reasonable
inhabitants: and with out all question, this ill had not
fayled to have befallen, had not God (who noe doubt hath
an especiall worck in the peopling of thes partes with
Christians), by his owne hand, in great mercy, swept them
all away in an instant, when it was least expected; for not
long after that the Gouernour (haueing thus receiued this
loathed report of this ratt-warre in Somersett, and being
at his non-plus of newe deuises to helpe himselfe), had
determined once againe to fall vpon another generall
burneinge of the whole ilands, to the extreame discontent
of all men, and especially of Mr. Lewes the minister, who
openly preached against it, so that the Gouernour could
neuer endure him afterwards; behold, by a soudaine fall of
great store of raine, and some cold northerly windes
bloweinge with all, in a moment, and when noe man durst
so much as hope for so happy a turne, thes mightie armies
of rauenous ratts are clean taken awaye, vanish, and are

scarce one to be found in a share; but in steed of them, shortly after, come in marchinge towards the houses whole troupes of great and fatt wild catts, who haueinge formerly found foode ynough vpon these vermin abroad, and so become wild and sauuage, are now againe in this their necessitie, and by want of wonted reliefe, forced to returne to their first tamenesse; sheweinge themselues herein like thoes vnthanckfull badd naturall men who neuer respect longer nor farther than to serue their owne turnes. And thus was this desperate wound recouered, beinge a blessinge which, comeinge indeed imediately from heauen, not only procured and established the well-fare and very subsistance of this colony, but with all (as fallinge out in his time), carryed with it an accidentall addition of much reputation to the Gouernour; for, in such euents, fewe men trouble themselues to looke out so far as the causes, but rest well ynough contented with the sence of the effects.

In the moneth of March next followeinge this good fortune (being a season aboue all others most subiect to soudaine gusts), certaine of the colony people, to the number of fiue, goeing out to sea in a calm munday morneinge to fish, on the sodaine ther arose so forceable and lastinge a storme, that the bote wherin they wer being forced of from all partes of the ilands, they wer neuer heard of after; although the Gouernour, vpon newes, sent out his owne bote three or foure leagues to sea, to make enquierye and search after them. In the same moneth, also, a bote belonginge to Smiths tribe was over-raked with the billowe and three men drowned.

Much about this time, the good ship called the *Neptune*, sett out (as you formerly heard) for the whale fishinge, arriued and moored her-selfe in the Kings-castle harbour, being very fully furnished with all things necessary for that purpose; so that fiue shalopes are manned, and fall instantly vpon that bussinesse, but with noe better successe than the former; for haueinge struck and launced diuers whales, not so much as the least peece of any one could be recouered, so that a sodaine cooleinge followed the heate of that affayre; the which, also, shortly after became, by a frozen dispayre, quite given over; although, perhaps (as some of good iudgement haue since affirmed), the triall and experiment was not so thorougly performed as was requesite, nor the proiect so hopelesse, as it is (to this daye) receiued.[7]

Vpon the layeinge aside of this whale-fishinge (and it may be in some part the cause of it), an alarme was giuen from Sommerseate of four sayle of shypps descried vpon that coast; whervpon, in all hast, the people in generall are called to armes, and in a hurry distributed to all the fortes; the towne of St. Georges, also, where the Gouernour rested, is very thoroughly manned, and for two dayes space so held before it was knowen whether they wer freinds or foes. At last, the weather groweinge calme, a bote is sent out to make a discouery; the which, sone after returneinge, brings a pleasciuge message and newes to the Governour, that the admirall of the descried fleet was Captaine Powell in the *Hopewell* (who, as you knowe, had bin employed to the Sauuage Ilands),[8] and that the rest were prizes of his; the which, haueing falne with in his reach, he could not hold from catcheinge at; and so, hauing seazed on them, had thus brought them to be ript vp in the ilands. The same eueninge, one frigate and another carucll of them gatt in at the Kings-castle: the next day a third frigate came in, into the Townes harbour; and, two dayes after, arriued Powell himselfe in the *Hopewell*, who by the wind scantinge

---

[7] Whale fishery was subsequently conducted on a considerable scale, both at Bermuda and the Bahamas. The reader will find very full details respecting it in my *Memorials of Bermuda*. A tax of £10 for each whale killed was a part of the Governor's salary down to 1740.

[8] Probably the Lucayas or Bahamas.

vpon him was in a shrewed possibilitie of hauing bin driuen of to sea, and therby to haue left his newe-gotten booty to the mercye of the place.

Thes ladds being thus gott in, the first inquisition that the Gouernour made vpon them was of their ladeinge; when findeing it for the most part to be meale and hides, with certain munition and some other furniture, all which sommed to gether might amount to a matter of some reasonable value, he resolued to sett a calme face vpon all things, and to make fayre weather with Powell; at least so long vntill he had fully and absolutely possessed himselfe of all such goods as he had brought with him; and this with all hast he pursued, causeing them to be for the best part vnshypped, and layd vp into his owne store-houses; the which was noe soner done, but presently he began to expresse himselfe in a contrary manner, and (partly the better to answer it in England, but especially hopeinge therby to fasten vpon some of this booty for himselfe), he sharpely questioned Powell of a mis-demeanour and litle lesse than a pyracye, for this his fact, askeinge him in plaine tearmes how he durst be so bold to bring in his stolen goods into his harbours. But Powell (who, indeed, was of a farr more dareinge speritt, although at that time vpon all the in-equalitie of tearmes that could be) answered him roundly that he had done noething but what he both could and would answer when time and place required: but as for being putt to it by him, he beleaued it might be refused, for the Admiralty of England only (as he tooke it) was the Court to which he was liable. This reply frettinge the Gouernour (who could neuer with the least patience endure the least contradiction wher he was in the wrong, much less being, as now, in the right), fallinge into an extreame fury, he replied, that he would teach him to knowe and feele the contrary, and ther vpon fetchinge out his commission, he willed him to looke and see whether by it himselfe wer not an admirall sufficient, within this his command, to call a better and an honester man than himself into question. Powell vpon vewe, haueinge found that true which before he suspected not, and wisely perceiueinge that noe good was to be gotten by a persistance in' his error and heate, in a far more mild and temperate straine, answered to this purpose: "Indeed," (quoth he) "I nowe see that your authoritie is far more extentiue and absolute than I imagined; in which respect I willingly and readily submitt myselfe vnto it in all things; neuerthelesse, I make noe doubt but that, as your forbearance in this kind must and shall deserue a freindly obligation from myselfe, so the Company in England will hold it duely and with meet caution referred vnto their censure; to whom, if any present harsh course be attempted against me here, I must bo forced to appeale. This speach wrought doubly vpon the Gouernour, on way to the asswageinge of his furie, by a kind of giueing way vnto it, but it had its cheife and maine operation vpon that touch of an appeale; the which, if he receiued not, he feared how the non-acceptance might be taken by the aduenturers; neither, to say truth, did he well apprehend or vnderstand in what sort, or by what formalitie of course, to put him to his triall if he should goe on to proceede against him; findinge it, therefore, the easier and safer waye for himselfe to be only the reporter of this his action to the Company, and there to leave it, he readely rested vpon that course; so that, at last, it was agreed vpon that Powell, leaueing behind him the best part of his prizes and his three frigates, should, with the rest, make his returne for England in the *Hopewell*, and ther receive his sentence from the interested Company, and accordingly, he dealt with all in the restitution. Vpon this determination (when he could gett no better), shortly after awaye goes Powell for England, and with him stole away one George Haynes, as also the gunners wife of the shypp, the which aggravated the Gouernours spleen against Powell, as (falsely) conceiueinge him priuy to their departure (such stealthes in those harsh and hard times being generally coueted, and with all care and watchfulness both feared and prouided against by the Gouernour), and especially he was madded at the departure of the woman (though it was with her husband), by reason that haueinge bin once his household seruant she had proved herselfe in certaine secret pointes too lavish of her tongue, and therefore mistrusted much more freely and broadly to fall into it againe at her nowe comeinge home. The very next daye after this departure of Powell, the *Neptune* also made her waye out of the harbour of the Kings-castle; and it was afterward rumored that she did this with the more hast, upon an intention that, if she could have mett with Powell abroad, to haue serued him as a pyrate, and made purchase of him, a proiect (if any such there wer) which certainely would have fallen out to both their costs, it being well knowen that Powells speritt (although neuer so much disadvantaged) would not easily haue stouped to base and abiect conditions. In this *Neptune* was also carryed for England the lieutenants wife of the Kings-castle; and very much doubted it was by some of the subtlest wher it was done with the Gouernours secret and close consent or not. True, indeed, that openly he seemed much enraged, and entred into some publick chafes with her husband: but yet, by reason of some especiall turnes of his that she serued him in, as well foulcinge Powell his bussiness at her arriuall in England, as some others, it caused many (as before sayd) to suspect the integritie of the carriage of the matter, and made the Gouernour to be conceiued a more politick and cunning man than perhaps he deserued.

Noe soner wer the harbours thus, as you have heard, cleare of shypinge, but the Gouernour (tickled with an ambitious and vaineglorious apprehension) began to fall vpon a project of bravery; for findinge himselfe possessed with two frigates and a caruell, left him by Powell, he conceiued that it would proue an action of reputation, if he who had bin a Cape-merchant in Virginia, should nowe sett out a vessell vnto them, as a Cape-Gouernour:[9] neither was it likely (thought he) to be taken in ill part by the Company of Adventurers at home; since euen at the worst it could proue noe manner of charge to them; aud chaunceinge well, might be a meanes of fittinge and furnishinge the colony with corne and cattell (which was the open pretence) without their trouble; with all extremitie of hast and vrgeinge, therfore, he caused one of thes vessells, the *Carwell*, to be trimmed up, and fitted with a halfe-deck and a fore-castle; the which being manned with twelve of the colony men (the same Walters that had bin one of the six Gouernours carryinge the name of master, but one Hellicott, a Frenchman, being indeed the only marrinour) was sent out for that voiage, an oath being taken by euery one of them, that they should vse their vttermost endeauours to make their sayd voiage with a speedy returne. But this shypfull being arriued at that English colonye, and after some staye and entreatie haueinge obteyned some fewe goates and hoggs; in puttinge out to sea againe, and makeinge some shewe of a returne, whether it wer through want of skill, so that they could not find the Ilands, or by the dislike of some of the cheife among them, that affected not to passe againe vnder the Gouernours command, after some weekes of tumbliuge abroad at sea, they bore vp againe for Virginia (from whence they came out), wher the barck and most of her passengers remaine vntill this day, and neuer returned to the Sommer-Ilands, to give vp their account to the frettinge man that employed them.

But Powell being arriued in England, and not long after him the *Neptune*, Powells cause is presently and primarily taken notice of, and variously disscussed in the court: at

[9] See note, p. 69.

last, vpon a testimony deliuered in against him by the fore sayd liuetenant's wife, who had bin with him at the takeinge of his first prize, and looseinge of her (and was the only wittnesse produced against him) all his actions in that kind are disauowed by the Company, and held irregular and beyond his commission; the which notwithstandinge, they wer contented, in respect of an especiall fauour and kindnesse ment vnto him, to forbeare to pursue any farther at that time, and vpon his good behauiour euer after only in respect of the dammage that the Company had receiued in generall by the willfull prolongation of his voiage, by going out of his course; and that also many perticular men had bin preiudiced in their supplies and other necessarys, which should have bin landed by him in the Sommer Ilands, and wer not; by way of redresse and recompence he was censured to lose his whole paye, and to forfeite all such goods and purchase whatsoeuer as wer left behind in the custodye of the Gouernour of the Sommer Ilands; all which they not long after sent for, and employed and appropriated to themselues; wherby as well the Gouernour's hopes as Powells wer frustrated, and thus was that affayre passed ouer.

But in the meane space, the Gouernour ther being ignorant of thes resolutions, and flatteringe himselfe with a conceite that a good part of thes sayd goods would fall to his share, began to putt in practise some experiments for the improueinge of them; he caused therfore a triall to be made for the tanneinge of the rawe hides with the bark of the mangroue tree; and to that end framed diuers cesternes of cæder, and appointed one or two of the colony people (who professed most for themselues and their skill that waye) to take that charge in hand; but all this proued so baddly, as not only the labour but many of the hides wer vtterly lost and spoyled, to the extreame enrageinge of the Gouernour and the punishment of some of the boasteinge tanners.

Giueing ouer this proiect, therfore, he fell to the buildinge of smale framed houses at the Towne, and caused the negroes to replant the suger canes. He sommoned also the holdynge of an assize: and because he would haue somewhat to doe at it, he sent his prouost marshall into the maine to apprehend the body of one Gabriell:[1] the cause wherof was this. It was discouered vnto him, by one Christopher Carter (that had bin one of the six Gouernours) that the sayd Gabry should tell him that the baylie of Pembroke tribe (being a gentleman bred up, and sent ouer by the earle of Pembroke) had used thes wordes to certaine of the people of that tribe, that, Rather than his folke should goe up to worck at the fortes, he himselfe would lie in yrons for them. Vpon this information, Gabry is apprehended and brought vp to the towne, and being examined very stricktly by the Gouernour, confesseth the heareinge of the sayd wordes from Mr. Pollarde (so was the bayly named), and thervpon is committed close prisonner, as guilty of the concealement of so dangerous a resolution. This committment of Gabry being noysed abroad, and comeinge to the eares of some prime men of the tribe, who had bin at the heareing of Pollards wordes as well as himselfe, feareing the euent and findinge themselues on the same predicament, they thought it was time to act somewhat that might recouer themselues out of the danger: whervpon, acquaintinge the baylies that wer next vnto them with the bussines (among the which one Mr. Riche, a kinsman of the Erle of Warwicks and the bayly of Southampton tribe, was one), of themselues they attached Pollards person, and instantly wer in action to carry him

[1] It appears, by the imperfect record of this Assize, still preserved in the Colony, that the incident occurred in 1617, and this conclusion is supported by the circumstance mentioned below, that "the ratts were still very busie". We have already chronicled their sudden disappearance.

by bote vnto the towne; but by the waye at sea they descrye the Gouernours shalope and himselfe in her (who was in a voiage downe into the maine, vpon a fresh apprehension of a priuate proiect of his owne interest, the which he shortly after pursued with all attention and eagernesse, as we shall see anon). Making signes, therefore, vnto him of important affayres, and some of them in a straunge manner, as by holdinge up of halters and the like, they at last caused him to make towards them, wher, being arriued, and with an angry harshnesse (according to his garbe) demandinge what they had to saye to him, in an humble but fearefull fashion they presented him with their poore amazed prisonner, beceeching him to take this their carefull (though somewhat tardy) duty in good part, the which should encourage and teach them to be euer hereafter both more vigilant and wise. But the Gouernour, lookeinge terribly vpon them, badd them only to carry him on forwards to the marshalls ward at the towne; "for (quoth he) I haue more serious thinges to thincke of at this time", and (withall, pointinge to Mr. Riche, to whom, vpon the very like ground he bore a greater spleene) "I make him ther also (sayth he) your prisonner; and vpon your perill, see that both of them be safely deliuered to the custody of the marshall, ther to attend my farther pleasure." Within fourteene dayes after which he makes his returne to St. Georges, and sodainely vpon it holds a generall assize, wherin fewe other bussinesse being haudled, the cause of thes much deiected gentlemen is especially aimed at and pursued: and first of all he begins with Nicholas Gabry, who formerly haueing fallen into a foule (but ignorant) contempt of the Gouernours warrant, and by him, for that time (as he thought) pardonned, is nowe againe at this assize questioned and endicted for it (for it was mistrusted that the matter of concealement in Mr. Pollards case would not sticke deepe ynough vpon him); and although at his arraignement, penitently confessinge his offence, he pleaded guiltie, yet the Gouernour (to expresse his mercye, as sayth the record) would needs haue a jury of twelve men to passe vpon him; who, makeinge no bones to find him guiltye of mutiny and rebellion, he receiued sentence to be hanged; but being carryed with a rope about his neck to the gallowes, and made to goe vp the ladder, (verely thinckinge to die), he was repriued by the Gouernours command: yet, vpon this irregular and vnwarrantable condition (contrary to the lawes and custome of England) that he should remaine a slaue to the colony (that is to say to himselfe) vntill, by his good future behauiour, he should deserue to the contrary.

This done, Mr. Pollard and Mr. Riche are brought publickly to the barre: Mr. Pollard is charged vpon the wordes aforesayd, that he should give out that he would rather lie in yrons than suffer any of his people to worcke at the fortes. To Mr. Riche wer obiected thes articles followeinge: 1. That he should taxe the Gouernour of injustice, for not doeing him right in a debate and controuersie betweene him and one Beamont, the master of the *Neptune;* but should saye, that if Sir Thomas Gates, or Sir Thomas Dale, had bin in his place, they would not haue suffered him to goe out of the harbour before it had bin done: to which the Gouernour replied, that he talked like a child, and that he should hold his peace; for (quoth he) I knowe what I haue to doe as well as they, and better than you can direct. Secondly. He was charged, that at the Gouernours comeinge vnto his house in the maine, he ther, a second time, fell into the same expostulation: at what time also (seemeinge to be in some passionate heate) he demanded of the Gouernour when the maine men should be commanded to the fortes, and how many of them at one time wer to be ther; to which the Gouernour answering, that it should be when he thought most conuenient for their best ease; and as for their number, some one or two at a tyme, accordingly as the tribe was furnished with inhabitants; and the rather *because the ratts wer still very busie:* that thervpon the sayed Mr. Riche should arrogantly reply, that if the people would be ruled by him, they would come all together, or not at all; and so, repayreing the fortes, they would make the merchants to pay for it. Thirdly, he was questioned, for that beinge one time at St. Georges, he should tell the Gouernour to his teeth that the fortes were to be repayred and maintained without the charge of the tribes, and that the maine men mainteyned the generalitic. Fourthly: that he should saye that the Governour denyed him justice in a certaine contention betwixt him and one Robert Walker. Fifthly: that the Gouernour, being at a certaine time in conference with him concerneinge Powell, at what time he told him that he looked to be sent for into England about that bussinesse, he then sayd Mr. Riche should answer, that if he were so, he would not suffer him to goe. Sixthly and lastly: that being commanded to cause his people to burne one of the brother ilands for ratts, the Gouernour himselfe and his people haueing done as much to the other, and being questioned why it was not done, his answer was, that he had somewhat els to doe with his people than to burne ilands. Vpon which articles being accused, and both of them putt to their answer, and demanded what they could saye for themselues (yet in noe forme of iudiciall proceedeinge, and without a jury passing vpon them), they thervpon, both of them (especially Mr. Pollard), fully and pitifully confessed their error, acknowledged their heynous offence (for so they nowe tearme it themselues), and submitted their cause wholy to the Gouernours mercye, the which (not without teares) they humbly supplicated; who, therevpon that he might shewe (sayth the record) that he alwayes proceeded with mercye rather than justice, not only remitted their heinous transgressions, but instantly restored them to their former places of command, in as full and ample manner as euer before; and truly he might well doe all this without giueing iust cause either of being censured ouer pittifull, or vnder-prouident; for well ynough and apparently knowen it was, that thes delinquents wer so honestly kind gentle-men and goodfellowes, that in any action of dangerous consequence, they would in such a case rather speeke out, more than they euer ment, than conceale any thinge they entended. True it is, that the Gouernour was euer after very suspicious and fearfull, least by meanes of their kindred and friends in England, they would proue some back freinds to some of his hopes: and it may be, indeed, that he felt some effects in that kind not long after; though certainely since his returne home, he hath found all thinges to cotten for him beyond his expectation, not to say desert.

I told you, euen nowe, of a proiect of priuate interest that hastned the Gouernour into the maine: the which (being nowe ridde of the tye of the assize, and haueinge slubbered up, as you haue heard, the bussinesse about Mr. Riche and Mr. Pollard) he from that time forward, with all dilligence and indefatigable paines, to the great burthen of the plant-ation, and the extreame secret grudgeinge of the people, continually pursued and sett forwards: and thus it was. The Company of Aduenturers, vpon his election to the gouernment, had promised him by waye of entertainement and reward, to giue him at the end of his tearme three shares of land; nowe a prime instruction of theirs was that he should presently after his arriuall in the Ilands, dispose and laye all of them out into tribes, and shares: (the willfull ommission wherof by Mr. Moore being as you haue heard a maine and principal cause of their distaste of him). This Gouernour, therfore, to auoid the like disgust of himselfe vpon the like occasion, was noe soner settled in any reason-able manner, but he fell vpon the performance of this talke:

whervpon, being of necessitie thoroughly to acquaint himselfe with one Norwoode, who was the only surueyour he had; he at last became so familiar and confident of him, as not only he imparted vnto him his promised reward from the Company, but solicited at his hand this intelligence, that vpon his through vewe of the whole ilands which he was shortly to haue, by being employed in the generall laying of them out, he would lett him knowe wher the principall and choice peeces of soyle was to be found, that so he might vse his friends in England for the obteyneing of his shares of reward out of that part: this being assured him by the surueyour, the bussinesse is quickly sett on foote: so that beginninge at the east end of the ilands, which boundeth vpon that generall land nowe called Tuckers Towne (being so tearmed by the Gouernour Tucker himselfe vpon his erectinge ther of two or three cottages of leaues and plantinge the liue-tenant of the castle and his wife vpon it) he went onwards towards the west, layeing out in that manner the tribes and shares as he went, without skip or interruption, vntill he came to the western-most part of that called at the present South-hampton tribe: wher findinge out that which the Gouernour had coniured him to seeke out for him, a fatte and lustye soyle, with a most delicate enlarged valley, he ther stayed his progresse, and returneinge to the towne, he told the Gouernour of his discouery, and withall added, that in respect of the stint and equall number of shares allowed and proportioned to euery one of the eight tribes which wer to have fiftie shares to euery tribe, he euidently had discouered that some surplusage of ground would be found; the which, if it could be cast to fall out within that so fruictfull a valley, it might both giue an oppertune conueniencye to himselfe to aske it, and withall proue very well worth the haueinge: in his opinion, therfore, he held it the best waye to giue ouer his first course of surueyinge from the east-end of the ilands, and (haueing already layd out seuen of the tribes that waye, and one only resting to be distributed) quite contrarye to his former waye to proceede, and begin at the farthermost end of the iland called Ire-land, and so to goe on toward the East: wherby it must of necessitye fall out, that what ouerplus soeuer should be left (as some ther would be) it could not but fall within the contents of this excellent vally.

The Gouernour haueinge receiued this welcome and deare intelligence, in much passionate kindnesse euen huggeinge the man againe and puttinge him in high hopes of extreame requitalls, in all hast returnes him to the prosecution of this proiect: the which being exactly performed, ther is found a remaindor of about some eight shares of the best ground in all the ilands, ouer and aboue the due belonginge to that tribe. This being thus done, and so all the tribes and shares disposed of, and the suruaye perfected; the plott thereof is by the Gouernour sent ouer into England to the Aduenturers, with an intimation in the last place, that in respect ther was some surplusage of ground, to the quantitie (as the Surueyour thought) of some three shares, ouer and aboue the due contents of euery tribe, it might well serue (as lieinge cleare of all interested partes) for the accomplishment of that reward, which they had promised him at his election : and the which for quietnesse-sake, and a publick good, he was willinge thanckfull to accept of. This suruaye, with the plott of it, arriueinge in England, gaue good content to the*Company, and presently they began to settle euery particular mans right vpon him, by casteinge of lotts. First therfore, eight of the cheifest persons and deepest aduenturers wer assigned to haue ten shares apeece in euery tribe, answerable to the quantitie of their adventures, and euery one of them (for honnours sake) to haue the tribe called by his owne name: and this, vpon the issue of the lotts, fell out in this manner. The first tribe, boundinge on the generall land of Tuckers Towne, fell out to the

Countesse of Bedford, and was called Bedford tribe; the which since beinge (vpon some secretts) passed ouer to the Marquesse Hambleton, is nowe tearmed Hambleton tribe. The second chaunced to Sir Thomas Smith, and is named Smithes tribe. The third to the then Lord Cavendish, and so named Cavendish his tribe; but since vpon his being created Earle of Deuonshire, it is by an order of Court called Deuonshire tribe. The fourth fell out to the Lord Pagett, and so named Pagetts tribe; the fifth to the Erle of Pembroke, and called Pembroke tribe: the sixth to Sir Robert Mansfield, at that time a forward Adventurer, but haueinge since in an humour sold himselfe out of the ilands, the name of the tribe hath bettered itselfe, and by an order of Court is giuen to the Erle of Warwick, and called at the present Warwick tribe. The seventh tribe befell the noble Erle of South-ampton, and is called South-ampton tribe: and the eighth to Sir Edwin Sands, and named Sands his tribe: between which and Southampton tribe lieth that portion of surplusage land which vpon the occasion aforesayd is still tearmed the overplus: part wherof (as you shall see herafter) hath since bin disposed to Southampton tribe, part of it to Sands his tribe, and the other part to Captain Tucker.[2] As for the remaindor of thes islands, lieinge to the eastward of thes tribes, being in quantitie as large or rather more than any one of them, it was and yet is allotted and reserued for the enter-tainement of publick expences, and thervpon stiled the Generall land: wherin standeth the towne of St. Georges to the eastward, wher the Gouernour keepes his residence: and on the west-end is Tuckers Towne, betweene which and St. Georges are erected thes peeces of fortification

---

[2] This division of Bermuda into eight districts called originally tribes, but now parishes, has been handed down to the present day; and the inhabitants cherish their local independence with a loyalty which a stranger has difficulty in comprehending.

followeinge: first, the kings castle, wherin on three platt-formes are mounted sixteene peeces of ordinance: nere vpon which vpon a high rock to the southwarde stands Charles his fort, wher are two peeces of ordinance; one of them commandeinge the landinge place vpon the castle, the other playeing of to sea: then haue you ouer against the kings-castle, and in flauncker vnto it, Southampton fort, wer lie mounted five pecces of ordinance, betweene which and the castle passeth in the chanell that leadeth into the harbour; which is thus secured and played vpon by three and twenty peeces of good artillerye. From hence (the coast trendinge to the north-easte) is Coopers island, wher standeth Pembroke Fort, and vpon it three peeces of ordinance: thence passeinge on, more northwards, you come to the harbours mouth of St. Georges, which is garded by Pagett Fort, and Smithes Fort, lieing opposite one vnto another and the channell passeinge in betwixt them: in Smithes forte are five peeces of ordinance: in Pagetts Fort six. About halfe a leauge more inwards into that harbour standeth the towne of St. Georges; which is commanded by Warwick Fort, wheron are placed three great peeces: and on the warfe, before the Gouernours house, lie eight more: besides one smale faulcon, planted at the foote of a trianguler-frame of timber, made to looke out to the sea for discouery of shyps, called the Mount, beinge the warneinge peece of the fortes: and lastly, on the north side of St. Georges island, is erected vpon a rock the smale fort of St. Katherines, in garde of a certaine sandy baye; being the same wheron the first that euer landed in thoes partes, first set their feete,[3] and in it are mounted two peeces of ordinance; so that the whole number of great

---

[3] "Sea-Venture Flatts", the scene of the memorable shipwreck of Sir George Somers, is still noted on the charts; but this is the first identification of the precise spot where the unfortunate party landed. It is still guarded by Fort Katherine.

pecces at the present vpon the fortes, and at the towne, are fiftie, many of which are whole culuerins; the rest demi-culuerins, sakers, minions, and some one or two faulcons. And thus haueing breifly deliuered vnto you the artificiall defence of thes ilands, which in part was touched before when we spake of the naturall, we will nowe returne from this digression to the former course of our first story.

After the Company, therfore, and Court of Adventurers had thus disposed and distributed euery perticuler mans shares by lott, and patronized and named the tribes; they fell at last into consideration of the Gouernours last clause concerneinge the bestoweinge of the ouerplus land vpon him, by waye of his reward, concerneinge which howsoeuer at that time they sented not any thinge of the mistery of the deuice, but receiued the relation and take their beleife of it accordinge to the letter of his letters; yet their wonted and certaine propertie of being slack and dull in point of recompence, saued them at that time from being cousenned: so that writeinge in auswer to the Gouernours generall letters, they giue good applause and approbation to his proceedings in generall; and as for the matter of reward, they wished him not to doubt but that he should find himselfe in seruice to a gratefull and respectfull Company, who would rather encrease their promised salary and entertainement to a deseruing man, as they hoped he would prove, than any way lessen and shorten it: only he was wished to attend the due and prefixed time and end of his tearme, accordeinge to the mutuall agreement; the which as yet, he had litle more than halfe gone through. And this was all that the labour of his best freinds could worck out for him at that time: many perticuler men of the Company beginninge to take diuers exceptions and disgusts at his proceedeinges, vpon some priuate respects and intelligences.

But whilst thes resolutions wer in trauerse in England,

the Gouernour in the Sommer Ilands, contrary to the aduise and opinion of his best and most entrusted freinds conuersant with him, entred vpon a precipitated course and action, the which, as in likely-hoode, so in effect, had well nigh quite ouerthrowne and frustrated all his best hopes in the perticuler of obteyneinge the foresayd ouerplus lands (for ouerweeneinge himselfe, accordinge to the nature and fashion of such who from but small estate, and noe high condition, find themselues in a grouth and a kind a being of both) he would needs assure himselfe, that, what with his owne deseruеings on the one side, and the strength of his freinds on the other, he could not misse of this his desired praye: beinge (as he tooke it) so well masked and disguised in the contriuement; and withall consideringe how beneficiall, both in respect of fame and gaine, it would proue for him: and besides the exceedeinge charge, and almost impossibilitie of doeinge it, being a priuate man: reiectinge all disswasions, discouragements and obiections, he absolutely resolued with all expedition to frame and erect a very substantiall and braue cæder house vpon this peece of delicate ground, the which he had thus already in the strength of his hopes deuoured for his owne. He expeditiously commands, therfore, great store of timber to be felled and towed to St. Georges from diuers partes of the ilands, especially from St. Dauis', the which being squared and framed ther, by the choysest worckmen pressed out of the whole maine, he caused to be conueyed in flotes as nere to the ouerplus as he could; and from thence to be haled, by the strength of men, to the place wher he appointed, to the great slackinge and disturbance of the generall bussinesse of the country, and extreame suffrance of the poore labouring people. Wherof many being vtterly spent with paines and fastinge, euen sunck under their burthens: neither was ther any recompence or pay so much as propounded; only sometimes, some of them wer well payed with sound cudgellinge by the gouernours owne hand, if he conceiued the best neuer so litle slack, tardy, or grudgeinge: but by this meanes, great store of materialls of all sortes are in a short time prepared and layed ready: and the buildinge goes nimbly forward and with speed is highly aduanced, to the much content and iollitie of the Gouernour, who sometimes would remaine absent from the towne and fortes two or three moneths together, in a continuall and indeed only employment of himselfe and all his meanes, this waye, and in this affayre.

The Gouernour being thus wholy taken up in the maine, the good shyp called the *Dyana*, sent from the Aduenturers with fresh supplies, both of goods and men, arriues in the townes-harbour: by her likewise was brought the Companyes answer to the Gouernours letters before-mentioned; as also, the first magazin to be sold for tobacco that euer thes ilands sawe; of which since ther hath bin euery yeare one, to the cost rather than profitt of the inhabitants; their folly, wants, and high enhancement of the prices, concurreinge to keepe the colony poore ynough as long as the custome and use of it shall be mainteyned. This shyp, after six or seuen weekes staye, cleares herselfe of the ilands, and makes her waye homewards, haueing laded vpon her about some thirtie thousand waight of tobacco, the which proueinge good, and comeinge to a luckye markett, gaue great contentment and incouragement to the vndertakers to proceede lustely in their plantation: for, for the most · part, without some such sweet sence and quickninges nowe and then they growe dull and tyred; as litle vnderstandeinge (the most of them) or regardinge any other more noble respects, what colours or shewes so euer are openly pretended. By this shyp, also, the Gouernour (among other thinges) in his generall letters, wrote to the Company concerneinge his owne returne, and of his desire to haue a successor: and yet notwithstandinge, in his most priuate letters to his fast freindes, he intimated a willingnesse of a prolongation of his time, prouided that they conceiued it might be beneficiall for him; of which he desired to haue perticuler information, and that accordingly they would worck it out.

Noe soner is the Gouernour thus ridd of the incombrance of shypeinge (although he found very smale incouragements, and noethinge indeed but fayre spoken vncertanties), yet findinge himselfe obiected to the publick eye, and both engaged and well stept into the action, his secret hopes also fedd with the beleife of his owne worth, and the power of his freinds still carryinge some litle life within them), but he resolueth what soeuer came of it to proceede in his buildinge proiect: a second time therfore he commands the appearance of the most able persons in the maine to the purpose: the ground is cleared on all hands; the frame of the house fitted and raysed: some are sett to their task in diggeinge of cellers, others in burneinge of lime and makeinge of mortar; others in makeinge of shyngles: some fiue or six of the best experienced in that kind are employed to make search and triall for fresh water, the which to their much content is hapely and plentifully obteyned. In breif, euery man is so fitted and bestowed to the actinge of a part; so hastned and godded on by the callinge and cudgellinge of the Gouernour, as that in a very short time the worck is brought to much perfection, and a large, hansome, and well contriued house (yet by farr the best in the Ilands) is erected and in good part finished. The burthen wherof laye so heauye on the shoulders of the poore inhabitants in generall, as that in secret (how perillous soeuer) they could not chuse but lament and grudge at the misery of their condition: and especially they deplore their estate to their preacher Mr. Lewes, who, compassionatinge them, not long after (after his manner) gaue an open touch at it in a sermon of his in the maine;

the which comeinge to the Gouernours knowledge, putt him into so high a choler, that at the preachers comeinge next to towne, meetinge him vpon the warfe, he could not hold, but takeinge him aside, he wispered in his eare that he was informed well ynough of his tricks and rayleings against his buildings: "But take you heed (quoth he) of and looke well to your selfe: for if you serue me so but once more, I shall tie your neck and heeles together vntill your back crack, and so helpe you to repentance." Vpon which terrible threatuinge the minister (whose speritt was not to be mannaged that way) presently replyeing aloud, "You knowe well ynough (sayth he) that I feare not your threatninge, and therfore you may vse them to such as doe: for my part I will freely performe the dutyes of my function, and when I have done will answer it also, as well (if not better) than you shall doe yours." Vpon which answer the Gouernour, although with much adoo he forbore him at the time, yet euer after he nourished a perpetuall heart-burneinge against him, the which vpon all occasions and opportunities he greedely manifested, not only dureing the time of his being Gouernour, but euen euer since his returne, so that it is knowen that he purposely went to a certaine byshop, and complained of the poore mans irregularities in not conformeinge himselfe in the Sommer Ilands to the booke of Common Prayer; the which, though the discret byshop seemed not much to regard, in respect the place was so farre remote of his diocesse, yet it sufficiently manifested the spleene conceiued and nourished by the Gouernour against the minister, neither did he spare to expresse it much more liuely for the space of their after staye together in the ilands; witnesse the passage that presently after ensued; at what time the said preacher takeing occasion in a sermon he preached at the towne, to say that it could neuer be well with that state and Gouerment, wher Moses and Aaron ioyned not together; the Gouernour, being at the hearcinge of it, stoode vp openly in the church as the preacher was at his sermon, and told him aloud that he was out of his text. Another time the preacher reproueinge in the same manner some of his auditory for gazeinge vpon the women; "And why not, I pray, sir? (cryes out the Gouernour in publick), are they not Gods creatures?"

Amidst thes iaugleings and fallings out a pitiful and desperate attempt was executed, the which for a time took vp all the talk, and added discontent to the Gouernour: for two poore and silly fellowes consorted only with one young woman (who, had she but bin possessed with the least correspondencye of inside to her outside, might well have bin tearmed excellent), stealeinge awaye the bote belonginge to the castle, the which one of them had in charge, and poorely victuallinge her, they committed themselues to sea, and so ranne awaye. Uncertaine it is to this daye towards what part they addressed themselues; for being neuer seene nor heard of after, by all likelyhoode they quickly made an end of their entended voiage, either in the bottome of the sea or in the belly of some great shark. It is true that some suspicions wer taken by the discouerye of a letter of one or two more confederated with them, and some enquiryes made by the angry gouernour about it; but noe profe being found of pregnancye, the matter was husht up, and noethinge farther spoken of. In the very next moneth after, the very like attempt plotted and concluded by six other of the colony people (so extreamely addicted wer most men in this man's gouernment to gett lose from the Ilands vpon any tearmes), but the conspiracye being reueiled by one of the faustinge confederates, the other fiue wer sodainely apprehended, and being indicted and arraigned at the next assize, which was shortly after, they wer all of them found guilty of rebellion (for vpon thoes tearmes ranne the indictment) and so receiued sentence to be hanged; but, being the daye after carryed to the place of execution with halters about their

I

neck, one of them only suffered death, the other foure wer repriued by the Gouernours warrant, and afterwards by him absolutely pardoned (for he vsually tooke vpon him to doe that too). The rebellion and mutinye layd vnto their charge in the enditement ranne in thes wordes: "That they had plotted and entended to runne awaye with the great bote belonginge to the Castle, and soe to goe for the West Indies, and ther to take a Spanish frigate, to which end they also ment to assault on a sodaine the Kings-castle, and thence to furnish themselues with munition and water-cask. They also made a vowe and swore one vnto another, that being once entred into the bote the would all of them die together rather than be taken aliue."[4]

Dureinge thes executions in the Sommer Ilands the *Dyana* arriues safely in England; the which, howsoeuer, she brought a good content to the aduenturers by her luckye bringinge in of good tobacco, yet passed it not without a leuen of offence and disgust in many perticuler persons against the Gouernour. Some of them accused him of vaineglory and presumption in buildinge such a flauntinge house vpon ground belonginge to the Company, others taxed him with his forceinge of the people in generall to that priuate worck, and with his rigour practised vpon them in it, and this they called noe lesse than oppression and crueltye; and some ther wer that stuck not to giue out that he was to be questioned about the abuse of the Companyes name in giueing out that this buildinge was made for their vse, and vpon thes tearmes, and under that pretence force-inge the poore people to their great grudgeinge against the Company, to labour and toyle out themselues in it, as also for employeinge many perticuler necessaryes out of the store which belonged to the publick seruice to that use; wheras it was well ynough knowen that his entendments in all this

[4] All this, as appears by the Colonial Records, occurred in 1618. John Yates was executed 24th July 1618.

affayre wer cutt out and modelled only to serue his owne turne. The vsage likewise of Mr. Riche and Mr. Pollarde wer taken in very ill part by their friends and famelies, in so much that euen at that time (although the most part of a whole yeare yet wanted to the accomplishment of his first tearme of gouernment, ther wanted not discources and conferences for the search and choyce of a newe one; the which, neuerthelesse, was for the present closely carryed, both by reason that diuers of his interested friends did earnestly mediate, and make all the fayrest weather for him, that possibly they could, as also in respect that his prefixed first tearme of three yeares was not as yet terminated; so that a shyp (called the *Blessinge*) being vpon the instant of a voiage thether, it was held noe good discretion either to discontent or vtterly dispayre him vntill they had him safe ynough from doeinge of them any harm. This I saye was the ground of the huslinge and close carryage of that entention for the present; but noe soner was the shyp departed from the English shore, and so all intelligences secured for that yeare; but the diuers parties began openly to discouer themselues against him. Among the which, one of them went so far as that in one of their ordinary and common courtes, a motion was made by a gentleman of worth and good note (some lords and many of the merchants of the Company being ready to second it), that in regard that the Deputy Gouernors limitted time in the Sommer Ilands was vpon an expiration, it seemed very fitt, by waye of a preparatiue, that in the meane time some courses might be thought on for the choice of a successor, to which end it was not amisse that some fewe persons wer publickly named to the Company at that instant, that so vpon notice of the men, inquisition might be generally made of their qualitie and sufficiencye, and therby the iudgments and opinions of all men the better grounded and assured against the daye of election, which was to be at their next generall and great quarter court. This proposition being generally approued and held very profittable and vsefull, the Gouernour of the Company (who then was, and yet is, Sir Thomas Smithe) was entreated, accordinge to the custome, to put it to the question; but he being at that time determinately bent by all meanes to hold in the old Gouernor, as well therby to scrue some turnes of his owne as to pleasure his friends (and cheifly Mr. Tucker, the searcher at Grausend), sodainly and sullenly replied, that, for his part, he found that motion vtterly vnfitt, both in respect of time and occasion, the Gouernour's tearme in the Sommer Ilands was neither yet finished, nor, if it wer, did he see wher they could be better prouided elswher; to which it being answered that howsoeuer that might be true, yet was it necessary and requisite that euery man should haue the libertie and freedom of giueinge his vote, and the which, without this meane of preparation, could not so perfectly and vnderstandingly be performed. He was, therfore, once againe desired to put it to a decision by erection of hands; vpon which second vrginge (expressinge much heate and passion), "Doe it who will (answers he) by me it shall not be done at this unseasonable time;" the which peremtory answer (it being a course and refusall vtterly vnexpected, and so tooke them vnprouided) though it caused a leaueing off of that action for that court daye, yet it was taken in so ill part by diuers of the great ones, and most of the honestest, as an order of court vpon occasion therof, not long after, was passed in a great quarter court at Virginia, that what gouernour, treasurour, or deputy soeuer should refuse to putt anythinge to the question, required by any member of the court, and iudged by the most to be fitt to be propounded, was, *ipso facto*, to be depriued of his office.

Much about this time, the shyp the *Blessinge* arriues in the Sommer Ilands, and by her comes the Gouernour to the knowledge how the world goeth with him in England, for although by the generall intelligence he receiueth noethinge but vncertaineties and a kind of spinneinge out of his hopes at length, yet by diuers priuate letters from his friends, he is told plainely, not only of the multiplicitie of disgusts taken against him by most of the Company and some of the great ones, so that it was likely it would goe hardly with him concerneinge the farther continuation of him in his place of command, but that also in the perticular about his fine house and fatt ground, it was altogether to be dispayred of, vnlesse he fully and nimbly cleared himselfe and satisfied the Company about his oppression of the people in generall, and the harsh course he had held with Mr. Riche and Mr. Pollarde; neither did they see how this possibly was to be done without his owne presence. Haueing receiued this vnwelcome aduise, and being much inwardly deiected, he first begins to thinck seriously of it within himselfe, at last he imparts it to some such as he conceiueth his most trusty fellowes, consultinge them principally in this perticular, whether it wer not the best course for him to passe in person for England with the returne of this shyp, and ther by a liuely appearance to cleare all thes impediments, since it might be feared that in so far a distance, his freinds ther wer not so officious and entertaine for him as wer to be wished; and this he found the rather necessary to belieue, by reason that haueinge wrote publickly to the Company concerninge his returne vpon the expiration of his first tearme, and privately to his freinds to receiue their aduise about it, he had receiued by this shyp noethinge but doubts and vncertaineties; wherby as on the one side he grew suspicious of the care and respect of his freinds, so on the other he verely thought that either the vndertakers would secretly and sodainely send him a successor, or, at least, would not bestowe an entreaty vpon him to a longer continuance, the which he highly but closely affected and hoped for, and of which he ment to make good vse. But this inclination of his towards agoeing for England being once discoucred to be in him, is sone after brought to a thorough resolution by a trick putt vpon him in this manner. Euery man in generall being exceedeinge couetous to haue him gone (his followers, that they might followe him thether, the rest to be ridde of him wher he was) it is agreed by two or three of the cunningest heads among them, one Wood, the ensigne of his company, being the prime plotter of the deuise (a fellowe that had a great deale more of good witt than he knewe how to vse well), that a letter should be framed as written to the sayd Wood from a deare freind of his in England in this tenor : " that howsoeuer he himselfe (as he well knewe) was neither of the court, counsell, nor Company of the Sommer Ilands), yet haueing some good freinds ther wer, he from them had receiued knowledge of a great difference and contrarietie of opinions among that Company about a certaine handsome house, that is sayd to be built on the Sommer Ilands by the present gouernour, with whom it was very likely to goe very hard, vnlesse either by some trustie and powerfull freinds, or his owne presence, a speedy and diligent care and pursute wer taken in hand and throughly followed, and thus much he thought good in his loue to him to let him knowe; that so, if the Gouernour wer his freind, and such a one as he had occasion to wish well vnto, he might accordingly inform him, if otherwise, he might also vse his pleasure." This done, and the counterfeite letter, which was excellently approued of by the rest of the confederates, coppied out in an vnknowen hand, Wood takes his time to impart it to the Gouernour, yet not without an extreame diligent attention for the nick of an humour, so that at the last findinge it, with a serious looke and a garbe promiseinge somewhat of extraordinary, he presents himself vnto him, and most humbly beseecheth him to afford him a fewe wordes in priuate. The Gouernour (caught with the manner) presently retireth himselfe into

his garden, and bidds him followe him, wher, being alone
together, Wood thus enters vpon him : "Sir (sayth he) I
haue had a conflict within me euer since the arriuall of this
shyp, vpon the receipt of certaine letters which tell me
thinges befittinge your eare to take knowledge of, and my
duty to make knowen vnto you; yet being somewhat vncertaine what to make of them, as not being assured of the
certainetie of the intelligence, I was a good while suspensiue
what to do, at last (as nowe) my respect and duty to you,
my Gouernour, hath ouerswayed all other suspensions and
feares; so that submittinge myselfe to be censured rather
for ouer-credulous and slight than neglectiue and wantinge
due regard of the least care of your good, I haue adventured
to impart it vnto you, and so to leaue it to your owne recte-
fieing iudgement." This prolouge ended, he tells him in
fewe wordes the contents of the letter, continually comeinge
in with this parenthesis, that it may be all this was but
some mistakeinge, and yet he knewe that the freind that
wrote it him was both iudicious and honest. But the Gouernour, although he noethinge smoked the secret of the
plott, yet being vnwillinge to haue it thought that this intelligence or the feare of it wrought anythinge vpon him, he
only, for that time, willed him to shewe the letter, the which
being quickly done, after diuers readeings and surueyeinges,
he at length (with protestations of thancks unto Wood for
his care and good will, whom formerly he could so ill abide,
as he professed openly he would hang him) told him plainely
and in direct wordes, that this report so concurred with
diuers others that he had receiued from England, as that he
found it necessary for himselfe to goe in person thether in
this shyp, vnlesse he would see, not only himselfe in person obiected to all publick scorne, but the best and mainely
affected fruicts of his labours to be bestowed vpon strangers,
if not his enemies; he was therfore firmely resolued to take
his leaue of the Ilands for a while; not doubtinge but to

cleare vp all clouded conceites and apprehensions by the sunneshine of his presence, and to frame all matters at his arriuall at home answerable to his mind. Full glad was this letter-coyner to find his inuention to worck so well vpon this impatient patient, the which how he afterward pursued and composed, you shall heare by and by.

But whatsoeuer the Gouernours resolution was in the Sommer Ilands, the aduenturers at home, for the most part, wer constant and intentiue to a newe election at the præ-fixed day: true it is that the persons wined at and desired wer sundry and diuers, accordinge to the affections and iudgements of thoes who wer to giue in their votes. But the competition especially rested betweene one Captaine Southwell, who mediated by the letters of great courtiers and fauorites; Mr. George Sands, who stoode very fayre, and likely, by the strength of his brother Sir Edwin, a popular man, a great speaker, and of wise estimation in their Courts; and one Mr. Nathaniell Butler, fauoured by diuers of the Lords of the Company, and in especiall long knowen to the Earle of Warwick, and by him well affected, so that much endeauour and canuasseinge for voices against the election day is used on all hands, by the lords openly, directly, and freely, aimeinge mainely at the good and well-fare of the plantation, by others with more libertie, layeinge hold on any occasion that might further their owne ends: in which humours and endeauours we will leaue them awhile, to take our leaue of the discontented Gouernour in the Bermudaes.

We left him, as you know, cuningly scrued into a reso-lution of giueing up his regencye, and a returne for Eng-land: but the partyes that had wrigled him into it, although they feasted themselues with so dainetie a beginninge, yet made account they had attainned but the one halfe of their waye, vnlesse they could also bring him to the institution of such a deputy in his roome as should proue only fitt for their turnes. *Hic labor, hoc opus:* the man, indeed, was ready ynough to be found, Mr. Miles Kendall; one that by lieing among them from the first of the plantation, and participateinge with them in all their sufferings, and many of their by cources, was generally very popular. His speritt, apprehension, and easinesse of nature was knowen to be very conueniently mannageable: noe great exactor of labour, wittnesse his time of being one of the six Gouernours; a good fellowe besides he was approued to be, and one that would not stick in company to be an *aqua vitæ* man sometimes. Behold the man, therefore: the mystery is how to catch him; his owne ambition they doubted not of, the Gouernours being brought to the choyce and admittance of him is the only feare. But this also (as in all other actions) seemed more difficult before it was attempted than it was found afterwards; for, ther being fewe or none to thinck of besides, and thoes that most desired him being such as wer only called to counsell (for who nowe but Wood with the Gouernour at midnight), the whole bussinesse, both for the old mans dispatch, and the newe ones receipt, is fully and absolutely concluded, to the good likeinge of the one partie, but the perfect content of the other, who scarce conteyneinge themselues within the meete limitts of forbearance, wer sometimes in a fayre hazardinge to lose their hopes, by an vntimely and oner-hastie discouery of their ioyes. But the prime men of all the colony being hastily called together to St. Georges, the (nowe vpon departinge) Gouernour relates vnto them the necessitie of his leaueinge of them (which none of them wept for), and withall tells them that he had fastened his choyce vpon Mr. Kendall, to leaue him deputy gouernour in his place, the which, mqst of them (some very fewe only of the honestest and wisest excepted) receiued with high applause: and thus, within a few dayes after, the newe Gouernour, being commissioned by the old, and settled at St. Georges, the old retired himselfe a shypboard, from whence he budgeth not vntill his departure out of the harbour with the shyp, which was not long after; the people haueing bestowed a gratuitie of tobacco on him, to the value of 1,500 weight, which was fetched in by his causeing diuers of his confidents to giue out that he had an order from the vndertakers to require a certaine quantitie of them at his gocinge awaye, the which he rather referred to their courtesies than his commission. And thus ended Captaine Tuckers gouerment, and began Captaine Kendalls.

Lib. V.—*Captaine Kendall; his deputy gouerment; being the fourth Gouernour.*

Before I enter vpon this mans atcheiuements, I must (for order sake) bring you back a little into England, that then you may returne with more satisfaction, for ther the fore-mentioned parties (not to say factions) fortifie and buckle themselues for the battell of election, which was about this time to be pitched, the difficultie and brunt whereof seemed to rest betwixt Mr. Sands and Mr. Butler; neither was it easie to saye to which side the fortune of the daye would fall. True, indeed, that the Lords partie, which was for Mr. Butler, as best vnderstandinge their owne strength, and withall propounding the noblest conditions, seemed euer most likely to carry it. Two maine passages only ther wer, that to interpose themselues. The first and cheifest was a jealousie conceiued by diuers inferiors of the Company, and secretly nourished by some subtle heads of the contrary faction, that this Mr. Butler was especially made choyce of, and thus earnestly solicited for by the Lords, that by this meanes he being once accepted of for Gouernour, the merchants might be wearied out of the ilands; the which therby fallcinge only and

solely to the lords and gentlemen, was imagined to be an
effect very much effected. The second was that Captain
Tucker, being (as they beleiued) still resident ther, and so
desirous to be, it was held by some a good saucing course
to continue him for three yeares longer, as they wer
allowed by their letters patents (although he was not so
pleasinge vnto them as they could wish), rather than be at
the charge of sendinge ouer a newe one. As for Captaine
Southwell, although he dayly renewed his forces by fresh
and continuall supplies of great mens letters, yet that
course being altogether distastfull in generall (as contrary
to the freedome of their Courts), little hope or none appeared. And vpon thes tearmes, for the space of some
monethes, stood this affayre. In this interim arriues the
Blessinge, and with her (beyond all mens expectation)
Captaine Tucker, whose arriuall putts a newe face, for a
time, vpon all thinges: for nowe the Courts are wholy
taken up with takeinge knowledge of the forsaken state of
the ilands, in what manner, and vnder what condition they
are left, and vnder whose direction and command; concerneinge which points, haueinge receiued a relation rather than
a satisfaction from Captaine Tucker, the treaty of all bussinesse become reduced to thes heades—about the future
Gouernours entertainement; the impartinge to Captaine
Tucker his promised reward of three shares, and the confirmation of Captaine Kendall in his deputy gouerment.
For the first, it was resolued that the former course of
giueinge of land by waye of gratification to such Gouernours
as wer sent successively must not be continued, for soe
in a short the meanes would be wantinge and fayle in
that kind to gratifie them; besides, they found by experience that those expectations in the last Gouernour had
produced but badd effects: it was therefore concluded that
their entertainement should be annual, to which end it was
ordered and confirmed by erection of hands, that sixteene

shares of land, conteyneing four hundred acres, should be laid out to that purpose; and this land to lye together in St. Georges Iland, being part of the generall land; and to begin at the east-end thereof, and so on west-wardes; thirtie two men of the generallitie being to be placed as tenants vpon it. The which allowance, howsoeuer, it was afterwards knowen (for they guided themselues at first only by the mapp), to be for the present of noe worth at all, both by reason of its being disabled for tobacco by want of due fences, and that it was also the only plott of ground vsed and fitt for the cattell and cowes; yet was ther noe heed nor care at all taken for either the reuerseinge of the order, or amendinge of it, so highly (especially when it rather makes than marres their owne priuate incomes) are the most of thoes that sitt belowe the half-pace in love with thes their owne Court-creatures. Concerneinge Captaine Tuckers reward, it was agreed vnto that three shares of land, according to their promise, should be bestowed vpon him, but whereas he had precipitately layd them out for himselfe without their lycence and approbation; and not only so, but with the sweat and extreame oppression of the inhabitants and cost of the Company, had erected and framed a stately house vpon them to serue his owne ambition, it was held altogether fitt and exemplary to putt him besides this his cushion, and to depriue him of so presumptious an expectation; wherupon it is ordered that two partes of this ouerplus land, together with the large house, should be appropriated to the Churche, the rest allowed vnto Sands his tribe, in recompence of some glebe land that the owners of that tribe had bought for Pembrok tribe; as also by reason that the iland called Ireland, being a part of the sayd tribe, proued for the most part barren and vnproffitable.[5] As for Captaine Kendalls confirmation and continuance in his deputy gouerment, it was held not

[5] The Report here referred to, known as the Lords' Arbitrament, will be found in the *Memorials of Bermuda*, i, p. 143.

only necessary but almost vn-auoideable; for, howsoeuer, he was generally esteemed vnfitt ynough, and by some soe openly professed, yet the entertainement for present Gouernours proueing so short and smale, how could it be hoped that any man of value would accept of it; for thus iudged the most of them after the sence of their owne aimes.

Thes resolutions vpon thes three maine pointes being thus hastely concluded, there was yet a rescruation and clause annexed, to alter, or if need wer, to reuerse them at the next great and generall Court, as they should find occasion; yet, notwithstandinge, they are in the mean time presently after shypped ouer by way of instructions to the Sommer Ilands for Captaine Kendall, by the shyp the *Gyllyflowre*, which was at the instant of her departure thether, and with them some congratulatory letters of some fewe interested freinds of his; among which, from a man of note, and one desirous to be so, wer thes informations and touches worthy obseruation; that by his meanes and powerfull operation, he was absolutely confirmed in his place for three yeares: that Captaine Tucker had as absolutely lost his house and land at the ouerplus, it being for the present assigned to the Churche; the which, notwithstandinge, he doubted not but one waye or other, either by exchange or some other proiect, to gett for himselfe ere it wer long, and therfore prayed him to performe a freind and kinsmans part, that in the interim noethinge wer embezeled from it; the which gaped for good newes, how hugged and made vse of at the arriuall, we shall let you see when we come to it.

But this shyp is noe soner gone, but the confirmation of Captaine Kendall in his gouerment in the Sommer Ilands, and the danger of it, began, by some of the most considerate and lesse passionate, to be looked into and throughly aduised on. The order, also, concerneinge the future Gouernours entertainement, and the weaknesse therof, fell into the consideration of such who had both engaged themselues and Captaine Butler to the day of election; and it began to be concciued that it might proue a wroung and dammage vnto him insteed of a fauour, if they should tie or vrge him to that voiage vpon so meane tearmes; neither did they thincke but that he himselfe, vpon the knowledge of it, would be vtterly vnwillinge withall. Resolueinge, therfore, to knowe his mind before they proceeded any farther, they freely imparted vnto him what they concciued, wishinge him, likewise, with the like libertie, to deliuer himselfe vnto them, that so accordingly they might shape their course; whervpon, in fewe wordes, he answered to this effect: That at the entrance into this affayre, and when it was first propounded, he offered himselfe (as they knew) to be disposed of by them in any honest (answerable) action that they found him capable of, prouided that he might haue meanes sufficient to vndertake and prosecute it to some effect and perfection. And wheras at that time, by way of encouragement, they putt him in good hope of gettinge an improuement of his estate, his reply was (if it please them to remember): that as for that perticuler, it should neuer worck vpon him, but on the bye, the former respects wer thoes with which euery honest man ought to be commanded: as for the other, if it came either by waye of reward, or for the better enablinge of him in the vndertaken employment, since he might warrantably and comfortably, he would not refuse them, but he hoped euer to carry that mind, as to ranck it farre belowe many other respects: and this profession he had not only made vnto them, but vnto all others also, that upon their knowledge, and by their appointment, had treated with him about it: and in this mind he rested at the present, neither would he cause any ill suspicious mistrusts of the sinceritie of it, by a mutation vpon grounds contrary thervnto. If they rested, therefore, in their first opinion of him they might go on in their first resolution; if not, but that they had found some ground and reason for a chaunge and alteration, he desired them to deale freely with him also in that perticuler, the which should be so farr from giueing him the least distaste or discontent, as he should find iust occasion and cause to acknowledge it for a fauour.

This answer being heard and receiued to content and satisfaction, a through resolution is taken, with all industry and perseuerance to pursue his election. Neither did it nowe meet with halfe the difficulties and oppositions that formerly wer expected; for first, Mr. Sands, either vpon his notice takeinge of the smale hopes of gaine, or that he misdoubted the strength of his partie, or both as far as could be learned, desisted wholy from standeinge for the place. Captain Tucker's freinds likewise, by reason of his vnlooked for comeinge ouer so sodainely, and the dislikes they found the Company had of him, dispayred (and so desisted) to doe any thinge for his returne : so that all thinges seemeinge to concurre for the effectinge of what they desired, at the very next court day a motion is openly made that the Company would be pleased to expresse themselues against the day of election, which nowe drewe nere, whether it wer not fitt (in diuers important respects) that a newe Gouernour wer sent ouer into their ilands; if it wer, that then some gentlemens names might at the instant be propounded to prepare mens iudgements, for the giueing of their voices at the appointed time. Bothe which propositions being receiued as conuenient, are presently vpon it affirmatiuely concluded by an erection of hands with a very generall approbation; only it was obserued that some fewe, who seldome vsed to sitt mute in any cause, wer found silent in this; but the reason also was as sone discouered, for they wer known either to be kinsmen to Captaine Kendall, or dependents vpon those kinsmen; yet neuerthelesse, noe notice being publickly taken, Captain South-well and Captain Butler are the men propounded, and the Company willed throughly to enforme themselues of them against the next great Quarter Court.

But betwixt this time and that, ther fell out an accident, which so cleared the waye for Captain Butlers election, as putt it quite beyond all opposition. It had its chiefest influence indeed upon Virginia, but yet not being without operation (both by reason of the propinquitie of the places and coniunction of the Companyes) in the Sommer Ilands, especially, in this perticuler, it is for perspecuitie and order sake necessarely to be also inserted in this my course of history. And from thes grounds it tooke its being: Sir Thomas Smithe haueinge from yeare to yeare, for a long time bin continued in his treasurour-shyp of the Virginian Company, it was found that many and great sommes of mony collected and brought in for the vse and behoufe of that plantation wer so expended and lost, as a very smale grouth and improuement of that colony could therby be any way discerned; neither (as it was sayd) could ther euer be gotten any perfect or iust account of thes disbursements. It was nowe, therfore, with somewhat more life and quicknesse than formerly, affected and required; to which end ther had bin chosen very substantiall auditors and such as wer thought and esteemed to be of great integritie and iudgement; and a prime one among the rest was Sir Edwin Sands. Thes auditors fallinge closely to their bussinesse, euen at the very first procure and giue many disgusts to Sir Thomas Smith. He tooke it ill that they held not their meetinges at his house in Phillpott-lane, as others had formerly vsed; he beleiued they ment him noe good by their so earnest requires for all old bookes of account; and to haue them deliuered into their hands, and left with them dureing their auditt: but the point that especially gauled was, that some of the auditors (and cheifely Sir Edwin Sands) made it their ordinary and frequent vse, to lament openly in the courts, that vnlesse they wer better attended, more freely enformed, and a truer correspondence practiced, it would proue altogether impossible for them to attaine to any perfect account : nay they sticked not to saye in plaine tearmes, that in steed of thes fayre and equall dealeings which they expected, they found noethinge but courses and endeuours dayly putt vpon them which aimed only (as far as they could perceiue) to breed delaye and intricatenesse, and to enwrape them in all obscurities. To which charge and imputations, howsoeuer, Sr. Thomas Smithes answer in publick was only, that thes conceiued difficulties and complaincts seemed rather to arrise from the want of experience and from insufficiencyes of the most part of the auditors, and especially the leading men (wherin he was well knowen to aime at Sr. Edwin Sands), than any other iust cause whatsoeuer : yet such a heart-burncinge and separation of affections (not to say spleene and malice) ensued ther vpon betwixt them, as for euer after, it was easily discerned and euen generally obserued, that the most of their motions and propositions tended more to crosse and snibbe one another, than to procure any fayre and good effects; as rather lookeinge after who it was that spake, than what it was was spoken : and to such a heighte of heate thes distempers became enflamed within a very short time, that all their meetinges and consultations seemed rather cockpits than courts.

But thes auditors receiueinge noe satisfaction nor content this waye, fell into another that lead nearer to the point : for first they began to wisper among themselues, than to spread it abroad by meanes of their fellowes and faction, that noe hope was to be had of euer perfectinge thes great accounts (so far behind they sayd they found them) so long as Sr. Thomas Smithe (the man cheifly to be questioned) remained thus in a perpetuall dictatorshyp : he was to be chaunged therfore, though it wer but for the time, and some other vn-interested gentleman or merchant to be put in his place. This proiect being by many of all sortes well ynough approued, and mainely prosecuted by the faction of the auditors, two difficulties only rested to be cleared: the one how to displace the old Gouernour, whom they well knewe had many great freinds; the other was wher to find a newe: for the first ther being three chcif parties in the Company; the first the lords and most of the gentlemen; the other of Sr. Thomas Smithes, and many of the merchants, especially thoes of the East-India Company; and the third that of their owne: it was held the only course for the facilletate-inge and surety of the carriage of their election, to vse and practice all possible endeuour to conioyne the lords and thes together. As for the man ther and thus to be chosen he was not long in findinge out euery man almost cast his eye vpon Sr. Edwin Sands.

The quintessence and perfection of this affayre, insist-inge thus vpon the vnion to thes two sides, it was quickly apprehended, that the fayrest and fleetest course for the accomplishment therof, was by giueinge the lords a perfect assurance, that if it would please them to ioyne their forces with theirs, for the assistance of electinge Sr. Edwin Sands to be the treasorour of the Virginian Company, a point (as they sayd) of maine necessitye for the wellfare and stabilitie of that plantation, they would be as constant and ready to doe the like for them in chuseinge Captaine Butler to be the Gouernour of the Sommer Ilands; the which, as perhaps it was fully as needfull, so by them (they imagined) noe lesse affected. This proposition and the condition deliuered and made knowen vnto the lords was willingly accepted; and after some fewe meetinges of the prime men on both sides, absolutely concluded; the forme and manner of the con-ueyance of it being also disgested and ordered, at what time (among other thinges) because it was certainely knowen that diuers perticulers of the Company wer willinge ynough to haue Sr. Thomas Smithe remoued, and yet durst not openly professe so much by erection of hands, by reason of their dependences vpon him some other wayes, it was held very beneficiall and safe to bring in vse the custome of a ballettinge box, the which some other Companyes in London practised to good effect, whereby men might freely deliuer themselues without being taken notice of.

Thes conclusions being thus agreed vpon by thes two parties, and the bussinesse openly propounded at the preparative Courts of both the Companyes, which are allwayes held the Wednesday seuen-night before the Quarter Courts, at the next days of election (the ballettinge box being brought in and placed on the table), Sr. Edwin Sands, Mr. Alderman Johnson, and Sr. John Worssnam (Sr. Thomas Smithe wisely refuseinge to stand in competition wher he knew it was to noe purpose), were putt in election for Virginia; Captaine Kendall, Captaine Southwell, and Captaine Butler for the Sommer Ilands. The balls being cast and counted, Sr. Edwin Sands is found to carry it for the one, and Captaine Butler so wholy for the other, as among three hundred balls three only wer found against him; neither was ther any other matter of moment handled at thoes dayes meetings in either of the Courts, saue only that in that for the Sommer Ilands, Sr. Thomas Smithe was continued in his gouernourshyp of the Company, contrary to the expectation, as it was thought, of Sr. Edwin Sands, who verely looked to haue had that also, for he stoode as a competitor; and that Captaine Tucker, by the sollicitation of his freinds and his owne extreme importunitie, obteyned a suspension of the former order of Court, concerneinge the disposition of his reward and the fayre house at the ouerplus; the absolute and whole orderinge wherof being now by the whole Court fully committed to the conclusion of some of the Lords, who not long after, as not willinge to discourage their newe Gouernour, nor to leaue the old vnsatisfied, nobly and freely gaue in their decree,[6] which was that the whole ouerplus being to be deuided into seuen partes, three of them, together with the house, should be allotted to Tucker; other two partes to Sands his tribe; and the other two for the glebe of South-hampton; the which order was afterwards put in execution by Captaine Butler, and so rests at this day. And thus, haueinge at last brought you to Captaine Butlers election, we will leaue him for a while in England in preparation for his long voiage, and returne you to the Sommer Ilands, that you may see how Kendall, Tuckers deputy Gouernour, behaues himselfe in the mean time.

Noe soner was the shype called the *Blessinge*, with Captaine Tucker, out of the harbours mouth, but a newe sayle is discouered both out of the shyp at sea and from the mount at land. The shyp presently makes towards her, neither did the other shunne the meetinge, so that sone beareinge vp one with another she is found to be English, and manned with English, being called the *Treasorour*, and her commander one and the same Elfry who brought in the frigate of meale (and the ratts to boote), in Mr. Moores time; sent out she was by Captaine Argoll from Virginia, wher he was then Gouernour, vnder a pretence of tradeinge all alongst the coast with the natiue Indians for skinnes, and at the Virgin and Sauuage Ilands for goates; but some of her people comeing abord the *Blessinge*, by some speeches vnaduisedly let falne, begett a suspicion in Captaine Tucker of a farther proiect than was openly pretended; neuer the leese, not findinge a ground, nor perhaps a power of stayinge

---

[6] "The Lords' Arbitrament" on this question is preserved in the Colonial Records. It is dated 24th July 1619, and refers to an Order of Court of 10th March of the same year. The date of Sir Edwin Sandys' election as Treasurer of the Company, and, as would here appear, of Butler's appointment as Deputy Governor for the Somers Islands, was 28th April 1619.

of her, after an houre or two of being together, they part;
Tucker sendinge some letters to Kendall by the Ilande
botes that wer yet abord, wherby he aduiseth and wisheth
him by all meanes, and in any case, not to suffer the sayd
shyp to enter any of the harbours, tellinge him of the perill
he thereby might fall into, as veryly assureinge himselfe
that she went not vpon any warrantable action. But the
Blessinge being once at sea, the botes belonginge to the
Ilands are easily entised abord the *Treasourer*, wher, lettinge
Elfry and his company knowe of Kendalls being deputy
Gouernour, and how kind a man he was to good fellowes
(the which himselfe also partly knewe by experience), they
easily perswade him to putt into the harbour awhile to refresh himselfe; neither was Elfry hard to be entreated, for
in want he was of many necessaryes which he hoped to fish
well ynough from Captaine Kendall, and especially a good
bote, some corne, sayles, wood, and water. Herevpon some
of the Ilanders abord him are preseutly dissmissed to certifie
the deputy Gouernour of the bussines, and the rest stay
behind to pilote him in; the which, notwithstandeinge, gatt
not into the harbour vntill two dayes after, by reason of
contrary winds. But howsoouer, the deputy Gouernour, by
the aduise of his newe and young counsellours, despiceinge
the admonitory letters of Captaine Tucker, and laughinge
at his wisdome, was well ynough contented, as it sone after
appeared, with the comeinge in of thes guests; yet, to let
the world knowe that he would be a commandour, he
caused all such of the maine folke (his owne gang only
excepted, whom indeed he should haue punished most) as
presumed to goe abord her, without his licence, and contrary to an article in that case, conceiued and prouided by
Captaine Tucker, to be bound ouer to answer it at the next
generall Assize, when how kindly and christianly he dealt
with them you shall see hereafter.

But the *Treasorour* being thus gotten in, is very kindly

entertained by the Gouernour, and passeth vnder the name
and title of the Erle of Warwicks ship. Many close conferences are held betweene her Captaine and the Gouernour
and his leaders, that Wood (formerly spoken of) and one
Yates being alwayes at his elbowe, and in his eare; and
verely beleined it is that Elfry, being in priuate with them,
and the aqua vitæ pott walkeinge, did freely ynough professe
some secret ententions, and possesseth them with many
pretie hopes out of the West Indies, with which being tickled
they are induced the readyer and willinger to giue care to
his motion for releife; howsoeuer certaine it is, that after
some six weekes staye, being furnished by the Gouernours
secret appointment with one hundred thousand eares of
corne out of the kings castle, which was to haue bin as a
continuall store ther, and euery yeare renewed by the
country, and by this meanes vaided with a good newe sayle
that belonged to the publick, and the which they shortly
after wer in pitifull want of, and a hansome bote built at
the charge of the aduenturers, he merely hoysed sayle and
makes his waye on his entended voiage; and well knowen
it is that the kind deputy Gouernour had noe other satisfaction from him at that time (nor that I knowe of euer after),
than windie promises, of straunge requitalls vpon a *bon
voiage*, the which he scorned so much as to question; and
vpon which it is sayd the good gentleman builded braue
castles in the aire, and held himselfe very well and sufficiently appayd.

The Ilands being thus cleared of shypinge, and want
beginninge to make both the towne and country sober, the
deputy Gouernour and his fewe select and beloued counsellours, who indeed wer the Gouernours gouernours, begin
to consider how that his authoritie being deriued and fetcht
only from the commission receiued from Captaine Tucker,
and the date of thes three yeares vpon expiration, it must
of necessitie followe that the validitie of his warrant must

also fayle and extinguish with it, was therefore altogether behoufefull to find out some newe meane of establishment; neither was this long in contriuinge, for concerneinge a generall likeinge and desire in most of the people to so easie and populer a gouerment, fittinge with the humour of the aqua vita men on the one side and the idle men on the other, and restinge assured that thoes fewe otherwise enclined, either durst not reueile themselues, or that, by reason of their paucitie, it would proue to noe purpose if they did, it is therevpon concluded that a generall appearance should be summoned to St. Georges; and, by waye of a newe election, euery man should be required to deliuer his voice, whether Captaine Kendall should be continued in his command and Gouernour-shyp, or some other man; this being as sodainely executed as it is contriued, and most of the maine comeinge in a hurry to the towne, wher they are wondrously welcomed and feasted with store of turkees and great bowles full of loblolly, some dramms of hott liquour squeazed out of the Gouernors seiler, enterlaced with all. The assembly is held vpon the day appointed in the churche, and the busines propounded, in a perswasiue oration made by Wood, wherein he tells them of the necessitie of addcinge a newe life to the nowe vpon dieinge commission giuen by Captaine Tucker, the which certainely, sayth he, cannot more substantially be acted than by the free choyce of a generall voice, to which you are now called; neither needed they to trouble themselues with lookeing out for a newe man, for who but Captaine Kendall, worthy, kind, affable Captaine Kendall (and he was in person to heare what he sayd) could be thought vpon; speake freely, therefore, quoth he, and speake out, whether this be not the man you all desire, hope in and wish for; this emphaticall speech is noe soner ended by Wood, but euery man cries out "a Kendall!—a Kendall!—who but noble Captaine Kendall!" The which being sufficiently hooped out, without the least

contradiction that could be heard, very heartye thancks is
giuen them all (good people) by the late deputy, now absolute
Gouernour, as he takes it; and a promise, publickly published, so to behaue and carry himselfe durcing the whole
time of his future regencye, as should giue them cause to
belieue and assure themselues that they had not mistaken
him in their election : and thus is ended and made vp this
great bussines of expectation, and the eueninge of that
blessed day solemnised with noice of great ordinance,
healthinge, and much braue triumph; and vpon this sandy
and formelesse foundation (not to saye tumultuous and
seditious) this Gouernour euer after, vpon his owne confession, more relyed and humored himselfe, than vpon any
other warrant or commission whatsoeuer.

The Gouernour being thus irregulerly confirmed, it began
at last secretly to be thought on by some of his most prouident contriuers how this act might be taken in England.
To help out the matter, therfore, and sweeten all distastes,
it was thought fitt that some publick worcks wer presently
sett vpon, and especially such as, being propounded and
vrged vpon him by Captaine Tucker at his departure, the
accomplishment of them was likely ynough to be warranted
by him to the Company at his arriuall, and so by them
reconned as good as done, whose expectation, if it should
be deceiued, might well make them very angry. Hereupon,
the people of the Maine being called to the execution, the
perfection of Smithes Forte is first attempted, the which,
being begun by Mr. Moore, then proceeded on by Captaine
Tucker, is nowe lastly sett vpon to be accomplished by this
man; but the rock wheron they wer to worck proueinge
exceedingly hard, and the layers out of the plott and ouerseers of it haueing but small experience in such affayres,
after a great deale of labour, and many moneths expence,
a fayre plattforme and a hansome redoubt is spoyled, and
in a manner left vnseruiceable, by being slubbred up with

dangerous and vnsure vpperworcks of brittle stone and rubbish, to the extreame hazard and perill, vpon the least occasion and great shott of an enemy, of all such as therin are to mannage and plie those ordinance. This thus made up, and the most part of a winter bestowed on it, the buildinge of a fayre framed church at St. Georges (a worck cheifly recommended vnto him by Tucker, and for which he had left and prepared for him many materialls) is determined, so that the prime carpenters of the Ilauds are consulted about it, and some timber appointed out for that purpose. But a sayle made from the Mount putts of that affayre for a while; for nowe other thinges are to be hearckned after, and dainties hoped for. To the discouery of this shyp, therfore, out goeth Wood (the Gouernours oracle in office, the Liuetenant of his owne company, and, a young hare-brayned fellowe called Danby excepted, whom he also makes Liuetenant of the Kings Castle, his prime minion); and not long it was (for his late goeingo out gives him a quick returne, the shyp meetingo him at the harbours mouthe) but the deed is done, and back againe comes Wood to give up his intelligence, whom the Gouernour moetinge, "What newes, my good Liuetenant," saythe he. "Nay," answers Wood, with a promiseing countenance, "before I tell you that, my esteemed Generall, you must graunt me three boones." "Propound them," replies the Gouernour; "I can deny thee nothinge." "Marry, the first is," saythe Wood, "that you bestowe four gallons of aqua vitæ vpon this your deseruing gang; the second, that you release Mr. Groue out of prison" (this Groue was a fellowe sent out of England by Sr. Edwin Sands, and it is sayd he was a ballade-maker and streete-singer of them ther, but now, by the wise choyce of the Gouernour, made the Prouost Marshall, though at that present, by reason of some sawecynesse, in some deiection); "the third is, that he should make much, very much, of his owne thrise worthy person for the (nowe I begin to find it)," saith he, "iudicious Company in England hath confirmed your ioyfull election here with their generall approbation ther; and long, long may you continue our Gouernour," the which last petition it is well knowen he spake from his heart. "And, for addition to this our happinesse," quoth he, "it is reported that Captaine Tucker is not likely to make hetherward any more; and, besides, it is said that he hath lost his flauntinge house at the Overplus. And thes daintye newes the sweete *Gylly Flowre* yonder hath brought in with her." For this shyp was she that (as you have heard) so presently departed after Captaine Tuckers first arrivall, as she carried away with her the first (suspensiue) resolution of the Court about the two perticulers of Captaine Kendalls confirmation and Captaine Tuckers depriuement, and so knewe nothinge of the reuersement of them, which was at the next quarter Court after.

But howsoeuer, thes wisht relations could not chuse but giue an extraordinary wellcome to this shyp, especially with the Gouernour and his retinue. Yet was ther another maine cause concurreing to rayse it to an extremitie with the most of them; for she was bountifully laden with stroung beere and hott liquours, and had a master also as bountefull, both in the takeinge of it in his owne person as in the giueinge of it out vnto others, so that ten butts of strong beere are drunk out aboard the shyp dureinge his short staye of a moneth, enterlaced answerably with drammes of aqua vitæ, rosa solis, and good sack, out of which fountaine ther flowed out vpon the master such a spring of affection from the Gouernours cheife officers and the most part of thoes commons, which for the most part wer (and I am affrayd are still) common drunkards, that it being afterwards demanded of some of them being in England in open court ther what masters of shyps they most effected to have sent vnto them, an vniuersall crye was raised for them that they above all men liked one Mr. Crayford (for so was the goodfellowe-master called) : the which the Court takinge discret notice of, by all means kept him from them; for the question was not made so much to giue them their choyce as to know whom they especially would desire; for although at the present they sounded not the true cause of their affection, yet was it generally thought to arise from some grounds of seruinge their owne turnes, and therfore especially to be prevented.

Dureinge the staye of this shyp here, this Gouernour (Kendall) held his first generall assize at St. Georges, and that wholly after Captaine Tuckers fashion, wherein I find upon record the triall of foure persons, endicted and arraigned vpon two generall endictments, the one for stealeinge of a sowe belonginge to the Gouernour, prised at three pounds sterlinge (as deare as a Scotts nag), the other for breakinge into a house wher the Liuetenants wife, of the Kings Castle, laye at the same time (her husband being at the same time in England), to both which, although the poore fellowes (hopeinge the rather therby to find mercye) pleaded guiltye, yet the Gouernour would needs haue a jury to pass upon them; whervpon, the bussinesse comeinge to a publick heareinge, they answered for themselves that, as for the sowe, they tooke her as their owne, because Captaine Tucker (whose then she was), at his departure, had giuen them her, and they knewe not that she was entayled to the Gouernourship, but thought she had been his owne in proprietie, and so, by a deed of gift, thers. Concerneinge their breakeinge into the house, they could not deny the fact; yet was it done without any felonious entent, for they offred not to take any thinge away when they wer ther; they only did it, therfore, to discouer whether Danby, the Liuetenante of the castle, his deputy Liuetenant, did not take upon him to be deputy Liuetenant with his wife also in his absence, a report much enlarged

and generally beleived, and whom at the same time they
found lockt up with her in very suspicious manner. Vpon
which answers, the jury, layeinge their heads together,
returned them guiltie of the felony, but acquitted for the
burglary. Whervpon (by the Gouernours command, and
well knowen it is how angry he was for his deare Danby)
three of them had sentence to be hanged; but being
carryed to the place of execution, with halters about their
necks, they wer at last repriued, and so left to liue condemned men, as some of them doe vnto this day. As for
the fourth man of them, he scaped by being sick, and had
neuer any thinge sayd vnto him. At the same time also,
one Browne (an old acquaintance of the Gouernours, and
held by him valorous, because he was wronge for the
violent pullinge of certaine fellowes out of the church
dureinge deuine seruice, and striking them at the church
dore, was censured to lose one of his eares, but the execution therof was absolutely pardoned; and yet another,
that threatned the same Browne to be his death was
bound to the peace. At this assize, likewise, fourteene of
thoes men who (as you formerly heard) had gone abord
the *Treasorour* at her comeinge in without the Gouernour
licence wer called into question; but the cause being heard
and confessed, they wer all of them clearely and fully pardonned; and it was thervpon remembred that they had bin
all of them forward men at his late election, and with thes
effects ended the assize. Presently after which, awaye goes
the *Gylliflowere*, and makes her returne by Newefoundland,
laden hether with passengers, and from thence with fish.[7]

Noe soner is this shyp departed but many discontents
and dreads begin to arrise and to be apprehended, secretly,
among the best sort of people; some of them wisper that
causes of all sortes wer carryed and discussed with litle in-
sight and lesse integritie by the Gouernour, and that the

[7] The record of this Assize is lost.

first tale alwayes bore it awaye; others sayd that so wholy he seemed to be lead by some fewe about him, as one would iudge that either he could not or durst not doe any thinge without them, and that in the examinations and hearings of controveries betweene party and partie, which wer brought or sent for to be heard before him, his Marshall Groue was so talkative, busie, and conclusiue, and himselfe so mute and quiett, as that the marshall appeared the iudge, and the Gouernour a cypher; many complained also of tricks and cousenages putt vpon them by his favorites in nimmeinge and hookeinge awaye from them their goods, and especially liquours; and that when they went to the towne to complaine they found themselues so threatned and terrefied, as they sawe it to be the safest course for them to returne without doeing it they came for, briefly noe accesse, nor redresse of any thinge, to be gotten without the mediation of two or three who only had the leadeinge of him; and such a kind of people they wer, and the waye to winne them so costly and vntoward, that neither honest men would vse it, nor poor men could; nor was ther any other hope of a recouery, vnlesse by the fallinge out of thes theiues the true men might come by their goods; of this, indeed, and only of this, some smale sparkes and glimpses of comfort appeared sometimes, the which was likely ynough to have a quick augmentation, in respect that ther was noe other tie of vnion than the loue of themselues and their owne lusts, the which being so rotten hands wer not in possibilitie to hold long. Diuers other the like mutteringes and complaincts runne closely abroad from hand to hand, the which either the Gouernour knewe not of, seemed not to knowe, or cared not for.

But whilst the Bermuda world stoode vpon thes tearmes, the Company of Adventurers in England, presently vpon Captaine Butlers election, tooke the opportunitie of a shyp that was to goe for Virginia, and vpon her shypped diuers passengers for the Sommer Ilands, and among the rest, a preacher and his family[8] (the Gouernour elect being shortly after to embarke himselfe in a shyp of the Erle of Warwicks, which was in triminge within the dock of purpose to carry him his voiage), so that in the meane time this shyp (called the *Seaflowre*), about the middle of July 1619, arriues in the Kings-Castle Harbour, the which, howsoeuer, she brings noe generall letters to the then Gouernour from the Company; nor scarce any priuate ones from his freinds, which so much as touched the great mutation in England, by the election of a newe Gouernour ther; yet euery mans mouth in the shyp being full of it, it came quickly to the Gouernours care, to the infinite discontent of himselfe and his followers, although true it is that the Gouernour for his part (as one that could not endure to believe what he could not abide to find), was the last man that would creditt it, vntill at last, by secret enquiries of perticuler men, and chiefly of the newe-come minister, he found that which he was desirous to lose. But vpon this intelligence of a newe Gouernour from England, two especiall effects of good to the plantation ensued, the one was a restraint of the former insolencyes committed by the minions of the Gouernour, who nowe found it behoofefull for them to deale more cautiously than formerly, for feare of being called to a more strict account than would proue for their ease; the other was a progression in publick worcks, and in perticuler in the buildinge of the newe church; it being conceiued that as that worck was much desired and expected in England, so

---

[8] Smith apparently did not know, or had forgotten, the name of this preacher, for he refers to his arrival in the same terms, without naming him, in his *General History*. We learn his name from a letter of Captain Butler's to the Company in 1620: "Touchinge our preacher, Mr. Lang, and his eloquent letters, as you stile them, this is the first time I knewe or heard either of them or his eloquence." There is no record of such a minister in Bermuda, and this name is an addition to those enumerated in the writer's *Memorials*, vol. i, p. 691.

the neglect of it might proue very prejudiciall and exclude all future expectances and hopes of fauour; carpenters, therefore, are on all sides employed about it. Tymber is felled and towed to the towne, and the forme and situation thereof layd out and appointed after the modell and direction giuen by Captaine Tucker; but very inconueniently and without due prouidence, by reason that standinge ouer-bleake, and vpon the top of a hill, it is of necessitie to lie open to euery gust and huricanoe, the which in the winters are not uncommon ther, and so therby not likely but to receiue continuall dangers and dammage; and besides, the windes bloweinge neuer so litle loud must needes cause so much bluster and noyce within the church, as the voice of the minister can by noe meanes be heard by the halfe of the auditory. Thes wer the effects I saye, of this hearesaye of a fresh election. But, howsoeuer, thes open carriages promised fayrely, yet passed they not without close and slie practices, entended to worck all that might be against the acceptance of the Gouernour elect; it is wispered about, therfore, and certaine pict companions are the possessed and possessors of others, that the Adventurers and Company at home (sittinge by their warme fires, and full flesh potts) delt vnrespectiuely and harshly with the colony here, continually in this manner to thrust vpon them, at their pleasure, newe and vnknowen men to be their Gouernours; wer ther none here among themselues fitt ynough to take that charge? had they not witt and iudgment sufficient to chuse for themselues? nay, was it not the fittest and most equal, that so they should doe? it was, therfore, to be consulted vpon nowe in time, whether they wer not to stand vpon their right; that so accordingly they might carry themselues at the approch of this newe man who was to be looked for by the next shyp, to which end some especiall ones are elected to grope the minde and affection of their old minister, Mr. Lewes Hughes, and to see whether it wer possible to winne him vnto an approbation of this course, that so they might vse him in his publick exercises to angle the peoples affection that waye. But he (as formerly he had euer honestly done) vtterly dislikeing and disclaiminge all such by wayes as dangerous, vnwarrantable, and seditious, and withall, haueinge a good hope of the future Gouernour, whose father and freinds he had knowen to be likely to breed him honestly; by his stiff refusall and earnest protestation against it, gaue a main blowe to their mutinous and confused proiects; the which neuer the lesse secretly kept themselues in some hopes, and a languishinge kind of life, vntill by a straunge and tragicall accident, which fell out not long after (as you shall see by and by), they tooke and receiued their finall blowe, and deaths wound. About this time also, a smale frigate descried vpon the coast occasioneth a present distraction from all other thoughts; and especially, after she was knowen to be a good-fellowe, manned for the most part with English, who haueinge played some slie partes in the West-Indies, and so gotten some purchase, part wherof consisted of negroes (a welcome for a most necessary commoditie for thes Ilands), she offered to leaue and giue them to the Gouernour, so he would be pleased to admitt her ingresse and egresse, that so she might carine her selfe, and take in some necessaryes, wherby to be furnished for a second voiage vpon the same place and tearmes; and not many nor long consultations wer held about this point; for, howsoeuer, it was doubted by some that this receipt might be ill taken in England, in respect that she was vtterly vncommissioned; and so in plaine tearmes a pyrate, yet the desire of gettinge surmountinge all other respects and feares, and nowe knowcinge they had but a smale time to preye for themselues; her admittance is absolutely concluded, only she is caused to retire herselfe into a by-rode; but yet within the command of the ordinance of Smiths and Pagetts Forts; that so some excuse, if need wer, might be made of the matter, as if this by-place wer none of the harbours; but her fourteene negroes are quickly fetched ashore and deliuered unto the Gouernour. Being thus gott in, her demands and requests are to be provided with some quantitie of corne, the which she was supplied withall, partly from the poore remaindor in the fortes, but especially with that sommers crop, the which groweinge vpon the common ground allotted for the sustentation of the Gouernours famely, was of due to haue bin reserued for him, that was nowe vpon comeinge, as haueinge noe other meanes to relye vpon, nor to rayse his winters prouision. She earnestly also, but more closely (bribeinge the minions officers to that end) sollicited for some helpe of munition, the which although at first (as being held a dangerous matter to graunt) was somewhat stoode vpon, yet at last, was in part yeelded vnto vpon the opportunitie followeinge.

For within fourteene dayes after her arriuall, newes is brought from Sommer-seate of a shyp falne foule vpon thoes north-west sholes, so that botes are on all hands sent out to take knowledge of her, and newe gapeinges after newe gettinges procured. Vpon discouery she is found to be a hansome pinnace, manned for the most part with Dutch, and some two or three English, who, haueinge long waited for prey in the West Indies, and all in vaine, fallinge into distresse of victualls, is perswaded by her English to make for the colonye, and so to refresh themselues; but wantinge a knoweing pilott to bring them in, when they fell upon the coast, found themselues ere they wer awaire engaged within the out-lieing rocks; so that dispareinge of themselues to free themselues, they make all their shyft, and aduenture vpon a drift to seeke for the shore, mooreinge their barck as well as they could to a rock, and shoote of a peece of ordinance to giue notice of their distresse. But by the waye they meete with the Ilands botes, and together with them returne to the forsaken vessell to see what may be

L

done for her recouery; wher, whether it wer the want of
diligence or skill, as some giue out, or that it was a trick
and deuice of the Gouernours quaint counsell therby to
make her a wrack, as others haue not stuck to affirme,
certaine it is that noethinge to any purpose was attempted
for her preseruation, so that being left and giuen ouer as
hopelesse and lost, she was left to the mercye of the next
storme, the which shortly after tore her in pieces; only in
the meane time some smale parcells of goodes are saued,
with certaine murtheringe peeces, sayles, and a cable or
two, the which fallinge to the Gouernours share serued him
fittly to furnish out the foresayd frigate, and so wer bestowed, and for which (as you haue heard) she had bin so
feruent a suter. In recompence wherof certaine presents
are made, as well to the Gouernour himselfe as others.
To him wer giuen a gold ring, like an aldermans, with a
great (and thought a good) redd stone in it; as also an
ebonye bedsteede, and a fayre chest, with God knows what,
to them, diuers and sundry implements, as apparell, linnen,
hatts, and a Negro or two, being all indeed that they had
in that kind; so that being emptied throughly this waye,
but better and beyond hope furnished with that they could
make more vse of, within a while they take their leaue and
depart with a promise (which was neuer meant to be performed), that if they spedd well in their entended voiage
(which they doubted not of), to make a second returne, and
make a better requiteall. As for the poore Dutch, they
continued in these Ilands vntill, about a yeare after, they wer
shypped awaye for England, and so for their country by
Captaine Butler, noe direction nor mention of them being
made vnto him by the Company in their generall letters,
although he had carefully and punctually written vnto them
to the same purpose.

Presently, after the farewell of this frigate, fell out that
tragicall accident, the which (as I told you even nowe) gaue

the speedeinge blowe to the sinister plotts and far-fetched practices contriued for the keepeinge of the newe-expected Gouernour. For one Wood (who as a prime man, and the prime witt, had a prime part to playe in this act) againgt the Gouernours goeinge into the maine had caused a saker mounted vpon the warfe to be laden to giue him an adieu (a fashion formerly vsed vpon euery such occasion, and since broken of by Captaine Butler as an idle expence of powder, of which, consideringe their slowe supplies in that kind, they had little need), and standinge before the mouth of the peece, questioninge the gunner whether he had putt in a shott, vnaduisedly and vngunnerlike (although he tooke a pride in being esteemed a good one), haueing a halfe pike in his hand, he thrust it into the concauetye of the peece, with the yron head fore-most, to trye whether he could find the shott; and makeinge diuers blowes to that purpose, and therby (as it was likely) strikeinge some fire, certaine scattered cornes of powder that laye behind the rest wer kindled, and so the peece makeinge her discharge strooke the sayd Wood, sorely wounded therewith in diuers places, into the sea, which was hard by the place; but being recouered from a drowneinge by some that stood near, within two or three dayes after he dies of those hurtes, to the extreame passionate griefe of the Gouernour, and to such a generall dismay of that pack of confederates as neuer after they so much as once mett together to thinck of the pursute of their former entendments; so that all thinges groweing calme and quiett, seemed to make waye for the receipt and accesse of a new Gouernour, who was nowe euery daye expected.

Sone after this, the shyp, the *Treasorour*, formerly mentioned at large, makes her second returne into the Ilands, and enters the harbour of St. Georges; but of her we shall haue occasion to speake farther in Captaine Butler his time, which now approacheth; for within two moneths after, and somewhat lesse, arriueth the Earle of Warwicks shyp, called also the *Warwick*, and is fast moored in the Kings-Castle harbour, before any iland bote makes out for her disconery; and in her the newe Gouernour, of whome we are nowe to speake. But because euery alteration and alienation of this nature must needs bring with it a newe world, and for the most part a new face, vpon all thinges, it is fit to pause a while, that so we may the fresher fall vpon it when we come ther; and, therfore, here will we end our fifth booke and begin our sixth.

LIB. VI.—*Captaine Butler, the Fifth Gouernour.*

Captaine Butler being thus arriued in the *Warwick*, anno 1619, vpon the 20th of October, the first act he did as Gouernour was to let them at the towne vnderstande that he was so. By the same bote, therfore, that came to discouer them, he sent word to Captaine Kendall by one Mr. Dutton, that came in with him, and was to be Bayly of Warwick tribe, that being come commissioned from the Company of Adventurers in England, by vertue of his Maiesties letters patents, to be the Commandour and Gouernour of thes Ilands, and his sayd commission being entred into force, vpon the very first houre of his being in harbour, hewas to take notice both of it and his arriuall, and to desist from all publick commands in that kind; and farther, that it was fitt that, with all conuenient speede, he did repayre vnto him on shypbord, to giue a full information and account of the present estate and condition of the plantation; and the rather, because he was resolued not to repayre to the towne himselfe vntill he had seene the shyp throughly voided of her passengers, his owne goods on shore, and his house at the towne putt in a readynesse and furnished for the receipt of him. And this through and quick message was thought fitt to be sent thus at the very first, vpon a secret intelligence giuen in, that certaine tumultuous requests would be made by the generall men, vpon such tearmes as might imply a conditional acceptance; the which relishinge of that ill fruict of the election of their owne Gouernors here was conceived by all meanes conuenient to be broken and crushed in its very birth.

But this relation beinge receiued with as litle shewe of disquiett and trouble outwardly as could be expected from such men, an answer is returned the same night by the same hand, that the newe Gouernour was very wellcome into the harbour, and so should be into the towne, when it pleased him; that Captaine Kendall would personally visitt him very shortly where he was; and that his house and all thinges els should be fitted for him against his landinge. The next daye, somewhat before noone, Captaine Kendall, the two ministers, and two or three more of the counsell, with diuers of the officers came abord, wher they are with all courtesie and kindnesse receiued and dined by the Gouernour, with his owne shyp prouisions. Diner is noe soner ended but the Gouernour withdraweinge himselfe in priuate with Captaine Kendall into the gallery of the shyp, had conferences with him to this purpose. He told him that the Company haueinge resolued with themselues to giue him a successor, he supposed that himselfe was noe lesse wellcome to him than another man, in which respect answereable to the fayre reports he had heard of him, he doubted not, but by his meanes to receiue (by reason of his long experience in thes partes) much light and knowledge about the affayres and bussinesse he was to fall vpon, and in perticuler he desired to be certainely and perfectly enformed concerneinge the receipt and admission of such straungers shyps as had bin with him since Captaine Tuckers departure, of which he assured him that the Company would be inquisitiue, and expect to be fully satisfied;

for which free and faire dealeinge he would vpon all occasions, either to the Company in generall or his friends in perticuler, make a thanckfull acknowledgement. Captain Kendalls answer was, that he thought the Company had done him wronge to putt vpon him so sodaine a mutation. Not yet six moneths past he had word from them of a confirmation in his place; now the quite contrary was manifest, he did not knowe of any cause of such an alteration in himselfe, neither if ther had bin could they knowe of it, and therfore he expected it not. The Gouernour replied, that howsoeuer it was not his part to take vpon him the defence of the Companyes decrees, but to execute them; yet he conceiued it might with ease be done in this perticuler, because that first confirmation of him was but with a relation and reference to a more generall approbation at the next quarter elective court, the which being otherwise determined of, then altered all the former conclusions; besides it was to noe purpose to expostulate this fact with him here, nor did he thinck he could obteyne any good by it any wher els.

But as they wer fallinge vpon some other pointes, comes one hastely in, and relates a misfortune which, at the very first, let the newe Gonernour knowe that in this employment he was to meet as well accidentall as naturall disturbances and crosses. For haueinge bin that morneinge at the Kings-Castle to vewe condition of thoes fortes, which wer to his smale satisfaction when they wer seene, the gunner (with the Gouernours meaneinge, for otherwise it is not likely he would haue suffered it, because he came then but in private) had made ready a peece of ordinance for his farewell, the which at his departure he gaue fire vnto; this haueinge done, and being ouer hastie to make after the Gouernour to the shyp, he carelessly left his lintstock with a cole of a match in it vpon the plattforme, the which fallinge downe vpon the plancks, which wer of ceder (and so apt to take fire), it began by litle and litle to kindle, and was not heeded vntill being all on a flameinge fire, word was thus brought to the Gouernour, who instantly, vpon the newes, caused all the botes about the shyp to be manned, and made thether himselfe also in his shalope; but, before he could gett to it, he found that the fire had so generall preuayled on all partes (most of the ordinance being also laden), as noe hope remained of saueinge any thinge, nor of doeing the least good; so that after an houres staye, he returned to the shyp from whence he came; the platforme and carriages of the great peeces being within a while after consumed to ashes: neither did this accident pass without secrett wisperings, and censures of prognostication, the time and place concurringe to augment the credulite.

But the Gouernour seemeinge litle or noethinge to be moued with either, the very next daye sends awaye the steward of his house (an honest and discreet gentleman, named Mr. Seimour Woodwarde) to the towne, with the most part of his house-hold stuff, to order his house and to lett the company knowe that the day followeinge, being Sunday, he ment to be a-shore with them. He wrote also a command to him that supplied the place of liuetenant to his owne Company, dureinge the absence of Captaine Felgate (who was not yet heard of, although he had sett out from England six weekes before the *Warwick*), to haue a gard in readinesse for him at his comeing on land, and to cause the shalope and bote-gang to be abord ouer night, and so in the better readinesse in the morneinge. In the meane time many of the best of the maine repayre to the shyp, and present their attendance vpon the newe Gouernour, and some matters and decisions belonginge to justice being likewise offred and entreated of him, he refused not euen ther to heare and determine such of them as the time and place allowed a possibilitie vnto, tellinge them pleasantly that he perceiued he should not liue idly among them, since they began so rarely with him in this kind.

Vpon the Sunday morneinge very early, accompanied with many botes of the Ilands, the Gouernour makes his waye towards the towne, the shyp giveinge him a farewell with seuen peeces of great ordinance; but, by the waye, a bote of the Company, being ouer-whelmed by the folly of thoes that wer in her, he caused a generall staye, and comes up himselfe to her rescue; which done, and noe harme ensueinge, he passeth on in his shalope, haueinge with him as many of the counsell and baylies as the smale vessell could containe. Arriueinge at the towne, he finds all things ready for his receipt. Captaine Kendall, Mr. Lewes (Hughes), the minister, (for the other came with himselfe from the shyp), foure or fiue more of the counsell, and all the rest of the officers, attendinge him close by the shore vpon the warfe; at his landinge he is wellcomed with two peeces of ordinance, and so passing betweene two files of shott and pikes, he directly takes his waye to the newe framed churche, which he findeth halfe finished, and ther causeth his commission to be read by the elder minister in a full auditory; which is noe soner done, but Captaine Kendall, who sate by him on his left hand, very hastily begins a broken speach to the company, and at the first dash falls vpon the point of grieuances; but, being sodainely cutt off by the Gouernour, he himselfe speakes vnto them to this effect:—"Countrimen, being a meare straunger (as far as I knowe) to you all, I am come thus farr (as you heard euen nowe in my commission) to be your Gouernour and Commander; and it may be that this ignorance one of another may begett and occasion some mutuall iealousies, especially on your part, who, if I proue otherwise than I should be, are likelyest to suffer first. It is true that myselfe also, findinge the like by you, cannot but find and meete with much discontent, though it wer but in this perticuler, of being forced to carry a heauier hand than (if you will beleiue me) sortes with my nature; to vse many wordes vnto you in myne owne behalfe by way of promise, wer but vanitie; since the worst men, as well as the best, can vse their tounges to serue their turnes. Only this much I will saye to you, that howsoeuer I am vpon no tearmes to be called to your expostulations; yet, if at any time dureing mine abode with you, I shall in the least manner be found to act a tyrants part, or wilfully peruert the straight course of iustice, I wish with all mine heart that the Company that sent me hether (vnder whose censure I am legitimately to fall) may call me to that account, as may make me an example to all others that may have the meanes to be faultie in the like kind here-after. As for you, I must tell you in plaine termes, I expect that you freely submitt yourselues to be ordered and commanded by me, and that without all capitulations, for it is not in you to putt it to the question in the least manner; as therefore, in matter of religion, I will endure noe recusant, so must I haue none in point of obedience. If ther be any of you that vpon some former grounds haue iust cause to find your selues agreiued, it must be your part and discretion to take your due time and place to shewe it, and then, too, in such a manner and temper as becomes you; the redresse whereof, although it may hapely proue beyond the limitts of my strength for the present, yet you shall not need to feare, but that by myne expression of it to the Company, and mediation for it (which shall be serious and faythfull), ther will in good time be obteyned an ample and reasonable satisfaction. It shall be in the meane time mine earnest prayer and endeuour that our behauiour and carriage may be such one vnto another that as it seemes ther be very fewe, or rather not any, that are discontented that we are thus mett at the present; so euery one may be sory in some respects when we are to part hereafter."

The Gouernour haueinge ended this short speech, which for aught that could be perceiued was generally well receiued, the elder minister proceeded to deuine seruice, and so to a sermon, wherein was briefly touched the necessitie of the magistracye, the submission due vnto it, the hopes and expectations of the future in perticular, with some other pointes fitt and proper for that day and action: the which being finished, the most part of the company attended the Gouernour to his house (a garde beiug made for him from the church thether), at the entringe wherof a very ready and well followed volley of smale shott was deliuered by thoes of his owne company, who wer all in armes: the counsell, the baylies of the tribes, and most of the officers dineinge with him at his owne table, the rest at others prepared for them.

But thes ceremonyes and feastinge were sone cutt of and ended with that night, so that the next daye the Gouernour, assemblinge the counsell and all the baylies, made perticuler inquirie of the estates of their seuerall tribes, and gaue them notice of such instructions and orders of court as he had receiued in charge from the Company to putt in execution, and wer fitt for them to knowe: at that time, also, he swore two newe baylies that came ouer with him, and so dismissed them all to their seuerall charges: the rest of that weeke, he bestowed in takeinge a vewe of the fortes, and of the munition, wherin it seemed that he found but smale content, being heard publickly to giue out at his returne to the towne, that he looked not to haue had the Companyes and his owne expectation so farre shortned and deceiued in that perticuler aboue all others; and that he was sorry to finde himselfe constrayned to write so vnwellcome newes vnto them hereof, as nowe he must. About eight or ten dayes after this a sayle is descried from the mount, and thervpon a warneinge peece is presently giuen from the townes warfe, and the shalope well manned out to make a discouery. About fiue houres after, the bote returned and brings word to the Gouernour that she is an

Euglish shyp and called the *Garland*, and by this time she had moored herselfe in the Kings-Castle harbour.

This *Garland* had putt out to sea from England about eight weekes before the shyp the *Warwick*, that brought the Gouernour, so that not being heard of vntill nowe, some misdoubts ther wer of her miscarriage, she haueing fallen vpon the Ilands three weckes before and within sight of them, but not seen from the shore, she was againe putt of by foule weather, and being forced to the south-wards, laye beatingc it vp so long that her water was almost all spent, and a great many of her passengers and seamen also sick and dead: being in which extremitie, and almost dispayreiuge to recouer the Ilands, she was vpon a newe resolution to make for Virginia (whether after her touchinge here she was also bound), but by the waye she meetes with a Dutch man of warre that had bin in course vpon the West Indies, by whom vnderstandinge wher she was (for she also had seene the Ilands), and that the harbour she looked for was within twenty leagues of her, receiueinge some quantitie of water in exchange of some wine and bœuf, followeing in that direction, she shortly after (haueing bin seuenteene weekes continually at sea) thus recouers her wished port. Being come in in this sick and weake condition, she putts the Gouernour from all other employments for that present to helpe and succour her and hers. His botes, therfor, are in all hast sent abord to fetch of her sick people which wer many and weake, who are in seuerall places bestowed in the towne, and certaine persons appointed to tend and looke vnto them: much of his owne perticuler prouisions, and all the milck of the cattell being for a while employed that waye. In this shyp, among some others of fashion, arrive also Captaine Felgate, the liuetenant of the Gouernours company, and Captaine Stokes, the captaine of the Kings-Castle.

Haueing thus in some reasonable manner settled this

businesse, the Gouernour makes a passage quite through the maine and tribes to hold a generall assize in Captaine Tuckers fayre house at the over-plus: and this place was chosen at this time for that purpose, partly that by that occasion he might by the waye take knowledge of the country, but especially that the towne of St. Georges might therby be eased from the burthen-some accesse of much people, haueinge already bin lately much oppressed, and euen eaten up with newe commers. The prefixed time of the assizes being come, the Gouernour would by all meanes that the forme and carriage of that action should for that time be wholy and altogether as it was wont to be in Captaine Tuckers time, the which (as it appeared afterwards) was either because he would not ouer-sodainly begin an innovation, or that therby he would discerne what that had bin, rather then that he ment to continue it so in his time; but not many either criminall or ciuill causes appearinge at this assize, it is fully finished in two dayes, which had wont to hold out for foure, and so the Gouernour makes a present returne to the towne, to be nere to the continuall occasions of the shyps.

Noe soner was he ther but diuers vnhappy and disasterous accidents began to assault him, one in the neck of another: for first by a most terrible storme and huricanoe the shyp the *Garland*, rideinge in the harbour of the Kings-Castle (which is ouermuch open to north-west windes), is forced from her safetye to cutt downe her maine mast by the bord, and (so maimed) to ride it out for her life; but the Erle of Warwicks shyp (moored not far of from her), all her anchors comeinge home, is driuen upon the rocks and vnrecouerably lost: you may iudge in what distresses the Gouernour felt himselfe vpon this blowe: which yet was not so much in regard to thoes that wer past as of the future, which ther vpon threatened him; for the shyp the *Warwick* being the magazin shyp, and thus lost, all that yeares crop of tobacco was likely to perish with her by want of exportation; and, besides, he conceiued that the adventurers not heareinge anythinge of them that winter, they might be held for lost by the waye, which could not but produce very ill effects: neither could ther be apprehended any other waye or meane of redresse than by riggeinge up the *Treasourour* to serue in her stead, the which, as it would proue both difficult, tedious, and dangerous, so it was plainely and euidently to be seene that the *Garland*, not being able to make her voiage to Virginia (in the case she was in) without the Gouernours helpe, she was of necessitie to be left destitute by his spendinge of all his meanes and store another waye. Here-vpon, sittinge in consultation with the whole body of the counsell, the master of the *Garland* is called in, who being demanded whether he wer able to make his entended voiage to Virginia of him without farther assistance of men, sayles, mast, cordage, victuall, and the like, his answer is that by no meanes it was to be done, but with apparent and certayne ruine both of shyp, goodes, and persons: whervpon being publickly assured by the Gouernours owne mouthe, that in respect of the losse of the *Warwick*, and the necessitie of trimeinge and fittinge up the *Treasorour* to serue in her steed, ther was noe possibilitie of affordinge of him any such releife at the present, it was at last concluded and resolued vpon (as the best course for all parties) that the shyp, the *Garland* (leaueinge all her Virginian passengers behind her) should be accepted for the magazin in steed of the wreackt *Warwick*, and so to returne directly for England, fraughted with the tobacco of the Ilands, being that sommers crop: and this she should doe vpon the same tearmes of threepence vpon the pound that the *Warwick* was: only the master petitioned that, if his owner who sett him out should, vpon his non-performance of his voiage, refuse to allowe him his out-ward fraught, that the Gouernour would be pleased to moue the Company

in his letters to make it vp vnto him by rayseinge one penye
more vpon euery pound of tobacco that he carryed home :
the which sollicitation was promised him and performed, as
hopeinge that his owner (who was also a brother of the
Company) would not exact so hardly vpon him, consideringe
the extremities that he was fallen into by God's hand ; and
that also he was likely to rayse a great crop of tobacco the
yeare followeinge, by the improuement of thes Virginia
men, vpon his vnsupplied land in the Ilands ; and thus was
this wound cycatrized. I denye not but diuers other apprehensions, both here and at home, wer nourished and embrased about the carriage of this affayre; for some conceiued that the speach of riggeinge up the *Treasourer* for
that voiage, which the Gouernour so openly and frequently
gaue out, was only to drawe in the master of the *Garland*
to accept the fraught of the Companyes tobacco vpon the
easier tearmes, as doubtinge least he would otherwise make
too great vse of the necessities and extremities that he was
fallen into; for, as for the *Treasourer*, it was well ynough
knowen in how rotten a case she was euery waye, and how
out of all trimme, so that it laye not in the strength of his
store to make her fitt and capable of the voiage, especially
being to be a winter one: some other secret reasons also
wer thought vpon, wherby it was conceiued that the Gouernour could not chuse, but hold her altogether improper
for the employment. Others ther wer, who, being of lesse
charytie, would needs haue all the consequence of this bussines to consist only of a plott betweene the Gouernour and
the master of the *Garland*, for the better blindinge and
beguileinge of his owners in England, and the helpeinge of
him to a more colourable and hansome pretence. But thes
and the like conceites, especially this last, seemeinge rather
as the fruicts and effects of ignorance, passion, or malice,
than grounded vpon any probable likelyhoode, are to be
slighted and contemned : for what need indirect tricks or

crooked polycies when fayre and straight courses offer themselues.

But this losse of the good shyp, the *Warwick*, was not the only ill that this cruell storme brought with it, for a generall blast of the winters crop of corne ensued, so that an exceedinge feare of want seazed on the inhabitants generally, and that not without cause : for howsoeuer the Ilands are prolefull ynough euery waye, and haue two haruests euery yeare : yet what with the improuident wastes that are growen to a custome among the most of them, and that the maine part of their standeinge and staple foode consists of corne (so that, for the number of people, I beleiue ther is scarce halfe so much graine eaten in any part of the whole world againe); if but any one of thes two haruests miscarry in any generall manner, a dearth and kind of scarcetie for some monethes is assuredly to be expected : and the rather grewe it terrible at this time, by reason that it was well knowen that both an vnusuall number of newe comers had bin lately brought in, and the most of them ill ynough prouided : as also that the fore-goeing sommer (in Captaine Kendall yeare) had bin miserably mispent in all kindes of wastes and ryotts ; neuerthelesse, the effect of all this became not so senceable vntill the monethes of February and March followeinge (1620) : at what time, not only the common sort but euen the Gouernours owne table (by reason of the wrongs done vnto him by Captaine Kendall, in giueing or rather sellinge away his due prouisions to the pyrate before his arriuall), was for some monethes some meales found without bread. At which season also it being discouered that diuers close fellowes, better horders than others, haueinge more store of corne by a great deale than would serue their owne peculiar turnes, vncharitably refused to communicate it, but at most vnconscionable prizes ; and that many sticked not to feede their hogges withall, while their neighbours wer ready to starue for want of it : the

Gouernour, for redresse hereof, graunted out a perticuler commission to his serieant maior and the stewart of his house (both of them being of the counsell), to make a strickt search through-out all the tribes, commandeinge that whersoeuer an ouerplus of corne was found, a conuenient competencye being allowed and left to the famely wherto it belonged, the residue should be sold, at a reasonable rate, to such of the same tribe as wer knowen to be in most misery and need. The which course, howsoeuer, it was at the first sinisterly taken, and so caused some secrett grudgeinges, yet was it sone after discerned to produce very excellent effects, euen to the saueinge of some liues.

About the same time also the Gouernour sent out two proclamations (the first that thes Ilands euer sawe from their Gouernours in that forme), the one for the recallinge and recouery of all such goodes as had bin embezeled out of the wreackt *Warwick*, and out of the *Treasorour* (whose ordinance also he commanded to be all of them brought to the towne); the other was for the newe nameinge of two of the tribes, Mansfeilds tribe being to be called by the name of Warwick, and Cauendish to take the appellation of Deuonshyre.[9] Not long after this the former sowre sauce is a litle sweetned by the findinge of some amber-greece, the which being honestly brought vnto the Gouernour, the finder thereof is as honestly payed: and this payement likewise was the first that euer was really performed in that kind, and this amber-greece also the first that euer the Gouuernour sawe here.

The Gouernour being bestowed in doeing his best towards the recouerye of his former hurts; and nowe hopeinge (the dearth only excepted) of some future amendment, so that he might find the meanes to keepe a quiett Christmas, which approached very neare; behold in the verye beginninge

---

[9] These proclamations have not been found. The earliest preserved is for the " Observacon of the Sabaoth day", dated 20 March 1620.

of it, arriseth vpon an extreame sodaine as great or greater violence of wind than euer before, wherin the *Garland* (the only shyp left with them seruiceable) is once againe brought into all extremities; for all her helpes giueing waye, and so being vpon drift, she falls within a cables length of the rumeinge rocks, and had vndoubtedly perished, but that one of her maine anchors, fastened to an excellent newe cable, by great good chaunce hitts foule betwixt two rocks, the which thereby fasteninge the whole stresse and waight of the shyp, so keepes her aliue the remainder of that hugh gust, which by deuine prouidence lasted not long after. At the same time also (for one mischeife neuer goes alone) a foure square frame of timber, called the Mount, and built vpon a high hill nere the towne by Mr. Moore (and by him much gloried in), seruing to good vse for the discouery of shyps at sea, and so the Eye of the Ilands, was blowne up by the rootes.

But it seemed that thes straunge and vnauoideable mishaps serued rather to quicken the Gouernours industry than to dull it, so that (haueinge finished the newe framed churche, which is a large and hansome one) with the very first of the newe yeare he begins a newe peece of fortification vpon a rock lieing in flauncker to the king's castle, and excellently commandinge the chanell that leades into that harbour, being a place that at the very first of the plantation, by an Order of Court, was enioyned to be fortified, yet not ventured vpon vntill nowe, by reason of the great dainger of landeinge of ordinance vpon it, and the feare of splittinge the botes. But which (in despight of all difficulties) he found most necessary to be performed, by reason that otherwise, shyps at their entraunce vpon the chanell might shroude themselues so nere and close vnder the high rock of the castle as that they could not be touched with thoes ordinance, which nowe they cannot doe without being played vpon by thes. And to the onsett of this worck, and

M

for the first fourteene dayes, he called all such passengers as wer to passe in that shyp for England, tellinge them that it was fitt and equall that they should doe some publick good ere they went, for he knew not whether euer they ment to doe it hereafter : to the ouersight of which worck (haueing layd it out first with his owne hands) he sent his Luietenant Captaine Felgate, being himselfe constrained to keepe at the towne for the dispatch of the shyp for England, the which not long after (haueing all the tobacco of the Ilands that was made in Captaine Kendall's yeare, laded upon her, being very much in quantitie, but miserable in qualitie), about the 23rd of January, an. 1620, cleares her-selfe of the harbour, and makes for England : and was saluted at her goeing out with a great peece of ordinance from the newe worck (wher the Gouernour was also in person), that so she might carry the report of it to the aduenturers : at what time, also, she was in danger in her passeinge out by fallinge too nere the Southerne Sholes, that lie at the harbour's mouthe, so that she rubbed vpon a rock, the which, by good hap, proueinge but soft and brittle, did her little or noe harme. By her, likewise, the Gouernour sends his first generall letters to the Company, wherein he giues them intelligence of the condition and estate of the Ilands at his arriuall, and especially laments the want of munition, and the weake case that he generally found the fortes in : as also the want of gunners, carpenters and colony men; desireinge a speedye and sufficient supply. He giues them perticuler notice withall of all such shyps as had bin entertained by Captaine Kendall; as the Dutch wrack, the roueing frigate, and how the *Treasorour*, haueinge bin vpon the coast at Captaine Tucker goeinge awaye, was admitted by Kendall; and so went to the West Indies, from whence she returned to Virginia, wher, not likeinge her entertainement, she conueyeth herselfe awaye secretly, and shapeth her course for the Ilands a second time, and arriueth extremely poore, haueinge all her vpper worcks so rotten as she was vtterly vnable, without uery much cost and labour, to putt out to sea againe. He attendeth, therfore, their iniunctions and directions (accordinge to the prescriptions giuen him in his instructions) concerneinge thes perticulors, that therby he might shape his course. And, indeed, he was very carefull to enlarge himselfe about the *Treasorour*, in respect that he had bin acquainted with some passages of bussinesse concerneinge her in England, and found the violent and captious courses that by some (to make good their owne endes) had bin practised against her, and therfore knew it very likely that they would doe the same with him vpon the same occasion, which by all meanes he endeauoured to auoide.

The magazin shyp, the *Garland*, being thus gone, the Governour falls closely to his worcks, so that within some fewe weekes the newe platforme is fully finished, and hath fiue good peeces of ordinance mounted vpon it, three wherof wer with infinite toyle, much danger, and some perticuler charge and expence to the Gouernours purse, waighed out of the wrackt *Warwick*. He built for it, also, a smale powder-house of cæder, muskett profe, and in nature of a redoubt, to secure the ordinance; and then honnored the whole peece by callinge it South Hampton Fort. At the same time, likewise (by the oppotunitie of an expert Dutch shyp-carpenter, falne vnto him out of the Dutch wreak, whom he hired to staye with him as his seruant for three yeares), he began to sett some newe bote vpon the stocks, of which not only himselfe at the towne, but in a manner all the captaines and gunners of the fortes, wer in dangerous want of. Being thus busied on all handes, a tall shyp is made from the hill wher the mount stoode, and a peece of ordinance (to giue warneinge to all the fortes) is discharged from the warfe; but the wind bloweinge a stiff gale at north-east, noe bote could possibly gett out to discouer her. She plied it vpon a tack, and laye close by a wind alongst the north side of St. Georges Iland, and had the rocks for her lee-shore, and so continued two or three houres, being at last falne so nere the rocks, as the Gouernour (who stoode all the while with his perspective glasse, veweinge of her from of Warwick Fort) fearcinge she would strick vpon them, went in person hastely to St. Katheraines Fort, meaneinge from thence to giue her a warneinge peece; but being come thether, he perceiued she had tacked about, and so stoode vpon the other bord, and at last bore vp before the wind, and made her waye south and by east, and was quickly out of sight. Much disputeinge ther was what this shyp should be. Some thought her to be English, and that she wanted a pylote to bring her in; others would needes haue her a Spaniard, and that she ranne in this manner alongst the shore to take vewe of the fortes, which lie all on that side. But most wer of an opinion (of which the Gouernour was one) that she was some Dutch man-of-warre, that in her course to the West Indies, fallinge with thes Ilands, and knoweinge them to be planted with English, stoode indifferently affected to her comeinge in; but findinge neither a bote to make out towards her, nor knoweinge of herselfe how to hitt so dangerous and intricate a chanell, she thus made awaye, and pursued her voiage. In the eueninge of the same daye, one of the colony people (a luckey fellowe, it should seeme that waye, for he had twise done so before) found eight ounces of very good amber-greece, and brought it to the Gouernour, who (accordinge to an Order of Court in that case prouided) payed him the full moyetie of the value therof, after three poundes the ounce in good English gold: wherby all men wer encouraged to looke out for so good a commoditie, and honestly to reueile it when they found it, wheras formerly, by reason of continuall and vsuall breach of promise, they euen openly professed the contrary.

Within two dayes after this, wer descried two smale frigates which came vp close by the shore on the south side of the ilands, and so the Castle gaue the warneinge peece, about sunne sett; whervpon the Gouernour manned out his shalope presently, and commanded to double the gardes at the towne all that night, abont the midst wheroof Captaine Felgate (who had bin at the worck vpon Southamptou Fort) comes to the towne, and being instantly brought in to the Gouernour, who was in bedd, he deliuers him certaine letters written in Italian from one Peter Scouten, a Dutchman: the contents wherof wer: "that being in seruice vnder his lordes, the States of the Vnited Prouinces, and haueinge bin in the West Indies for the same entent, and nowe falne vpon thes Ilandes (which he tearmed a Promontorye), he desired assurance vnder the Gouernours hand of ingresso and egresso into the harbour, that so as a friend he might carine his barkes, and take in some fresh water, and be gone." In his company also (as captaine of ye other frigate) was the same Powell that you heard so much of in Captaine Tuckers time, and by whose aduise and encouragement the other was thus piloted in. The Gouernour haueinge receiued thes letters, and throughly enformed himselfe by Captaine Felgate of the burthen of their vessells, and the number of their people, and especially enquireinge whether they wer well victualled and free from all infectious diseases; after some time of thinckinge with himselfe, he towards morneinge returned by the same hands this answer, written also in Italian: "that being here vnder his Maiestie of England, the Commandour of thes Ilands, he was to carry himselfe a freinde to his freindes, and an enemye to his enemyes; if therefore he could shewe for himselfe and his a lawfull sufficient commission signed by the States of the Vnited Prouinces, who wer freinds and allies to his king, of his being nobly and honestly employed by them in thes partes, he and his should be welcome, and (behaueinge themselues as honest men) should find all the securitie they desired or could expect, otherwise they wer to looke for seuere justice and to enter vpon their perill." Vpon which answer, within two dayes after (the wind not sufferinge them vntill then) they both of them came in at the harbour of St. Georges, and preseuted themselues and their commissions to the Gouernour; who, findinge them very ample and authentique, caused them to be coppied out, and gaue the straungers his best entertainement. And this he was the rather forward to doe, as findeinge them the men he had need of, for percciueinge them extraordinarily well furnished with victuall, and especially with a good quantitie of oyle and bacon, he delt with them about the sale of it to the needye inhabitants (who by this time began very many of them, to haue a deepe sence of a scarcetie, and came running daly vnto him, with lamentations), the which both of them (espccially Powell, who had alwayes shewed himselfe a good wellwiller to the plantation) very readily and willingly consented vnto; so that ther was sold out and deliuered vpon trust and creditt to such as had most need of it diuers and sundry commodities, to the value at the least of six or seuen hundred pounds sterleinge, to the much refreshment and great content of the people. Concerneinge the which, and how the payment thereof was afterwards carryed, we shall speake when we come to lett you knowe how the receipt of them was taken and apprehended in England by the company. Thes shyps, haueinge rested here about the space of seuen or eight weekes, tooke their leaue and departed; Scouten back againe to the West Indies, and Powell first for the Lowe Countries and then for England; by whom also the Gouernour wrote priuate letters to diuers of the Lords, and some others of his freinds, in his behalfe and fauour.

The whilst these thinges wer in action in the Sommer

Ilands, the Company of Aduenturers in England make out many a long looke for the *Garland* and *Warwick*, much wonderinge at their long staye, and especially they wer in great feare of the *Warwick*, as carryinge their newe Gouernour, and being the magazin shyp; at last the *Garland* arriues, and by her they receiue the perfect knowledge of all the former mentioned euents. By her likewise, they haue Captaine Kendalls yeares crop of tobacco, the which proueinge extreamely badd, and (to say troth) for the most part little better than starck rotten; and withall comeinge to a very lowe markett, giues them a great and generall both distaste and discouragement, so that they presently fall into many distrusts, and almost dyspayres of the subsistinge of that plantation, especially by the meanes of tobacco; it is resolued therfore that newe proiects for newe commodities must speedely be found out and putt in execution, or els all thinges ther would sodainely fall in pieces; the which what they wer, by whom first propounded, and by whom vndertaken, you shall see when we come to the arriuall of their next magazin shyp, which was almost a whole yeare after.

But in the interim, the Gouernour ther, being cleared from the distractions and impediments of shypinge, goes liuely on with his worcks of fortification; and haueinge fully finished Southhampton Fort, he remoues the people to the Kings Castle for the restoreinge of the burnt redoubt and the makeinge of a large plattforme vnder it, the which, after eight weekes of hard labour by thirtie men, he absolutely perfecteth; and then plantinge vpon it seuen peeces of excellent ordinance vpon newe cæder carriages, wherwith to playe and commande into all nookes of the harbour to which the aduantage of the site serued very opportunely; he causeth it to be called Deuonshyres redoubt. About the which time, haueing received some requests from some of the baylies of the tribes, which petitioned the surcease and adiournement of bussines of this nature, in regard (as was pretended) of the hardnesse of the time, and scarcetie of corne, he tooke occasion by waye of satisfaction for all the rest to answer the Baylie of Warwick Tribe, who had wrote vnto him to that purpose ; the which answer he also caused to be secretly and vnderhand dispersed abroad, and was deliuered in thes followeinge wordes :—

"I haue receiued your letters ; in the very beginninge whereof you are so obscured as you giue me not present meanes to answer you to that perticuler. I must therfore wholy ommitt it vntill I see you next; only it seemes somewhat odde wher you write, that that loue of mine which (you saye) I haue vnto you, should any waye preiudice you, or make you obnoxious, and especially (as you to seeme to implye) guiltie ; it was not wont to be so infectious. I hope I shall euer affect to place my loue vpon deserts, the which when I find the grounds answerable, is not easily shaken, nor can be. In the second part of your letters, you become a vehement, if not passionate counsellour against the progression of the fortes this yeare ; but I must tell you plainely, your reasons appeare to me both vnseasonable and vnsounde ; they are vnseasonable in regard, that after two moneths worck, wherin (I dare be bold to saye) as much hath bin performed, to as much purpose, and vpon as much necessitie, as in thirteene weekes by some others ; you would haue me giue them ouer vntill after haruest ; that is as much to saye vntill the next yeare ; for I cannot doubt, but you vnderstande, that after the midst of Aprill, the people are so wholy to apply themselues to the plantinge of tobacco, to the gatheringe in of their corne, and the summer labours, as it wer pitty in deed to distrackt them, and besides the heate of the season in this eleuation is altogether vnsufferable in thoes monethes for thes labours. To leaue the fortes therefore, the which (thancks be to God) are so well forwarded, vntill the next winter, wer to lose what soeuer hetherto hath bin done vpon them ; for who knowes not but that in the meane time the winters great and common windes will blowe the most part of the rubbish into them againe, and so the layinge out of the worck be altogether defaced and to seeke ; the ordinance also that lie dismounted ready to be planted vpon them must needs be halfe buried in the dust and sand ; the ten newe carriages that I haue already almost finished at St. Georges lie scattered about, and many peeces of them (in despite of all care) dispersed and lost, the portage and reportage of the mattocks, spades, beetles, wedges, tents, and such like necessaries, proue a double labour. You knowe that this bussinesse was not attempted nor begun without mature aduise and deliberation : it was publickly propounded at the assize ; you your selfe had your place and voice at the meetinges of the counsell without me about it: you did approue of it then—why are you altered nowe? will you saye it is by reason of the present want of corne you see amongst vs? who was he so blind, weighinge the extreame wastes of the yeare before my comeinge in, the generall blast of our late winter crop, and the thrustinge vpon us so many ill prouided newe comers, but foresawe as much long since: haue you not heard me diuers times to speake as much in publick?—haue you not seene me lament it in priuate?—why did you not diswade me then, when it was timely?—or why doe you nowe so out of season? And wheras you saye, that you presume I would forbeare this worck if I but knewe the necessities of the time; is ther any man in thes Ilands a more publick man than my selfe? or doe you thinck I can be senceless of that which I euery day feele? Ther are not fewer than fortie persons that feede dayly on my store, the third part of them extraordinary men, entertained for publick worcks. I spend not lesse than 1500 eares of corne weekely, whereas I feare me (so ill haue I bin delt withall by you knowe whom) my whole remainder ammounts not to 1000 in all;[1] we are resolued therefore to liue some monethes without bread, and are contented, submittinge our selues to Gods good pleasure, who hath layed this affliction vpon vs, to teach vs to amend our selues, and to learne wise prouidence, not that we should forsake our important worcks. Neither, to saye truth, doe I perceiue how the present labouringe at the fortes can any waye aggrauate or encrease our sufferings in this kind, or cause the sword of famine (as you tearme it) to wound us any whitt deeper; can fiue men taken out of Warwick Tribe for fourteene dayes, starue the tribe? must they not eate at home, as with me? Oh! but you will saye, that lesse would serue them at home; it may be so, and yet it may rather be suspected not so. It is true, indeed, that it is requesite for such as come to the fortes to be furnished with some quantitie of corne to serue their necessities in foule weather when noe fish can be had abroad, and is it not so with them at home also? my meaneinge is not, when I command prouisions from you for the fortes, that you should glutt them with them; a conuenient proportion will suffice, and the rather because I doubt not but to take fish for them when you cannot come by it. As for the present necessitie of the speedy repayringe of the old worcks of fortification, and the rayseinge some newe, iudge you your selfe what it is, when of twenty peeces of artillerie, the which the aduenturers in England conceiue to be seruiceably mounted in the kings castle, ther are not three that can be aboue three times vsed or discharged in a fight; besides, I can assure you that ther are more plotts and proiects vpon thes ilands than you are aware of, and I am forewarned of some not fitt to be publickly mentioned; neither are thes doubted dangers (as you call them) so far of as you imagine. Hold fast therfore your first opinion and ioyne

---

[1] *Sic* in MS. Probably 10,000.

with the rest of your fellowe counsellours, by all meanes, care and encouragement, to farther the speedy perfectinge of thes so needefull and concerneinge peaces. In vaine doe we build houses, and churches, plant tobacco, sett corne, vnlesse we prouide for the keepinge of them when we haue done; and ther is noe earthly meanes to doe this but by the sufficient forteficinge of the mouthes of the harbours, and this I hope shall be in reasonable manner performed by Easter next. Howsoｦeuer I will not trouble you of the maine beyond that time, but rather then fayle, perfect the residue with myne owne seruants and the generall men. Concerneinge the slaunderous tounges of some wherwith you goe about to scare me, I would haue you knowe I can easily contemne them; ther was neuer any honest or worthy action but found such base calumniators; and yet let such knowe and take heed least in ther misvse of me, they proue not sawsye with the place of command that I hold here vnder his Maiestie, from whom, next vnder God, all power and authoritie is deriued; for howsoeuer I can easily passe ouer a priuate iniurye committed against mine owne person, yet I neither dare nor will endure it, when it toucheth and extendeth so far as to question my command. I am senceable, I take God to wittnesse, euen as deepe as my heart, of the least greiuance and endurance of this people; but when I cannot free them wholy, I must chuse the euill that is least. Encourage them, therfore, as it becomes you, both by precept and example: and therby, as in all thinges els, make your selfe still more and more capable of that place in mine affection, the which you (not vntruely) are senceable of to be well begun, and which shall willingly, also, be euery day more and more expressed by your loueinge freind,

NATH. BUTLER.

And thes wer the contents of this answer vpon the occasion of the bussinesse of the forteinge, the which sone passinge abroad from hand to hand, gave a good fortification in this perticuler, and caused a more willinge and free puttinge forward of themselues that way than otherwise would haue bin; so that by the latter end of the March followeinge, the Gouernour, findeinge thes works at the Gurnetts Head and in the kings castle very well forwarded, and the heate of them ouer, he dismissed the people of the tribes, and accomplished the remainder within a while after by thoes of the towne, by which time he had cutt out two newe plattformes, built a newe redoubt, made fifteene newe carriages of cæder, and mounted twenty peeces of ordinance, which all of them before laye either vtterly dismounted, or mounted vncerviceably, and soe to noe purpose. Neither did thes martiall employments so wholy take vp the Gouernour but that he also found time to bestowe his thoughts for the setlinge of other matters; and in perticuler concerneinge the churche affayres, perceiueinge that neither of his two ministers would by any meanes subscribe nor vse the booke of common prayer, or liturgie of England; and that not only so, but wer also different, and in noe good and fitt agreement betweene themselues in the formes of administration of the sacrements and marriage: the which differencies, though they wer noethinge substantiall, yet many of the common people wer therwith troubled and disquieted, some beginninge to question the validitie of them, others to growe into factioninge and disputes, which of the two did best, and many of the worst sort to make a scoff and jest of both, he found that it was time, if it wer possible, to reduce them to some vniformitie: but dispayreinge to bring them to that here, which all the byshops in England could not doe ther, he at last bethought himselfe of the liturgie vsed in the Ilands of Garnesey and Jarsye, the which being of his maiesties dominions, and by him tollorated, he conceiued would not be ill-taken if (for the time) he putt it in practice here; beinge also in good hope that his ministers might be both of them brought to the vse of it, in respect that all thoes perticulers wer therin ommitted at which they tooke so much exception and stumbled at. Callinge them both at once, therfore, priuately vnto him, he told them that he was verye sory to find them in no fuller consent one with another in the vse of the seruice, and in especiall in the forme of the sacraments and marriage. He graunted, indeed, and knewe well ynough that their disseutions wer noethinge essentiall, yet could they not but proue uery scauudalous and offensiue, as well to some in England, as to most of the inhabitants here.

In England it would be obserued, how that being but two of them only together, and so far remote from their country, that yet the prouerbe might be verefied vpon them, "So many men, so many minds"; besides, it was not vnlikely but that the hearesayo of it would occasion some such iniunctions from thence as would displease them both. As for the people here, they well knewe how ill the effects wer that this their disvnion had already bred among many of them, and the which wer likely euery day to growe worse and worse. He had bethought himselfe, therfore, of a waye and meane to cure this ill, the which he doubted not but would proue uery acceptable to themselues also; and it was by propoundinge the punctuall vse and practise of that forme in the vse of the sacraments and marriage which was vsed within His Maiesties dominions in Jarsye and Garnsye, beinge one and the uery same with that of the French Protestants, thoes of the vnited prouinces, and euen Geneua itselfe. This was it, that, without all inouation and alteration, he would haue them for the time to vse here, and this was that which he hoped would quench and make up all the infectious heates and dangerous breaches that otherwise might ensue. And, truely, it seemed that this proposition had a peaceable constellation in aspect at its birth, for noe soner was it borne than gladsomely receiued by both the ministers, who instantly promised the Gouernour all conformitie in the acceptance and vnitie in the practice. Whervpon he himselfe translateinge it verbatim into English, out of a French Bible which he brought ouer with him, he caused the elder minister to begin the vse therof at the administration of the Lords Supper, at St. Georges, vpon Easter Day next followeinge, at what time himselfe, many of the counsell, the officers, and a great auditory communicated together, a speech by waye of introduction being also deliuered by the minister out of the pulpitt about the receipt of it, and the ground and causes therof expressed. And this forme was generally obserued throughout the whole Ilands (the Gouernour endureinge noe variation) in thes perticulers of the sacraments and marriage all the time of his gouerment ther, and for aught I knowe, so continueth vnto this daye.

Presently after this Feast of Easter, 1620, the Gouernour, haueing made and launced a newe cæder bote, to rowe with foure oares only, and built of purpose to goe well vpon the oares, the nimbler vpon all occasions to serue for a boate of aduise, he began to thinck of preparations towards the erectinge of a newe mount, in lieu of that formerly blowne downe, and to be raysed in the same place. He sent away, therfore, the liuetenant of his company, Captaine Felgate, into Harrington tribe, and gaue him a commission to fell cæder ther for the same end, the which wer conuayed to the towne in flotes. He made also a presse of carpenters, the best he could heare of, and commanded them vp to St. Georges, wher he conferred with them about the sayd worck, and propounded diuers fashions and formes to be considered, which of them was the fittest and most sightly, both in respect of strength and hansomenesse. At last, the trianguler forme, being most generally approued, the bussinesse is sett on foote on all hands, the timber squared on the warfe, and from thence, with great toyle and labour, haled and drawne up the hill wheron it was to stand; from which time forward it was so continually and closely followed as that, within one moneth after, this frame is once againe accomplished, and becomes seuen foote higher than it was before; and (to preserue it from the like fortune) is stroungly keyed at the three corners belowe, with very substantiall posts; and playsted and whited at the top, for the better discerneinge of it out to sea; at the foote therof, also, vpon a cæder plattforme, is mounted a peece of ordinance, taken out of treasorour, to serue as a warneinge peece to all the fortes, vpon the discouerye of shypps from thence, and the which, by being so loftely placed, is the better to be heard on all sides; and so this worck, being absolutely finished and perfected, is named by the Gouernour Riche-Mount, which hath already stoode stiffly in many a terrible storme, without the least dammage that can be discerned, and may be hoped to doe so in many more.

At the same time, the Gouernour dedicated a smale peece of worck to the memory of the dead; for, walkeinge about the towne to see the worckmen, one Mondy very early, accompanied with two or three of his officers, he espied a great crosse of wood pitched, slopeing into the ground, in a by-place, all ouergrowne with bushes and rubbish; wher-vpon, enquireing what it ment, it was told him that Sir George Sommers (who, as you haue heard, was one of the very first of the discouerers of thes Ilands, and certainely the prime anthor of their plantation) dieinge here, his heart and bowells wer buried vnder that crosse; the which, some freinds and followers of his had fastned ther, in memory therof; to which relation, howsoeuer, the Gouernor made noe other replye at that present, but that so noble a gentleman deserued a better monument; yet, within a day or two after, haueing found out a hansome marble stone (that had bin brought out of England, and laye almost buried in the sand), he caused masons to be sett on worck about it, and takeinge downe the crosse, and cleareinge the place round about, he raysed, in the same place, a plaine, long-square of hewen stone, about three foote in height, hansomely and conueniently contriued, and vpon it caused the sayd marble stone to be layed. Vpon the top, and in the midst wherof he cutt out in a plate of brasse, which he sent for out of England, this epitaph followeinge; sayd to be composed by himselfe :—

"In the year 1611,
Noble Sr George Sommers went hence to Heauen,
Whose well tride worth, that held him still employde,
Gaue him the knowledge of the world so wide;
Hence 'twas, by Heauens decree that to this place
He brought newe guests and name to mutuall grace.
At last his soule and body being to part,
He here bequeathed his entrayles and his heart."[2]

[2] There is an error in this epitaph, perhaps not uninfluenced by the exigency of the rhyme, which has been the parent of much confusion. Sir George Sommers died 9th November 1610. The " handsome marble stone" has long since disappeared; but tradition has apparently been constant as to the site, and the writer, when Governor of Bermuda, replaced it by a marble tablet bearing the inscription following:—

NEAR THIS SPOT
WAS INTERRED IN THE YEAR 1610,
THE HEART OF THE HEROIC ADMIRAL
SIR GEORGE SOMERS, KT.,
WHO NOBLY SACRIFICED HIS LIFE
TO CARRY SUCCOUR
TO THE INFANT AND SUFFERING PLANTATION,
NOW
THE STATE OF VIRGINIA.

TO PRESERVE HIS FAME TO FUTURE AGES,
NEAR THE SCENE OF HIS MEMORABLE
SHIPWRECK OF 1609,
THE GOVERNOR AND COMMANDER - IN - CHIEF
OF THIS COLONY FOR THE TIME BEING
CAUSED THIS TABLET TO BE ERECTED.
1876.

Another inscription, of scarcely inferior interest, which was extant in 1671, and "set up in the Governor's Hall over his chair", has also disappeared:—

CONDITVR IN HOC LOCO NAVIS PER REICHARDVM
FROBISHERVM ONERIS 70 QUÆ VIRGINIÆ
DESTINATOR (sic), NOS OMNES HINC
TRANSPORTABAT ANNO 1610, MAY 4.

See a tract, entitled *Description of the Last Voyage to Bermudas in the Ship 'Marygold', S. P., Commander.* By J. H. London, 1671." And *Memorials of Bermuda*, ii, p. 341.

Some topographical details will be found in the Appendix.

In the beginning of May next followeinge, which was about some eight monethes after the Gouernours first arriuall, he sent out his generall warrants for the holdinge of an assize at St. Georges, vpon the 6th of June after; and because he found many defects (not to saye absurdities), in the forme of this great action, as it had bin formerly carryed in Captain Tuckers and Kendalls times, he resolued to doe his best to redresse them, and as nere as possible could be, to reduce the whole course therof to the vse and fashion of England; in which respect also (as beinge a newe thinge, and vnseene in that manner in thes Ilands vntill nowe), I am resolued to describe and deliuer it vnto you somewhat at large. He caused, therfore, a graund jury to be warned, consistinge of the most able and sufficient men of the tribes; to whom all bills whatsoeuer wer to be presented, and by them examined, before they wer offered vnto the Court; a course formerly wholy omitted. He appointed, also, two petty juries (wheras, in former times, ther neuer was but one) to be sworne; the one for the triall of causes criminall, and pleas of the crowne; the other for the decysion of actions of dept, trespasse, account, and the like controuersies between partie and partie. Vpon the sixth of June (the sett daye), after a sermon in the framed churche, the Gouernour, attended with all the counsell and baylies, with his ordinary garde of 12 halberds, resorted to the sessions house (a place very conueniently fitted for that seruice), wher himselfe first takeing his place alone, after three proclamations or oyeres, the counsell and balies are seuerally called, and tooke their seates on each side of him accordingly: then the grand jury is empanelled; the which done, and sylence enioyned by the crier, the Gouernour himselfe sittinge as judge (this being the first time that euer Gouernour was knowen to sitt so here, both Captaine Tucker and Kendall allwaies deputeinge others to act that part), with his owne mouth, he gaue them their charge;

the which, in respect of the noueltie of it here (hauing, by the meanes of some freinds, procured a coppy therof), I thought fitt also to insert, and was verbatim, as followeth:—

"This is the second time (as you all knowe) of my holdinge of an assize or generall gayle deliuery among you, which is an action tendinge to the glory of God: obedience and loyaltie to our Souerainge Lord the King: and to the peace and tranquillitie of our selues. Breifly, for the vpholdinge of justice, for the rooteinge out of vice, and rendringe of all men their due. Nowe, ther is noe man, at least noe sober man, but will confesse that it is one of the fayrest happinesses in this world, to liue vnder the subiection of good lawes. How much cause haue we, therfore, to blesse and prayse God, that being thus far remoued and planted from our natiue soyle, He hath not only brought us to a good and happy place, floweing with milck and hony; a place wherin, certainely, we cannot want any good and necessary being (prouided we be but industrious to gett it, and prouident to keepe it), but also hath vouchsafed us the meanes and libertie to liue vnder the conduction and guidance of our owne lawes; lawes inuented and established by our owne auncestors; such lawes as are, in themselues, euery waye excellent; and such as hauing bin borne and bred vnder, we haue noe pretence nor excuse left us, either of ignorence, or mislike. For mine owne part, I haue euer told you, and I hope to make it good vnto you, that I am resolued, by all possible endeauours, to reduce all courses of justice, and to passe all decissions and determinations by that square; and at the present, in this perticuler of an assize, I haue, as you see, empannelled and sworne (according to the laudable custome of England) a grand jury, which, hetherto, you haue not; and they are men (I hope) of integritie and judgement, such as both vnderstand themselues and the seruice they are employed in; such as knoweinge the bond and high nature of an oath, and makeinge a conscience of it, will not be leade, either by partialitie on the one side, or malice on the other, to committ the least action which may burthen their consciences, transgresse against justice, or disturbe the wellfare of this plantation. and you, my masters of this enquest, you are to take due notice of the value and eminence of the place you hold. In this important action, you are the eye of the action; for you are to looke out and discouer all such thinges as you shall discerne necessary and becomeinge the knowledge of it. You are also the ears of it, by giueinge ready admittance to the informations and iust complaincts of all such as find themselues distressed, and haue occasion to use your mediation: and lastly, you are, in some sert, the tounge of it also, for you are freely to vtter, without all passion and affection, whatsoeuer is offered to your eye or eare, that may concerne the maintenance of justice, and the redresse of abuses. In vaine sitt I here to iudge and decide such controuersies as are bred and growne dayly amongst you; to reward the good, and punish the badd, vnlesse yon shall present and manifest them to my knowledge, that so I may knowe who are the good, and who the badd. You are, therfore, I saye, to receiue all bills of endictment offred vnto you, as also to frame such as fall within the compasse of your owne knowledge, and findinge them fitt and proper for the ears of the Court, you are to deliver them in vnto the clearck of the assize, that so they may receiue their censure. But because you may the better vnderstand thoes perticulers which you are especially to take notice of, I shall, as briefly as I can, remember them vnto you; at least such of them as more nearely and peculiarly belong and are pertinent to you of this plantation; wherin you may well beare with me and mine oratory, if I fayle to obserue the quaint methodes and nice eloquence practised by common publick speakers; or not so fully reckon vp all thinges vnto you as you may perhaps expect. For my breedeinge hath bin rather in action than wordes; and since my comeinge hether among you, my memory hath been putt to thinck of more matters than one. For your better apprehension, therfore, and my remembrance, I will deuide what I meane to speake vnto you at this time, into thes three heads, vnder such thinges

as concerne
{
The Person of God.
The Person of the King.
The Person of our selues.
}

"By such thinges as I ranck vnder the first head, I entend only those that most directly belong or strike at the sacred god-head, which is the vnitie of essence, in the trinitie of persons. I saye most directly (for otherwise all thinges whatsoeuer are to tend and aime at God's glory, a *Ioue principium*, and I will adde *et omnia*). And among thes, in the prime place, are athists, a generation who not only, with Davids Foole, saye in their heartes ther is noe god; but being among their companions, and in their roreinge brauerye dare pronounce as much with their blasphemous mouthes, thinckinge to gaine a reputation of being more profound than others, by being more prophane than others; a viperous kind of broode they are, and by all meanes to be rooted out, as, indeed, not worthy to treade vpon the face of the earth; nor to breathe any aire but the fire of hell. Blasphemours, likewise, of God's holy name, by barberous oaths. Irreuerent speakers therof, and the like, are to be considered vnder this head. Hereticks also, holdinge or maintaineinge any opinion contrary to the articles of our Christian fayth, or against the doctrine of the sacred Trinitie, receiued by the Churche of England. And here also may be rancked all such as shall refuse to come to churche, to heare deuine seruice; or being ther, shall behaue themselues disorderly or vnciuilly. Such also as interrupt the minister and preacher of Gods word dureinge the exercise of his function. Thoes that are common and ordinary prophanours and breakers of the Sabaoth.

"Such as fight or quarrell in any churche or churche-yardes. All thes, and the rest of this kind, you of this inquest are mainely and principally to take notice of, and to present them, that by the hand of justice they may receiue condigne and deserued punishment.

"As for such delinquents, as in their plotts and misdemeanours, strike most perticulerly at the sacred person of the King our Soueraigne Lord, they are suche as transgresse in facts of treason.

"Ther are two sortes of treason { High Treason.
                                  Petie Treason.

"High treason is committed when an attempt is deuised and made against the vniuersall and generall maiestie of goverment, and especially towards the person of the king, his queene, or issue. It is high treason, also, to counterfcite the kings coyne, to wash or clipp it. To forge the kings hande, or any of his scales, is treason. To refuse the oathe of allegeance also, after it hath bin twice offred. To denye the kings supremacye, by mainteyneinge the Popes, or any other forraigne princes authoritie, which, in his Maiesties dominions, is highe treason. To kill any of his Maiesties cheife officers, sittinge in the place of justice, and in the execution of his place, is highe treason. The rayseinge of mutenies or rebellions, agaiust his Maiestie, or any of his deputies and cheife officers, is of the same nature. The deuiseinge only, and plottinge of any attempts preiudiciall and dangerous to their liues, is high treason. And such as are found guiltie in any of thes, by a jury of twelue men, are by the lawe sentenced to be drawen, hanged, and quartered. You of the inquest, therfore, you are diligently and carefully to make enquirye after all such, and to present them, that they maye recciue their iudgements accordingly; and this, at mine hand, they shall be sure of. And these are facts of high treason; some other perticulers ther are besides, of the same nature, which you may remember of your selues.

"As for petie treason, it is committed when any bloudy and heinous offence of willfull murther is practiced and perpetrated by an inferior vpon any such a one, being his superior, as hath a dominion, and a kind of maiestic and regalitie as it wer, in ruleinge ouer the sayd partie. As for a child to murther his parent; a scruant to kill his master, or mistris; a wife to murther her husband. It is likewise petic treason for a man out-lawed of felony to breake prison, and therby sett at libertie any one emprisoned for treason; and in case of pyracye, a straunger, being captaine of an English shyp, wher in also wer certaine Englishmen, and they, together, robbed at sea; this was adiudged felonye in the straunger, and petye treason in the English, who wer drawen and hanged. You may apply the example of your selues, and to some of your selues. The frigate that was here this last sommer, before mine arriuall, who had bin, and nowe is a rouciuge in thes partes, without any commission at all from any prince or state; at her being, as I haue heard, she colourably gaue a Dutchman the title of her captaine; but it is well ynough knowen that an Englishman was her cheife commandour, and Englishmen her only strength; it was very vnaduisably and dangerously done to relieue such; and had 1 bin here, as I am nowe, she should neuer haue followed her ill trade any longer. For my part, I knowe not how it can be answered by such as wer then in prime command, and would be loath to giue such aduantage to any against my selfe. As thus much touchinge petie treasons, the punishment wherof is to be drawen and hanged; and if they be women, burned aliue. The forfeiture is, that the king haue all his goodes; and for his lands, the king likewise is to haue them *annum diem, et vastum*, as the lawyers saye; and the escheate ther of shall be to every Lord of his owne proper fee.

"Now, besides thes two sortes, high treason and petye treason, the lawyers mention a third kind, which they tearme misprision of treason. If any one, therfore, presume to drawe his sword, although but with an entcut only, to wound, strike, or kill any of the kings magistrates or deputyes sittinge in the place of justice, or to strike a juror in the presence of any magistrate sittinge in iudgement, or to refuse any one so offendinge, this is misprision of treason; as also for one man to strike another in any Court of Justice is misprision of treason. It is also very properly misprision either of treason or felony when one knoweth that another hath committed or is about to committ any treason or felonye, though not consentinge ther vnto, and yet will not nor doth not discouer the same to the magistrate. The punishment of misprision of treason is that the offendor forfeite to the king all his goodes and chattells for euer, and the proffitts of his lands durcinge his life, and also shall be perpetually emprisonned. And thus farre of the high offences of treason, petye treason, and misprision of treason, which, belonginge to the person of our Soueraiuge Lord the King in perticuler, strike as it wer directly at his crowne and diguitye.

"As for thoes crimes committed against the person of one man towards another, they are infinite as vice is infinite. I will only at the present make mention of such as I find more neerely and peculierly to concerne and touch the wellfare of this plantation, of which you of the jury are especially to enquire, that they may be brought out in their censures.

"Of thes, the cheife and prime one is murther, and he is to be held a willfull murtherour who takes away the life of any one vpon malice forethought; and yet stabbeinge another man, if he be killed therby, although it be sodainely done, and without malice forethought, is by a late statute made willfull murther ; and it seemes that herein the statute hath an eye to the basenesse of the action, as being generally the worck and act of a coward. The penalty of murther is hanginge. If you find any such, therfore, you are bound to present them, that they may fare therafter.

"But because euery killinge of a man is not vpon malice præpensed, the lawe in that respect addmitts a distinction. If, therfore, a soudaine quarrell and brawle ariseth, and so one man killeth another, without all former hatred or malice, in a sodaine heate of fury, this the law maketh manslaughter, in which case the offendor is allowed his booke, and saueth his life, if he can reade, by being burned in the hand. But if an infant, one that is an ideott, or a lunatick person, chaunce to kill a man, this is neither within the compasse of murther nor felony, for it is *felonia quia fieri debet fellio animo*, and it is to be thought that neither of thes are capable of it, it is in this case, therfore, accounted homicide. Marry, if a druncken man killeth one in his fitt of drinck, this is felony, for it is a voluntary ignorance in him, and by the lawes of some countryes it hath bin heretofore doubly punished, as carryinge with it a double sinne, drunckennesse and bloud.

"Another kind of killinge ther is, called homicide by misaduenture, or chaunce-medly, and this is when any person, being in a lawfull action, without any euill entent, chaunceth to kill a man, as if a man shooteinge to trie his muskett, and by the swerueinge of his hand the shott falleth wide of the entended marck, and striketh a man, and so killeth him. This is homicide by misaduenture, or chaunce-medly, and so of the like. But if a man be doing of an vn-lawfull action, and in doeing therof, chaunceth to kill a man ere he is aware, and not with any entent, yet this is felonye at the least, if not murther.

"Besides thes, ther are other distinguishinges in this, as casuall deathes, by the fall of houses, or by being killed with a beast, and the like, in which case the cause of such casuall deathes is forfeited to the king and taken for a deodand, as it is called, because at first it was giuen to the Churche. Ther is likewise a homicide vpon necessitie, as when the justice of the lawe commandeth a man to be putt to death, or when a iudge pronounceth the sentence of death against an offender attainted by due course of lawe, or when an inferiour person is enioyned to be the executioner of this sentence, that is to saye, the hangman ; and this leaueth the name and nature of murther or homicide, and is tearmed iustice, or rather iudgement, which is the lawfull execution of iustice. It is, therfore, straunge and seneelesse the nice custome which is taken up in the world, of such hateinge and abhorreinge of the hangman and publick executioner. In some places, as in Italy and Germany, the people will scarce so much as eate with him. In most places it is a very odious office. Here amongst us, I find that euery man flies from the office of a whipper more than from the crime which causeth the whippinge. I saye it is altogether vnreasonable, and a mear conceited foolerye this, for certainely, whosoeuer he be that hath this office imposed vpon him (and some one must haue it), if he be an honest man, he is neuer the lesse so, any way, for his office; indeed, if it be inflicted vpon him for some delinquencye and crime, he weares it as a badge, and it serues almost in the nature of a burneinge of the hand. And thus much of murthers, manslaughters, homecides, and other casuall and accidentall deaths.

"The next to be rancked vnder thes are felonies and burglaries. Felonie is a fraudulent takeing awaye of the goodes of other men, the prize of the sayd goods ammountinge the value of tweluc pence, doing it with an intent to steale them. Burglary is committed when in the action of the felonye, the dore or wall of a house, although neuer so weake, is forced and broke open; and thes two offences are by the lawe punished with death. But if the prize of the stolne goods ariseth not to the worth of twelue pence, this pilferinge is called petit larceny, the punishment wherof is whippeinge and the like, at the discretion of the magistrate. And truely, you of this great inquest, you are with all care and diligence to looke about you in thes cases. Theeues and idle persons are the worst vermin that a plantation can haue; they are farr worse than the ratts. How is it possible, thinck you, that any honest man can preserue his goodes or life in any securitie and enioyement, especially in your weake palmitoe houses, vnlesse seuere and strict inquisition be made after thes disordered persons? Neither is it in my power to procure any redresse of thes misdeamenors vnlesse you of the graund iury shall carefully looke out and present them. You also that are petie iurors in the trialls you passe vpon them, shewe yourselues both discret and conscionable of your oathes. Take heed, least either by fooleish pitty or partiall affection you suffer them to escape you by your straunge and sencelesse acquittinge of them. I am sorry to find such a number of thes malefactors in my time, and to see so many prisoners at the barre. I graunt that this hard year hath bin an occasion of this encrease, and I belieue that many haue played the theeues to fill their bellyes; besides, we haue had ouer many ill chosen and ill prouided newe people huddled vpon us this yeare. It behoufes you, therfore, so much the more to looke well vnto it, for I can assure you that if ther be discouered and perceiued neuer so litle conniuancye and tolloration of them on your part, they will sodainly encrease with that violence vpon you, as it will proue ouer late to repent of your kindnesse, or rather indiscretion, not to saye vnconscionablenesse, in not respectinge the duty of your oathes. For mine owne part, if I shall discouer any such fooleish and dishonest haltinge tricks practised either by you that are iurors, or you that are to giue in your euidence against the prisonners, I shall be compelled to take up such courses as will distaste you; for I would haue you knowe that whilst I am here, I neither dare nor will endure that iustice be baffelled or betrayed among you. Take warneinge, therfore, you especially that haue bin robbed of your goods, and are bound ouer to preferre your bills of enditement, take heede, I saye, that ther be noe shufflinge up vnderhand of matters of this nature; for you are to knowe, that whosoeuer he be that shall receiue back any stolne goods, though they be his owne, before he hath prosecuted against the theefe that stole them, makes himselfe guiltye of the steeleinge of his owne goods, and may be hanged for it.

"One beastly vice I had almost forgott (and sorry I am to haue found so much cause of remembrance). I meane the foule and vnnaturall sinne of . . . . It is a most barberous and inhumane practice, and by all lawes punishable with all seueritie, and in the highest kind; by noe meanes to be borne withall. If I shall find that any one dureinge my time is by sufficient profe found guiltie hereof, and that he be capable of due triall, he shall be sure to feele the seueritye of the lawe. It is filthie and impious ynough but in the least manner to attempt or come nere it, and I shall find inflictions to make such a one smart for it, but the act and perpetration therof is altogether intollerable.

"Nowe, besides thes notorious delinquents, who by the lawe are the most part of them punishable with death, there be many other, the which howsoeuer of an inferior degree and lower ranck of ill, yet in a well-gouerned place are by noe meanes to scape scott free, or be wincked at. And amongst thes, the very worst of them all is periurye. Periured persons are thoes who whittingly and willingly falsifie their oathes, therby either for fauour, affection, desire of gaine, or the like, to serue their owne base and vnworthy ends. Thes wretches and bane of all societie and good order are by all meanes to be rooted out. We haue noe other waye nor meanes left us to discouer, decide, and iudge the causes of highest nature than by the oathes of men; and all lawes haue entended that noe man who professeth God to be his Creator, Redeamour, and Sanctifiour, comeinge into the presence of this all-seeinge, allmightye, and all-powerfull God, and before his deputye on earth, the magistrate; and being by him enioyned to sweare to tell the truthe, the whole truthe, and noethinge but the truth, that such a one so called and so sweareinge will dare to proue such a wretch and presumptuous vilaine as to call Him that is the Father of Truth, nay, Truth itselfe, to wittnesse and auouch a knowen and determined falsshoode. It is a wonder that God, in his iust iudgement, strikes not such a one with a thunderbolt instantly to hell. Iurors also which have taken their oathes (as you nowe) to iudge iustly, according to your consciences, and trye equally, without all respect and partialitie betweene partie and partie, after the profe of their euidence, when, for any respect or commoditie, they shall doe otherwise, contrary to their owne consciences, what doe they but (as much as in them lies) endeuour to make euen God himselfe a lier. All thes, therfore, are, with all possible diligence, to be made after, and found out, that so, according to lawe, they may be seuerely punished, and made examples to all men.

"Oppressors, likewise, are euer found a dangerous kind of beasts, especially in a newe plantation as this is, and therfore, with all might and maine, to be hunted out. Oppression (that you may rightly distinguish it) is a wroung or hard vsage, practised by one man vpon another, beyond lawe, conscience, and charitie: as for example, when an incrochment is made vpon other mens landes or liuelihoodes: or when one man taketh aduantage vpon the need and necessitie of his neighbour therby to gripe him; as haueinge a commoditie which he may conueniently spare, and the other is in extreame want of, he either refuseth to sell it him, hopeinge still for a dearer markett and enhauncement of the prize; or, if he doe sell it, after much importunitie and entreaty, he cutts his throate with the rate; and in this nature are all enhauncers and engrossers of corne, especially in deare yeares, as this is one. Tradesmen also, who (by reason of the scarcetie of them in some places, and the necessitie of them), when they encroach vpon their poore neighbours, and make vse of their wants to make them paye vnreasonable rates; and so to sett them (as they saye) vpon the tenters; what are they but extorters? as when smithes shall refuse to make hookes to fish withall, or any other the like necessary toole, that the people cannot liue without, vnlesse they be payed at their owne vnconscionable prizes and pleasure; this is a biteinge vsury and horrible oppression: and the very same it is in all other tradesmen, practiseinge the like course. Thes, therfore, and such as thes, if you meet with them, you are to present, that they maye be ordered as justice requires.

"As for decciuors and cony-catchers, who (I feare) are too rife among you; they are, by you of the graund inquest, with care and diligence to be looked after; and of so many kindes they are, as scarce to be sommed in a whole day. I will only, therfore, name some of them; such are they who falssifie waights and measures; such are the practisers of cunninge and cousennage in any kind of commodities and merchaudice. And amongst the rest may iustly and properly be comprehended the false makers up of tobacco, and such as vse base and dishonest tricks, to giue it a hausome shewe for a while (thes sawe-cers of tobacco), when they knowe too well that it will be rotten within one weeke after. It was a pitty and shame to see what a deale of base stuff and rascally ware was made by you here, and sent into England the last sommer, in Captaine Kendall's yeare. You will call it cuff-tobacco, and it hath carryed that name with it into England; and it was good ynough, you sayd, to be payed vnto Cuffe, the cape merchaud for the magazin. But take you heed, least it Cuffe your selues most. I am affray'd it will proue a meanes so to vilifie and abate the prize of your best tobacco, and to discreditt it in generall, as therby both your vndertakers willbe discouraged, and your selues vndone. For the time that I am to staye with you and ouer you, I shall assuredly take all the courses I can deuise and apprehende to redresse this encreaseinge disease, and to cure this wound. Looke vnto it, and let this be a fayre warneinge vnto you all; whensoeuer and whersoeuer I shall hereafter find such bashawe and vnmerchandable stuffe, I will rather make bon-fires of it at your dores, than suffer it to be exported. And you of the inquest, you are to employe your vttermost skills and knowledge to enforme against this abuse. It is a great part of your oathe, and I see not how you can cleare your selues from the foule taxe and imputation of periurye, nor be able to acquitt your selues if you neglect it.[1]

"It is your duty, also, to present and haue a vigilant eye ouer such vn-conscionable fellowes on the one side, and vnsatiable swine on the other, as either sell or buy their liquour at vnreasonable and vnmeasurable rates, and especially after such as mingle it with water, euen salt water. Dureing the being of the shyp the *Garland* here, this last winter, diuers made their complaincts vnto me about this abuse; and I examined some of the most suspected marriners about it, but could not find any pregnant profe against them; generally, they affirmed that it was either done by your selues to vent it so againe, and to make it hold out measure; or by some that you entrusted to bring it vnto you, who, tiplinge the one halfe of it by the waye, wer forced to make it up againe on that fashion. I cannot tell how to beleiue thes saylours: onlye thus much I must needs saye, that I finde thes good liquours so deuillishly bewitchinge and powrefull ouer many of you, that it proues stroung ynough to violate all the bonds of trust and freindshyp. I protest (be it how it will), could I finde out some of thes water-brewers, I would make them seuere examples to all the rest. I beleiue, verely, it hath bin one of the maine causes of the much distemper and sicknesse that we haue had amongst vs this shypinge time. It is yenough, and too much, that we so extreamely abuse our good liquours with ouerdrinckeinge, we need not add this kind of ouerbreweinge it also. I haue sett downe (as you knowe) certaine prizes and rates, the which, in the buyinge and sale of them, wer not to be transcended, because I would neither haue you abused by others, nor haue you abuse your selues: but you haue found out a trimine trick of equiuocation, to frustrate mine

---

[1] This abuse was never eradicated, and contributed very greatly to the loss of reputation and ruin of the plantation. It affords one of many illustrations of the short-sighted policy which bolsters trade, by manufacturing frauds and deceptions.

entention, and to cheate your selues; which is, that by waye of bargaine
you will paye noe more, but, by waye of goodwill, will giue as much
againe; well vse it whilst you will, it will at leangth appeare, that as
on the one side you ouer-bye your driuck, so on the other you will ouer
drinck both your witt and wealth; and at last (as many of you doe
already), looke as if you were halfe sodden, with scarce a ragg to hang
on your backs.

"Ther is another ill-fauored vice and custome rauiginge amongst
you, which by all meanes is to be suppressed: and it is an itche of
tounge, and a kind of base delight to depraue and slaunder the actions
and good names one of another. By the Statute Lawe, this is punished
with emprisonment: and besides the partye wrounged maye haue his
action of slaunder against the foule-mouthed man: and in some cases
by a discreet and vnderstandeinge Jury, deepe dammages are allowed.
Thes kindes of talkers are by the laweyers tearmed common barrettors.
And if the deprauations extend to men of place and command, very
seuere and sharpe punishments are inflicted: and with good reason, for
howsoeuer it is true, that wordes are but wind (as they saye), yet experience tells that oft times they proue the fire-brands of all other ills;
for *a verbis ad verbara:* it may be that some busie heades and factious
discontents haue bin the breeders and sowers of this ill seed among you:
but let them take heed least at length it produce hempe, to make a rope
to hang themselues.

"And thus as breifly as I could I haue sommed up vnto you such disorders, offences, and crimes, as by you of the graund inquest are stricktly
and in conscience, by vertue of your oathe, to be looked after and presented vnto this Court. Some others ther are which of your selues you
may remember to your selues: as the want of due cleareinge of the path-
wayes, the negligence vsed by such as are entrusted with your botes, a
dangerous disease infectinge ouer many of you, and the carelessnesse
and stupide negligence of such people is seuerely to be punished; for
botes, next fortification, are the most important, beneficiall, and vsefull
instruments that thes Ilands can possibly haue, and therfore the more
warely and diligently to be vsed and preserued. You are also to present
such as by their wreacklessness shall suffer the ratts to encrease and
growe stroung vpon them in their grounds, to the annoyeance both of
themselues and their neighbours; as also the dammage and misrule that
may arrise by the sufferinge of hoggs to goe lose, the carelessnesse of
gatheringe in of corne in due time, and of due houseing of it likewise.
Breafly, whatsoeuer, you in your discretion shall find necessary, for the
good and wellfare of this plantation, you are with all care and conscience
to giue this Court knowledge therof, that so all thinges being ordered
after justice and equitie, ther may ensue, by Gods blessinge, peace and
tranquillitie.

"For my part, I shall require at your hands, that you carefully and conscionably discharge this your charge: take heed, therfore, of slightinge such dutyes as by oath you are bound to performe. I hope you are so discreet and honest, as that by your care and integritie shewen in the seruice, I shall find the meanes and opportunitie to settle many thinges for the good and wellfare of this litle Common-wealth: and so to leaue them setled when I am to leaue you, as not easily to be shaken. In doeing wherof, as you shall giue great satisfaction to my selfe, so you shall performe an especiall part for the free passage of iustice here, without which it is not possible that any societie can long subsist; for, vnlesse good men be cherished, the badd corrected, and the incorrigible cutt of, all things must needs come sodainely to confusion and ruine."

And this was the effect of the charge, deliuered in the very same wordes; the which (as I haue sayd) I thought properly and duely inserted into the body of this Historye, as well in respect of the noueltie therof, in regard both of substance and forme; and being giuen by the Gouernour himselfe, which formerly neuer was vsed: as that also by diuers touches therin, may be vnderstoode and perceiued the condition of the people, for the most part, and the sicknesses that they are infected withall (I feare me) euen to this day.

But this charge being thus ended, the gayle was called ouer, wherin wer eighteene prisonners for criminall causes; a number very extraordinary for this place, but nowe occasioned by reason of the hard yeare, and the ill-supplied newcomers (as you heard in the charge), the which done, the Court brake up for that morneinge. Presently, after dinner, the Gouernour returned to the bench, and so did euery daye for two dayes after, and then finished the assizes, wherin diuers and sundry actions of controuersie betweene partie and partie wer tried and decided; some contempts and abuses in that nature censured to the whippeing post and pillery; others for petye pilferings, saued by their booke and burned in the hand; two only of the most heinous and notorious offendors wer condemned to die; whereof the one of them (vpon some especial considerations) was by the Gouernours precept repriued; the other hanged. The daye after was bestowed in a generall muster, and all the able men exercised in armes; the which being done, euery man was dismissed to his owne home. The rest of this moneth of June, and the other that followed, wer wholy spent, by the Gouernours command and direction, in makeinge of botes, in mountinge and remoueinge of ordinance, and in repayreinge and makeinge of carriages; at the same time, also, he made diuers trialls for the recouery of some goods out of the lost *Warwick* (ther being noe possibilitie of weighinge up any more of her ordinance, vntill the shyps carkasse be quite rotten, by reason they all of them wer made fast to the sides of her, and cannot be come at), some butts of beare only (being boyant ware) wer not without some adoe gott out of her; some of which, although they had layne almost six moneths vnder water (beyond expectation), proued very good. About the same time, or not long after, writts wer sent downe to all the baylies, for the summoninge of the generall assembly at St. Georges; and for the choice of burgeoises against the first of August (1620) followeinge, when it was to begin.

Presently after, a messenger was sent from the serieant maior at Sommer-seate, to the Gouernour at the towne, that two sayle wer seene of to the westward of that Iland, and that they stoode alongst the side of the Southewarde; who was presently dispatched back againe, with command to the serieant maior to haue a continuall eye vpon them, and to stande vpon his garde for feare of their landinge vpon that coast with shalopes. The next day, both of them are seene from the mount, one comeinge close up by the shore, and within a cables length of the rocks called the breackers, the other keepeinge of a leauge more to seaward. Whervpon a warneinge peece was giuen from the foote of the mount, and the shalope manned and sent out to discouer them. Within fiue or six hours after word was returned that one of them was the same Dutch frigate that had bin formerly here with Powell; the other a smale barck of the west country of England, belongeinge to a merchant that was of the Company of the Sommer Ilands, and by him purposely sett out for thes Ilands. The daye followeinge, the both of them gatt in at the harbour of St. Georges, and the English barck fell close up, and rode before the towne; as for the other, being poore and ragged, she had noe mind to shewe herselfe, but kept at an anchor, close vnder Smithes Fort, only her captaine (a very well fashioned and well quallefied gentleman) came ashore, and demanded leaue and libertie of the Gouernour to carine her ther, the which the Gouernour graunteing, and comfortinge him for his badd voiage, she shortly departed for the Netherlands. But by the English barck, the Gouernour receiued diuers priuate letters from his freinds, that gaue him perticuler notice of the occurrents and passages in England: by her, also, he was enformed of the approach of the Magazin shyp; she was fraughted cheifly with passengers, and the most of the well chosen labouringe boyes for apprentices, for which she came to a good markett; she had, besides, a smale magazin of goods, the most part wherof was appointed for her owners owne people, and the remainder to be sold for tobacco.

But the Gouernour (although he was somewhat diuerted by the comeinge in of thes shyps) was at this time cheifly taken vp in fittinge and disposeinge of bussinesse against the meetinge and session of the generall assembly, which nowe drew neere; wherin, at the very first, he mett with many and materiall difficulties; for, haueinge prepared certaine of the ancientest Ilanders, who wer best knowen, and best entrusted by the people (the elder of the ministers being a prime one among the rest), he employed them to gett all the knowledge they could, what the maine pointes wer that would be generally shott at at the assembly; by whom, haueing for a certainetie bin assured that the cheife aime and generall scope and drift of most of the bills that wer entended to be preferred, would beate vpon the enlargeing of themselues and their liberties, and the enfringeing and curbeinge of their vndertakers in England; a course and endeauour which he well ynough knewe would proue as well effectlesse as sencelesse, and neuer be able to worck the entent it was plotted for; and besides, could not but giue great discontentment to the Aduenturers. He endeauoured, therefore, by all meanes to diuert it, and to possesse the burgeoises with the vanitie of it, and the impossibilitie of doeing any good that waye; and this he did, as well by the meanes of those men aforesayd, as by his owne mouthe and person, all conference with many of them; to whom also, to the same end, he shewed the perticuler instruction that he had receiued from the Company in England, concerneinge the holdinge of this assembly, which ranne in this manner:—

"We require you, that as sone as you maye after your arriuall in the Ilands, you doe assemble your counsell and as many of the ablest and best vnderstandinge men in the Ilands, both of the clergie and laitie, as you and your counsell shall thinck fitt, wherin we wish you rather to take too many than too fewe, both because euery man will more willingly obey lawes to which he hath ycilded his consent; as likewise because you shall the better discouer such thinges as haue need of redresse by many than by fewe: and that in this assembly you deliberately consult and aduise of such lawes and constitutions as shallbe thought fitt to be made for the good of the plantation, and for maintenance of religion, justice, order, peace, and vnitie among them. As also vpon what penalties you thinck fitt, the performances of each lawe be enioyned: wherin we aduise you to be very moderate, allwayes so proportioninge the penaltye to the offence, that the greatnesse of the punishment doe not encourage the delinquents to offend out of hope of pardon, as it falleth out wher this rule of moderation is not obserued. And what in assembly shall, by the maior or better part, be agreed vpon, we would haue you distinctly to aduertize us of by the returne of the next shyp, that they may be ratefied and confirmed by the authoritie of the Court here, is such manner as by his Maiesties Letters Patents is limmited and appointed, with such alterations, explanations, or amendments as to the sayd Court shallbe thought meet and conuenient. And this course of assemblinge of the grauest and discreetest men in thoes Ilands, to consult and aduise with you and your counsell of such thinges as may conduce to the generall good of that plantation, and to the well gouerninge of the people ther, we aduise you to hould at least once in euery yeare, and of your resolutions and determinations from time to time to aduertize vs, that they may be established and confirmed by order of our Courts here as a foresayd : and in the meane time you shall not need to doubt to putt in execution any such wholsome Orders or Constitutions as shall by the maior part in the sayd assemblies be agreed vpon. Prouided that the same be not repugnant to the lawes of England nor contrary to thes your present instructions, or to the standing lawes already by us established."

Haueing read this instruction, perticulerly directed for the holdinge of the assembly, vnto some of the prime ones, who wer the leadinge speritts of all the rest, he especially and punctually obserued vnto them that clause, wherin it was enioyned that the Aduenturers wer to be distinctly aduertized of what so euer was by the maior partye agreed vpon, that so it might be ratefied and confirmed by the authoritie of their Courts in England, in such manner as by his Maiesties letters patents is limited and appointed : therin "first you maye see (S'rs sayth he) that by his Maiesties letters patents, the vndertakers in England haue power and authoritie to giue us lawes: as also that howsoeuer they haue giuen us licence and libertie to propound here, and prouide some peculier ones for our good and wellfare, by this our generall assembly, yet they haue so restrained us, that whatsoeuer we enact amongst our selues, it shall not, nor cannot, stand in force, vnlesse it be by them ratefied and confirmed ther; so that whilst you endeauour and practice thus to aduantage your owne ends only, and to giue your selues your full content, and them noethinge but the contrary; what doe you els, saue only discouer your minds and good wills, or rather ill-wills, towards them, by giueinge them to vnderstande, as it wer, in plaine tearmes, that you care not how much they be streightened, so you may be free, and as you would haue it: all which they shall noe soner heare, but with holdinge vp their hands only, and a dash or two of a penne, shall wholy be annihilated (nay) perhaps be a cause that the quite contrary be concluded; and this is all that you can gett by this course, that you so generally affect. It is mine aduise to you therfore, that this affayre be carryed in a better temper and with more moderation and equanimitie: and that the benefitt and commodite of the Aduenturers may be so mixed and enterwouen with our owne, as they may proue impossible to be seuered: and this course will certainely be a meanes not only to winne them to a ratefication of what we ennact here; but to ioyne with us also (euen by our example) to carry and leuell all bussinesse and conclusions with an indifferent hand, without which (I doe assure you) such is the reciprocall bond betwixt you and them, ther cannot long continue any hopefull subsistance to either side."

This speache seemed, euen at the instant, to gaine well vpon them, so that desireinge the Gouernour to giue them leaue to impart and make it knowen to the rest of their fellowes, which in a while after they iointly returned this answer, that they had well considered of what he had deliuered vnto them, and found it so fitt and necessary to be followed, as they wholy resolued to referre the whole conduction of this affayre to his guidance: and that noe bill should be preferred by any of them to the Assembly, but what by him should first be seene and approued, the which resolution gaue the Gouernour good content, as findinge himselfe more than halfe through the waye he was to make by so luckye a settinge out.

Vpon the first of August (being the prefixt day) the generall Assembly began, and was held at St. Georges, in the newe framed churche, fitted for that purpose. In which, before I let you knowe what was done, it is meet I should tell you how it was done. The forme and composition therof was therfore as followeth:—

The persons wer, the gouernour, the counsell, the baylies of the tribes, two burgeoises out of euery tribe, chosen by plurallitie of voice, a secretary, to whom all the Bills presented, and by him openly reade in the House, and a clearck to recorde the Acts.

The order (appointed and prescribed by the Gouernours direction and command) was :—" The first daye (after a sormon in the morneinge) the burgeoises, the secretary, and the clearck tooke their oaths. The secretary was openly sworne by the Governour himselfe, whose oath was that he should receiue all Bills presented vnto him, or to be presented, and as opportunitie serued, distinctly, and word for word, with an audible voice, to reade them publickly in the Assembly: that he should dilligently obserue and take especiall care that all Bills wer openly reade three seuerall dayes before they wer putt to the question, and came to be decided by plurallitie of voices; that he should heedfully and faythfully take account of all such Bills as by most voices should be passed and ennacted for lawes; that he should conceale the secrets of the House, and neither directly nor indirectly reueale or discouer them to any person whatsoeuer not being a member of the Assembly, all which he should duely and truely performe and keepe to his vttermost abilitie, so helpe him God."

The secretary, being sworne himselfe, he gaue the oathe to the clearck, which conteyned :—" That he should diligently, exactly, truely, and faythfully, as nere as possible he could, engrosse all such Bills as should be deliuered vnto him to that entent by the secretary. He should assist and ayde him, the sayd secretary, in all such employements and affayres as (belonginge to the present Assembly) he should haue occasion to use his seruice. He should not reueale any bussinesse or affayre handled or determined by the Assembly, being within his hearcinge or knowledge. Thus two being sworne, the secretary gaue the oathe to all the

o

burgoisses, which was, that being to be members of that
generall Assembly, they should sweare to vse and employe
their best endeauours as a furtherance therto; that all such
propositions as by them or their meanes should be offered
vnto the consideration and discussinge therof should especially be entended and leuelled at a publick wellfare; that
they should not be leade by any partiall affection, or respect
of priuate gaine or interest, to oppose or hinder the estab-
lisheinge or ennactinge of any lawe aimeinge at the refor-
mation of any disorder and abuse; that in all such actions
as they should practice and contriue dureinge the whole
time of their assistance in that seruice, they shoulde striue
to discharge a good conscience in all equitie and integritie;
that they should by all meanes conceale the secretts of the
House, and not impart nor discouer, either by word, writte-
inge, or any other meane, directly or indirectly, to any one
not being of the present Assembly, the passage or carriage
of any affayre or bussinesse that should be treated of and
disputed dureing the time of the whole sittinge and continuance of the sayde Assembly. All this, and euery part
therof, they should promise and sweare to keepe and performe to their vttermost power and abilitie, so help them God."

The whole Assembly being thus sworne, wer called ouer
by the secretary, and so tooke their places in the House, the
counsell sittinge next the Gouernour, and the rest as they
came. All of them being seated, and in quiett, the Gouernour declared the cause and benefitt of the Assembly, and
the duty and due aime euerye particuler member therof was
to carry and bring with him, together with some instructions and aduises to that end, in thes wordes followeinge:—

" Thancks be to God, that we are thus mett, to so good an end as the
makeinge and ennactinge of good and holsome lawes; and I hope the
blessed effect will manifest that this course was inspired from heauen
into the hearts of the vndertakers in England, to propound and offer it
vnto us, for the singuler good and wellfare of this plantation. As
for the forme and regularitie to be obserued herein, you haue heard it

read vnto you euen nowe by the Secretary: and I hope you are well skilled in it; for to that end I gaue coppies therof vnto the baylies at the last Assizes. Concerneinge the scope and aime that we are to bring with us hether, I shall (God willinge) briefly deliuer somewhat vnto you at this time: and hereof, the principall and maine part is, the Glory of God: wherein we are to ponder and resolue of all such thinges in generall, as may promote true religion and beate downe the contrary, which is sinne and prophanenesse. The second aime we ought to haue is the maintenance of our fayth, obedience, and alleigeance to our Soueraigne the Kinge; and therfore are to prouide against all such courses and actions as may lessen the respect due either vnto his Maiesties owne person, or any such as by his authoritie are placed ouer vs. In perticuler, we are to take heed and to scourge, if need be, that dangerous opinion (which hath too ouerboldly been wispered and nourished among you) of choseing and electinge your owne Gouernour here. Thirdly, it is our dutyes, and will proue our wisdome, to conclude vpon some such courses as may best secure the vndertakers in England from many abuses and wrongs, which (I must tell you plainely) are by many planters offred vnto them. It is therfore an vn-wary and vn-wise affection, that some manifest, while they striue to haue all thinges to be carried in this Assembly to the gripeinge of the aduenturers and proffitt (as they fallsly thinck) of themselues; ther is noe thinge, I can assure you, to be gotten that waye; it serues only to discouer your selues vnto them, to your owne disaduantage: for you must knowe that it is but in vaine to enact or conclude any thinge here, vnlesse it be confirmed by them ther. We are to be honest, therfore, and discreat, and soe to mixe our owne good and proffitt, and theirs together, as may make it inseperable, by being fully receiued by both sides: and this you will find to be the true way, for the firmeing of this plantation. Fourthly, we are to endeauour and aime at the good and benefitt of our selues in perticuler. I meane at the generall good and wellfare of the inhabitants of thes Ilands wherin we liue: and herein, in the first place, we are to prouide against the attempts of all forraigne enemies, by secureinge our harbours, and all places of access by botes or shypinge: and this is done by sufficient fortification, and well manninge of them, as also by makeing of our selues in generall to vnderstand how to defend ourselues, that is to saye, to be soldiers: otherwise, I see not with what comfort we can plant tobacco, and take paines to make it good (as we ought to doe), vnlesse we prouide to keepe it when we haue it. Me thincks, that euery married man that hath a childe borne to him here should (if it wer but for his childs sake) be ready to keepe it a freeman: and ther is noe earthly meanes to doe it better than by this. It may be, some of you conceiue and flatter your selues that all thinges this waye are well ynough already, and that ther needs noe more to be done then ther is. It is a deceitfull and dangerous apprehension this; and you doe noe lesse than betraye yourselues and your owne safetye by it. You heare by this barke that is newely come in vnto us from England, of the rumours and likely-hoode of great warres in Christian-doome. If it should so fall out that any soudaine breach happen betweene England and Spaine (and who knowes how sone this may be), ther is not any place that it will breake out vpon soner than vpon this. The pyrates, likewise, haue a longinge eye after thes Ilands, and knowe well how behoufefull they would be for them; let us, therfore, so prouide for our selues, that come an enemye when he will, and be what he will, we may be able to giue him a braue wellcome. And thes are the foure maine pointes and aimes that we are to respect and looke after in this action we are nowe to enter vpon. Nowe, the waye and meane to be prepared for them is, by takeing due notice, euery one of us, that we come not hether for our selues only, and to serue our owne turnes, or any mans els in perticuler, but to serue and regard the publick. We are, therfore, to riddle our selues from all base desires of gaine; we are to despice all priuate interests, thus farre at least, as to cause them to giue place to the generall. It may well be that some men chosen to be burgeoses here may find some bills preferred into this Assembly that may strike at some gettinge and in-come of theirs in perticuler. If they doe so, let them yet remember their oathes; let them not shame themselues, and the place they hold here, by doeing the contrary. If, in their owne consciences, they find that hetherto they haue done iniurye to a common good, let them not augment it by obsti-nacye. It is in vaine to striue against the streame; for in this case, I hope they shall allwayes find the currant to runne against them. I graunt that ther is a freedome of speach and opinion, with modestie, to be held by euery man here. It is laufull and expedient also, that all men should deliuer their censures and judgements vpon any bill whatso-euer, as their discretion shall induce, and their opinion carry them; but yet I hope ther is nce man here amongst us so wedded to his owne con-ceites as to affect and delight in opposition, much lesse to thinck it a waye and course to obteyne the repute of a wiseman by holdinge straunge and extrauagant opinions: to be singuler on this fashion may be a meanes indeed to make him a noted man; but such a noted one, as for my part, I should be full loath to be. It is after that fashion as if one of you should walke through Cheapeside at noone day, all to be be-painted and stuck with feathers like an Americane, wher he may be sure to be looked at, but laught at; it behoufes us therfore to haue our iudgements rectified in this point as well as in all others, and the meanes thervnto are principally three:—

"The first is, by comeing hether, without all preiudication. We must bring equall mindes with us; that is to saye, without haueinge our mindes so preoccupied and taken up before, as noe roome is left for justice and right. Secondly, we are to giue attention and diligent care to suche reasons as we shall heare deliuered, either for or against any bill whatsoeuer. Thirdly, we must ingenuously and quiettly submitt our judgements and suffer our opinions to be ruled, swayed, and ledd by the truth, force, and reason of thoes reasons, and so accordingly giue our votes. And certainely thes are the true wayes, this the only clue to conduct us out of the pitt of passion, darcknesse of error, and laberinthe of selfe-loue. Let us beseach God to inspire us with peaceable speritts, and such thoughts and desires as become honest, loyall, and wise men, such as may be for his glory, and the formeinge of this hopefull and forward plantation. We ought to knowe that somewhat of worthe and value is expected from this action, and from us the actors in it; and this, bothe by the Company in England and the inhabitants here. Let us make it, therfore, our master peece, and not thincke the time long that we bestowe on this seruice. Deuines saye that in point of religion ther is noe standeinge at a staye, but that men goe either forward or backward, and surely euen in this ciuill affayre I maye well saye thus much, that our condition and estate here cannot but hereby either be bettred or empayred. It is our parte to prouide for the best. Let us therfore take heed, least by peruerse obstinacye and foolish willfullnesse, we cause that to proue a poyson, which was entended a medicine. But, let us followe and embrace that excellent counsell of the wisest king that euer the world had, or shall haue, the which he deliuered thus:—

"'Be not ouermuch just, nor make thy selfe ouerwise.

"'Wherfore shouldst thou be desolate?

"'Be not wicked ouer-much; neither be thou fooleish. Why shouldst thou perish not in thy time?

"'It is good that thou laye hold on this, yet withdrawe not thyne hand from that: for he that feareth God shall come forth of them both.'"

This speach being thus finished, the Assembly rose for that day (for they satt only in the morneinges), the afternoones being bestowed either in consultation with the Gouernour in his house, or vpon some perticuler committees to frame bussinesse against the next daye.

At the next meetinge of the Assembly, the secretary reade all such Bills as wer propounded, the which done, whosoeuer would rose up and spake either for it or against it, in which action this order was obserued. He that entended to speake, stoode up (vnlesse it wer the Gouernour), bareheaded, wherby it was discerned that he had a meaneinge to speake. If more stoode vp than one at once, he that was iudged to arise first, was first heard. Euery man was to direct his speach to the secretary, and to be heard without interruption. He that had once spoken to a Bill, though he wer presently answered and confuted, might not replye that day, so that none might speake twise to one and the same Bill in one daye; and this was to auoide ouer-much and tedeous disputes, and tautologies, and losse of time that waye. In speakeinge against any mans speach the partie spoken against was not personally to be named, to shunne therby heates of contention, and the giueinge of distates one to another. Noe reuileinge nor nipinge speaches wer to be vsed vpon any occasion whatsoeuer. All Bills wer to to be reade three seuerall dayes once, and but once before they came to be consigned and concluded of by voices, that so in the meane time they might be aduisedly examined, and euery man haue space to deliberate, and so to accept or reiect them when they came to be put to the question. After a Bill was read three seuerall dayes, and sufficiently disputed vpon, the secretary was to demand whether it should be putt to voices or noe, the which being graunted, the sayd secretary was to hold up the Bill in his hand and to saye, "All you that will haue this Bill to passe for a lawe let them saye soe; as many as will not let them saye the contrary"; if the then crye affirmatiuely yea, wer found apparently greater than the negatiue noe, the Bill was passed for a lawe, if on the contrary, it was dashed. If it proued doubtfull which crye was the greater, the secretary was to saye thus: "As many as allowe the Bill, stand up on your feete; you that refuse it sitt still"; and then bothe the numbers being counted, the most carried it. And, in this fashion, all the Bills wer decided dureinge the whole session of the Assembly. Vpon the last daye, all the Acts that wer passed wer reade, the which being done, the Gouernour dismissed and brake up the Assembly with a short speach, accordinge as the former passages of bussinesse had giuen him occasion.

And this order and forme was punctually obserued dureing the whole time of the Session, dureing the which fifteene seuerall Acts wer, with a very great and generall vnanimitie, agreed vpon and enacted; the titles wherof only with some breife annexed reasons occasioninge them (for breuitie sake), shall be inserted in this history, referringe the reader for a large vewe (if he be so minded) to the bookes of statutes and the publick records, kept in the Ilands for the information of all men that are to liue vnder their subiection.[2]

I. The first wherof was an Act against the vniust sale, and lettinge out of apprentices and other seruants, the which especially respected the rightinge of the vndertakers in England, it being obserued that diuers inhabitants here haueinge committed vnto their trust, by their vndertakers in England, certaine seruants and apprentices to be placed and settled vpon their shares, the one halfe of whose labours wer to redound to the benefit of the vndertaker, the other to the planter; the sayd planters made it a common vse and practice to let out to hire the sayd apprentices vnto straungers, and many times to make sale of their whole time for some certaine prize, without the knowledge, and contrary to the intention, of the vndertaker, wherby it was conceiued that dammage might ensue to the sayd vndertaker, as well by a secret concealement of that halfe of the hire which was to be receiued for the sayd seruant so let out, and which ought to belong vnto the vndertaker (the bayleife of the tribe, in that case, being not able to discouer the deceite); as also by a lower emprouement of his labour than otherwise might be for the remedye and redresse of the sayd wrong and abuse, this Act and statute law was enacted.

II. The second concerned the disposeinge of aged, diseased,

[2] The Acts are given at large in the *Memorials of Bermuda*.

and impotent persons. For it being considered that by the vnheedefull and carelesse choice of some vndertakers in England (who, this waye, caught at all they mett) ther had by some late importations, diuers such bin throwne in and forced vpon the colonye; and more wer still to be euery day expected, not only to hindrance of thoes that so tooke them up, but to the great disturbance of orderly Gouerment and the generall slackeinge, if not chokeinge of the grouth of this newe hopefull plant; it was thought fitt, by waye of causeinge and procureinge, for the future, a greater respect in their choice, and to deliuer the plantation from so vntimely a burthen; that all such persons so sent ouer should be presently shipped back againe, and that at the only charge of him that sent him, or els to be maintained here vpon the sayd vndertakers land, and in the interim to be freed from the paiment of all supplies.

III. The third Act was for the necessary mainteininge of the Kings-Castle. The importancye of the preseruation and makeinge good of which place, being duely weighed, it was found altogether vnfitt, and a strannge improuidence, to leaue the gard therof, and of three twentye peeces of good ordinance, vnto the care and mannagement of one poore half-blind gunner and his wife, as in former times it had bin; whervpon it was ennacted that twelue able and sufficient men should be continually resident ther, in the nature of a garrison; and that for their foode and entertainement thirtie thousand cares of corne should yearely be raysed, and one thousand waight of tobacco, the which is at the present executed; and the captaine of the castle, together with his famely, commanded by the Gouernour, to be continually in person ther, over and aboue the said number.

IV. The fourth prouided against the makeinge of rotten and vnmerchantable tobacco; triers of tobacco being yearely to be sworne in euery tribe for the discouery of all bashawe and vnsendible ware, all which by the sayd statute is enioyned to be burned at the owners dore.

v. The fifth cnioyned the erection and frameinge of certaine publick bridges, and the maintenance of them. And this was found necessary, as well for foote-conueyeance and vnion of the people one with another for their publick and priuate occasions, as for the better answeringe of any alarme, and the conuenyance of the women, children, and impotent persons vnto the fortes and places of saue-garde, if any botes and shalopes should land vpon them in the mayne.

vi. The sixth statute was for a continuall supply of resident corne in the fortes. The which, haueing formerly bin exacted and receiued, but wholy exhausted and spent in Captaine Kendalls disorderly yeare, was nowe againe thought fit to be reuiued (without intermission) by an Act of a generall assent (which might stop the mouthes of all grudgers), that therby it might serue as a legicy store for all publick occasions and necessities, and the fortes neuer suffered to be vnfurnished with some necessary prouisions to entertaine all comers, either for defence or offence.

vii. The seuenth appointed two fixed dayes in euery yeare for the holdinge of the generall assize; the which was done by Act of Parliament, vpon due and considerate choyce of the most proper and easefull times and seasons, that so, therby, publick notice and answerable preparation might be had of them, and noe mutations moued nor allowed.

viii. The eighth commanded the makeinge of highe wayes, and prohibited the goeing ouer mens ground; and this was for the redresse of a common practice, in making an ordinary passage ouer mens corne and peeces of tobacco, to their much dammage and spoyle, and also for the better answereinge of all soudaine alarmes, and the drawinge of the people together, vpon any occasion, to any place of rendeuous, and especially to the King's-Castle.

ix. The ninthe was for the preseruation of the breede of tortoyses, the which being an excellent and daintye fish, wer, by the liquorousnesse and wastefullnesse of many persons, killed ouer young and scared awaye, the which this lawe prouided against.

x. The tenth punished vagabonds, and prohibited the entertaininge of other mens seruants.

xi. The eleuenth enioyned the settinge of a due quantitie of corne for euery famelie, and a collection and keepeinge of a publick store in euery tribe, the which was looked into, vpon notice taken of the improuidence generally crept in amongst the inhabitants, both in the prouideinge for it, and the keepeing of that litle they had.

xii. The twelfth Act respected the care of the corne being sett, and, therfore, commanded the keepeing in of poultry dureinge certaine weekes, and vntill the corne was growen past their damnifieinge, which formerly had bin much preiudiced by them; and many poore men, which had noe poultry, extreamely oppressed by their neighbours this waye, who had more than ynough of them.

xiii. The thirteenth was for the maintenance of sufficient fences, and against the fellinge downe of marcked trees appointed for boundes; it being conceiued an ill incrochment, which diuers persons (either out of carelessnesse, or vnconscionablenesse, or both) began more and more to practice to the danger of breedinge many confusions and much contention, and, therfore, by this Act, prouided against.

xiv. The fourtenth graunted a leuye of one thousand pounds of tobacco towards the payments of publick worcks for the yeare 1620.

xv. The fifteenth was bestowed in enioyneinge an acknowledgement and acception of resident Gouernours, and for their warrantice, in case it should fall out that the date of their commissions be expired before the arriuall here of a legitimate successor from England, the which was apprehended very necessary and of great importancye, bothe for the auoideinge of the dangerous confusions that an anarchye, by a vacaucye of gouermont, might bring vpon the whole plantation; as also for the cuttinge of of all coulours and pretences of vnmeet and presumptious elections among themselues. In the same Act, likewise, a certain clause was inserted (by waye of entreaty to the Aduenturers), that the future Gouernours, in succession, might, for a moneth or two before their receipt of the helme of Gouerment, remaine here as priuate men, and so, by lookeinge on and obserueing (dureinge that time) the settled fashion and manner of the carriage of the publick bussinesse, they might (as their iudgements should lead them) either approue or refuse it in their after courses; and this was humbly offered vnto the determination and consent of the Honorable Company; that so, from thence forward, an answerable date might be obserued in all their commissions, by them to be graunted vnto the sayd future Gouernours. Prouided alwayes, that the quondam Gouernour remained and stayed the sayd time and tearme of two moneths in the ilands; the which, if he did not, that then the sayd commissions might, vpon the instant of his departure, be of full power and authoritie.

And thes wer the contents of the fifteene Acts conferred and ennacted dureinge the Session of this generall Assembly, the which, being digested (as it is sayd by the Gouernours owne hand) into a conuenient methode, wer sent into England by the magazin shyp, the *Joseph*, an. dom. 1620, ther to receiue their confirmation and ratification by the Company in their courts ther, in such manner as, by His Maiesties letters patents, is limited and appointed; and, in the meane time (as he was warranted by his instruction), the Gouernour did cause the sayd Acts to be publickly reade in all churches, and so to stand in full force, vntill he heard the contrary from England.[3]

[3] To appreciate the judgment, firmness, and caution evinced by Captain Butler in the conduct of this General Assembly, the reader must

Noe soner is this bussiness ouer, but the magazin shyp is discouered vpon the coast, and the warneing peece giuen from the mount to all the fortes. The same daye, towards night, she came into the harbour of St. Georges, but in a very weake and sickly state, haveinge cast ouer bord twenty or thirtie of her people, and some of them men of good account; and among the rest, a neare kinsman of the Gouernours, being his sisters sonne. And so violent was the infection growen among them, that the most part of the people and marriners wer either so sick, or so dismayed, or both, as the master of her himselfe confessed to the Gouernour, that if they had stayed aboard but one weeke longer, he verely perswaded himselfe she could neuer haue bin brought in, for want of hands. Vpon her wer shypped and arriued diuers gentlemen of fashion and their wiues, but most of them very crazie with the voiage, wherof, howsoeuer, the most part, by the bounty of the aire, sone recouered; yet some ther wer that died presently after they wer ashore, it being certainely the nature and qualetie of the place either to kill or cure quickly, wher it meetes with infected bodyes. By this shyp also the Company sent a supply of ten persons for the generallitie, but so ill chosen they wer (for they had bin taken out of Newgate), that smale hope of good was to be had of them, and it was secretly

---

remember the entire novelty of Colonial legislation at this time. With exception of the Virginia Assembly of 1619, the proceedings of which had probably not reached Bermuda, as they were only ratified in London in April, this Assembly at St. George's is the first in our Colonial history. Its powers were ill-defined, principles of constitutional liberty were struggling into day, but not yet acknowledged by the Crown or readily granted by the Company, and the Burgesses were wholly inexperienced. These difficulties invest the first experiments of legislation, humble and minute as are the subjects of it, with an interest beyond their intrinsic importance.—See a paper by the writer in the *Archeologia*, or the *Proceedings of the Society of Antiquaries*, for 1879, not printed when this sheet passes through the press.

muttered about that they wer the occasion of the shyps infection.[4]

The Gouernour found himselfe some-what distressed with this sickly accident, being once againe putt to the releiueinge of great numbers of thes sick people; and not only so, but by reason of the continuall employment of his botes in fetchinge them of the shyp, many of his owne men, and especially thoes of his botes gang, became infected also, and for some weekes wer not able to doe him any seruice; and truely, ther could noe other iudgement or censure passe vpon this infectious disease than that it was the plaine plauge, the purple marcks being plentifully discerned vpon many of them. And without doubt, had it bin almost in any other place, it would haue enlarged it selfe to a dangerous desolation; but the exceedinge excellent salubritie of the ayre (than which I belieue the whole world hath not a better) surmounted all thes dangers and difficulties, and in a fewe weekes became such a conquerour as this dreadfull infection wholy ceased, and the former wonted health of the Ilauds was fully recouered; for well knowen it is, that diseases (vnless meerely accidentall) are straungely and, indeed, wonderfully rare and vncommon here, except it be in shypeinge times, when it is many times thus brought in and thus recouered. But, howsoeuer this could not passe without disquiett, yet other occasions ther wer that came packt up in the generall letters by this shyp which far more discoutented the Gouernour; for the Adventurers in England,

---

[4] The Treasurer, Counsell, and Company of Virginia, in their anxiety to people that plantation, addressed the Lord Mayor in November 1619, to provide, as he had done the previous year, "one hundred children from the superfluous multitude to be transported thither, there to be bound apprentices, upon very beneficial conditions"; and the city granted £500 for their passage and outfit. At the same time, by the king's order, one hundred convicts, from various prisons, were sent out also, and the Bermuda Company was prayed to provide for a portion of them. —See E. D. Neill, *History of the Virginia Company of Loudon*, p. 163.

haueinge receiued such a rotten shypfull of Captaine Kendalls yeares of tobacco as would yeeld them litle or noething, and withall haueinge aduertisement from the Gouernour of the meane and weake condition that he found the Ilands in the point of fortification, wherby they sawe it likely that the redresse therof (which was so vnauoidably necessary) would proue a matter of charge, they became (I saye) well nigh in an vtter dispayre of the subsistance of this plantation, and the rather because this drugge of tobacco, wheron (as their staple commoditie) they had fixt their hopes, like a rotten reede, came into their hands (not to saye hearts) when they especially wer to be vpheld by it. It was, therfore, the generall cryo and conclusiue apprehension amongst them that some newe commodities must be sodainely sett on foote to serue in poore tobaccoes roome: marry, to tell what this should be was (indeed) the mistery. Whervpon Captaine Tucker (who, by being a dilligent commer to the courts, became priuye to all this), catchinge hold of this opportunitie the very next court-daye after, proposed a pretie proiect of makeinge of suger, the which he offered vnto the Company vpon thes tearmes: that himselfe in person would goe that voiage, and carry with him, vpon his owne purse and the purse of his friends, a sufficiencye of men and materialls to erect an injenio, in consideration wherof he demanded the one halfe of all such suger as by him should so be made, tellinge them wonders of the hopefull increase of the canes ther, and what a great quautitie of ground he knew to be fitt for them. This proposition was at the first highly approued, and in great likelyhoode to be generally swallowed, had it not come interlaced with some odde prouisoes vpon the by, among the which one maine extrauagant one was that himselfe and all his might be absolutely freed from all commands of the Gouernour, the which was held as well extreamely and vnreasonably ambitious, as vtterly irreguler and impossible; sortinge, indeed, only to make that boast good which he had not forborne improuidently ynough to vent dureinge his rule here : that by some such slight as this, by him fastned vpon the Aduenturers, he would make his returne to thes Ilands, and dwellinge in his braue house at the ouerplus, ther braue the Gouernour, who so euer he wer, to his face. But, howsoeuer, by reason of thes distastes, this captaine was not accepted of for the suger vndertaker; yet went that bussinesse on by other meanes and other hands, as we shall see hereafter. The only point herein that especially disturbed the Gouernour was that by reason therof, being stricktly enioyned, and the Kings name vsed vnto him to that purpose, to employe and (in a manner) force the people (who wer extreamely vnwillinge and backward vnto it, and did litle lesse than laugh out at the proiect) to betake themselues to a generall planteinge of suger-canes. He not only doubted that the Aduenturers would find themselues farr shortned (if not quite deceiued) of their golden hopes this waye, but also plainely found that he was of necessitie to giue ouer and desist from all such entendments in matter of fortification, as he was fully resolued to haue prosecuted that winter, and found the Ilands in want of, as being very desirous to leaue them in sufficient case and condition in that kind before his leauing of them.

Another point in the generall letters that disgusted the Gouernour was the fastnesse and constancye that he found in the Company to the non-diuident of tobacco here, for haueinge at his comeing awaye receiued from them an order of court, in thes wordes :—

" That to preuent wroung to the owners, all tobacco and other commodities which wer to be diuided betweene the owners and tenants, should be sent into England vndeuided, with a note vnder the Bayleyes hand, what portion belonged to each person ; accordinge whervnto a iust diuision and distribution should be made, as the same should be sold in England, etc., at his arriuall"—

he found so many inconueniences, difficulties, and litle lesse than impossibilities in the effectinge of it, together with the infinite discontent that he should generally giue vnto the people by it, as he gladly and greedely layde hold vpon an excuse (luckely offered) of freeinge himselfe from the execution therof for that yeare ; and in the interim, writeinge very earnestley to the Company for the reuerseinge of and employeinge the assistance of his ablest freinds to that purpose, he was in good hope to cleare himselfe absolutely from so odious a taske, when (contrary to his expectation) he finds by thes letters a newe re-inforcement putt vpon him, enioyneinge the strickt and exact prosecution therof by all meanes possible.

Some other perticulers ther wer in them also that liked them not, as the ouer-credulitie he perceiued among most of them, in their receipt, naye, welcomeinge, of all false and groundlesse informations, the ill expression and bad coherence which he obserued in the very letters themselues, as seemeinge rather contriued with artificiall obscurities and incompatible iniunctions, wherby he might rest confounded and entrapt, than plaine and direct dealeinge to giue information. But because you may the better iudge whether thes grounds of his discouragement and discontents wer truely and causefully taken or noe, and that withall you may the more succinctly and perspicuously vnderstand howe he behaued him-selfe in them, and in what manner and fashion he continued the passages and carriage of thes affayres, I haue thought it not amisse to deliuer vnto you the true coppies of the generall letters, together with his replye, verbatim ; and this the rather also that the garbe and forme of the writeinge one vnto another may be seene in their natiue and true dressinges and trimme ; and first (as the occasion and ground of the replye) of the generall letters written vnto the Gouernour, the stile wherof was—

To the right worshypfull, our very good freind, CAPTAINE NATHANIELL BUTLER, ESQUIRE, *Gouernour of the Sommer Ilands.*

The contents of the letters as followeth :—

"Sir, we receiued your letters by the *Garland*, which arriued here about the third of March, being glad to hear of your safe arriuall, with your company, whose proceedeings we praye God to prosper. The first that we obserue in your letters is, that certaine Dutch and English vessells fell vpon your Ilands; which, as we vnderstande by others, wer victualled out againe, for their seruices and proceedeings vpon the West Indies; wherby we conceiue the Ilands are the more vnfurnished with victualls for the inhabitants and thoes rouers ayded by you to thoes ill seruices, for which we are here accused and charged by the state to be accessory to Pyracye, whereof we saye noe more, till we come to speake of Powell and his consorts. We are sory for the losse of the *Warwick*, and for the burneinge of the platforme in the Kings Castle, and thoes other disasters you mention, which we hope you will endeuour with all diligence to repayre. Your agreement with the *Garland* for threepence fraught vpon tobacco we haue performed, and threepence more we sett vpon it, to defraye charges for the publick, as by the invoice vnder the husbands hand may appeare vnto you. Many necessary men you write for, as carpenters, smithes, gunners, etc., and many prouisions to be sent for the publick, the which for want of a publick store we cannot accomplish; for, in truth, the whole returne being noethinge but a quantitie of very vile condicioned tobacco, neither well cured, nor well made vp, noe man would consent for all the perswasions could be vsed in two generall courtes, to yeeld aboue three pence for the publick charge; which three pence, and that other for fraught, many men esteeme to be more than their rotten tobacco is worthe, whereby, for a great part of it noethinge at all is payed, and so it remaines packt vp in ware-houses and sellers, wher for ought we see, the owners entend to let it lye, rather than giue six pence to fetch it out; whereby you may iudge of our abilitie and the planters of our incouragement. We knowe it was not your fault, as being done before you came thether, but we rest vpon your word and creditt that the next shall be better to make amends; and for returne thereof we haue nowe furnished and sett out this magazin shyp, in this calme time of the yeare, as your selfe desired, that she may be ther in such due time as to bring awaye the first and prime crop of tobacco, and to arriue with all here before winter shall approach; as for their second crop, which we perceiue they putt altogether, it doth but spoyle and discreditt all, better to cast it awaye than send it.

"We haue resolued here by an order of a great court to take in hand a newe course for the benefitt of that plantation, which we doe earnestly recommend to your dilligent care to see effectually performed, wherby the people may be withdrawne from their excessiue toyle and plantinge about tobacco, which brings vs neither proffitt nor reputation; which is, that euery share of land, one acre at least of such ground as is fittinge, be planted with suger-canes, and in like manner one acre at least be planted with vines. Heere are those who haue vndertaken to goe in hand to erect an injenio to grinde and boyle the canes into suger, and if need be to erect another or more injenioes in places more conuenient for the planters to bring their canes to grinde; the worckmen to haue one-third part of the suger brought to such perfection as we haue agreed, and the other two-thirds to owners and planters. And for the vines, being once growen to beare, the planters shall haue sufficient instruction to make their wine wholy for themselues and their owners. We vnderstand ther is good store of suger-canes in sundry places of the tribes, we praye you fayle not to take some course that, vpon reasonable tearmes, ther may be a distribution from them that haue plentie to thoes that want, wherby we may vnderstande by the next, that all shall be furnished with more or lesse, and that they be all charged expressly to multiplye and encrease their beginninge of plants till all be complete, and also to keepe both them and their vines fenced and weeded from annoyance of cattell and vermine, and also from the force of violent windes that may shatter them in pieces. This to begin and effect, shall be your reputation and exceedinge creditt, not without recompence, for which wholy we relye vpon you and leaue it to your charge.

"Sundry complaints are here made of the bayliefs, by planters and owners, as that they are not diligent in their places, especially as touchinge the tobacco, betwixt the masters and their seruants, that therin they doe not farther seruice than to take the thirtieth part, due to themselves; for which, to satisfie the complainants, it is agreed that the sayd bayliffs shall relinquish the sayd thirtith part, and shall noe more exact it as their due, but in all other thinges shall doe their dutyes belongeinge to their place. We haue here with all sent a magazin of goods, though not so great as we would, yet accordinge to the meanes and smale encouragement sett out by a fewe priuate men, and with all a Cape-merchant, the bearer hereof; we praye you, let him not want your assistance to followe his commission giuen him, as well in sales as gettinge in debts for this and old accounts, as he shall haue cause to vse your helpe.

"We haue, for this once, accepted and payed your bill of exchange £22, being the first, and we hope the last, president in that kind.

"Diuers men write from thence that you want corne, which by this we haue in some measure, as well for the publick as by porticuler men to their famelies supplied; but it hath cast a great aspersion and discreditt vpon our plantation, that, after such plenty ther as formerly hath bin boasted of, ther should now, by their slouth and negligence be a wast.

" Diuers of the tribes haue written that if we will send them for euery tribe a preacher, they will maintaine them at their charge, euery tribe, one; for they hold it too much for them and theirs to goe so far to deuine seruice when three tribes are tied to one congregation. If that be generally their opinion, we desire it vnder the hands of the cheife of the tribes and in what manner of competencye they will maintaine them, and we will endeauour to satisfie their desires with as much expedition as we can.

" Here is also complainct made of impositions layd vpon planters for warrants, passes, and such like, which some inferior substitutes doe exact of them; we praye you suppresse such incroachments, that ther be noe cause of farther complaincts.

" We doubt not but the decree of the Honorable Lords is ere this time put into execution touchinge the ouerplus land to be deuided, which we would haue performed, according to the lordshyps arbitrement.

" We pray forgett nott to doe right in this point of your instructions, that men complaincinge of their seruants for refuscinge their seruices, and betakeinge themselves to other men, may be redressed; and by name we recommend vnto you the case of one Nicholas Gabry, sometime seruant to one Mr. Caswell, who was transported at his charge, and supplied by him, now resident at Pembroke tribe; this man is here chalenged by Mr. Caswell, and to haue justice done him, which we desire you may be performed, being the second time we haue written in this case. And also one Roger Llwellin to be restored to Mr. Roberts, whose seruant and apprentice he is testified to be.

" Ther was a communion cup, with other furniture, sent as a guift to Pembroke tribe, we pray you returne certificate from your selfo and some cheife of that tribe, which may be here registered, to satisfie the world that that tribe is possessed with it.

" All the negroes left ther by Captaine Argolls shyp and the other pinnace, let them be deliuered to the right honorable the Erle of Warwick, his officers, or seruants, as his lordship himselfe shall direct, and the marriners of the treasorour sent home, they payeinge their fraught.

" John North and Nathaniell his brother, which haue bin long ther, and, as is sayde, take great paines in fishinge and other labours, are desired by their freinds here, with great importunitie, either to be remoued to the tribes, or so disposed in the generall, that as they labour for others so they may take some benefitt with them for whom they labour.

" Here is a note annexed from Mr. Daniell Tucker, subscribed with his name, conteyueinge a perticuler of such thinges as he desireth may be rendred vnto him, which he ther left behind, as belonginge and due vnto him, which the Company haue thought good should be recommended vnto you, not doubtinge but you will cause him to be righted, that he may noe more importune nor complaine of iniustice. We cannot perticulerrize in our letters euery mans case and complainct, therfore we have resolued that an order of Court hereafter and the coppy therof sent vnto you, vnder the secretaryes hand by whomsoeuer shall signifie so much vnto you, as if our letters did mention the same.

"We pray you let thoes of the generallitie employe themselues in plantinge of suger-canes and vines, as well as others, that by their industry therin they may be mainteyned hereafter.

"Complainct is made that here to fore there hath bin an abuse of shooteinge of the ordinance, wherof so much hurt hath ensued, and prodigall expence of powder in the ilauds vpon euery slight and vaine occasion to salute the comeinge, and goeinge, and landinge, and jollitie of gouernours, captaines, and shyps, which custome and abuse his maiestie hath here forbidden vpon the Thames at his comeinge and goeing from Greenwich and other places which are intimated vnto you, as an example to followe, which we doubt not but that in your wisdome and prouidence you will.

"We haue sent you a smale remembrance, which you shall receiue by the master, viz., one rundlett of sack and two suger lofes.

"The order of Court for all tobacco to be sent into England and deuided here, hath bin considered of, and is agreed shallbe continued and be of force.

"The last thinge we mention vnto you is that we cheifly recommend to be remembered, and it is vpon occasion of Powells being with you, whom your people call Captaine Powell, and by whom we lately receiued letters from you; this man as you knowe hath his recourse by commission from the States, with other Dutch and English, to the West Indies, from whence they haue retired, and made their rendeuous at the Sommer Ilands, wher bringinge suger, oyle, and other victualls gotten by trade or pillage, we knowe not whether, but being such thinges as please the people well, they willingly entertaine him and such others with great applause. Against thes enterprizes and practises we haue here to fore giuen you speciall warneinge and directions in your instructions, which we meruaile you doe not better obserue, nor see the danger that may ensue. And amongst others, that Mr. Lang, your preacher,[5] should so applaud and seeke by his eloquent letters to winne vs to the likeinge and approucinge of thoes courses, sayeing we must by all meanes endeauor and seeke to weaken our enemies, and help to pull downe the members of Anti-Christ, with other such like reasons, the common obiections of our modern theeues when they meane to robbe the Spaniarde. Once againe we admonish you, and praye you that this affectinge of such purchase may be layde aside, not alone for the vnlawfullnesse of it before God, but likewise for the danger may hereby

---

[5] The preacher recorded to have arrived in the *Sea Flower* (*ante*, p. 142). He is not otherwise known.

ensue to us, by complainct of the Spanish that we suffer and abett you in thes courses, wherby his maiestie may rightly recall our patent for abusciuge of it, but cheifly to your selues, by sufferinge such to haue accesse, to be familier with your entrance and land strength, as may sone consort with others like themselues to surprize your fortes on a soudaine, and to make thoes ilands theirs, which may proue a strouug fort for thecues and a greater plauge for christians than is Algier by the Turquish pyrates, than which, if such a meicheife should so fall out, it had bin better they had neuer bin borne that are the causes of it. And assure yourselues, though carelesse securitie maye make you not to feare it, yet thoes pyrates abroad haue an aimeinge at it, and your owne people by knoweing them too well, will yeeld to take their partes, when you shall not be able to with stand it; and the Spanish knoweinge the entercourse of rouers to thoes ilands (as they doe already), doe hold it intollerable to be suffred, and is likely will iustly make an attempt to roote you out, when neither you nor wee shall preuent it. If all this may not suffice to cause you to banish all entertainement of thes, that they may not so much as harbour in your rodes, nor come ashore, and that you doe not stricktly restraine your owne to goe out in such cases, wee shallbe forced to take such farther courses and direction from his maiestic as shall be requesite in this case to redresse it.

"We would glady receiue from you and your counsell a note, specific-inge what number and manner of ordinance and munition is ther at this present for the safetye of the ilands, for we find that a great quantitie and number haue bin thither sent and left, and wer at Captaine Tuckers comeinge thence, and store of powder.

"Mr. Caswell has here moued the Court to write vnto you in the be-halfe of his brother in lawe John Ward, who formerly was in question criminally, and afterwards pardoned, which the Court approueth so far forth as their letters patents allowe, and doe pray you in his behalfe that he may be well reputed and esteemed ther, so far as he behaues himselfe orderly and well, without any imputation of thinges formerly passed.

"Also we desire that the requests of Mr. George Smithe, accordinge to an Order of Court, may be effected. We earnestly praye you that this shyp may not be stayed ther, but dispatched to returne with all speede possible. If this litle magazin be not better respected and satisfied by the inhabitants noe man will hereafter aduenture, they puttinge all their trash tobacco vpon it. And so leauinge you, together with your charge, to the protection of the Almightie, we rest your very loueing freinds.

Subsigned with diuers of the Lords and many of the cheife of the merchands, wherin the pointes that the Gouernour found, in his opinion, strange and vnreconcile-able, wer; first, in that place wher he is enioyned that all the tobacco be sent undeuided into England; and yet presently after, in two other places, he is prayed, admonished, and charged, to haue an especiall care for the good of the magazin that the payments be made in good tobacco, that ther be present pay, and old debts gotten in by his assistance. He sawe not how he could act the one but must violate the other. If all the tobacco wer sent for England, accordinge to that first iniunction, how could the magazin be presently payed, as the second required, if the magazin wer presently payed in good tobacco, and old debts recouered, how could all the tobacco be sent for England? Another perticuler (which he apprehended to be perplext and obscure) was concerneinge Powell and the receipt of the Dutch. In the beginninge wherof thes very men and shyps are by themselues confessed to be commissioned from the states of the vnited Prouinces (allyes and freinds to his maiestie), and yet sodainely after, by the same hands, they are styled pyrates and rouers, and strickt commands (not without threats) imposed vpon him by all meanes to keepe them out of his harbours, and in all thinges to vse them as enemies, by which course he nowe found him selfe to seeke how to distinguish in thes kinds betwixt honest men and theeues, if such as had lawfull and authentique commissions wer to be held as pyrates, who wer the seamen and marriners that he was to take for honest men? If men lawfully commissioned wer to be esteemed and used as honest men, why are thes with such feruour excluded? And, besides, who could haue imagined (vnlesse by inspiration) that thoes wer to be held for knaues, and shutt out of dores, in thes Ilands, when the very same passe for true men, and are dayly receiued into all harbours of England, and vsed as freinds?

Some other thinges and passages ther wer besides (as he tooke them) that gaue him iust cause to wonder at the letters, and misdoubt for himselfe, for which I will referre you to this his ensueinge answer, thus entitled:

To the right noble and worthy the Lords and others of the Honorable Company of Aduenturers, for the Summer Ilands.

"Right Honorable Company,—I begin thes my letters wher my last ended, at the *Garlands* leaueinge of us, when findinge noethinge more important than some newe worcks of fortification and renewments of the old, I presently fell vpon them. This last past yeare therfore I haue in this kind perfected thes pieces followeinge :—First, I have sunck a plattforme vpon that rock which flaunckers the Kings Castle, being the very same that by an Order of the Court you haue here to fore enioyned to be fortefied, yet neuer aduentured vpon vntill nowe, and upon it I have planted fiue peeces of good ordinance, three wherof wer with much toyle (and some perticuler charge to my selfe) weighed out of the wreackt *Warwick*, and now they all of them playe with great freedome and aduantage vpon that harbours chanell; their carriages are all newe of cæder ; I have, besides (as an accomplishment of that worck), raysed a smale redoubt of cæder, muskett proofe, to secure and gard thoes ordinance, and haue honored the whole peece (being such a one, I hope, as may aduenture it selfe vpon a censure) by nameinge it South-hampton Fort. This being perfected, I began the recouery of the burnt redoubt in the Kings Castle, which is restored, and vnder it I have cutt (out of the maine rock) a conuenient plattforme, wheron, vpon newe carriages, I haue mounted seven peeces of great ordinance, which are of great vse, for the foundringe of any shyp that shall attempt a passage by force, as being lodged to shoote into her hould ; and besides they command into euery nooke of the harbour, and I haue bin bold to call it Deuonshyres Redoubt. From hence I went to the other plattforme, that shootes it selfe more out to sea-ward, wher, findinge scarce two peeces seruiceable, I haue newed and renewed all of them with substantiall carriages, and remounted the peeces. So that you haue at this present three and twentye peeces of ordinance in gard of the harbours mouthe, wher you had not fiue any way seruiceable at mine arriuall ; and nowe I dare (modestly) affirme it to be sufficiently fortified. As for the harbour of St. George's, it is too far short of being so, yet must rest as it is, vnless you will allowe meanes to succour it. I haue also this sommer finished the framed Churche at St. Georges, and when you send me bells, it shall haue a steeple. The mount likewise is up againe, and seuen foote higher than before. I hope it will proue long-liued, to which end I haue giuen it a trianguler forme, and keyed it at the corners below with substantiall postes. You have also a newe storehouse vpon the warrfe at St. Georges. I have builded, likewise, eight newe botes, and dispersed them to the gunners of the fortes whoe had none before, and the rest are with me at the towne to answer all occasions.

"And thus hath this yeare bin expended in thes kindes of worcks, the which I layd hold vpon the accidentall helpes I then found, and am nowe to part with all, so that nowe I knowe not how to serue you any farther this waye, for nowe I haue not meanes left me so much as to manne out a bote to sea, nor hands ynough to sett my corne, especially being of necessitie to cleare ground in St. Dauids Iland to that end, wher I haue layd out accordinge to your order of Court two hundred acres of land, for the reliefe of the owners of Bedford tribe, and I haue sent you the plott of it, and the overplus land is also punctually distributed, after the Lords decree, wher are twentye acres of excellent good ground, more (I thinck) than you expected.

"This yeare also (being instructed by you) we haue held our generall assembly at St. Georges, in the newe church, and all the Acts passed therein, are presented to your confirmeinge approbation, and in hope we are that you will not stricktly examine our defects, but consideringe it was our first, rather encourage us to a second.

"We haue also (thancks be to God) fully recouered our plenty of all thinges, and have a good hope to haue it secouded by this winters crop; yet we thanckfully acknowledge your care of us in prouision of meale, which (though we haue corne ynough besides) shall not be abused in excesses, to which I am a sworne enemye; the truth is that thes your prolefull islands cannot (vnlesse extreamely wroung'd by wasts and negligence) lye long vnder that burthen, and therfore all the aspersions and discreditts you mention, duely placed, are indeed to fall vpon the persons, not the place; yet let me tell you that you vnderstand it not amisse when you stile some mens reportes of their well leauciuge of them to be but boastes.

"Being thus growen ready for the magazin shyp, and soner than ordinaryly in the yeare lookeinge out for her (as hopeinge that some of our meane aduertisements might be fastened vpon you), we made a sayle, which fallinge with our harbour of St. Georges, proued a smale barck belonginge to one Mr. Delbridge, a brother of your Company, fraughted she was with well chosen country boyes, and a smale magazin of goodes cheifly ordained for his owne people here. By her we had newes of your magazin shyps approach.

"Vpon Munday, the one and twentieth of August, we had sight of this your *Joseph*, who, although she came merely in vnto us, yet made us sadd when she was come, for she had throwne ouer bord twenty of her passengers, and was full of sick folk, so that diuers of them haue not only died since on shore but also began an infection amongst us; the which notwithstanding (by Gods mercye and the bountye of our ayre) we wer sone ridd of. In all other respects, bothe herselfe and goodes wer well conditioned.

"By her I receiued your generall letters, wherin the first ill newes I mett with was the misse of my neccessary men, as carpenters, smythes, especially gunners, without which how can the continuall decayeinge carriages of your ordinance be supplied, or so much as hookes made for your people to fish; or to what purpose haue I fiftie good peeces of ordinance nowe well mounted within three miles compass of me?

"As for the last yeares rotten crop of tobacco (if you please to remember) I wrote to you suspiciously of it then, and sory I am I proued so true a prophet. But the imposition of three pence on the pound is yet obserued to amount well nigh to a thousand pounds sterlinge, and glad the people would haue bin to haue found a litle more of it bestowed towards a publick securitie. I am bound vnto you for your acquittinge of me from that of which I hope I shall neuer be guiltie: I meane of being the least cause of this badd ware; nor shall I fayle you in my word nor breake creditt with you, but performe my very best and most attentiue endeauour, so far as my skill and authoritie can exact an amends; but I doe not remember that I wrote so absolutely of this point, as you tell me of.

"Your newe resolution in your great Court about sugar-canes and vines I wish may fall to your wish, yet I hold myselfe bound to tell you freely that I find not the grounds therof answerable to your hopes. True it is that the canes at St. Georges and els-wher growe conueniently well saue that they are extraordinary short in the iointes), but ther can not be found one share among twentye that will afford one acre fitt for them; yet shall I giue life to your injunction with all diligence; and to this end I have already made a passage through the tribes where I find the people generally in distaste of it, and many of the best vnderstanders altogether dispayreinge of any good effect, and much they seeme to wonder that any experience fetched from hence should begett such a proiect. As for certain propositions produced in open court, pretended vpon thes respects, but entended to enfringe the commission, it hath pleased you to hold me capable of, and with all fallsly conueyeinge close imputations to the woundinge of my reputation, I shall neuer belieue that so noble and iust hands as yours will euer subscribe to their passage, nor I hope shall I euer deserue it.

"Concerneinge vines here, I confesse they conserned me much this Springe, for so admirably wer they taken and sett at the first, that I verily thought to haue presented you with a vessell of Sommer-Ilands wine, and to that end had them diligently tended and fenced, but when I expected their matureing, not one cluster of fiue hundred came to perfection, but groweinge into a kind of harduesse and shyneinge like a horne, they still proued rotten instead of being ripe. Whence this cause of miscarriage and sicknesse proceedes some vigneron must tell you.

"But since you are so graciously inclined to proiectors, giue me leaue to proue one among the rest. I am perswaded that there is not a fayrer hope of any staple commoditie from hence (besides tobacco) than the makeing of silcke; the sweet aire and excellent temperature which we enioye are exceedinge naturall for the wormes. The mulberry trees also (as far as I remember) are altogether resemblant to thoes I haue seene in the best silck makeinge places, and they encrease exceedingly and will be quickly in infinite numbers. Neither is the obseruation to be slighted, much lesse despiced, that such spiders here as worck abroad, make perfect silck, both in respect of strength, substance, and colour. As for the discouragements you haue formerly receiued herein from one Peter, a Frenchman, I am credibly informed by diuers here that protest they heard it from his owne mouthe in London, since his returne, that he hath sayd that ther are not better trees nor a better place in the world than thes Ilands for that end; and being asked why then he reported the quite contrary vnto you, his answer was that otherwise he should neuer haue gotten home to his country, and that he staruedthe wormes on purpose to that entent. Ther is noe great cost belongs to this experiment, and if you shallbe pleased to make it once againe whilst I am in your seruice, I shall not fayle you in any part hereof belonginge vnto me. For the desire you haue to drawe the people from their excessiue toyle and plantinge of tobacco, you saue me that labour, and haue taken the best of courses for it by your non diuident order of tobacco, as I shall farther manifest when I come to that poynt, and you will find I feare the next crop doe I what I can.

"Accordinge to your commands, the bayliffs are commanded from their thirties, euen this yeare, for so some ioyfull and not lesse than insultiue letter of priuate men expound your generall, which eles might haue bin more charitably enterpreted; yet are they enioyned to the due execution of their places (as your will is also), at which they shake their heads and quote scripture to me, that the labourer is worthy of his hire, and noe man goeth on warfare vpon his owne cost; and truly I am perswaded if they had bin but heard before they had bin condemned (I meane the most of them), they would not haue appeared so vnworthy as you deliuer them unto me. Full well you knowe that none are more obiected to malice and slaunder than publick men, and I haue heard that the inconuencies are many and weightie that may ensue the giueinge awaye, by an ouer-ready beliefe and applause, to the traduceinge of such. Howsoever, sure it is that it must needs make ill for me and my commands when all my subordinate officers are to serue me thus, vpon their owne purses, as voluntaryes.

" I haue recouered as much amber-greece as amounts in all to twentye eight ounces three quarters and a halfe. I haue payed the finders here their moyetye, after your Order of Court), the which at the rate of three pounds the ounce (for so much I haue allowed them) ariseth to fortie three pounds six shillings three pence. You allowe me, by the same order, ten groates on euery ounce which cometh to foure pounds and fifteene shyllings, so that the totall due to me is fortie eight pounds one shillinge and three pence. The amber-greece shallbe presented into your court, if it please you to make payment vnto the bringer therof of my part of due and disbursements for you, it is all of it yours. If you thinck I have payed ouer much for it at three pounds the ounce, I will buy your part at that rate, and so make it all mine. Likely it is that by reason of the dryeinge by keepeing, ther will be some losse in the waight, which I leaue to your consideration.

"The bill of exchange I charged vpon you the last yeare (which it seemes you misliked) was forced vpon me vpon thes grounds. At my first arriuall I found a generall wast, not only in perticular for my priuate famely, but in stuff for botes, in sayles, netts for fishinge, cloathes for your negroes, and the like publick vses. Vpon pittyfull complainct in thes cases, I made enquirie after courses formerly held, and was generally answered that whilst ther was generall magazins the custome was to take up so much for such vses as was found needfull to supply thoes necessities, and so to returne it vpon the aducuturers; wherupon, conceiueing this to be the same in effect, and haueing as great a necessitie layd vpon me as euer had any, I presumed to followe thoes presidents, which you nowe tell me you neuer found before, and are in hope neuer to doe againe. Informe me then, I beseech you, how shall your publick botes attendinge the fortes be furnished? how are your negroes to be kept from goeinge naked? and what meanes els are ther to recouer mattocks, shouells, grabbinge axes, and the like tooles requireable for fortinge? For it is not your meaninge nor expectation sure, that the Gouernours peculier entertainement (especially being at the passe that mine is) shallbe lyable to this change? if it be, he will haue but a very hard bargaine of it. You haue three hundred and odde smale shott in thes Ilands, which continually require trimmeinge, for ther is noe place (by reason of the aire of the sea) that more cankers arms than this, and yet you neuer allowed me one drop of oyle towards it. Hetherto I haue performed it with mine owne store, but can doe it noe longer.

"The impositions for warrants, passes, and the like, which you mislike so, were neuer made other by me, or any of mine, than I found presidented vnto me by my predecessors, euery one of them. The secretary is allowed one halfe pound of tobacco only vpon a warrant, and (me thincks) he deserues it, consideringe his penns, inck, paper, and paines. I protest vnto you if I find any of mine officers a dishonest incroacher in any of thes iniurious kindes, I shall make him an example, and I belieue they expect noe lesse.

"As for the wastes you feare of powder, and the jollitie (as you tearme it) of Gouernours, captaines, and shyps, I thinck (though indeed I haue found more cause of doubt this waye than euer I could imagine)

that noe tounge hath presumed to be so bold with you, as to informe
againſt me in that kind. Myselfe and your gunner practice with dumbe
signes to saue your powder, for well we knewe what smale quantitie we
had, and nowe feare how litle we shall haue. I questioned Mr. Kendall
about the overmuch lessinninge (for one yeare) of that store of powder;
as it is sett downe in the inuentory, left him by Captaine Tucker,
whose answer was that Captaine Tucker at his goeinge awaye commanded that all the ordinance in your Islands should expresse (as all
thinges els did) a ioyfull partinge, and that thence grewe both that wast
of powder and dismountance of your ordinance; when I depart, therefore, I will doe it sylently.

"I have recciued the one rundlett, and two suger-lofes, which it
pleaseth you to style a smale remembrance, but thanckfully I hold it a
great one, because it comes from you. Your constancye to your owne
order of Court, against the dindent of tobacco here was no soner here
but in the tribes, and scarce had I reade your letters before many
lamentyinge men came vpon me. Sir (sayth one), I am a kind of
chirugien, and haueinge cured many this yeare vpon creditt, I nowe
heare I am to goe into England for payment. I haue lent corne (sayth
another) this last hard winter, to be payed in tobacco this yeare, and
saued some liues with it, must I goe to London for it? A third tells
me in plaine tearmes, that since matters are come to this passe, he will
not sett one plant of tobacco all the next yeare, whom (for example
sake) I clapt by the heeles. But vpon thes forewarneinges, aduiseinge
with the counsell how to satisfie you, and keepe a quiett here, it was
thus resolved, and is answerably performed, I hope, without offence to
you. First, that noe man shall diude his tobacco, vnlesse he can produce
vnder his vndertakers hand an admittance and couenant for a diuision,
or giue in a certificate vpon oathe, that he hath recciued noe supply at
all this yeare from England. Secondly, that in respect of many detts
growen betwixt partye and partie vpon most vrgent occasions, as to
smithes for fish-hookes and tooles, carpenters for botes, etc.; it was
found necessary that for this yeare all single detts vnder the value of
fiftie pounds of tobacco should be discharged and payed out of the
lumnipe of euery such deptors crop, a note being to be putt in that so
much is to be defaulked at the diuision with you out of his part. And
I earnestly craue that in theis deuisions with you ther may be all equall
and iust respect had to the content of the people here, otherwise I haue
much cause to feare that their clamours will proue both loude and
dangerous.

"As for the extraordinary Dutch and English that haue bin here this
yeare, I must confesse myselfe mistaken in the receipt of them; and yet
I aduised with your instructions before their admittance; wher findeinge the title pyrate giuen to such as wer to be excluded, and authentique

commissions with these, I therby became (I nowe perceiue) ouer bold to distinguish ; and with the more ease was I hurried to this boldnesse, as well in respect that at that time we wer in great and vrgent need of their refreshments, as also that such and the very same are harboured euerywher in England itselfe. But I will noe farther diue into this secrett; for the future your will shallbe absolutely performed, so that I hope to giue you noe farther occasions to meruaile at my misobseruances.

"Touchinge our preacher, Mr. Lang, and his eloquent letters, as you stile them, this is the first time I knewe or heard either of them or his eloquence.[6]

" As you would gladly receiue, so I haue as gladly sent you a note of all the ordinance and munition we haue, as well good as badd, and you may creditt it and call me to account; you haue the counsells hands to it also. Compareinge it likewise with the note you had from me the last yeare, in my generall letters, you may finde how I haue carried myselfe in matter of expence that waye, I desire, therfore, it may be publickly reade.

" You haue sent you also a certificate of the receipt of the communion cup, belouginge and bequeathed to Pembroke tribe.[7]

"That I haue not bin forgettfull of that point in your instructions which concernes seruants alienateinge themselues from their masters seruice, mine actions may witnesse for me, as also that lawe to that end ennacted in our generall assembly. As for the perticulers in this nature commended to my redresse I haue disposed of them after your prescriptions for I durst not vary; and yet I must needs saye that vpon due examination I found some materiall partes, and diuers circumstantiall, farr dissonant from what (I believe) you were possessed with all, so that I could wish (if not in my time, yet in some other mans hereafter better entrusted) that your absolute commands in thes kindes might be sweetened with some wholsome prouisoes and references ; for you can instruct me of the perill of groundinge a definitiue censure, vpon the hearesaye of one side only, and will teache me that euen very good men oft times are willfully blinded with selfe loue, and their owne interests.

"The annexed note you send me, subscribed with Mr. Daniel Tuckers name, conteyneinge a perticuler of such thinges as he desireth to be rendred vnto him hath had its full due from me: and yet haueing thus fully righted him, how can I be sure he will noe more importune nor complaine? if he hath charged me with iniustice in this point or any other (as your letters seeme to implye), I shall looke to be righted by him also. Straunge it is to me that you are pestred thus with plainctiffs

---

[6] See *ante*, p. 165.   [7] This cup has disappeared.

as you speake of: truely the grounds could not be fetched from mine (only) two monethes time, but it may be ther was noe other cause at all, saue their own willfull malice, or fond credulitie. The shyp, indeed, that went out from us the last yeare, I find (by some priuate informations) to be as fouly fraughted with falsse reportes as rotten tobacco; but I would it wer as well within my power to cure the one, as you may the other, so should ther be noe discontent. It is performed on your part, if you be but pleased to practise a suspension of beleife and censure, remembring that I am your publick seruant, and three thousand and some hundreds of miles distant from mine accusers.

"The crop of tobacco sent vnto you by this shypinge, hath a very generall hope settled vpon it of restoreing you to some contents what the courses haue bin, that I haue held to that end may appeare by a lawe enuacted to that purpose in our generall assembly, and it hath had its due execution. If we fayle nowe (which God forbidd) I shall find reason to encline to the commone voice that all our tobacco is absolutely spoyled at the sea, and this may either be by takeing in of salt-water, as certainely it did the last yeare, or (which I rather thinck) by being ouersone packt into the hott hould of the shyp, and so being newe and greene, and not haueinge had its due worckinge abroad, it becomes ouer heate, and so worcks out the very heart of it; and the rather I am induced to this beleife, vpon an experiment in mine owne case the last yeare: when haueinge bought a smale parcell of tobacco vpon the choycest iudgements here to present my freinds with all when it came into England, it proued as badd as the worst: when yet a rowle of the very same lumpe reserued, remains to this daye, exceedeinge well coloured, and very strong and good. If you will haue, therfore, perfect tobacco from hence, I am perswaded, you must be contented to lett it rest with us one winter before it be exported, and so fetch it awaye in the spring: neither should I one iott mistrust this our present crop, wer it not for being ouer hastely shypt. This I am full sure of, that at its partinge from us, it appeared to all mens vewe as fayre, likely, and well conditioned as need be. Well knowen it is that the Spanish tobacco remaines for the most part a whole yeare before it be shypt awaye: you may doe well (especially if you find yourselues still agrieued) to make a triall with us, by sendinge one bark (as hitherto) about September for the moyetye of our crop, and to leaue the other halfe vntill the spring, and then send out a second bark for that part, and so accordinge as you shall find cause and proofe to proceede or relinquishe. The charge of this course (the vessells being but smale) will be all one with the former, and besides one maine encouragement may be added herevnto: that as the season of the springe will be lesse dangerous, and more agreeable for your fresh-water soldiers and passengers, so the returne of your shypinge vnto you more certaine and opportune, and their staye and attendance here in harbour farr shorter, and so lesse chargeable. The winds likewise in the moneths of the springe are, for the most part, easterly with you, and so serue fayre to bring your shyps hether: and being here they seldome fayle of findinge of them fauorable homewards. For mine owne part I protest vnto you; I haue taken all the care that I posssble could to give you content in this perticuler. If I fayle for all this, I will account it one of my misfortunes, and yet will not dispayre of a fauorable censure, since it is not within the power of any one man in the world, nor of all of them to preuent all accidentall ills.

"The smale credence I find giuen in pointes of the highest nature, together with some captious apprehensions that I heare of, teach me to stand vpon my garde in the meanest. I pray, therefore, giue me warrantize what shallbe done concerneinge your ouer many bulls here: we haue of them almost as many of the one sex as the other. This yeare you haue fiue calues, and three of them bulls; it is apparent that they not only hazard a spoyle and miscarriage in the cowes, but by their continuall fights endanger one another. If I shall cause the old bulls to be gelt, it is ten to one but they die with all; but if not, and that they should scape, yet hereby will they sone make the only ground that we haue to breede them on (which is the only ground you allott me to make tobacco on), too straight and narrowe to sustaine them. In truth I must confesse I am not able to apprehend what benefitt may arrise to this plantation (in the peaceable condition it breathes in) by nourishinge steeres, or barren cattle here. Some ther are (they saye) that would possesse you with the excellencyes of makeinge them draught beastes for the plough; it may well be that they haue had more experience in that occupation, and are truer bred to it than myselfe, yet reason tells me that neither the vneuen surface and posture of our Islands, nor the exceedinge lightnesse of the soyle can either allowe or require them. To your absolute iniunctions in this, as in all other the like, I submitt mine executions here (for I would be loath to be found guiltye of the least contempt). Since, therefore, you haue me thus at your command, it followeth that you become the more aduised and wary in your commands; and soe we are on both sides likely to doe well, neither is ther lesse danger on the contrary.

"And thus (as I take it) I haue giuen you the full account of my submission and obedience to your general letters and orders of Court, as also of the general employments of myselfe in your seruice this last past yeare. Many other occasions, both for your publick and mine owne priuate, vrge me to enlarge myselfe vnto you as an humble suter, but I haue spedd but ill hetherto, and loath I am either to disquiett or discontent you in being solicited, or myselfe with being denied, and therefore with a resolute patience I forbeare, and attendinge all opportunities to expresse mine affectionate seruice, rest most ready to be commanded to my vttermost abilities. NATH. BUTLER."[7]

But before the ensealinge or writeinge of thes letters, within some fourteene days after the magazine shyps arriuall, the Gouernour made a passage through the tribes; the which he did, partly to take order for the generall plantainge of sugar canes, to acquaint the people with that iniunction, and to take a vewe of what quantitie of ground might be found proper for them, and partly to see the choyce of the triers of tobacco, and accordinge to the newe statute in that case prouided, to giue them their oathes, which being done, he returned to the towne; and presently vpon it, the first crop of tobacco (which he only looked after) being finished and made up, the triers fell generally to their taske, so that much falsse and badd ware was burned at the owners dores, notwithstandeinge findeinge both by heare saye and eye-sight, that the affayre and execution hereof was not so throughly and stricktly carried, as he entended it should be, and expected from them as sworne men, he caused newe quickeninge warrants for ye redresse of this conniuence to be directed downe to all the baylies the second time, the which once more sett the bussinesse on foote, so that fresh bonfires ensued, and some that had escaped the first brunt payed for it at the second. Within a while after, the people generally (being generally hasted and vrged by the Gouernour) brought up their tobacco to the shyppinge, the which being done, and about some sixtie thousand waight therof laded vpon her, after seuen weekes staye, she cleared herselfe of the harbour, and made her waye for England, the which was the shortest time for staye, and sonest time in the yeare, that euer magazin shyp yet made in thes Ilands since the plantation.

[7] There is no trace of this vigorous letter, or of the one to which it is a reply, in the *Colonial Records*, now extant; hence, it has no place in the *Memorials of Bermuda*.

Ther went passengers in her for England the quondam Gouernour, Captaine Kendall, and Mr. Lewes [Hughes], the minister. About fourteene dayes before her, the smale barck of the west country of England (formerly mentioned) had taken her leaue, and vpon her had bin laden to the quantitye of about ten thousand weight of tobacco more.

Noe soner wer thes shyps departed and of from the coast but a new sayle is discouered, and proueth the same of which intelligence had bin giuen by the magazin shyp. She was called the *George*, and came fraughted only with newe men and supplies. She came in generally well conditioned; only in the action of fallinge vpon the shore she was in danger, for haueinge not carefully ynough lookt out for the Ilands, and the wind bloweing a stiff gale at southeast all the night, she found her selfe by breake of day so nere to the rocks, which was her lee-shore, as justly made her affrayed; so that the Castle gineinge the alarme by peepe of day, the Gouernour, at the heareinge therof, concluded that if it wer a shyp that occasioned it, she must needs be in perrill, and therupon presently went in person up to the mount; by which time, the daye beginninge to breake and cleare, she was discerned close under the land, and within a cables length of the rocks called the Breakers. Whervpon she shott of a peece of ordinance for a pilote, but by reason that the sea went so exceedinge high, and the wind blewe fiercely in at the harbours mouthe, noe bote could gett out to her, though diuers essayes wer made, and the Gouernour himselfe at the fortes to vrge them vnto it. She was putt to it, therfore, to trust to her owne skill and fortune, the which proued so well, as within two houres after she safely moored herselfe in the Kings Castle harbour. By her the Gouernour receiued his second generall letters from the Company, the most part wherof consisted of reinforcements of the contents of the former; and in perticuler that point was vehemently vrged that concerned the ex-

Q

clusion of all straunge shyps, the feruencye wherof gaue occasion to the Gouernour to apprehend that some other secrett causes and motions masked vnder the colour of thoes published reasons were the life-giuers to that so elaborate and diligent a prohibition, in so much as to some of his most entrusted freinds he sticked not to saye that he perceiued well ynough that by such courses as thes the aduenturers aimed and entended to hold the like tie vpon the inhabitants of thes Ilands that the Spaniarde doth vpon his West Indies; and that they determined and ment to keepe them in a continuall necessary need of them, and affected not to haue them ouer-riche. He wondered also at that clause in the letters that enioyned him to send all Powells debts due vnto him from the people here vnto them into England, and was not sory that he had apparently noe meanes to effect it, at least, that yeare. By this shyp also the certaine knowledge of such as wer vndertakers of the proiect for suger-canes was brought, and a certaine refiner of suger was sent ouer to make an essaye, who, although he had (by his owne confession) neuer seene a suger-cane in his life (so little care is ther generally taken for a through experimentall knowledge in thes kindes), yet being presently sett on worck, and by the Gouernour assisted with canes and men, some smale quantitie of browne suger, which they call panele (and which with refineinge they saye proues very good) is produced, and sent ouer for an incouragement.

This shyp had not long biu in harbour before (by the well-nosed drunckerds of the Ilauds) she was discoucred to be well stufft with liquours, for the master of her (who was a true water-ratt), with his mates, and the rest of his compagnions, vnderstandinge the quick and nimble vent of that commoditie, had aboundantly prouided for themselues that waye; and, indeed, it is iucredibly straunge to report what a huge quantitie of thes hott composed waters are (mis) spent yearely in these smale Ilands. Will it euer be belicued (in England it selfe, which is yet too neere akinne to Germany in this; in Spaine and Italy certainely it can neuer) that twelue hundred persons (wherof the one halfe almost are women and children, and so noe drinckers in this nature) should in three moneths space only consume and emptye two thousand gallons of this hartburneinge geare, by powreinge it downe into their vaste mawes? And yet this is the least that (truely) can be sayd of it. Howsoeuer, certaine it is that the Gouernour, apprehendinge that by this meanes, through the extreame greedinesse of the people that waye (all the tobacco being already exported that was worthe any thinge for which it was wont to be bartred) that that smale store of coine which by diuers importations was gotten in amongst them would be exhausted and carryed awaye which was nowe (by reason of the non-diuident order) the only meanes left them of entercourse and commerce one with another, he caused a prohibition to be sett vp vpon the maine mast of the shyp, that noe marriner whatsoeuer should sell any thinge for mony, but that all sales should only be made by waye of exchaunge and bartringe for such commodities as the Ilands afforded of themselues, or vpon creditt; and this vpon the penaltye of the forfeiture of all such goodes and mony as (contrary to the sayd iniunction) should be found so to be bought and sold; all which notwithstandinge, ye contrary and breach hereof being aduentured vpon by some that hoped in a concealement, discoueries wer made vpon them and the penaltie inflicted, to the example of others.

This shyp made staye here of eight or nine weekes, vpon idle pretences and vaine excuses of her master, who, scrueinge by the moneth, cared not how long he lengthened out his voiage in a harbour. But at last (haueinge receiued some harsh speeches from the Gouernour in check of his negligence) vpon the first day of the newe yeare, he weyed anchor, and cleared himselfe of the Ilands, makeinge his voiage homewards by Spaine (being so enioyned by his owners), to the much wonder of many who held it a dangerous improuidence. And thus, also, ended the first yeare of Captaine Butler his gouerment.

With the very first of his second yeare he held his third generall assize at St. Georges; and (as at the former) a grand iury was empannelled, and two petye jurys. The Gouernour himselfe also gaue the charge, and satt as cheife iudge. At this session fewe criminall delinquents wer found at the barre, the which (as it seemed by his open profession) gaue him good content. The cheife act of note was concerneinge the bayliffs of the tribes, who wer all of them endicted vpon a neglect and breach of the newe statute in that case made and prouided, in not giueinge a beginninge and entrance in due time to the worck and buildinge of the publick bridges, to which, they pleadinge guiltye, wer fined by the Court in ten poundes of tobacco a man, to be bestowed towardes the erection of the sayd bridges; and this occasion was the rather layed hold on that by it (by waye of example) others might take heed how they offended in the like kind; for, since the bayliffs could not be spared, how wer others to expect it. Dureing this assize, it was also ordred, at the counsell table, that, wheras it had formerly bin a frequent practice to carry about in the night time palmitoe leaues, fired and flameinge, to the much feare and danger of honest ciuill people, in fireinge their houses and groundes; that from thence forward the sayd ill custome should be absolutely left of, and that vpon the penaltye of one hundred pounds of tobacco, to be inflicted vpon euery master or a famely or haluer so offendinge; and that all hired seruants, apprentices, and boyes in the like case should be carryed to the constable of the tribe and wipt. It was likewise concluded that all handy-craftsmen, as smithes, carpenters, and the like, were to take such paye as the present condition of the place could afford, that is to saye, tobacco, corne, potatoes, etc., and wer not to stand vpon tearmes of refusall to worck unlesse they had payment in ready mony, which was rarely to be had, as formerly they had used to doe. A rate also was proportioned and sett downe for the paye and alloweance for the ferry at Burnt Point, which was as that euery person from sixteene yeares old and upwards should paye one pound of tobacco by the yeare to the ferry-man, or whosoeuer els did vndertake to keepe it and discharge it sufficiently. At the same time an iniunction was layd vpon the churchwardens of all the tribes that they should meete together, at two generall prefixt dayes in the yeare; and so to giue information of all abuses concerneinge breaches of the Sabaoth, drunckennesse, incontinencye, and the like crimes, vnto some one man destinated and appointed by the Gouernour for that seruice; that therby their presentments might be the better prepared and fashioned against the time of assize. Diuers other controuersies wer nowe also heard and discussed, being matters of plea betweene partie and partie; and so, after two dayes expence, the sayd assize was finished and dissolued. The daye after was bestowed in a generall traineinge, all the bayliffs and prime men of the whole plantation being commanded to be in armes. They wer leade into the fieilde by the Gouernour himselfe, wher he likewise in person (for encouragement sake) exercised the battell of pikes, and commanded his liuetenant to doe as much with the shott, which, being done, he caused the whole company to be equallye deuided into two smale battalions, and to be opposed one against another; and then caused the wings of shott to be drawne out in single files to a skirmage, after the Irish fight, the which he openly mainteyned to be most proper for the Ilands, both in regard of the uneuennesse of the ground as the generall thick couerts; and, thus haueinge held them in the feild about foure or fiue houres, they

wer with commendations (as in truth many of them well
deserued, being for the most part very readye men) discharged and dismissed, euerye man to his owne home with
good content.

The towne being thus cleared of people, the Gouernour
presently began to pursue some other affayres; and with
the first (vpon notice giuen of the abuse and spoyle which
ensued by sufferinge of hogges to goe lose, especially to
the corne, suger-canes, and potatoes), he set out a proclamation of restrainct, wherby libertie was graunted (by waye of
penaltie vpon the offendor) for any man to kill and carry
awaye all such hogges as (after the date of the said proclamation) should be found runneinge lose abroad; but yet
with this prouisoe, that within foure and twentye houres
after, the partie so killinge of any of them should giue
notice thereof to the bayliff of the tribe, and produce profe
of due occasion. He at the same time made three newe
carriages for the ordinance in the lower plattforme of the
Kings Castle, and spent two dayes ther in clearcing of one
of the best peeces which had layne cloyed ouer euer since
Captaine Tuckers time, the which, with much difficultie and
after many trialls, was at last effected, the shott being much
rusted in the concauitie of the peece, and her touch-hole
fouly cloyed with peeces of yron. He then also caused
diuers peeces of newe ground at St. Georges to be planted
with suger-canes and vines. He built, likewise, a newe
large storehouse of framed cæder in a smale Iland, licing
nere vnto the townes-warfe, and fitted it for the receipt of
all generall newe supplies from England by euery shypinge,
the which was made with two dores for the easier conuay-
ence of goods in and out; by the former want wherof the
people had sustayned much spoyle and dammage in their
prouisions, which wer sometimes, by scarcetie of botes and
lack of staires, windes to carry them awaye, forced to lie
open to all weathers, a moneth or two before they could be

carried into the maine. Great store of lime was also commanded to be burnt, and the fort commanding the towne, called Warwick Castle, began to be repayred and perfected, the which being left vnfinished by Mr. Moore, and neglected by Captaine Tucker, was conceiued by this Gouernour as a necessary accomplishment, both in regard to its being a sea marck as also that therin the women and children might be bestowed, and preserued from any soudaine fury of an enemye (it being a strength not hastely to be surmounted, but will require the mountance of some ordinance, and with all that it might appeare, so much the more worthy of the noble appellation it was distinguished by. This done, he made five newe carriages for the ordinance of Smithes-Fort and mounted the peeces upon them, the old English carriages (which wer of elme) being rotten and unseruiceable. From thence he went to Pagetts Fort, where he layd a newe plattforme vpon the topp of the redoubt, and beateinge out a large and hansome porthole he mounted a good peece of ordinance vpon a newe carriage in the same place; and this was done by reason of the vnscruiceablenesse of the old plattforme lieing vnder it; the which, by being ouer-streight, afforded not any due mannagement of the ordinance, and by its lieinge ouer lowe, and too nere the sea, was so annoyed with the billowe, that euery fresh gale at east and northeast (which are the only proper windes to bring in shyps into that harbour, and so most require the vse of it), fills it halfe full of water, and so altogether disableth the ordinance from worckinge any good effect. This forte being thus releaued, the Gouernour begins to erect a newe fayre house of hewen stone at the towne, the which he makes with a flatt roofe, after the fashion which he had scene in other countryes in paralell with this, and he built it of that substance and forme also, by waye of example and envitement of others to doe the like, as most proper for the nature of the place and climate, in respect of titenesse against the violent dashes of raine, of strength against the mightie windes and soudaine hurricanoes, and for coolenesse, by the thicknesse of the walls and the forme of the roofe; and, besides, most necessary in regard of the substance; for the saueinge and preseruation of timber, which in a short time (if wasted as heretofore) must needs fall out very short and geason[1]; and yet, in all prouidence above all other thinges to be made much of, both for the vse of carriages for the ordinance and ye makeinge of the botes, wheras of stone ther is an unexhaustable store, and lime most easily burned. This house (when it was finished) he destinated to the publick seruice, and thence called it the Towne House, wherein was contriued (and fitted for the purpose) one very fayre and large roome (of 32 foote in length, and 22 in breadth) for the holdinge of the Generall Assembly.

Whilst thes thinges wer thus on foote in St. Georges Island and at the fortes, the bridges (which, as you haue heard, wer enioyned by an Act of Parliament, and the bayliffs ammersed and shent[2] for their neglect therin) are now throughly sett forwarde and in action in the maine, diuers carpenters being, by the Gouernours warrant, pressed to the purpose, and the tribes, in order, brought up to the worck, so that, after some moneths of being closely followed, foure very substantiall and conuenient bridges are erected and finished, three of which wer so large and stroung that, although they wer of fortie, fiftie, and fourescore foote in length, and had their foundations, and part of their arches in the sea, yet a well laden horse might safely passe ouer them. At the same instant, also, the generall high-wayes (enioined likewise by a statute) are cutt out, and

[1] *Geason.* A very uncommon word, which Johnson found only in Spenser: "It to Leeches seemed strange and geason."—*Hubbard's Tale.* The sense here seems to be "inferior".

[2] *Shent:* pret. of the verb *to shend*, now obsolete.

"Such dream I had of dire portent,
That much I fear my body will be shent."—*Dryden.*

And see *Hamlet*, Act III, scene 2, *ad fin.*

in all places pursued and perfected, by which time the season for the entrance into the common employments about corne and tobacco comeinge vpon them, euery man is dismissed to pursue his priuate and home affayres. Much about the same time, the Gouernour commanded all the powder at the towne and the fortes to be broken vp and vewed. Such wherof as he found required it, he caused to be layed abroad in the sonne and dried, the which was done as well for the preparation, preseruation, and strength of the powder, as to be surely enformed both of its qualitie and quantitie, least otherwise halfe filled barrells and dust should be recciued and relyed vpon in lieu of good seruiceable and good store. A proclamation came then abroad also for the preseruation of wilde foule, and in particuler for the white hearnes, for their breedinge time draweinge nere, it was doubted that, by the encrease of newe commers, and especially boyes, a great waste might be practised upon them by the takeing awaye of their egges and spoyleinge of their nests.

In the moneth of May 1621 upon Whiteson Twoesday (being the prefixt and firmed day by the statute), the Sommer Assize began at St. Georges, and lasted two dayes, wher-at wer impleaded and tried by juries of 12 men, about some twenty seuerall actions in ciuill causes. Diuers indictments also vpon diuers of the newe statutes being made, found, and presented by the grand inquest, wer sentenced accordingly. Some matters likewise in the nature of contempts wer censured by the Gouernour and counsell, sitting openly on the bench, and about ten criminall persons wer arrayned vpon seuerall felonies, and petit larcenyes, fiue whereof (who had bin house-breakers in the daye-time), being found guiltye and condemned, wer saued by their bookes and burned in the hand; the rest openly whypt. Lastly, at the breakinge up of the assize, two orders (which had been debated and concluded at the counsell table) wer openly published by the Gouernour himselfe, the one of them about

tobacco, as that ther should not be suffred to growe nor
be made vp, vpon any one stalk, aboue the number of ten
leaues at the most; and that in the cureinge and makeinge
of it up, a distinction should be diligently practised of two
kindes, a better and a worse, or a prime and a latter sort,
and so not to mingle and confound one with another, as it
had formerly bin; but yet so that the worst part was to be
allowed for merchantable tobacco, by the censure of the
triers, or els to passe to the fire. The other order was occasioned by an abuse ordinarily practised by some contentious and branglinge speritts, who continually troubled the
court with friuolous slight and malicious idle actions and
sutes; and by it was decreed that, from thence forward, in
all ciuill causes between partie and partie, which came to
their triall by twelue men, the side cast should allowe vnto
the jury to the value of foure pence for euery person. And
thus ended the Assize; and presently vpon it, as well for
the divulginge and strengtheninge of the fore-mentioned
order about tobacco, a proclamation was sett forth, the
which also I have thought fitt to deliuer vnto you verbatim,
that by this one the manner and forme of all others ther
vsed may be knowen and censured as being first in vse in
this Gouernours time, and by him introduced; and it was
as followeth :—

By the Gouernour.

"It being apparent that by the negligence and abuses heretofore vsed
and practised in thes Ilands in the cureinge and makeinge up of tobacco,
the credit and estimation therof is brought into contempt, and well
nigh vtterly lost, to the much dammage and discouragement, both of
the vndertakers and planter. And although (for the redresse and recouerye therof) ther hath lately bin enacted in our generall Assembly,
an Act and Statute Lawe especially framed and contriued to that end
and purpose, yet it being considered that noethinge can be done too
much for the cure of so infectious and dangerous a disease, after due and
mature consideration and aduise, both with the counsell and other discreet and experienced persons in this affayre, it is concluded and commanded by the vertue hereof, and for the entent aforesayd that from
hence forward (beginninge at the date of this present) noe person nor

persons inhabitinge or being within any of this llands doe presume or practise in the dressinge, primeinge, and shreddinge awaye of the suckers from their tobacco plants, to nourish or suffer to growe aboue the number of ten leaues at the most vpon any one stalk, as also that in the cureinge and makeinge up therof, they stricktly and carefully obserue to distinguish and seuer it into two sortes and kindes, that is to saye, into a prime sort and a latter, or a better and a worse; and yet so as that that latter and worst sort be found also, and allowed by the triers, for merchandable ware, accordinge to the entent and meaneinge of the statute, in that case made and prouided, or otherwise to be burned at the owners dores.

"And wheras, vpon the performance exacted by this proclamation in the perticuler of the makeinge up of two sortes of tobacco, thus distinguished, and by occasion therof, some vnconscionable and peruerse people may be found who being to paye their debts will doe it in the worst sort of tobacco only, and reserue all the best for themselues, wherby it is conceiued that much discontent, discouragement and discommoditie may ensue, especially to manuall trades-men who are by all good vsage to be cherished and enuited to come amongst us.

"Thes are in this respect also to ordaine and appoint that all such debts and payments as aforesayd be equally made and performed, the one halfe of them out of the best and prime kind of tobacco, the other halfe out of the latter and worst sort. And thes premises, and euery seuerall and perticuler clause of them to be carefully and respectfully obserued and followed, vpon the penaltye of one hundred waight of tobacco, for euery breache and transgression therof, of which sayd penaltye the one halfe therof to be giuen to the informer, the other halfe to be employed in publick worcks; and also farther corporall punishment to be inflicted as shall in justice and discretion be thought fitt, and as the nature of so high a contempt deserueth.

"Straightly chargeinge and commaundinge all counsellours, bayliffs, constables, and all other inferior officers, as also all triers of tobacco that shall at any time hereafter haue an oath administered vnto them to that purpose, that they doe diligently and heedfully examine and looke after all such offences and offendors as shall any waye violate and transgresse the contents and meaneinge of this present proclamation, and vpon the disconery of them to bring them out to justice. As they will answer their neglect and contempt of this so necessarye a seruice at their vttermost perill. "Giuen at St. Georges, Maii 29, 1621.

"(Signed) NATH. BUTLER."

And thes wer the contents of this proclamation, the which I the rather insert, in respect that some of the young and rash heads, who fondly esteemed themselues riche rather in a great quantitie of tobacco than a good, secretly grudged and grumbled at this limitation of ten leaues vpon a stalke; but not dareing to aduenture vpon a breach therof, they wer left in their discontent vntill not long after by experience they found an ample recompence in the largenesse of their leaues, goodnesse and strength of their tobacco.

Much about this time it was that a soudaine alarme was taken at the towne of St. Georges, and from thence speedily deliuered vp to all the fortes, a peece of ordinance being shott of to that purpose. For one eueninge, about eight of the clock at night, the watch being vpon settinge, and the Gouernour ready to goe to bedd, the mount-keeper (who hath an oath giuen him to keepe his due houres of lookeinge out to sea from the mount, and an entertainement of an hundred pounds of tobacco by the yeare for that seruice) came hastely in vnto the Gouernour, and informed him that he had made a discoucrye of certaine botes and vessells lieing a hull (as he take it) to the northwards of St. Katheraines Point, as far out to sea as he could possibly kenne; whervpon the Gouernour, as well in regard of the time of the night (so that ther could noe farther vewe be taken of them from the mount), the fittnesse of a light moone, and the fayrenesse of the winde, which then blewe an easie gale at northeast, as that in his owne opinion, he euer held that place and that course the most likely to breed danger and offence (being withall not vnwillinge vpon any meet and due occasion to trie the readinesse and speritt of his men) secretly callinge for the drumme of his owne Company, he commanded him, in steed of his wonted settinge of the watch, to beate an alarme, the which being well and speedely answered by the garrison at the towne, and all of them quickly brought together and in armes vpon the warfe, they were deuided into three equall partes, wherof one part of them being deliuered to Captaine Felgate, he was commanded presently to carry them by bote to the manninge of Pagetts Fort, and in his waye to giue warneinge to thoes of Smiths Fort to stand also vpon their garde; another part was appointed to Liuetenant Buckly to lead ouer by land to St. Katherains Fort; and the last third part the Gouernour kept with himselfe at the towne, wher he held them in armes all the whole night, himselfe in person being very often with them vpon the garde. Sentinells also wer euery way sett out, and Warwick Fort (which commands the towne) manned. And in this manner being held together vntill the nexte morneinge, at the ordinary time of dischargeinge the watch (after he had caused a through vewe to be taken all about from of the mount) they were dismissed vnto their seuerall employements. Neither was it knowen for the present what vessells thes wer that caused this alarme vntill within a day or two after they wer found to be certaine botes of the inhabitants of Hambleton and Pembroke tribes, who had layne out all night at sea to fish for sharks, of whose liuers they vse to make oyle, to serue them in their lammps; and this was then their arrant.

Sommer being nowe well come on, and the weather calme, the Gouernour made newe trialls for the recouerye of more goods and ordinance out of the wrackt *Warwick;* but by reason her timbers wer not yet throughly rotten, nor her hold broke up, litle or noethinge could be gotten up at the essaye. Only certaine yron potts, kettles, croes of yron, halfe pikes, and the like, and one peece of ordinance (being the fourth that had bin fetched from her) wer weyed, the which peece was afterward mounted at the dore of the Corps du Garde in the Kings Castle, and serueth opportunely to playe vpon the landinge place ther.

Toward the end of this moneth (warneing haueinge bin giuen to all the tribes) the Gouernour made a passage through the maine, beginninge at Sands his tribe, whether he came by bote from the towne of St. Georges; and in all places as he went, he tooke a vewe of their corne and to-

bacco, and gaue a very strickt chargo concerncinge the
well cureinge and makeinge up of the one, and for the care
and preseruation of the other. By the waye, he also swore
the triers of tobacco; and wheras formerly ther had bin but
two of euery tribe, he nowe encreased them to the number
of three, that so ther might be a castinge voice. In the
beginninge of July, he caused the port-holes of the ordinance in the lower plattforme in the Kings Castle to be
repayred and enlarged, that thoes great peeces might the
better and with more facilitie be trauersed, and the battlements lesse damnified, which had formerly bin much shaken
by being ouer streight. Then and ther also he began to
rayse and contriue a stroung and conuenient house of hewen
stone for the receipt of the Captaine of the castle and his
famely, who formerly had bin very meanely lodged and
pestred in a poore smale frame, which was nowe turned
and fitted to serue for a Corps du Garde. He caused likewise a corne house, for the receipt of the prouision for the
garrison, to be sett up vpon that smale iland, wherin
standeth Charles his Fort; and at the same time he made
such another at the towne, and repayred the shalope-house
ther, which was much ruined.

Vpon the first of August next ensueinge, two sayles
being discouered from the westerne partes of the Ilands,
the Serieant Maior in all hast sent vp word therof to the
Gouernour at the towne, and about noone the same day
they wer discried from the Kings-Castle, wher the Captaine (accordinge to the Gouernours direction in such cases)
gaue warneinge with two peeces of ordinance, and was
answered with one from the foote of the mount. Towards
night they came both of them to an anchor, and rode two
miles out in the open sea, vnder the shore, ouer against the
harbours mouthe of St. Georges; and presently the admirall
sent of a small bote, the which arriuinge before the fortes
that command that chanell, and being haled by the com-

mandors ther, made answer that she came from Captaine
Powell, who was abord the admirall (and this was the same
Powell so oft mentioned here-tofore), and from him had
brought letters to the Gouernour, whervpon she is commanded to putt in at Smithes Fort, ther to staye vntill the
Gouernours pleasure was farther knowen. And not long it
was but the Gouernour (who had bin in his shalope at the
castle, and made his returne that waye) was arriued at
Pagetts Fort, the which being so nere vnto Smithes, the
straungers wer quickly brought ouer thether vnto him, and
presently their letters, which wer to this effect, that being
of Zealand, and commissioned by Prince Maurice, he had
bin at the West Indies, and nowe vpon returne, being falne
into distresse of water, by reason of calms, he humbly
desired admittance to refresh himselfe in that kind, for
which he would giue all content and satisfaction. To which
the Gouernour (instantly returneinge the bote) sent this
answer with her in wrightinge, that he was not ignorant
that Powell was not ignorant that (since his being here the
last sommer,) not only the Company of Aduenturers, but
the King himselfe also, had giuen him absolute command
for a generall exclusion of all such as he, and in perticuler
of himselfe by name. In which regard he much wondered
to find soe little vnderstandinge of himselfe, and respect
vnto him, as either to hope for any such matter, or to offer
it. It was noe meruaile, therfore, that Powell was nowe to
find the vanitie of his presumption by the effect; for he was
to seeke his refreshments els wher, and that without farther
delaye, vnlesse he ment to staye vpon the tearmes of an
enemye. He had done improuidently and rashly ynough
to send in his bote in that manner; and had it not bin that
some remnants of his former freindshyp, mixt with pitty,
wrought vpon him, he would assuredly haue stayed her, and
sent back his reason by the mouthes of his ordinance. And
with this resolution the bote is dispatched, so that within

two houres after the barcks both of them waye anchor and depart, and, being seene cleare of the coast by the Gouernour himselfe (who rested at the fort to be an eye-wittnesse of it), he then returned to the towne, wher already he found diuers of the maine-men posted up with the hopes of newes and supplies, of which they are in continuall neede. But being thus frustrated of both, they hang downe their heades, and stormed at the merchands, stickinge not to saye (as publickly as they durst, for feare of ye Gouernour) that the most part of their vndertakers would neither doe them good themselues, nor suffer any body els.

And to speake freely it seemeth a course of much stricktnesse in the company of aduenturers (not to saye oppression) thus to tie the colony, not yet ten yeares old, and soe remote from all neighbours and to make it destitute of all hopes and supplies, saue such only as they themselues send only once a yeare from England when they fetch away the tobacco; and then too so lamely and niggardly, as should ther, but at any one time (which God forbidd) fall out a miscarriage by the waye (and that waye is of three thousand miles in length), the most part of the poore people must needes vndergoe many and great distresses; and numbers of them (which wer an ill and misbecomeinge sight among Christians) be found in a shamefull and barberous nakednesse. True it is indeed (and an obseruation not without wonder with all thanckfullnesse to be acknowledged) that hetherto (in a good houre be it spoken) such hath bin God's great mercye to this his owne worck, ther hath not any one shyp miscarried either in her goeing or comeinge vnto thes Ilands; but certainely we shall be founde to make but very unworthy and base use hereof, if it make us presumptuous, since neither colony nor company doe or can deserue that God should worck miracles for them. As for thoes common and thred-bare allegations as that by a more generall admission, a dangerous discovery might be made vpon our weakenesses, and the secretts of our chanells, harbours, and fortes ouer-largely diuulged it is well ynough knowen that neither such a knowledge is nor can be wantinge by many other meanes and occasions not to be preuented; nor we in any such case or condition as we shall neede to feare (if the fault be not only in themselues) whatsoeuer this waye can either be knowen or discouered. The true cause therfore of this so enforced and terrible a prohibition springeth from some other groundes and motions, the which because they are well ynough vnderstoode and perceiued, for all their seuerall maskings and disguises, by the most of thoes, they are so sought to be putt vpon; and being also in part (though very succinctly) touched and pointed at heretofore, shall not need a second time to be mentioned farther in this place, omittinge therfore all farther disputes upon so odious an argument, we will returne whence we haue digressed.

Towards the end of this moneth of August the Gouernour began to sinck two newe plattformes in Penistones Iland: one of them vnder the redoubt of Pagetts Fort (vpon the top whereof he had a litle before made a small plattforme, and planted vpon it an excellent saker) which was to succour that old one ther which had bin spoyled by Capt. Tucker, and was uery unceruiceable; vpon which he mounted two sakers: the other was layed out vpon a point of that Iland lieinge out to the northwards; and vnder a smale redoubt called the pigeon-house, which being erected by Mr. Moore and left forsaken and in ruins by Capt. Tucker who robbed it also of a peece of ordinance to bestowe it elswher, was at this time renewed and the peece restored, as findinge it of good and requisite vse for the command of shalopes, which by a smale and narrow chanell might otherwise passe up vntouched into the towne harbour, and very towne it selfe, and for thes peeces, he made three new carriages of cæder.

Noe soner is this done, but the magazin shyp is descried

R

from the mount, and the shalope manned out vnto her from
the towne; but the wind at the instant scantinge vpon her,
and with all groweinge to a storme, she was forced to make
her waye round about the Ilands; but the bote haueinge
bin abord her with very much adoo gott in againe the next
daye after in the eueninge, bringinge newes of the losse of
many of her people, and in perticuler of her master, as also
of a newe minister, and the prime man for the suger apprehensions, and with all a straunge rumour of much complainet
in England against the Gouernour, with an expectance of
Tuckers returne by the next shyp to succeede him : within
eight dayes after the shyp her selfe getts in at the Kings
Castle Harbour (great fiers haue bin continually kept in the
night by the Gouernours strickt command, to direct and
shew her the coast) and then the Gouernour receiues letters
from the company, in which although he found not any
thinge that could confirme the former reports brought in by
the bote; yet by some priuate letters from diuers of his
noble and sure freindes, he was giuen to vnderstand the
cours and certainety of thoes proceedeinges, the which being
straunge and altogether vnexpected could not chuse but, as
they did, giue him much discontent, the groundes and origi-
nalls whereof, together with the practices and seuerall encite-
ments moueinge thervnto we shall nowe succinctly deliuer
vnto you. Captaine Kendall with his crue, being (as you formerly heard) shypped away for England the yeare before,
noe soner is gotten thether but hieth himselfe to his cosen
Sir Edwin Sands, (a man as well in the Virginia as Bermuda
Courts very loqueut, and by many and himselfe thought
eloquent), to him Kendall makes a pittifull complainct of
being depriued by the Gouernour in the Sommer Ilands of
fourteene negroes giuen him by the pyrate Kirbye; enter-
lacing withall some other most false and scaundelous grieuances. Sir Edwin, greedy to embrace any bold occasion of
wrangle against the noble Earle of Warwick, vpon some for-

mer disgusts betwixt them (whose negroes they wer adiudged to be) encourageth Kendall and shewes him the way to frame and present a petition into the Court about it; Kendall, proude of being thus backt, shewes himselfe at the very next Court, with his petition, and presents it, the contents wherof wer that wheras diuers Moores had been giuen him by one Kirby, they wer, contrary to reason and equitie, deteyned, and taken from him by the then present Gouernour of the Sommer Ilands, Captaine Nathaniell Butler, for which wroung and hard vsage he humbly craued the justice and redresse of that Honourable Court. And in seconding hereof, Sir Edwin Sands standes up and speakes to this effect, That true it was that his cosen Kendall had receiued much iniury in this perticuler, but that the Gouernour of the Bermudoes was to be cleared herein, for (quoth he and he sayd truly) " whatsoeuer he did herein, was by order from England, and that ther wer some mens hands to that order, who would be loathe to iustifie what they had done." Wherin it was well ynough knowen that he apparently aimed at Sir Thomas Smithe and Alderman Johnson, with whom he had not for a long time held any good quarter. Vpon this speach of Sir Edwins, Sir Nathaniell Riche (a nere kinsman to the Earle of Warwick, and a very temperate and honest gentleman) demanded of Kendall what Moores thes wer he thus layde claime vnto, and whether they wer not of the number adiudged as due vnto the said Earle: if they wer, that then it was a bold and sawcye fashion of him to deliuer that petition in that Lordes absence. Hervpon much dispute and contestation ariseth betweene Sir Nathaniell and Sir Edwin, so that Mr. Lewes Hughes the minister (who had departed for England together with Kendall), being present at thes broyles, and conceineinge that some abuse and wrong might hereby be wrought against the Gouernour of the Sommer Ilands dureinge his absence, he enformed the Gouernours brother, called Mr. James Butler (who was also at the same Court), of a certaine note giuen him by the Gouernour at his departure from him, wherby was manifested how irregularly and dangerously Kendall had demeaned himselfe during his smale time of his deputy-gouerment in thoes Ilands, and howe vnworthy to receiue any reward from the Company. The contents of the note were: "That the said Kendall had sold munitions to the pirate Kirby; had disfurnished the fortes of their allowance of corne to furnish him withall; had deliuered a bote vnto him belonging to one of the colony; and had let him haue some sayles: in recompence wherof he had receiued diuers negroes, certaine chests, one ebony bedsteed, and a gold ring, with some other thinges not knowen; in it was also mentioned how the sayd Kendall had caused himselfe (after the departure of Captaine Tucker, who had left him Deputy Gouernour), to be tumultuously chosen Gouernour by the people; and that he had bragged that he relied more by far vpon that election than vpon Tuckers commission." This note being shewed by the Gouernours brother vnto Sir Nathaniell Riche, it was thought fitt that it should presently be giuen into the Court, although Mr. Butler was not very willinge withall, alledgeinge (with good reason) that his brother the Gouernours name was not subscribed vnto it, and that although he confessed it to be written with his owne hand, yet knew he not whether it was his brothers meaneinge to haue it published; wherin certainely he very well vnderstoode himselfe, and was in a true aime at the Gouernours intention, who writte it only for a note of remembrance for Mr. Lewes, and the which he was only to vse in that nature; but, the opinion and importunitie of the rest preuayleinge, the note was thervpon publickly produced, and reade in open court, whervpon most of the auditors (as they had iust cause) wer very much moued, and the matters therin obiected against Kendall held very foule and worthy to be well looked into: to which end it was demanded why the Gouernours hand was not subscribed vnto it, sayeinge that it had bin well done, that thoes informations had been taken by commission ther, and so from thence sent vnto them by the Gouernour. To which his brother answered (very truly and discreetly) that the minister, Mr. Lewes, beinge one of the counsell for thoes Ilands, was in Court ready to iustifie whatsoeuer was therin written; and which was the cause (as he conceiued) why his brother the Gouernour had not subscribed vnto it; and, as for the punishinge of the sayd Kendall ther (which some wished had bin done), he told them it was very likely that it was foreborne, in respect that he, haueing personally and basely wrounged the Gouernour not long before by false and scandalous reportes, it might hapely haue been sinisterly taken by some of his passionate freindes, and blazed abroad as an occasion layd hold of to make good a priuate reuenge; in which respect it might well be that this reference in this case had rather bin to the Company in England. And, in truthe, ther could not have bin made a more true and exact interpretation of the carriage of this affayre than this was, howsoeuer at that time guest at only by the Gouernours brother, the Gouernour haueinge bin heard to saye, diuers times after Kendalls departure, that he looked to be taxed of the Company for not questioninge of him about the pirate Kirby; and that for his part he had only to alledge for himselfe thes two reasons: the one in respect that he euer found the sayd Kendall exceedinge silly, and easyly led any way, especially to the worser part; and that, therfore, it might well be that he was abused by some of his knaueish counsellours, who noethinge cared how far they engaged him in any action so they might pillage for themselues. The other was the case. Vnworthy and base iniuries received from him in his owne person, in regard wherof he esteemed it a course, freer from scandall and misinterpretation, to referre him to the Company in England than to deale with him himselfe, especially because he well ynough was acquainted with the humours of some of his cheife freindes in England (populer men in the Bermudo Courts), who wer not lesse affectionate and passionate in defendinge and palliateinge the errors and offences of such as they embraced, and wer in faction withall, than in exclaimeinge and plottinge against others. And, in truthe, this last apprehension of the Gouernours was fully confirmed, not long after, by a letter, which came by chaunce into his hands, written to Captaine Kendall from Sir Edwin Sands, by the shyp the *George*, an. 1620, wherin he signified vnto him of the hearesaye of all Kendalls traffique with the pirate Kirby, as of his sellinge vnto him ordinance, corne, botes, sayles, and the like; wishinge him, in any case, to deale plainely and confidently with him, and to let him knowe, as sone as he could, how far he had proceeded in thes courses, and that in soe doing he should be sure to find him a fast and sure kinsman and freind; and that if in the meane time any course of iustice wer taken against him in the Sommer Ilands, that he should appeale from it vnto the Company in England, and then let him alone to make a good partie for his securitie. The which aduice and direction seemed altogether dissonant from his open courses in that kind, and very much misbecominge a man so eagerly affectinge and professeinge the reputation of an vpright and excellent common wealthe man as Sir Edwin doth in all places, especially in this particuler, wherin it is well knowen how fiercely he hath expressed himselfe against straungers, and though nowe he is found not only a forbearour but a supportour when the case toucheth vpon one of his owne.

But thes informations of Kendall against the Gouernour rested in quiett, and seemed to be vtterly quayled vntill the great Quarter Court next succeedeinge; at what time it was againe discouered that much secret plottinges and close sideinge practices had bin contriued against him vnderhand, and that many associates had bin drawen into a conspiracye and faction against him in the meane time: among the which the prime ones wer Capt. Tucker; one Smithe, a grocer; and one Melin,³ who being but a meane seruant to one of the vndertakeinge merchants, was yet as proude an one and of as many wordes, and as sawcely peremptory as any master of them all; and in that regard cheifly cockered and made vse of by Sir Edwin Sands, who certainely was the cheife mouer, and principall backer of all thes impudent back-biters.

At this Quarter Court (wherin contrary to his owne knowledge and meaneinge, the Earle of Southampton was chosen Gouernour of the Company, and Sir Thomas Smithe remoued) the Gouernours brother began to make a motion to haue certaine promises performed which had bin made vnto him by the whole Company. But he was (somewhat im-

---

³ Elsewhere called "Meddling Mellinge". Mr. Thomas Mellinge was a somewhat prominent member of the Virginia Company. In November 1622, Dr. J. Donne, Dean of St. Paul's, preached before the Company at St. Michael's, Cornhill, "after which sermon ended, it is also thought fitt and agreed the custome they begun the last yeare shalbe continued, namely, to supp together, and for that cause have entreated Mr. Caswell and Mr. Mellinge (who last time so well performed it to all the Companies content) being assigned with Mr. Bennett and Mr. Rider to be stewards this yeare also, for prouidinge and orderinge of the supper, and buissines thereunto belonging, and of the place where it shalbe kept, and accordingly to giue notice thereof vnto all the Companie by sending the officer with ticketts that are to be printed for this purpose, notifyinge the time and place, and what each man is to paye, which is now agreed shall be iijs. a peece, as finding by last yeares experience it cannot be lesse to beare of the full charge; and for that at such great feasts venizon is esteemed to be a most necessary complement, the court hath thought fitt that letters be addressed, in the name of the Company, vnto such noblemen and gentlemen as are of this Society, to request the favour at their hands and withall their presence at the said supper."—E. D. Neile, *History of the Virginia Company*, p. 361.

The Feast was held in Merchant Taylors' Hall, " whither many of the nobility and council were invited, but few came. They spent twenty one *does*, and were between 300 and 400 at 3s. a man."—*Id.* see *Nichols*, iv, 781.

prudently and irregulerly) sodainely interrupted by Sir Edwin Sands, who made an earnest request vnto the Court, that his cosen Kendall might haue admittance to reade his answer to thoes former accusations inserted against him in the Gouernours note, the which he thought could not otherwise be esteemed of them as a meere lybell, in which respect the Gouernour deserued to be sent for home, and to haue a bill preferred against him in the Star-chamber : to which heady speeche (being noe lesse passionate than when I heard him, being treasorour of the Virginia Company for one only yeare, to tearme the whole Company vniust, and after glad to expound himselfe fauorably, the which by his good freinds was admitted him), the Gouernours brother calmely and pertinently replied and manifested vnto the Court, that that note was only giuen by way of remembrance to Mr. Lewes, who being a sworne counsellour of estate in the Ilands was ther ready to iustifie whatsoeuer had bin written in it, and that therefore it could neither be a lybell nor a lye. But the Court being ready to rise ther was noe farther dispute thereof at that sittinge.

But this cluster of confederates, not meaneinge to let it passe so, but being mad in their malice against the Gouernour, who was three thousand and three hundred miles from them, and litle dreamed of any such proiects, and with all to make way to their owne perticuler and diuers ends, wherof euery one of them had one by himselfe, as Sir Sands to thwarte the Earle of Warwick, who he knew truely loued and respected the Gouernour, as also to helpe out and cleare his cosen Kendall, and so by sending him back againe quickly to be ridd of him ther for feare of a farther burthen : Tucker likewise for his part, that therby he might make good his maine ambition and longinge desire to be returned once more Gouernour thether: Smithe, also, to reuenge himselfe for being noted vnto the Company by the Gouernour for his want of due respect, and for his clamerous behauiour against him without all cause or occasion: Medlinge Melling, because the Gouernour had snibed him to the quick, in an answer to one of his sawcye letters: and, lastly, Mr. Kendall, as being a man mainely marchinge downe hill to all dunghill actions, sencelesse of reputation, and vtterly vncapable of all noble respects; the associateinge vnto them, besides, one Carter, a very simple fellowe, but a perfect drunckarde; one Williams, a mutinous hare-brayne, and one easily wonne any way with a meales meate; as also one Hind, who, at the same time, had three wiues liueinge in London; one Groue, a ballad-singer, sent ouer by Sir Edwin Sands into the Sommer Ilands, and made marshall ther by Kendalls wise choice and discretion dureinge the miserable yeare of his deputy gouerment-shyp, and then displaced by Captaine Butler for his insufficiencye and knauerie; and, lastly, one Danby, a most especiall young minion of Kendalls, and a beloued bedfellowe of his,. God knowes wherfore. This crue (I saye) stroungly combined themselues together, and after many meetcinges at tauernes and alehouses, at last forged and hatched up certaine delicate articles to the number of one and thirtie, the which, within two Courtes after, wer dressed up and launced out into the Court against the absent Gouernour of the Sommer Ilands in this forme. The title of them thus:

> A Cataloque of diuers wroungs and iniuries committed and done by Captaine Nathaniell Butler, Gouernour of the Sommer Ilands, vnto the Company in generall, and to diuers planters, as also of diuers extortions and exactions of vnlawfull fees, taken or receiued by him or his ministers in the sayd Ilands.

The sappy pithe as followeth:

1. He hath made noe Act of Parlament or Lawe in his Assembly, either for the seruice of God, or for the obseruation of the Sabaoth, which ought to haue bin done before all thinges.

2. He hath confirmed noe lawe made here in England at our Quarter Courts for the gouernment of the people ther in Christian peace and amitie; neither confirmed any former lawe made in the Sommer Ilands, either for the obseruation of the Sabaoth, for the seruice of God, or for the execution of justice in the Ilands betweene the planters and the owners of the Ilands.

3. He sold this yeare the caske belonginge to the whale fishinge at vnreasonable rates for tobacco, fane to his owne vse; as also the colonie botes, likewise one barge, to one Llewellin for 140 lbs. of tobacco, which he tooke to his owne vse.

4. He keepeth a Dutch carpenter that was cast away in a Dutch pinnace to make botes vpon the publique, and sells them away for his owne vse at unreasonable rates.

5. He caused this yeare, by vertue of an Act of Parliament made in the sommer, 1000 lbs. of tobacco or more to be taken from the planters and owners of the best tobacco, before any diuision was made towards the payment of the men that built the mount; which sayd mount did neuer cost him 250 lbs. in all, and formerly noethinge.

6. He caused this yeare, by his warrants, collections towards watch and ward to be made through out all the tribes, a thinge neuer heard of before.

7. He caused a collection to be made for Mr. John Yates for the ferry; the said Yates returned about 900 lbs. of tobacco, and one John Dutton sent home and entred this yeare about 1700 lb., being but a bayliff, and carryinge ouer with him but one boy.

8. He sold cordage belonginge to the whale-fishing this yeare for tobacco, and sayles, and other implements, belonginge to the treasorour and frigate that was cast away in Captaine Kendalls time, and yet layeth the same vpon the sayd Capt. Kendall.

9. He sent in the' beginninge of this haruest into all the tribes the Prouost Ottwell and Woodward to collect his debts before any diuision was made, some of which sayd debts were oweinge for tobacco lost at dice.

10. He tooke extraordinary fines of some offenders this yeare, as of one Nash 50 lbs. of tobacco, who stoode also upon the pillory; likewise one Robert Tap and one Legge; and sequestred dead mens goods into his own hands as due to him, without giueinge any accompt of the same.

11. He hyred out the poore Dutch men formerly cast away and tooke the proffitt to himselfe, as also the *Treasorours* men this yeare.

12. He maketh such as haue warrants to goe for England vsually to pay 1 lb. of tobacco for his warrant.

13. He causeth the Marshall to erect extraordinary fees, vpon all men committed, the fees being written in capital letters in the Marshalls house; if the offendor be a counsellor or captaine he pays 20 lbs. of

tobacco fee and 1 lb. of tobacco a day for his diet; if a liuetenant 15 lbs. fee and 1 lb. of tobacco for diet; if an ensigne 10 lbs. fee and 1 lb. for his diet; for a common man 2 lbs. of tobacco fee and 1 lb. of tobacco for his diett.

14. He conccaled theft committed by one Crowther his man, for goods stolen from one Woodall, for which he was neuer punished nor questioned.

15. He furnished Captaine Scouten, a Dutch man, with some men and gaue him a bote of Captaine Hindes, and payed noethinge for it, and at his returne from the West Indies victualled him home for Holland.

16. He gaue to one Captaine Baker, a pyrate or Dutch man of warre, a warrant vnder his hand to haue a free trade with a magazin in the Sommer Ilands from the Lowe Countries, who is gone this yeare againe for the Sommer Ilands.

17. He tooke of John Powell, another English captaine, one chaine of gold, one wedge of gould, two siluer candle sticks, one silver ewer, one rapier and dagger, the hilts one of silver, which some Spanish rialls, with some veluett silck grogram, and silck stockinges, with diuers other thinges, in consideration whereof Powell sold his other commodities at excessive rates in the Islands, watered and victualled.

18. He hath reported in the Sommer Ilands that he was his Maiesties liuetenant, and not the Companyes Gouernour, and that he scorned to serue so base a Company as this is.

19. He made out seuerall warrants to the salters to gather in old debts before any diuision was made, and so seazed the best tobacco for the debt for his owne vse.

20. He hath taken some men seruants from their masters lands for his owne vse, and some he hath sent home without order from the owners, contrary to his first Act of Parlament.

21. He setteth publick men vpon the overplus and other mens lands takeinge the benefitt of their labours to him and them, neglectinge the plantinge of the publique land, the absence of which people doth dayly indanger the whole Islands if any enemie should approach, ther beinge fewe or none left to plye the ordinance, or tend any other seruice whatsoeuer.

22. He letteth out botes to hyre to bring downe tobacco from the maine to the shyp at extraordinary rates, refused 20 lbs. of tobacco of Mr. Gores man this yeare to bring downe but a tunne of cask, which is one p. cent., and noe botes are left for lesse than ten pounds of tobacco.

23. He freed such men from publique worck as would giue him ten pounds of tobacco a man, but such as did not made the great fort, and did other worcks, wherof he boasteth.

24. He hath killed two of the oxen in the Sommer Ilands, and shott some of the goates with his peece, and cate them, without order from hence.

25. He is a common dicer, and giues entertainement to any that will play in his company for money or tobacco, either in his owne house or els wher.

26. He beate Old Needham, and drew his sword vpon him at the Gouernours owne house. He beate likewise one Batt Payne, when he was a prissonner, and one Robert Williams, whom, when he had beaten downe, he trode vpon his neck till he was like to be straungled, because he would not kneele and aske for forgiuenesse.

27. He suffred Otwell, by exactinge of fees this yeare, to gaine 1,000 lbs. of tobacco, and also a man and a boy to be his bond-slaues, because they were not able to paye their fees; the one was Mr. Scotts boye; the other, Mr. Delawries man.

28. He suffred at the comeinge in of the *Joseph* noe man to goe abord but Otwell, the marshall, to buy up the aqua-vitæ, and oyle, etc., who keepeth a tap-house, and sells thes thinges againe for mony at extraordinary rates.

29. He seazed vpon all Mr. Ferrars prouision, and sold them awaye for his owne at extraordinary rates.

30. He tooke this present yeare from Captaine Hind 100 lbs. of tobacco towards payment for scoureinge and keepinge the armes, and also for powder spent in exercizeinge the men, a thinge neuer knowen before.

31. He tooke this present yeare of one Allen, a planter, on the publique land, for a warrant for his passage for England 50 lbs. of tobacco, and this man came without any warrant. He tooke also of one Downham, who had a warrant likewise, 50 lbs. of tobacco.[4]

Thes libelous articles wer handed into the Court by that Smithe, the grocer, formerly mentioned, yet without any hands at all subscribed vnto them; so that being vewed by the deputy and some others of the assistants, sitting abone the half pace, it was by them demanded of Smithe how he came by them, and who they wer that would take vpon them to be the authors; who answered, that he knewe noethinge, and that he only found them licing in his shop; whervpon it being thought altogether vnfitt to haue them

---

[4] The reader will find these articles, but without the replies of Captain Butler, printed from a defective copy found among the Colonial Records, in the *Memorials*, etc., vol. i, p. 272.

read in publick, a committe was selected to examine them, the which, after diuers sittinges about it, findinge noethinge of profe, nor any thinge to make any matter of, the heate of the businesse and noice of the clamour became husht and smothered up; only the Gouernours brother haueinge procured a copy of the sayd articles, sent them into the Sommer Ilands to the Gouernour, who, by the returne of the same shypinge, returned them vnto him, thus answered.

The arrant Articles answered by NATHANIELL BUTLER.

"To the first article of the one and thirtie, it is answered, that if the wordes seruice of God, here vsed, be meant restrictiue to a forme of churche seruice (for otherwise who knowes not but that all ciuill lawes tend to the seruice of God); then behold the only article among them all without grosse falssification; for it is true that we made noe lawe in our generall Assembly against the breach of the Sabaoth, nor for a forme of churche seruice; noe more did we for felonies, murthers, nor treasons. And our reason was that the lawes of England haueing, with so great iudgement and iustice, prouided in thes cases; it had bin (as we tooke it) an highe presumption in vs to haue meddled with any of them, and therefore applied our selues wholy to such perticulers as touched vpon our selues, and which the lawes of England could not take notice of, becauso euery climate hath somewhat to it selfe in peculier. And yet, howsoeuer, I see not with what integritie or discretion this article was preferred against myselfe in perticuler, since, for my owne part, I had only one single voice as all other men in this our free generall Assembly, the which also I practised spareingely as haueing bin informed that they are seldome the best parlamentall men that are allwaies in orations.

"To the second it is replied that indeed we confirmed not in our generall Assembly (for alone and single I neuer tooke vpon me to be a lawe-maker) any of your Quarter

Court orders, because we held them allwayes sufficient of themselues without our approbation, and so approued of them by our submission. As for a certaine sort of articles, formerly hung up in the churches by Captaine Tucker, and wholy deuised of his owne braine, I confesse I neuer could find in my heart, nor durst call them lawes, much lesse confirme them to be soe, since in many perticulers they wer both dissonant from the lawes of England and all equall distribution of justice, euery petit-larceny and two peny pilfery being equally rated with the highest felonies, and censured with death.

"To the third it is sayd, that true it is that vpon a generall and pittifull complainct of the want of tubbs and cask to wash in and pack up tobacco in, findinge in a certaine iland a heape of cask staues that had layne ther three or foure yeares, I caused a cooper to make some of them into tubbs and cask, the which I caused to be sold vnto the people at a reasonable rate, the one halfe therof being to pay the cooper for his worck, the other for publick seruice; so that to the much ease and content of the people, about 200 lbs. of tobacco in all was recouered this waye, and which, if it had not bin done, the people had bin much distressed in thoes prouisions, and by this time thes cask-staues had bin vtterly rotten and nought worthe As for my bote-sellinge, I deny not but that I sold that only one rotten barge to that one Flwellin mentioned in this third article for 120 lbs. of tobacco, yet not before I had made another in her roome, worthe 250 lbs.

"To the fourth it is confessed that I hired a Dutch carpenter to staye with me dureinge my gouerment here in thes Ilands, and that to the exceedinge benefitt of the plantation, as the effect shewes, for he hath multiplied their botes (of which ther is noethinge more needfull nor important) into fiue times the number that I found them. Yet is it most false that by his meanes I made botes vpon the publick to sell them againe at vnreasonable rates, since all the world here can wittnesse for me that I euer constantly refused to doe this, although much sollicited by the country in generall, because I would auoid all colour of scaundall this waye; but nowe I perceiue it was all in vaine, because impudent malice dare saye any thinge.

"To the fifth it is answered that, haueing built the mount, raysed Southampton Fort, cutt out Deuonshire plattforme, made fifteene newe carriages for your ordinance, our generall Assembly (assembled by your iniunctions and iustructions) found it iust and equall to present me with 1,000 lbs. of tobacco towards the 1,500 lbs. which it cost me, the which was afterwards respectfully leuied by the baylies of the tribes without any warrant of mine at all. As for the worcks done in Mr. Moore's time, in thes kindes and how they wer done, that they cannot be done so at the present, you selues may wittnesse for me.

"To the 6th, although I could sufficiently answer this article and most of the ensueinge, with giueing them a plaine negatiue lie, and makeing it good too when I haue done; yet, because I euer held it a word of an ill sound, I haue rather chosen (for reuerence sake) to saye that in good truthe, ther was neuer any suche matter; for that the watch and ward here mentioned was euer payed by mine owne purse, yet was it kept for a generall preseruation, and therfore will in time noe doubt (accordinge to reason) be made a generall charge.

"To the 7th it is protested that ther was neuer any such collection made as the article talks of, nor did the said Mr. John Yates (beinge one of the counsell) euer receiue any thinge of the people, for his keepeing of the ferry (for which he dwells most opportunely of all others) saue a willinge beneuolence of whatsoeuer euery famely pleased to giue him, the which (as he protesteth) neuer ammounted to halfe the value here articled. As for Mr. John Dutton (one

of the counsell likewise) he is ready to iustifie vpon oathe
that for the yeare here mentioned, in steade of the 1,700 lbs.
of tobacco, sayd by him to be sent home, and entred, ther
was not so much as one pound, and yet he brought ouer
with him three boyes, over and aboue that only one instanced by the informers.

"To the 8th it is affirmed that ther was neuer sold to my
knowledge of the whale-fisheinge cordage, beyond the value
of fiue pounds sterlinge; and that was done vpon the extreame want and pittifull importunitie of certaine poore
planters, whose botes wer in continuall danger for want
therof; as for sayles or implements belonginge to the
Treasorour or Dutch frigate, I neuer sawe any durcinge my
time worth the sellinge, and therefore could sell none, so
that if any such thinge was done, it was done by thoes that
had the first fingringe of them.

"To the 9th it is answered and avowed, that I neuer sent
any officer in my life to collect any debts of mine or any
other mans before the generall diuision; nor did I euer vse
to playe vpon the tickett, beyond that which I cared not
whether I wonne or lost.

"To the 10th it is auouched that ther wer neuer any fines
imposed vpon any one, but by the publick censure of the
whole body of the counsell in open assize; nor did I euer
sequester any deade mans goods, farther than the duty of
my place required, the goods being orderly prized, and as
iustly giuen account of.

"To the 11th it is answered, that thes Dutchmen here
mentioned wer most of them hired out before I came here;
and thoes of the *Treasorours* people wer euery way as well
vsed, and went vpon as good tearmes as any of mine owne
people.

"To the 12th it is sayd, that ther was neuer taken more
for any warrant to my knowledge than I found presidented
vnto me by my predecessors.

"To the 13th, that the fees allowed vnto the marshall wer held bothe by myselfe and the Counsell to be very reasonable, and it was thought a good discretion, to make men answerable for their faults this waye : that therby they might learne to keepe themselues faultlesse; since many esteeme their purse more than either creditt or any thinge els.

"To the 14th it is replied, that the quoted Woodall lending certaine tobacco to Crowder, the said Crowder (vpon present occasion) in the absence of Woodall, presumed to take it of himselfe. This being taken in snuff by Woodall, the controuersie is brought before me; and being found as you haue heard, was ordered accordingly, noe felloneous entent at all appeareinge in Crowder, nor Woodall making any such accusation.

"To the 15th it is affirmed, that vpon the extreame importunities of one of mine owne seruants called William Warman being at the same time very sickly : I suffered him to passe for England with Scouten (behold how he was furnished with men): I chaunged a bite with him also, but to his cost, for euery child here can saye I had by far the better bargayne : as for any victuallinge he had from hence, it is so groundlesse and false a tale, as it very well and truely resembleth the Fathers.

"To the 16th it is answered, that this baker who came in the Dutch pinnace in Kendalls yeare, had neuer any warrant at all vnder my hand, nor euer the least promise of trade, without the Companyes addmittance; and surely, if it be true (as this Article talks of) that he made out for thes Ilands the last yeare, he hath lost his waye, for hetherto we neuer sett eye on him.

"To the 17th, concerneinge Powell it is sayd, and not denied, but that Powell, at his being here, made certaine presents vnto me, as Gouernour (a custome not straunge any wher in the like case) as a rapier and dagger with yron

s

siluerd hilts in steed of the Articles siluer ones, and also certaine silck stockinges, which it is well knowen wer giuen to the bringer; in requitall wherof I returned vnto him by the same hand, an excellent sword and two fayre equinoctiall dyalls. As for the one chaine of gold, the one smale wedge of gold, the one siluer candlestick, which these fine informers haue made two, and the one siluer ewer; I bought them of the sayd Powell, at the prize of fiftie pounds sterlinge, as appeareth by a bill signed by myne hand, the which my brother and others haue seene in England, and payed him part of the sayd mony, the whole not being to be payed vntill my returne; how impudent, ther fore, is the sequall of this article; as that, vpon consideration hereof, he was to haue libertie to sell his commodities at excessiue rates, since ther is noe greater discontent among the people than that the Company hath prohibited them any more such good bargaines.

"To the 18th, it is confessed that I haue deliuered publickly, that by vertue of his Maiesties gracious letters patents, graunted to the Honorable Company, and their graunts to me, I was, as his Maiesties Deputy Lieutenant here, and so to be obeyed; as for denyeinge my seruice to the sayd Company, much lesse puttinge the tearme base vpon so honorable a Societie; I trust I shall neuer be found so foolishly base, as once to thinck it; hetherto, I am sure I haue neuer spoke it, nor is ther an honest man in the world that will affirme the contrary against me.

"The 19th Article being about giueing out warrants before the diuision of tobacco, hath had its full payment in my former Answer to the 9th.

"To the 20th, it is graunted that at the first returne of shypinge after mine arriuall, entrusteinge myselfe vpon Capt. Kendall (who of purpose it may be, sorted the most vnfitt), ther was an errour committed in gineing a libertie of returne to some that ought to haue bin deteyned; but this, since my better experience, hath bin carefully auoided; yet did I neuer take any mans seruants from his masters land for mine owne vse; but, as all knowe here, by all meanes endeauoured to doe all right in this kinde.

"To the 21st, it is answered that thes malicious enformers knowe well (though myselfe could not doe it before I sawe it) that, that only part of publick land allotted vnto me as Gouernour, to place my men vpon and plant tobacco, is the very same that pastoreth all our cattel; neither is ther (as yet) any other place, through want of water and grasse that can doe it besides. Thes cattle, both by former and late orders from you of the Company, are by all meanes to be preserued. So that being hereby of necessitie to forbeare my land, I was forced to followe the course lead me by my predecessors, and to suffer thoes few of the Coloney men, that I could find at the 32 promised vnto me by the Order of the Court, to bestowe themselues abroad wher they best liked, prouided that it wer done without endammageinge of any others. And yet for all this (as all honest will beare record for me) the fortes wer neuer so stricktly looked vnto as at the present, nor the ordinance in half so good plight.

"All the 22th Article is whole-lie inuented by the informers, without all coulour or shewe of ground.

"The 23th, also, is very fittly coupled with the former, being iust of the same stuffe; for I neuer tooke one pound of tobacco in my life for the release of any one, from any publique worck, nor neuer came neerer it, than only to suffer lazie and vnseruiceable fellowes to hire seconds to worck in their roome; but how they agreed with their seconds, and what they payed, I neuer looked after.

"To the 24th it is answered, wher ther is mention made of my killinge of two oxen, that ther was neuer two of them in the Ilands before I came; since, indeed, ther haue bin made diuers; yet deny I not, but that upon certaine assurance of the miscarriage of the cowes, by being ouer-harried with ouer-many bulls, I killed two very old ones, wherof one had bin gelded not long before, and truely wer thes cattle myne owne, I should sone sett foure or fiue more of them on goeing the same way, for the same cause; and yet well ynough knowen it is, that I am noethinge so greedy of bulls beefe as thes Plaintives are of aqua-vitæ. It is true also that I killed an old he-goate, and shott him through the heart with my peece, because he would not be taken otherwise. But it was done vpon a beliefe that he occasioned the rest to miscarry; though since it is per-ceiued that the poore beast had great wroung, because most of the rest of them haue died without my helpe, and it is thought to be with takeing ouermuch tobacco.

"As for the 25th, it need not be denied but that at my first comeinge I vsed to play at dice, sometimes in mine owne howse, and sometimes at my liuetenants, both for money and tobacco; yet not so commonly, nor with any such common fellowes as most of thes articles; and when-soeuer I did this, it was done fayrely, and with a contempt of gaineinge by it; neither did I conceiue it vtterly vnne-cessary for a time, to practice this familiaritie among mine officers; because, by it they might find that I could be both sociable and honestly merry among them, the which since they haue found to be true: I also haue almost utterly left of, this course of lettinge of them to knowe it.

"Touchinge the 26th, it is confessed that vpon an inform-ation of much wroung, offered me by old Needham, he comeinge in the nik, and I being angry, strooke him, yet not with my sword (which I scorne to vse vpon an old man), but with my hand; but since, haueing found that I was abused by a false tale, I haue satisfied him, by ac-knowledginge myne errour, which I hold the part of an honest man. As for Payne, I bestowed my truncheon vpon him indeed, but duely, for his sawcey connayeinge away of certaine vessells of wine, reserued for the ministers, and entendinge to tiple it with his ˙compagnions, and then laugh at them; yet was he not a prisonnour then, as it is impudently affirmed, for I only found him in the marshalls house. Robert Williams, also a peremtory fellowe of very insolent behauiour, and of a scuruye kind of mutinous speritt, for his takeinge vpon himselfe in a brauery the foule fact of another, I strooke once or twise with a reede I had in myne hand; yet neither beate him downe nor trode vpon his neck, but only clapt him by the heeles vntill I had taught him to find his errour. It may, perhaps, be censured by some of an irregular course for a magistrate to vse blowes with his owne hand; yet well knowen it is that the most temperate commandors that euer wer haue sometimes bin putt to the vse of their truncheons; and in truthe should all men that vsed to deserue it here, at mye first arriuall haue bin clapt in prison, I should hardly haue found prison-roome ynough to haue conueyed them; and besides, bothe mine owne worck, and the vndertakers would haue bin much hindred; for so accustomed they had bin to the cudgell by Captaine Tucker, as a good while it was before they could be brought into any order without it; but nowe, haueing generally learned a better lesson, I also haue quite quitted that kind of discipline.

"To the 27th it is answered, that Ottwell, my Prouost Marshall, hath offered to take his oathe that he gained not by his place, or fees, in any other yeare, yet aboue 100*l*. of Tobacco, which thes informers haue made a thousande. As for Scotts Boye, and Delawnes man (who wer both felons) they wer only left vnto the Marshall, vntill they had earned out their due and equall fees; the which they haue done long since, and are restored; and thes diligent informers in their 13th Article, rubbed vpon this very point once before; and nowe they have here about with it againe.

But it may easily be guesst at why such kinde of creatures as they are so full of inuectiues against this kind of officer; and it is a wonder they rayle not against my causeinge to be erected a newe payre of gallowes, a cage for drunckards, a pillory, and a whyppinge post.

"Touchinge the 28th, I confesse I held it not fitt that suche kind of people as thes Articlers should be suffred to neglect their tobacco bussinesse at home to gadd abord euery newe come shyp to be drunck, and therfore caused the Marshall continually to keepe good rule ther; if being ther he bought any aqua vitæ, wine, or oyle, I protest it is more than I knewe or euer heard before; only, this I am very sure of, that he dares not keepe any tappinge disorders in his house, whatsoeuer thes wide-mouthed men dare affirme in England, since he and all others here are sufficiently giuen to vnderstand that I am as fierce an enemie to all such practices, both in mine officers and all others, as euer was any Gouernour here yet.

"The 29th is a most cunning and insinuateinge trick. For not only Mr. Ferrars owne people, but all the world here will beare me wittnesse that I neuer touched any part or parcell of any of his prouisions in my life, otherwise than by a carefull layeinge of them vp for him in our publick store, neither did I sell so much as one penyworth of meale to any one, all that whole deare yeare.

"To the 30th it is sayd, and willbe mainteyned that ther cannot be a more worthlesse nor vngratefull man in the world than this Hinde, if he affirme what this Article reports: for all men knowe here, that whatsoeuer he gott and carrid with him honestly, he had it by my fauour and pitty of him, being otherwise wreachedly poore; and surely I haue euer yet bin fauoured with a better condition than to haue need to robb the spittlehouse.

"As for the last Article of this bunch, the 31th beinge the game on the head, it is yeelded vnto, as an answerable conclusion to the rest of the buildinge. For this Allen articled for was a colony man, who, pretendinge newes of his father's death, and much dammage to be sustained by absence, cryed vnto me to goe home againe. I pittyinge of him, gaue him leaue; yet neuer tooke a pounde of tobacco more of him than fiftie pounds, which was for his yeares worck, as euery one knowes. And thus I have sent you answered as impudent and groundlesse Articles as (as I thinck) the world euer yet had; wherby not only my selfe (dureinge mine absence) haue receiued most vndeserued cowardly wroungs; but the Honorable Company and their Court also, a notorious affront, and of very ill example."

And vnto the sinceritie, and in verification of thes answers, all the counsell and officers of the Ilands subscribed, protestinge their readinesse to affirme as much vpon their oathes whensoeuer they should be called ther unto, euerye man pressinge to giue in his testimonye, for the disprofe of thoes impudent and malicious articles, which generally wer much detested ; so that the Gouernour rather wanted paper than handes to expresse his iustification.

But the ale-hauntinge articlers in England, perceiueinge they could not by their scriblinge produce the reuenge that they desired; not restinge so, they fell vpon newe tricks and proiects, to make good their malice and spleene against the Gouernour, and of these, Tucker was indeed a stoute leader and a braue captaine. First of all therfore (conceiueinge himselfe a very gracious man with the Company), he sued into the Court for a patente, wherby he would be made sole Gouernour of the common land, as also Gouernour of the fortes; but this was sylently and with a scorne reiected, euerye man knoweinge him to be a better gardiner than a Gouernour. That fayleinge, he gaue out by himselfe and his twang that it was certainely knowen that the Gouernour (vpon disgusts receiued from the Company) resolued to forsake the Ilands and his charge ther by that yeares shypinge. In which regard, it being very dangerous to haue the Ilands left at six and seuens, it was very requesite that either a newe Gouernour should be elected and sent by that shypinge, publickly professed, or that a select committe of six men should chuse a man secretly, whose name should be closely sealed up in a boxe, haueing a large commission giuen vnto him, which he should vse accordinge as he found occasion when he came ther, and not to be knowen who he was untill then, the which fiue man he ment should be himselfe. But the Company sone smelt out this his rare deuice also, and larght at it, in so much as he was generally stiled vpon the Exchange, and in many other places, the Jack in the Box. Being thus growne poore and bare, his third shyft was, that he might goe ouer to liue upon his owne land, ther, as a priuate man, but freed and priuilidged from the Gouernment ther, and not any way answerable to the justice of the place ; the which also being held altogether irreguler and without example, as rather being a request fitt for knaues and outlawes than honest and worthy men, he became absolutely frustrate and putt of from all his deepe deuises, and grewe altogether in dispayre ; yet had he so confidently relied vpon them, and so promised vpon himselfe a certainetie of their takeinge, as he not only wrote vnto his planters by the first shyp, that he would assuredly come vnto them, in spite of all enemies, by the second shyp (haueinge shypped some barrells of beere vnto them also, to entertaine him at his arriuall, which wer afterwards merrily drunck up by such as rather wished their company than his), but also had bin abord the sayd second shyp himselfe, and ther pointed and sett out his owne cabbin, together with his wiues and his maydes, which he determined to take very speedely, and to dresse up for the voiage. But being thus generally frustrated of all his delicate hopes, he remained behind at home to plott and deuise newe lies and practices against the next yeares returne. The cheife and almost only discontent that the Gouernour receiued by all his packinge being from the readynesse and procliuitie that he therby perceiued and found to be in many of the Company to apprehend vncharitably and rashly of him and his proceedinges, wheras he expected (accordinge to reason and common vse in such cases) to haue found them his patrones and protectors; but in this also he was much releiued and comforted by being assured that they wer generally and almost only of the sitters beneath the halfe pace, being shop keepers and pedlers, who still fawne vpon and cocker their Gouernours when they are newe, and sodainely after endeauour as much to disgrace and canuas them. But we will nowe returne to the magazin shyp, who (as we have sayd) was gotten in in a very sickly estate into the King-castle harbour. The very next dayes night after whose arriuall, the Gouernour, about the middle of the night, receiued hastie newes by a dismayed messenger from Sands his tribe, that one hundred Spaniards wer landed vpon that part, and that diuers other botes and some shyps wer discouered to lie of at sea. Whervpon (haueing first well manned all the fortes) he instantly made thether in person, with some twenty men in their armes, determineinge as he found cause to drawe together more men by the way out of the maine, and gett thether by the breake of the next day, when, insteede of an enemy which he expected, he mett only with a company of poore deiected Portugalls and Spaniards, who, in their passage from Cartageua in the West Indies for Spaine, in company of the Spanish fleete, by the very same storme that had endangered our owne shyp (as you have heard) had lost theirs vpon our terrible rocks. They wer to the number, men, women, and children, of seuenty, and had saued themselues partly in their shypbote and partly vpon a raft; soe that (by Gods great mercy) not any one of them perished, although they had forsaken their broken and tattered shyp at least ten miles of at sea. Some of thes wer found people of fashion, and some women ther wer much to be pitted, wherof one of the cheifest was within three dayes after brought in bedd of a boye.

The Gouernour receiued them with all the comfort and releife that was possible, causeinge all such goodes of theirs as had bin pillaged from them by some of the baser sort of his people (who had begun to be fingring with them) to be restored; and in perticuler, haueing vnderstoode by the captaine and pylote that the meaner sort of their owne marrinours, vpon the first apprehension of their danger, had stolne from them in the shyp-bote, and not only left them to the mercye of the seaes, but carryed away with them also all such monyes as could hastely be gotten, so that the better sort, who had most right vnto it, wer therby vtterly destituted. Vpon justice by them, herein discretly demanded, the Gouernour caused a soudaine search to be made among all the sayd marrinours, and recouered from among them all to the quantitie of one hundred and fortie pounds sterlinge, or ther abouts (the which before wittnesse) he deliuered into the captaines hands, to be employed in a generall purse towards a generall keepeinge of them durcinge their abode here; and so billeted them abroad among the people of that part, wheron they wer fast cast, at the rate of a doller, or foure shillinges English, by the weeke for a heade. Only the captaine, pilote, and some others of the cheifest, both of the men and women, he caused to be conueyed to the towne, wher they liued the most of them at his owne table for nine or ten weeks, vntill he shypped them away for England, as we shall heare hereafter, haueinge giuen command and direction to all the fortes as by the waye they came any thinge neere them, that they should speake loude vnto them with their ordinance, the which, though they perhaps might enterprete as a biddinge of them wellcome, yet he entended it as a lettinge of them knowe that he was able to giue it, both them and their shyps, in what fashion he listed, nourishinge them with all in all the ignorance he could concerneinge such perticulers wherin their knowledge might be any way preiudiciall, and on the contrary, puttinge on the best face he was possibly able vpon all thoes thinges that might any waye speake the strength and reputation of the Ilands.

The Gouernour haueinge thus settled this affayre, turned himselfe to the occasions of the shyp; and first of all he caused all her sick passengers (which wer very many) to be had on shore, where they wer releiued and looked vnto; then the magazin goods (of which ther wer reasonable store, though the most of them none of the fittest), and the two Cape merchands (being more by one man euer ther vsed to be one shypinge) wer appointed their residence in a newe store-house, built of purpose by the Gouernour this yeare to that end. This done, precepts are sent downe into the maine to vrge the people to their worck, and with all conuenient speede to bring up their tobacco to the shypinge, wherof not lesse than twenty thousand waight had bin torne and spoyled in the feildes by the former storme. In this shyp, ther wer also sent by the Company ten boyes apprentices, to be placed on the generall land, and by the Company wer appointed also to the custody and ouersight of the gunner of Smithes-Fort, in regard wherof, he was allowed the one halfe of their labour, and for the other to stand answerable to the Company; but with this condition, that the whole yeares crop should be sent home vnto them euery yeare in lumpe, a course the which, as being newe and straunge, bothe caused a loathnesse and difficultie in the gunner to receiue them upon thoes tearmes (which certainely he had not done but for the importunitie and vrgeinge of the Gouernour), and also gaue an apparent

euidence to the Gouernour himselfe that the Company litle
ment or entended to make good their promises, by order of
Court, vnto him in the supply of his men (wher of he
allwayes wanted twenty of his due number), since they thus
tooke up a newe deuice and course to frustrate and auoid
him, not doubtinge but that this addle egge had bin hatched
and brought up by the plottinge and suggestions of some
of his talkatiue opposites in their Courts, who endeuored
noothinge more than how to discontent and discourage him.
With this shyp ther arriued likewise about one hundred
newe planters, some wherof were people of good fashion,
and very well supplied and prouided. The Gouernour also
at the same time receiued fifteene barrells of gunpowder
from the Company, and some great shott; but expectinge
farther (accordinge to an intimation of such perticulers in
the generall letters) to haue found some store of rozin, tarr,
fishinge lines, course oyle for the armes, and some other
necessaryes, he found himselfe vterly deceiued; only the
tarr and rozin came (very ill conditioned) by the next shyp,
wherby he perceiued a bold negligence (not to say worse)
in the husband of the Company, who, being by them entrusted to see such thinges prouided and shypt ouer, either
regarded not the charge imposed vpon him, or mis-applied
it to his owne perticuler, to the great danger and hinderance
of the plantation.

In the moneth ensueinge, the second shyp of this yeare,
called the *James*, was discried from the Mount, who that
day came in into the townes harbour; and she also, by the
heates of the season, had by the waye lost her master, and
diuers of her passengers.

In her ther returned into the Ilands Mr. Lewes [Hughes],
the ancient minister (who had bin here from the very
beginninge of the plantation, and taken great paines and
done much good, and yet at this time, contrary both to all
reason and expectation, found himselfe very harshly and

vngratefully vsed euery waye by many of the Company), as also (to all wise mens wonder) Mr. Kendall, the captaine of the forementioned informers, who (as being euery waye conscious of his owne miscarriage) had procured by meanes of his cosen Sands a certaine note of recommendation or protection to be inserted in his behalfe vnto the Gouernour in the generall letters in thes wordes:—

"We recommended Captaine Kendall vnto you, and very earnestly desire you (as he hath faythfully promised us) to sett apart all discontent and euill will for former unkindnesses past either here or ther, betweene you, which we cannot thinck on without greife soe that priuate discontents may not be any hindrance to the aduaucement of ye publick affayres; and in perticuler we must require you, that you doe not vse the authoritie of your place to the recentment of your priuate iniuries; a thinge very vnworthye of a Gouernour; and such as noethinge could be more odious vnto us; especially in the case of Capt. Kendalls, who comes vpon the publick securitie of our Court, which we haue giuen him, not as a thinge needfull, for we are assured, your good disposition is such as would not haue proceeded otherwise than iustly, and as a worthy man ought: but for his owne and friends satisfaction we could doe noe lesse."

Vpon the presentment of which by Kendall, and before the Gouernour either knewe it, or sawe it, lookinge vpon Kendall he used thes wordes vnto him: "Howsoeuer, Captaine Kendall, I confesse I did not looke to see you here at this time, by reason of some straunge thinges that I haue heard of you, since your departure, practised against me in England, and which you knowe also I cannot be ignorant of; yet since you are come, you may assure yourselfe that you shall liue vnder a moderate and iust Gouerment and vnder a Commandour that doth much scorne to make vse of his authoritie to serue (how iustly soeuer) his priuate and perticuler ends."

Afterward, haueing vewed the note, and well considered of it, turneinge vnto Kendall, "You see, Captaine (sayth he), by the assurance I gaue you at the first dash, that this, your protectinge note, might haue bin spared." To which purpose also, in his answer to the Companys generall letters

comeinge to this point, he told them that he was to thanck
the Honorable Company for remembringe of him that he
held not his place here to serue his owne turnes; yet was
this a lesson that he had both learned and practised before
then as holdeinge it vtterly vnbecomeinge him, not only
as he was a Gouernour and a Christian, but as he was a
man, in such cases as thoes to deale vpon such aduantages;
in which regard he vowed unto them that their Courts pub-
like securitie might haue bin spared and forborne; and that
yet the aduenturess of some other of that confederacye, by
a returne into the Ilands without it dureinge his time,
might sufficiently proclaime vnto the world that they knewe
him otherwise than they spake him."

But, howsoever, Kendall and his consorts escaped thus
freely from the touch of the Gouernour, yet could they not
(especially Kendall, as being the most notorious) keepe
themselues so cleare from the tounges and talke of the
people, some sayeinge that he came like a theife, with his
pardon about his neck; others, that if they had bin in his
case, they would rather haue gotten a liueinge with sellinge
of stinckinge fish than, after haueinge proued himselfe a
base and false informer and slandourour of his commandour,
behind his back, to sue pittifully, and make freinds for a
protection when he had done. Thes, and such as thes, wer
the common censures of the very common sort against him.
As for thoes of better fashion, he was altogether and generally neglected by them and despiced of all, euen of such as
had formerly bin his very great and affectinge freindes, so
that noe man enuiteinge him to house, nor scarce receiueinge
him when he came vnbidden, it became his owne report
that he was almost starued whilst he stayed at towne.
Yet had the Gouernour wished him not to forbeare his table:
but his owne guilty conscience forced him (as it should
seeme) to make noe vse of that enuitement, for seldome
went he thether, nor to the very churche it selfe, but makes

awaye as sone as he could to his home at Sommerseate, wher he is noe soner arriued but falls most desperately sick; so that being in all mens iudgments held as a dead man, it comeinge to the Gouernours eare, he of purpose sent the minister vnto him to comfort him, and for quiett of his conscience, to assure him that if any act done against him in perticuler did any way trouble his minde (as he conceiued it might well be), that for his part he did fully remitt it, and absolutely forgiue him. For which message, although for that present with a hollow voice (for he could scarce speake), he seemed to giue the Gouernour much thancks; yet noe soner became he a litle recouered, but (to let all the world knowe that it was done with a more hollowe heart) he gaue it out amongst some of his rabble of Sir Edwin Sands, his planters, that the sayd minister had bin sent vnto him to grope him in his weaknesse; and that for his part he had neuer done the Gouernour any wroung, nor would acknowledge it, though he had: of such a base mettaile is the man made of.

In this shyp came ouer likewise diuers newe planters, and among them certaine young maydes (or, at the least, single women), sent ouer at the cost and by the pious intention (as the generall letters sayd) of some Aduenturours of the Company to make wiues for such single men of the country as would paye one hundred poundes of tobacco apeece for euery one of them. Ther wer also two Virginian virgins (one wherof died by the way at sea) shypped by the Virginia Company, and very well supplied by them, who wer by that Company recommended vnto the Gouernour, as being not only one of the Company, but a sworne counsellor in that plantation, that by his care and authoritie honest English husbands might ther be prouided for them (a harder task in this place than they wer aware of), who together, after some staye in the Ilands, might be transported home to their sauvage parents in Virginia (who wer ther no lesse than petie kingos), and so be happely a meanes of their conuersion.[1]

Towards the end of this moneth of October appeareth vpon the coast a smale shyp of Barstable, in the west country of England, belonging to one Mr. Delbridge, a brother of the Sommer Ilands Company, and wholy sett out by himselfe. She came into the townes harbour, and was very well conditioned, and with her a conuenient and well chosen magazin and a Cape-merchant, or, rather, captaine of the barck (for so he was stiled by a commission procured from the Company), being an allyance of the sayd Delbridge: the which magazin, the most part of it (although it arriued somewhat at the latest, and by that meanes gott none of the best tobacco), was sold to the inhabitants out of a boothe, almost a mile from the towne, the remaindour

---

[1] Pocahontas was accompanied to England by three young Indian maidens, who remained after her death a considerable charge to the Virginia Company for four or five years. One of them died of consumption in 1620, the other two remained until June 1621, when we have the following entry in the Records of the Virginia Company:—
"At a great and general Quarter Court, held the 13 June, Itt being referred to this Courte to dyrect some course for the disposing of two Indian maydes havinge byne a longe time verie chargeable to ye Company, itt is now ordered that they shall be furnished and sent to the Summer Ilands, whyther they were willing to go with our servants . . towards their preferm't in with such as shall accept of them with that meanes—with especiall dyrection to the Gouv'nor and Councell there for the carefull bestoweing of them.'"—E. D. NEILL, *Hist. of the Virginia Company*, 1869, p. 104.

By an original clerical error in some transcript from the parish register at Gravesend, the death of Pocahontas is commonly placed in 1616 instead of 1617. The date of burial is given in the Register March 21, 1616, or March 21, 1617, as we now divide the year. This has been read May 21, 1616 (see *Notes and Queries*, 3rd series, vol. v, p. 123. E. D. Neill, *History of the Virginia Company*, 1869, p. 98, and the same author's *English Colonization in America* 1871, p. 83.) I am indebted to the Rev. R. Joynes, Rector of Gravesend, for verifying this correction, which reconciles her death with the well-known fact that she was present at a masque performed before the Court in January 1617. *Domestic Corresp.*, Jac. 1., vol. xc.

therof being afterwards to be carried for Virginia, as you shall heare. By her also ther returned two or three more of the Kendall crue, and among the rest that Carter, before mentioned, who, being one of thoes three that at the first of the discouery of thes Ilands wer left here behind to keepe possession (as you haue heard), and then findeinge a great quantitie of amber-greece, to the value of fiue hundred pounds sterling, which was taken from him by the Company, he at his time by infinite importunitie in recompence therof, receiued of the Company in gift for three lines (who found that he began to vndertake some dangerous courses, by the counsell of some wiser than himselfe) a smale Iland called Coopers; but with such cuninge conditions, one whereof was to keepe continually a certaine number of resident men vpon it, to be vpon all occasions at the seruice of Pembroke Fort, which stands ther (the forte with the appurtenances being neuerthelesse excepted from him) as let the world knowe, bothe how well they could laye about for themselues, and with what a foole they had then to deale withall. By this barck, also, are brought some fewe more new inhabitants as likewise single women to sell for wiues, and young boyes for apprentices, the which to such as would and could giue most.

The fifth day of Nouember followeinge (being the day of that damnable gunne-powder treasons discouerie) was this yeare (that the Spaniards might take notice of it) obserued here with a kind of solemnitie; the Gouernor, goeinge to a sermon in the churche that morninge, with an extraordinary garde of halberds and musketts; all the straungers of fashion, bothe men and women, dineinge with him, as also all the officers, and the cheife of the towne at what time, a health being begun by the Gouernour, to the Kings Maiestie, and the prosperitie of all his dominions, ther was vpon it deliuered a very good and quick volly of smale shott, the which was answered from the fortes with great ordi-

T

nance, and then againe concluded by a second volley of smale shott: neither was the afternoone of that day without musick and danceinge, and at night many huge bonfires of sweet wood.

By this time, the most part of the tobacco being shypped, the Magazin shyp, the *Joseph*, is ready to be gone; at what time also the Governour entendinge that bothe shipps should goe together (as a good meanes of safety and prouidence for them bothe (vrged the shyp, the *James*, to a dispatch; and to encourage her the more, promiseth her the fraught of the most, and all the better sort of the straungers; for, findinge their generall purse and stock almost vtterly exhansted, and that of necessitie they wer all of them to be furnished with some warme cloathes for a winter voiage; and besides, holdinge it vtterly vnfitt, that by a longer staye, either they should become farther acquainted with the place or the people with them; he resolued to shyp awaye, either all, or the most part of them, by this shypinge. But the master of the *James*, being very fearefull of the discharge, and due pay of his fraught by thes straungers when they arriued in England; and the sayd straungers not being able by any meanes to make present payment of it here, the Gouernour was constrayned (rather than to be any longer troubled with them) to engage himselfe for it vnto the master, by leaueinge a good part of his yeares crop of tobacco in his hands, vntill the sayd fraught wer by them discharged; the which, although the straungers protested honestly and speedely to performe after their arriuall at London; yet the Gouernour thought it not amisse to intimate as much to the Company in his generall letters; praycinge them, since it was for a generall good, that if it should proue that they delt otherwise than well with him in that perticuler, they would be pleased to interpose their assistance to the Spanish Embassador resident in London, for his proseruation; to whom also, at the earnest entreaty of the straungers, he wrote letters in Spanish in their behalfe and fauour; the which, notwithstandinge he enclosed (vnsealed in his perticuler letters to the Earle of Southampton, the Gouernour of the Company), not knoweing whether otherwise it might be sinisterly interpreted by his enemies for a Gouernour in this place especially, to write to the Embassador of a forraiuge Prince, and cheifly of that Prince, without acquaintinge thoes that had employed and entrusted him thether.

And thus are these accidentall guests packed away, haueinge bin very curtuously entertained by the Gouernour (though not without some grudginge of the common sort, who sayd openly that they would not haue vsed them in the like case) durcinge their whole abode here, the which also they seemed themselues to be so seuceable of as that their departure, they presented the Gouernour with an act in writeinge, signed with all the prime mens hands; by which, as towards and by way of an expression of their thancks, they made a full and absolute deed of gift vnto him, of what so euer, either was or should be recouered out of their lost shyp left behind them; and this they manifested to be and rest in their power to doe, in regard that bothe by their owne safe arriuall on the shore, and their leaueiuge of diuers liue creatures, as hogges and dogges abord behind, the shyp could not be taken nor held as a wrack. Fiue persons only of all this number wer detcyned vntill the yeare followinge, and vnder a pretence of want of roome for them in the shyps; though many conceiued that it was rather done to find out in the meane time whether any discoueries might by their meanes be made of any Spanish intentions vpon thes Ilands from the West-Indies or els wher; and the rather (perhaps not causelessly), it was guest so by reason that these fiue men wer saylours, and had long bin conuersant in thoes partes and soe most likely to attaine to the knowledge of it if any such thinge wer in talke.

T 2

About the fourteenth of November, both the shyps, the *Joseph* and the *James*, beinge in two seuerall harbours, gatt out and mett at sea; yet neither of them without some danger: for although the weather was at the same time so calme, as they wer forced to towe them out with botes and strength of men, yet the chanells being very narrow and the currant great, the *Joseph* found her selfe to be falne ouerneere a rock, and so was putt to it to let slipp an anchor, and so shyffted for her selfe. But the *James* (wherin most of the Spaniards wer), by the willfullnesse of her Master, who regarded not the Iland-Pylotes aduise, caused his shyp to be towed vpon a rock which laye hid a fathome under water, wher she strooke seuen or eight times, to a generall dismaye, but especially with the poore straungers, some of the women lamentinge, and cryeinge out to be gotten on shore againe, and sweareinge that they would rather die in the Ilands than aduenture awaye with such perill. But the seas (by good hap) being extraordinary still and quiett (otherwise she had certainly bin lost without all redemption), she was at last towed of, with very much adoe, and that without the least harme and dammage that could be discerned: which caused the Gouernour to saye (when he was told of it) that he was noethinge sory for the aduenture, since the shyp escaped so well: "for", quoth he, "it letts the Spaniard knowe, that besides our good fortes and store of ordinance, we haue secrett and stroung walls vnder water, on all sides to giue them a rude wellcome if they come vnbidden, vnlesse they looke well about them: the which thes their countrymen haue found true to their cost by loseing their owne shyp and goodes on the end of the Ilands, and beinge putt into a second feare of loseinge of their liues in one of our owne shyps at the other end."

In the moneth next followeinge the barck of Barnstable also takes her leaue of us, but leaues her Captaine or Cape-merchant behind, who (from some former infection) dieth in the Ilands. She made her course for Virginia, whether (as you haue heard), after her dispatch here she was bound. By her the Gouernour sent two large cæder chests, wherin wer fitted all such kindes and sortes of the country plants and fruicts, as Virginia at that time and vntill then had not, as figgs, pomegranates, oranges, lemans, plantanes, suger canes, potatoe, and cassada rootes, papaes, red-pepper, the pritle peare, and the like : one of which sayd chests he directed to the then present Gouernour, with letters of this tenor followinge.

"To my worthy Friend, Sir Frauncis Wiatt, Gouernor of Virginia.

"Sir,—If your name deceiue me not, we knowe one another. Howsoeuer your neighbour-hoode and affinitie of command inuite me to wellcome you, and to wish you all happinesse, in this your onerous Honnour.

"Our plantation commenceth a commerce vnto you, for by this shyp I haue sent you suche of our prime fruicts as (I heare) you haue not, but assure my selfe you would haue; nor is ther ought els with vs, but (dureinge my tearme here) you shall, as brethren command it. And (although your owne climate giues a beleife you can haue noe badd aire) I cannot chuse but wish you the temperature and salubritie of ours, the which I dare pronounce to be equall with the best of the world; and with it also communicated our bothe naturall and artificiall strengthes. I doubt not but that you haue your good wishes for vs likewise, as a participation with you of a spatious continent, goodly pasture, fayre riuers, necessary yron mines, and (perhaps) some other secret hopes : We are glad and thanck you for it, and let vs still iointly goe on to wish one anothers good, and to act it, and God second our honest endeauours. And thus (noble sir) you haue hastely and heartely recommended the true and faythfull affection of

"Your assured freind,
"St. Georges, in the Sommer Ilands,   "NATH. BUTLER.
"Decemb. 2, 1621."

The other chest being alike fitted and ordered as the former, he sent vnto Sir George Yardly, whose time being newly expired, Sir Frauncis Wiatt arriued ther this yeare, being chosen by the Virginia Company to succeede him, Sir George retireinge himselfe, as a priuate man, to liue vpon certaine land of his owne in a hansome house which he had built dureinge the time of his Gouerment. The contents of which letters wer as followeth :

"To my worthy freind, Sir George Yardly, in Virginia giue thes.

" Worthy Sir,—This bearer (who loves you well) assureth me that you ment vs well the last yeare, and that you sent out a shyp of purpose to let vs know it, of which howso euer we wer depriued by the ignorance of the pylote, yet your noble entention ought to be and esteemed as an act done to encresse my thancks. I haue nowe sent you some of our country fruicts, and I wish they may multiplie with you; they are of our choice ones, and such as giue vs much content here; wher, and euery wher els, I shall by all meanes expresse my selfe,
" Your affectionate freind,
" St. Georges, in the Sommer Ilands,   " NATH. BUTLER.
" Decemb. 2, 1621."

The Ilands being thus cleared and voide of shypinge, and the Gouernour at some litle leysure, he presently goeth into the maine, and so out to sea to the lost Spanish shyp. He had bin once there before, within two dayes of her first ruine; but even then findinge her (contrary to all expectation) shyuered all to pieces (for neuer had shyp a more soudaine death), and most of her goodes either under water, or floted away, he found noe possibilitie of recoueringe any thinge of value, saue one anchor, one cable, and two very good sakers: Nor spedd he any thinge better at this time, for the wind beginning to blowe loud, and the least gale disablinge all attempts that waye, by reason of the great swellinge of the billowes in that part, and its beinge so far out to sea, he was constreyned to returne without any great effect: only three murthering peeces wer weyed and brought to the towne, the which afterwarde wer knowen to be the very same that Kendall had sold to Kirby: whervpon the Gouernour, demandinge of the fiue Spaniards that wer left behind how their shyp came by them, it was answered that the sayd Kirbie, being long on roueinge vpon the Islands of the West Indies, was at last discouered in his haunt, and two good shyps sent out from Cartagena to entrappe him ; wherein their Pilote had bin cheifly employed : so that at last, being taken on the soudaine, most of his men wer slayne and hanged, his frigate borded and carried awaye, and himselfe, being shott through the neck with a muskett shott, forced to runne into the woods, wher he sone after died of his hurts : by which meanes whatsoeuer he had formerly pillaged was made a praye to the conquerours : thes murtherours fallinge to the share of their Pilote, who thus brought them to his shyp, and his shyp to us.

The Gouernour is noe soner returned out of the maine to St. Georges, butt he setts twenty men of his owne people on worck at Southampton Forte, the which after six weekes of hard labour is absolutely perfected, and the whole worck shutt in, and ordinance secured, by three smale bullwarcks, two curtaines, and two ravelins : the which not only (being thus putt together) maketh a very fayre shewe out to sea, but is, with all (the naturall site of rock exceedinglie well concurringe) very stroung and defensible : being (to saye the truth) the only true peece of fortification in the whole Ilands.[1] By this time Christmas being come, and the prefixt day of the Assizes, the fifth generall gayle deliuery (since this Gouernours time) is held at St. Georges, wherin diuers ciuill causes betweene partie and partie, in the nature of nisi-prius, being heard and decided, some delinquents are condemned and sentenced to the whypinge post : others to be burned in the hand accordinge to the natures and severall qualities of their offences. Three young boyes only, for sundry felonies, as stealeinge of pigges, meale, potatoes, and breakeinge open some cabbins to that end, are sentenced to be hanged ; but being carried ouer to the place of execution and made to goe up the ladder, and their eyes banded, lookeinge verely to die and being exceedingly

[1] This Fort still exists, abandoned, but in fair preservation, and is among the most interesting of the historic monuments of Bermuda.—*Ed.*

terrified, thoir reprive is shown to the Marshall, who ther vpon returneth them, the Gouernour sayeinge to some that wer about him, that he could not find in his heart to hang such young knaues for stealeinge only for their bellyos, since it might well be, that either the cruelty, pouertie, or at least want of fitt gouernment in their masters, wer chiefe occasions and motiues of this ther pilferinge: an apprehension iustly and with all reason grounded vpon the carelessnesse and indiscretion of diuers vndertakers in England, who appoint boyes to be commandours and ouerseers of boyes. But the only matter of note at this Assizes, was, that the same Crowther, about whome it was suggested (as you haue heard) by the Articlers of England, that the Gouernour should conceale his felonye, haueinge at the sitting of the Court entred an action of slander against one of thoes informers, for giueinge out some such thinge of him, here since his returne, the Gouernour caused the sayd action to be so withdrawen (although ther wer diuers wittnesses ready in the Court to depose for the cleareinge of the sayd Crowther), sayeinge that himselfe being interested in the cause, it was not fitt nor proper for him, being the Judge of the Court, to haue the heareinge of it; and that therforo he must, together with himselfe, haue patience vntill their returne into England, wher he might assure himselfe to find good and sufficient justice in good time to right them bothe.

The Assizes being broken up, the Gouernour, with the the first of the newe yeare, sends downe his Linctenant into the maine, to distribute the armes to able people, and such as wor fitt, and affected to be soldiers. And to that purpose, giueth certaine orders for the rendeuous, and answeringe to all alarmes, which wer hanged up in all the churches in the maine and wer to this effect: "That fiue of the tribes, vpon the disconery of an enemye, should resort to the ouerplus house with their armes, ther to be furnished with powder, bulletts, and match ; the charge wherof was committed to the neerest Counsellour dwellinge ther-abouts: and from thence they wer to be conducted by their leaders, accordinge to direction from the Gouernour, and as occasions required. The rest of the tribes wer to repayre either to the Kings-Castle or the towne of St. Georges, to be prouided ther in the like manner, and accordingly commanded. And euery man to whom armes wer committed wer at all times to keepe them fixt and in point, vpon the penaltie of one moneths imprisonment, and to be withall disgracefully cassired: and were also vpon the like penalty to make their appearance at all exerciseinge dayes and places."

About this time it was (though by meere chaunce and ill husbandry, too), that an experiment and inuention of much importance and benefitt for the whole Ilands for the keepinge and preseruation of their corne (which is the Indian maiz) from the flie and weauell which infinitely spoyled it, and hitherto vnauoidably, was found out and discouered. For the Gouernour haueing giuen out a proclamation the yeare before, that all corne should be housed and gathered in by a certain day, vpon the penaltie of the forfeiture therof: which was done vpon due information and certaine knowledge, that very much corne, by the lazinesse of diuers idle persons (who more diligently looked after Aqua-vitæ than Panem-vitæ), had by that meanes bin lost and spoyled euery yeare in the feilds, and, with all, proued a great nourishment and maintenance of the increase of ratts, a vermin euer dangerous, and to be carefully looked after in thes Ilands ; at this sommer haruest (ther being generally great store of corne vpon the ground, and a goodly crop) very many of the inhabitants (none of the best husbands), who had hastely gathered in their corne before the day of forfeiture, for feare of vndergoeinge the penalty, haueing so gott it in, did as hastely cast it into out houses, vpon heapes, and altogether vn-husked, as it came from the foild, so lett-

inge it be vnheeded foure or fiue monethes, by which time
all the good husbands through out the whole Ilands, who
had diligently and painefully husked and hung up all their
crop, began euery wher to complaine and lament the ruine
and spoyle of it by the flie and weauell: only thes good fellowes, who neuer cared but from hand to mouthe, wer iolly,
and held up their heads, makeing their boasts that not a
graine of theirs had bin touched or hurt: the which (beyond
all beleife) being, indeed, found visiblye true, some fewe (who
looked into the causes of actions) apparently perceiued that
the former common vse of huskinge and hanginge up of the
corne (which both tooke up much time, asked many handes,
and hindred other bussinesse about tobacco) had bin the
only meane to prostitute it to the flie, who, by bloweinge
into it generated the weauell; the which weauell, after it
had deuoured the inward substance of the graine like a
viper, eates out its way, and became a flie it selfe: from all
which the corne was sufficiently preserued by being left
lieinge in its naturall coate-armour, the husk. Herevpon
this ill-bestowed vnproffitable labour of huskeinge and hanginge of it up becomes totally left and giuen ouer (for you
may be sure that euery man would greedely followe a lazzie
trick, especially being gainefull with all), and therby the
former wonted plauge of the decaye and ill keepeinge of it
excellently avoided: an experiment among many others,
which lets the world to vnderstand that mis Fortune hath
euer had, and will haue, a greater strooke and hand in in-
uentions than either witt or industry. Much about the
same time, also, excellent fresh water is luckely found out
both in Cooper Iland and St. Dauis, to the great ease and
benefitt not only of the places themselues and the inhabitants ther, but of all the neighbouring fortes, which haueing
bin long and often searched after in former times could
neuer be mett with all vntill nowe.

In the moneth of February followeinge, certaine iniunctions wer directed from the Gouernour to all churche wardens and sidemen to this purpose:

"That wheras the sayd church-wardens and sidemen wer to assist the ministers in lookeinge to the liues and conuersations of the people, being a principall meanes for the suppressinge of prophanenesse and vngodlynesse, that therfore the sayd officers wer carefully to take to their charge, and to goe vnto, or send for all suche person or persons as should be found to absent themselues from the churche, or refuse to recciue the communion, or wer an open prophanour of the Sabaoth, or an obstinate swearer, notorious drunckard, disorderly and riotous gamster, enraylour, slaunderous or idle busie-body, a make-bate, one vehemently and vpon iust grounds suspected of an incontinent life, or liueinge any waye offensiuely, the which sayd delinquents, they wer first in mild and loueinge sort to admonish and exhorte in the feare of God to refraine from such vnchristian behauiour, and in case they amended not, but still continued in their former disorders, to present them at the generall Assizes, ther to receiue such open punishment as the qualitie of their offences should be found to deserue. And farther, the foresayd officers wer to present all such readers as regarded not to keepe a true register of all marriages, christeuings, and burialls, as wer made in ther generall parishes, or did not euery Sabaoth day teache and catechise such youthes and people of the younger sort as wer most ignorant in the principall of Christian religion, and to saye the Lord's Prayer, the articles of the Christian fayth, and the ten commandements by heart, as also all such prime men of famelies as did either refuse or neglect to send their people and seruants at the time appointed for the sayd readers to teach and instruct them."

In the same moneth, also, the Gouernour augmented the number of his garde from twelve to twenty, and gaue them one Mr. Seymour Woodarde for their captaine, a very honest and ciuill gentleman, and a rare man (in that regard) in thoes partes, who was the first captaine of the garde in the Sommer Ilands.

In the moneth of Marche followeinge, a small barck was discouered vpon the south-west side of the Ilands; the which the day after gatt in at the townes harbour, being sent from Virginia. Her ladeinge was aqua-vitæ, sack, oyle, and bricks; in exchaunge wherof she desired plants and herbes of all sortes, potatoes, ducks, turkeyes, and

lime-stone: she brought with her also letters from the
Gouernour and some of the Counsell ther to the Gouernour
here, in her behalfe and fauour, wherin mention was made
(with muche thancks) of the receipt of the former supplies
sent (as you haue heard) by the Barstable shyp, exceedingly
crauinge a second and an enlarged quantitie in the like
kindes.

In the interim of this shyps abode here, the marriage of
the Virginian mayde, recommended vnto the Gouernour by
the Virginian Company resident in London the shypeinge
before, was consummated: she being then married to as fitt
and agreeable an husband as the place would afford, and the
weddinge feast kept at the towne, in the Gouernours newe
house, and at his charge, wherto not only the Master of the
newe come shyp, and some other strauugers wer inuited,
but not fewer than one hundred persons wer made guests,
and dined with all sortes of prouisions that the Ilands could
afford in very plentifull manner. And it was thought to be
done in a more fasionable and full manner, that the
straungers at their returne to Virginia might find reason to
carry a good testimony with them of the wellfare and plenty
of this plantation: as also that the kindred and freindes of
the Virginian bride, who wer prime commandours, and not
lesse than Viceroyes among the neerest neighbouringe Indians to the English colony ther, might receiue a certaine
knowledge of the well being of their kinds woman, and by
the good respect and kind vsage shewed vnto her among
the English, be encouraged both to continue and augment
ther former freindshyp, and to become Christians themselues: to which ende also, the Gouernour wrote letters of
aduice to the Gouernour in Virginia, and caused the mayde
herselfe likewise to doe as much to her brother, who, by her
fathers late death, had succeeeded in all his royalties and
commande.

At the same time (this nuptiall feast being ouer) an

essaye was putt in action by the Gouernour for the killinge of wales, who (dureinge the monethes of Marche, Aprill, and May) are in huge numbers found vpon the coast: and it was attempted at this time, vpon the Master of the shyps report of his owne sufficiency and his mates that wayc who wer both of them employed in it; but noethinge effected, as well by reason of the misse of due meanes, as due skill: otherwise it being in all likelyhoode a bussinesse very faysable, and of fayre hope; and that as well in regard of the extraordinary number of the whales as of the richnesse of them, haueing (noe question) for the most part store of sperma cœti.

After fiue weekes staye here this Virginian barcke cleared herselfe of the harbour to make a returne into Virginia, being deeply laden with the natiue commodities of the Ilands, for the releife of that plantation: for she was ballasted with lime-stone, the best in the world for that purpose; and had besides twenty thousand waight of potatoes at the least, great store of ducks and turkeys, some fewe conyes, all kindes of plantes in great varietie and quantitie, as likewise store of the Cassada roote, and a good proportion of corne, and of which also she might haue had much more. For the Gouernour, haueinge receiued secret and sure intelligence, by some priuate letters, written from thence, that the people ther in generall wer in much distresse by want of breade, freely offered vnto the Master of the shyp to spare him twenty thousand eares of corne out of his owne store, and one hundred thousand from the country; but the Master (being as it should seeme scooled to a concealement) would by noe meanes confesse nor acknowledge any want at all in that kinde, and so went awaye worse prouided than (perhaps) sorted with the wishes and expectances of many of the inhabitants, especially of such as being but newe commers thether might well find a smarte sence of this dissimulation, and wish that ther had bin lesse outfaceinge of a want in that nature, especially with their neighbours being Englishmen.

The monethes of April and May followeinge wer spent in fully accomplishinge and perfectinge the newe stone house at St. Georges; in buildinge of a strounge and large prison of framed cæder; in digginge of a newe well, and empaleinge of it; and in scowreinge of the fresh water pond ther. The Gouernour also, at the same time, sent downe his Liuetenant and the Captaine of his garde to attempt the weyeinge of the rest of the great pieces at the ruined Spanish shyp, wher, after fourteene dayes expence of twenty mens labour, foure very good sakers wer recouered, and gotten to the towne.

Sone after this began the generall Assize at St. Georges, wherin wer decided not fewer than fiftie ciuill (or rather vnciuill) actions betweene partie and partie : and twenty criminall prisonners brought to the barre, to the great discontent (as well as trouble) of the Gouernour, who plainely found by thes vnexpected ill fruicts of the misvse of his former wonted clemencye, that a wraunglinge and stiffnecked people, as the most of thes proued themselues (being, to say truth for the greatest part, improuidently and wreatchedly raked up out of the London kennells,[2] wer not to be mannaged with so smoothe and gentle a snaffle as he (out of his naturall disposition) had thetherto only employed,

[2] See *Calendar of State Papers, Colonial Series*, pp. 12, 19-23, for indications of the reckless measures employed to obtain labour for Virginia and the Sommers Island at this period, to which many of their disappointments were traced. Among others, the king ordered one hundred men to be pressed, "notwithstanding the many inconvenyances which Mr. Ther (Treasurer) alleadged would thereby accrew unto the Company, that they could not goe in lesse than fouer shipps for feare they beinge many together may drawe more vnto them, and so mutiny and carry away the ships, which would stand the Company in foure thousand pounds"...... Memorial to the Rt. Hon. Sr Wm. Cockaine, Knt., Lord Maior of the Citty of London, 17 Nov. 1619, applying for a further grant of one hundred children. E. D. Neill's *Virginia Company*, p. 160.

and, therefore, openly professed himselfe happy, and a glad man that he was so shortly to leaue them. And the rather he became fully assured hereof, by the cryeinge and outrageous crimes, that three of these foresayd prisoners wer nowe in hold for; wherof the one was endicted and arrainged (and as straungely, to say truth, acquitted by a sencelesse jury, though one of the best the place could afford) for the rape of a married woman; the second and the third, after a large heareinge, and due and fauourable triall, wer acordinge to their desertes hanged: and vpon iust cause...... And as an addition to all this, much about the same time likewise, two chickings wer hatched, the one wherof had two heades, and the other crowed very loude and lustely within twelue houres after it was first gotten out of the shell.[3]

A litle before this Assize also it was that a certaine desperate fellowe, bound ouer thether to answer for his stealinge only of a Turkye (a fact that could not haue cost him more than a burneinge in the hand, whether it wer out of meere madd folly, or of being conscious to himselfe of some other guilt), aduentured, rather then to come to his triall, to steale away a hansome newe bote belonging to his Master (who was his surety for his appearance), and in her (being single and all alone) to committ himselfe to sea: the which he did, but to what part he intended, and with what forecast, could neuer be yet discouered, for hetherto he was neuer heard of, nor without an exceedinge wonder litle short of a miracle is he euer like to be.

It was much about this time (accordinge to an Order of Court sent from England, and receiued by the Gouernour the shyppinge before) that the office of the baylies was putt

[3] I here follow the judicious example of the Richmond reprint of Smith's *Generall Historie of Virginia*, Ed. 1819, in omitting the details of abominable crimes and incredible prodigies, which are given in that work in terms identical with the present narrative. See *Memorials of Bermuda, etc.*, vol. i, p. 159.

downe, who being remoued from their sayed places, in their roomes, and steade wer chosen, by pluralitie of voices, two men in euery tribe, who wer after the same fashion to be newly chosen euery yeare, and wer tearmed ouerseers, being especially (nay only) to looke to the diuident of all suche commodities as wer to be yearely shared betwixt the owner and planter. And it was found very straunge and much wondered at by all suche who, neuer so litle, looked into the generall carriage of affayres in thes Ilands, that the ad- uenturers in Englande, who, for the maine part of them, are well ynough knowen to be very ententiue and open-eyed for their owne aduauntage and gaine, and hereof some what vncharitably suspitious, and therfore extreamely iealous of being iniuried in thes kindes by their tenants here, should thus on a soudaine decline, and forsake the care and con- science of the former baylies who, for the greatest part, wer elected and appointed by themselues, and the rest by the Gouernour (being certainely not only the most sufficient, but the most honest here to be found), to throwe themselues thus and their confidence vpon such men who wer only to be culled out by a generall choice (which is generally the worst) taken from the mouthes of thoes very people whom they wer thus to trye and ouersee. How could it be but apprehended but that this their election, thus brought forth, must of necessitie produce all the effects quite contrary to their aimes and desires: neither could it be imagined by what meanes and fortune this galemafry became thus dis- gested, vntill at last it was remembred that the most part of the able iudgement of the Company by their being els wher tooken up and bestowed by the actiue times and high affayres at that time on foote in England, this bussinesse and contriuement fell necessarily vpon the refuse and rest of them; who, for their creditt sake, thinckinge to doe some what, at length, after much sweateinge, lighted vpon and hatched vp this broode of new orders about thes fresh ouerseers, the which in all probabilitie is most likely (if it hold out but a yeare or two) to stinge and vexe thoes that sate so close vpon it, euen in thoes very perticuler partes, wherof they are most tender and so most chary.

The office of the baylies thus ceaseinge, that part of their former charge which belonged to publick justice (for they had formerly in their peculier tribes, serued in the nature of Iustices of the Peace) was by the Gouernours iniunction layde vpon the sworne Counsellours and a perticuler Counsellour appointed for euery tribe, who, within their limitts, wer to doe justice in petie matters, and so to saue the people from the labour of runneinge vp to the towne vpon euery slight occasion. And this course he was forced to take, as findinge that the newe annuall ouer-seers, in all likly-hoode would be allwaies vtterly vnfitt for this seruice, and that bothe by reason of their choice, as chaunge; and therfore thought noe waies fitt (although the vndertakers had entrusted them with their tobacco) at which notwithstandinge he much wondred) for him selfe to doe the like by them, in pointe of justice.

In this moneth of Iune, the botes are once againe sent downe from the towne to the Spanish lost shyp (being almost fortie miles of) for the recouery of the rest of her ordinance; but, the weather falleinge out very vnanswerable both in respect of winde and raine, after eight dayes attendance of twentye-men, one only saker, and another murtherour are brought up to the towne.

Presently vpon this returne the Gouernour began to hewe out of the maine rock a payre of large and handsome stayres, for the conuenient landinge of goods and passengers out of botes, the which after one weekes hard labour of halfe a score of people of his owne, wer fully finished, to the much both beauty and benefite of the towne.

This done the Gouernour employed two of his botes, manned with twenty of his best men, with two excellent diuers, and went in himselfe in person, to attempt the recouery of more ordinance out of the wreackt *Warwick*, being the shyp that brought him in. But she was found so vnluckely lodged as all the remaindour of them wer burried vnder her side, and not one of them to be found; so that one only small murtheringe peece was gotten vp at that essay. But not contented with this ill fortune, he, the same day, caused thes same botes and men to passe out to sea, and to make a discouerie vpon the rotten ribbs of a shyp called the *Sea-Adventure*, which (as you formerly heard) had bin wreacked about some thirteen yeares before.[4] The which beinge founde out, and his diuers sent downe to the bottome (which was three or foure fathome deepe) to see what was to be done, at the very first profe, there was, by great chaunce, discouered a very fayre saker; and with very much adoe (though not without some danger of mens liues (euen of the Gouernours, who stoode nere vnto the guun) by the breakeinge of a rope, such is the miserable want of respect in such of the Company, as, by the Lordes and others are improuidently entrusted with the prouideinge of suche necessaries) the sayd peece was safely recouered and landed at the towne; haueinge notwithstandinge her long lieinge vnder water, receiued litle or noe harme. At the same time and place also, a great shete anchor of hers was weyed; as also diuers barres of yron and steele, with some pigges of leade; to the great benefite and vse of the poore Plantation in that perticuler, whereof at that present it was in great and gripeinge want, by reason that for diuers shypinges before, scarce any at all of soe vsefull and important a commoditie had bin imported, through the carelesse wreatchlessnesse of the greedy vndertakers, who neuer regard how litle of such necessaryes they send vnlesse it returne an vnconscionable gaine into their vast cofers; nor how much

[4] Singular that the writer does not think it worth mentioning that this was Sir George Sommer's vessel.

of vnnecessaries, nay preiudicialls, so it pay them accordinge to their pedlinge phrase, with cent. per cent., at the yeares end, as it commonly doeth.

This yeare, towards the latter end of July, the Gouernour with diuers botes in his company sayled downe vnto Sands his tribe; from whence he caused diuers searches to be made out into the sea at the Westerne End of the Ilands, for the carkase of a certaine shyp, the which by sundry inhabitants of thoes partes had bin seene, and was reported to lie with her hull suuck vnder water, vnbroken up, and her hatches spiked downe; but by noe meanes could she be found out. Only three fayre sakers more wer weyed out of Spanish wreack, which laye all in pieces not far of from thoes quarters; the which done the Gouernour returned to the towne, takeinge his waye through the Tribes, at what time he tooke a vewe of a certaine newe Ingenio proiected by some of the vndertakers in England, vpon their vaine hopes of suger canes; the which he found more than halfe finished.

All this sommer also the Gouernour employed two of his people to look out for bedds of oysters, and to make triall for the findinge of perle; wheroof a certaine quantitie of seede was presented him (and which was very straunge out of one only smale shell, about six score smale seede) besides some other perles of a reasonable size and roundnesse, only they wer found somewhat defectiue in their coulour, and wanted that orient lustre and shyne which cheifly giues them their prize and value.

It was much about this time that certaine letters, signed by the whole body of the Counsell, wer presented by the Minister, Mr. Lewes [Hughes] unto the Gouernour at St. Georges, being (verbatim) of this tenor.

"Right Worthy Sir.—This poore plantation, haueinge nowe almost for three yeares had its liuely hoode and being from your noble and iudicious Gouerment, wee assure ourselues that your wisdome hathe long since taken due knowledge of thoes griueances wherwith this litle common wealthe is most oppressed, for which (as we by our place present the body of the plantation) we stande bound in a generall behalfe to seeke all lawfull redresse. To that end thes are presented vnto your vewe, and our selues in generall become petitioners, requestinge your lawfull fauour (although we must confesse that in respect of your selfe, your care, trouble, and gouerment, might iustly end all at once), that so you would be pleased to take into your consideration our poore condition and estate, so that when you shall leaue and surcease to be any longer our noble Gouernour, you would vouchsafe to remaine our most worthy freinde, in presentinge our discontents to the Right Honorable the Lordes of the Company, and so, vpon occasion, to proceede by waye of humble petition to the Kings Most Excellent Maiestie (the relcife of the oppressed), by whose gracious fauour we hope (through your assistance) to be made happy by a true setled government. So shall not our selues only rest obliged vnto you in all thanckfullnesse (as the only meane of our deliuerance), but the generall inhabitants also of thes Ilandes be for euer bound to eternize the remembrance of so good and beneficiall a deede and most noble an action; and thus, worthy Sir, presumeinge on your fauourable graunt herein, we cease from farther troublinge of you by heapes of wordes, and rest with remembrance of our seruice. At your noble commande."

And thes wer the contents of thes letters, of which the Gouernour haueinge considerately aduised, he returned an answer by the same hand that brought them, that the Counsell (from whom they came) should determine of a generall meetinge in some place in the maine, wher he himselfe would not fayle to be present, and so to giue them his resolution by his owne mouthe. At which assembly (being about eight dayes after), after he had made mention of the message receiued from them and the perticulers therof, he told them that findinge the motiues very forceable and vrgeinge, and their manner in deliuery of themselues fayre and honest, he could not (haueinge vowed himselfe to the good of the plantation) but yeeld to their so generall a sollicitation; only in regard of important priuate distractions which might befall him in England, wherby he might be forced to a lesse attendance vpon the bussinesse than was requesite and he desired, he thought it very behoufefull that they would select two of their company to be ioyned with him to helpe to beare out that burthen ; and that, with all, letters of credence and intimation should be iointly written from them all to the Lordes of the Company, which might expresse their meaneinges and desires in some breife and generall tearmes. The which aduise being receiued and followed, the men wer presently made choice of, and the letters drawne to that purpose as followeth :—

"May it please your Honnours. We shall be humbly bold to expresse and make knowen vnto the noble Lordes of the Company thoes heauie lodes and weightie pressures which, by the disrespects and impositions of the generallitie of the Company, doe dayly fall vpon vs and make vs to grone. And since this expression of our selues proceedes from most loyall and quiett mindes, and is to be offered to most noble and true iudgments, we cannot but assure our selues not only of a favourable construction but gracious acceptance ; and the rather in regard that (being sworne councellours for this poore plantation) we act (as we conceive) noe improper part. Yet not to be tedious to your Lo., but takeinge due notice of your highe affayres, we haue chosen in thes our suppliant letters to fall only vpon generall tearmes as to lament vnto you our being defrauded of the foodes of our soules, neglected in the safety of our liues, censured by orders of Court, contrary to his Maiesties lawes, frustrated in our important and neerely touchinge couenantes, impouerished and made naked by being forced to buy our necessaries at most vnreasonable rates, and lastly that our children, when any of us die, are left here behind vs in a condition but litle better than slauery.

"The perticuler euidences and profes of which generallities we leaue to Captaine Butler, our late Gouernour,[1] to single out vnto your Lordshyps whensoeuer you shall be pleased to require them, whom by our ioint and earnest intreaty we haue sollicited and wonne to this charitable office, and haue also ioyned with him the Captaine of the Kings-Castle and the Captaine of Southampton Fort, being bothe of them our fellowe counsellours, most humbly beseechinge your noble Lo. to vouchsafe them your beninge audience and full credence, that so, vpon due examination, we may (by your gracious fauour and protection) find our redresses (accordinge to our hopes and prayers) from your honorable Lo., or at least (if vpon necessitie) your Lo. (who we well knowe are noe

---

[5] This expression is used in anticipation. Butler's time was nearly expired, and he, in fact, left the Island about a fortnight before the arrival of his successor Captain Barnard, which occurred early in November 1622.

way conscious of our wrounges and sufferings) shall admitt and direct us to proceede farther, by waye of humble petition to his sacred Maiestie in that behalfe, that then your Honnours will vouchsafe to be so far from being parties against us as not so much as to rest neuters, but to be pleased to compassionate our greiuances, and to receiue vs and this whole plantation as most oppressed but most respectfull clients vnder your aidefull patronage and protection, towards whom in all humble duty wee shallbe allwaies ready, by all possible meanes to be expressed.

" Your Honnours most affectionate seruants."

And thus wer thes letters of credence, wherin to giue a fuller satisfaction to the Lordes concerneinge the grieuances noted vnder generall heades in the foresayd letters. Some choyce perticulers wer instanced and proued vnto them by a second writeinge, signed likewise by the whole body of the Counsell, which I haue thought good also to deliuer vnto you, and wer as followeth :—

" 1. We are defrauded of the foode of our soules, for being not fewer than fifteene hundred soules, dispersed into a lengthe of twenty miles, we haue at the present but one only minister, neuer had but two together, and thoes two, alwayes so shortened in their promised entertainements, as but for meere pitty, they would certainely haue forsaken vs, and so haue left vs desolate.

" 2ly. We are neglected in the safety and preseruation of our lines.

" By want of all sortes of munition, for we are not allowed so muche powder as can maintaine all our ordinance in three houres fight. We haue nine fortes and two plattformes, and fiftie three great peeces seruiceably mounted, and but one only gunner in the Companyes pay to plie them all, yet hathe ther bin not lesse than two or three thousande poundes raysed by impositions vpon our tobacco within thes three last past yeares vnder the pretence of supplyeinge vs with thes necessaries.

" 3ly. We are censured contrary to His Maiesties lawes, as it may appeare by thes instances followeinge in steede of many others.

" One Paul Deane, being indicted, arraigned, and condemned for the stealeinge of a peece of cheese valued and prized (with all stricktnesse) at about two shillinges six pence, pleadeinge the benefite of his cleargie accordinge to the lawes of England, is rigourously denyed it, and so hanged vntill he was dead in Captaine Tuckers time.

" One Nicholas Gabriell, endicted, arraigned, and condemned (in Captaine Tuckers time of Gouerment also) vpon certaine mutinous wordes, as was pretended, being repriued from the execution of the sentence, was in lieu ther of censured by the Gouernour in direct tearmes to remaine a slaue to the colony, contrary to the lawes of Englande, which alloweth noe slaues, nor any such censure.

"One Steuen Painter, vpon an action of trespasse only, sayd to be committed against his vndertaker in England, without so much as being first admitted to speake for himselfe, is by an Order of Court from the Company in Englande censured, not only to make a full payment and reparation of the sayd pretended tresspasse, but also to be (ouer and aboue) examplerly punished. The coppy of the which sayd sentence is sent ouer by the Company ther to the Gouernour here, to be by him putt in execution vpon the sayd Painter.

"4ly. Wee are frustrated in our important and necrely touchinge couenants.

"For one John Dutton, comeinge ouer hether, vpon hopes of a commission giuen him vnder the handes of the perticuler Aduenturers of Warwick tribe, wherby he was enabled for three ensueinge yeares to be bayliefe of the sayd tribe, and by waye of recompence for his paines in dischargeinge of the sayd office, to receiue the thirtith part of all suche parcells of tobacco as should yearely dureinge the sayd tearme be made up in the sayd tribe, the sayd John Dutton is notwithstandinge, by an iniunction in the generall letters, sent ouer hether the very next shypinge after his arriuall, absolutely prohibited to receiue or meddle with the sayd thirties, and yet enioined to execute and performe the sayd office and charge without any one penny proffitt. It is also (as a farther vndeniable profe of this grieuance) a case generally knowen and felt in thes Ilands, that many poore planters, haueinge couenanted with their under-takers in England (and comeinge ouer hether vpon hopes therof) to deuide their yearely tobacco here, and only to be accountable vnto the moyetie, are neverthelesse (contrary to the sayd perticuler couenants) forced, by newe generall Orders of Court, to send ouer their whole crop of tobacco into England vnto their undertakers vndeuided, from whom the most of them neuer receiued but very lame and wretched accounts, to the vtter vndoeinge of the sayd poore planters.

"5ly. Wee are pinched and vndone by vnreasonable rates of necessary cloatheinge, houscold-stuffe, and other goodes.

"For, notwithstandinge that our tobacco (our only mony) is by the Aduenturers valued at a meane rate here, vz., at two shillinges six pence the pound, yet their owne commodities sent ouer hether are by themselues pitched at what prize themselues please, and so sold here, viz., salt, six shillinges the bushell ; vinegre, at three poundes of tobacco the gallon ; oyle, eight shillinges the gallon ; aqua-vitæ, three poundes of tobacco the gallon ; and that without all allowance of leakage, weareinge cloathes also, and all other the like necessaries being answerably rated.

"6ly. Our children, the parents dieinge, are left behind them, and kept here, in little better condition than slaues.

"For poore planters, comeinge ouer hether, and sometimes bringinge ouer with them diuers children, if any of the planters chaunce to die (as diuers haue done, and allwaies will doe), their surviueinge children are for many yeares employed and helde as slaues or drudges at best to their landlords for the only discharge of their dead fathers debts, beinge in the meane time instructed in noe trade, scarce so much as to the makeinge up of tobacco, but left in the handes of rude and mercilesse young fellowes, vtterly vnfitt for the least charge in that nature, who, insteade of allowcinge of them necessary cloatheinge to couer their nakednesse, and due foode to fill their bellies, teache them only suffrance and patience, to the great ruthe and pitty of all honest eyes that behold and consider them."

After the profe and manifestation of which greiuances, ther was last of all (by a thirde writeinge signed as before) offered vnto the considerations of the sayde Lordes of the Company a course and waye of redresse and case of the foresayd wrongs, expressed in the wordes followeinge:—

"An Humble Proposition, submitted with all due respects vnto the true iudgements of your Honnours for the true redresse of thes suffrances.

"Wherin we are far from that insolent arrogance as to prescribe any course iu this kinde to your Lo. wisdomes, only in confidence of your gracious goodnesse, we are bold to present our meane apprehension; but yet in the nature of a rude chaos to receiue its forme and perfection from your Lo. direction and approbation.

"In regard therfore (as it is most apparent) that all thes ills and neglects proceede from the carriage and conclusion of all affayres, by multiplicitie of voices in the Sommer Ilands Courts in Englande, wherby not only all holsome and necessary motions (especially if they succour of neuer so litle charge and expence) are cried downe by number rather than waight, but also that this course, as being in its selfe full of confusion and error, is directly contrary and opposite to the noble Government of a Monarchy, vnder which we haue bin borne and bred, and desire alwayes to liue; it is our dayly prayers (and we hope without all offence) that it might please His Sacred Maiestie, in steede of this anarchy of Gouernment nowe practised in the Sommer Ilands Courts in England, to institute and appoynte the body of a Counsell, selected and composed of you the Honorable Lordes, the Gentlemen, and some of the worthy Merchants of the Company, who beinge thus His Maiesties Counsell for thes Ilands, and haueinge their certaine and knowen dayes of sittinge, all the rest, bothe of the Aduenturers and planters, may (vpon all occasions) haue their recourse thether (by petition) for iustice; and that from thence all orders, lawes, and iniunctions concerneinge the Gouerment and perticularities of thes Ilands may haue either their beinge or alloweance.

" And from hence (we find all reason to assure our selues) ther will vndoubtedly flowe as from a pure and naturall fountaine thes blessed and holsome streames.

" 1. That we, the poore inhabitants of thes Ilands, shall be supplied with a meete sufficiencye of Ministers, and they sufficient men, and sufficiently payed and contented.

" 2ly. That we shall allwaies haue a due quantitie of munition, some skillfull gunners, and an answerable number of generall men to manne and attend the fortes.

" 3ly. That the pure and smoothe currant of His Maiesties lawes shall passe amongst vs without interruption either of ignorance or tyranny.

" 4ly. That by a free trade and lawfull admittance hether of honest men and shypinge, the excessiue and gripeinge prizes of all necessaries will of themselues fall to an honest abatement.

" And this (as we wish, so we hope) may, without all inconuenience or violence to His Maiesties gracious letters patents, or iniury or detriment to any one in perticuler, be graciously graunted by His Most Excellent Maiestie; and so willbe, shall it but please you, the honorable Lordes of the Company (to whom we are, in the name of the whole plantation, most humble suppliants in this behalfe) to vouchsafe it and vs your necessary assistance and opportune mediation.

" For which high and pious fauour, the whole inhabitants of this poore plantation (at the present languishinge vnder thes vnsupportable burthens) shall continually offer up their earnest prayers to Almightie Godd (as they haue due cause) for your Honnours happynesse and prosperitie, bothe in this world and that which is to come."

And in this manner and methode was this affayre contriued and fashioned for its carriage, mannagement, and dispatch in England. What the issue was, and effect that followed herevpon, must be looked for hereafter.

But this bussinesse was noe soner ouer but the Gouernour found himselfe intreagued in a second, and that of noe lesse consequence; for not long before, haueinge caused a certaine fellowe named Thomas Harriott to be bound ouer to the next assizes vpon certaine seditious wordes by him vttered to one of the Counsell, and some others which might tend to a stirringe vp of the people to disobedience

and mutinye, he at this time, by letters sent vnto him from
that parte of the Ilands and the same counsellours, found a
soudaine and dangerous encrease of the same ill by the
same delinquent, causeinge not only a boldnesse and irre-
gularitie in the common and worse sort of speritts in that
quarter, but also a dishearteninge and feare in the best, the
contents of which letters (for the fuller expression of this
motion) I haue here also inserted, aud are as followeth :—

"Right Worshypfull.—At your last being with me at my house, at
the binding ouer of Harriott, you gaue me charge to haue an eye vnto
him in the point of his followers especially, since which time how iolly
and carelesse he hath shewed himselfe, his great feasteinges and the like
it is not vnknowen vnto you. But at the present he so exceedeth, and
is growen to heighth of insolence, as he dares to question your worshyps
gouernment, to interrupt the minister in the pulpitt, to disobey my commands, and hath angled the people to that passe, as some haue bin heard
to saye they would they had more Harriots; others that they would be
of Harriotts side, and the like. True it is, Sir, that thes thinges I heard
not myselfe in person, but Mr. Lewes can (I dare say) verefie as much
to his greife, and Captaine Yates also, vnto whom, as I haue heard, he
spake straunge wordes before the whole tribe. I confesse, Sir, it had
bin my part to haue seazed upon his person presently, and to haue sent
him up prisonour vnto the towne; but I conceiue with all that, if it
shall please your worshyp to send your marshall to fetch him up by land
in yrons, all his confederates will be much daunted; for to say truth,
they are all so out of order as they cry with loude voices after Mr.
Lewes that Capt. Tucker will come too morrowe, nor can I apprehend
any other issue hereof than some violent sedition, vulesse your wisdome
take a speedy course of preuention, for so many seemes to stand up with
him, as it may be ynough to cost vs all our liues; for ther are so many
poore snakes (but desperate withall) that seeme ready to take his part,
as if he should be suffred vntill your time should be expired, before the
comeinge in of your successor, it is to be feared that euerye one would
be a Gouernour, and all thinges come to confusion. I beseech your
worshyp to examine all that Mr. Lewes and Capt. Yates can saye herein,
and to consider of that and this, and what more may be founde in this
compact, that so both he and they may be curbed in time, for otherwise
I must needes saye our case will sone proue most miserable.

"Your Worshyps in all humblenesse,

"S. P."[6]

---

[6] Probably Stephen Paynter, one of the principal people at this time.

The Gouernour being quickned with thes letters, and findinge it necessarie to shew himselfe to be so, instantly sent downe the Liuetenant of his owne company, together with the Prouost Marshall, who sodainely apprehendinge the sayd Harriott in his house brought him to the towne, wher he was made a close prissonour; wherupon an especiall Commission being directed to two Counsellours, for the full and perfect examination and takeinge knowledge of his cause, the whole body of the Counsell was assembled, who, together with the Gouernour, sitting in open Court, the sayd prisonnour was charged with these sixteene articles followeinge, and vpon the charge had free libertie to make answer for himself.

"Certaine articles, tendinge to sedition and mutinie, obiected and proued against Thomas Harriott of Southampton tribe, tobacco-maker, being brought to the barre, before the Gouernour and Counsell, openly sittinge in Court, etc., vpon the 7th of September 1622.

"1. That the sayd Harriott did giue out that the Gouernour should saye that he would call a Martiall Court, and hang him the sayd Harriott if he could.

"The which sayd article was proued against the prisonnour by the oathe of two witnesses, and found a mere slaunder of the Gouernour.

"2. That he should report ther wer noe counsellours allowed in thes Ilands, nor to be so held to be, saue only Capt. Felgate, Capt. Stoakes, and Capt. Kendall, but that the rest wer of the Gouernours makeinge, and therfore durst not but yeeld to whatsoeuer the Gouernour liked, least he should take them by the arme and turne them of, and therfore they rather chose to saye as he sayth, and sitt with their hatts on their heades, than by displeaseinge his will to be made to stand bare. And in scorne he called them a company of wise men.

"Proued by the deposition of two witnesses.

"3. He hath sayd that the Counsell in generall stand but for ciphers, and doe more hurt than good in their places.

"Confessed by the prisonour.

"4. He affirmed that the Gouernour sold corne out of the publick store to the Spaniards that lost their shyp vpon the coast last yeare, and tooke mony for it.

"Confessed by the prisonnour, but the contrary proued.

"5. That he aduised one Mris. Faucett, widowe, to redemande certaine corne that her husband the yeare before had payed into the publick store, accordinge to a leuye appointed by statute, saying vnto her to encite her thervnto, that it was as good mony as any in her purse.

"Proued by the oathe of two wittnesses.

"6. That he hath publickly reported in a disdainefull manner that the Gouernour would haue euoughe to doe to answer for himselfe vnto such matters as ther would be obiected against him, viz., for loadeinge the people with payments. And that for his part he would make him to answer him for certaine corne that he was forced to pay the last yeare.

"Confessed concerneinge the first part that the Gouernour would haue ynough to doe to answer for himselfe, and his owne reason was because (quoth he) I haue gone ouer with two Gouernours from hence, and they wer bothe of them troubled by the Company; and so he beleaued would this be. As for the rest, that the Gouernour loded the people with payments, and that he would make him to answere for his corne, he denied them bothe; but that he had notwithstandinge so reported was proued by the oathes of two wittnesses.

"7. He hath sayd that the Gouernour this yeare did demand 30,000 eares of corne of the country, and the Counsell did taxe the country at 42,000, which was 1,200 more than the Gouernour required; but that the sayd Counsell should be made to pay it back, and farther he hath ignorantly affirmed here vpon, that the whole body of the Counsell wer in a premunire.

"A sufficient cause being shewed for the leuy of the ouerplus of corne, the prisonnour was found guiltie of article by his owne confession.

"8. He affirmed that the Gouernour should saye that without himselfe his Counsell could doe noethinge, but that he, without his Counsell, would doe any thinge, wher vpon he inferred that the Gouernour would make himselfe more absolute than the King.

"Found to be a meere falsehoode and slaunder of the Gouernour, inuented by the prisonnour.

"9. He hath sayd that the Gouernour called the Ferry at Burntpoint a royaltie belonginge to the Company, and therfore he tooke 250lb. of tobacco this yeare for it of Captaine Yates; but (sayth he) the Gouernour dares not call it a royaltie in England.

"The article confessed wholy by the prisonnour.

" 10. He hath sayd to Captaine Yates, by waye of aduise, that he should not paye one ounze of tobacco vnto the Gouernour for the foresayd Ferry.

" Confessed to haue giuen him the sayd counsell.

" 11. He publickly gaue out that wheras the Gouernour told him that he had gotten his mony with tappinge he kept, himselfe kept a tap-house vnder his nose, and an extortinge fellowe to begger the country with payinge the extortinge host; and that he prayed God that the Gouernour proued not a kind of host himselfe, for he thought it would proue that he had a hand in the buyeinge and sellinge of the wine, which the last yeare was solde so deare.

"The whole article found a meere slauuder, inuented by the prisonnour, of which he was found guiltie by his owne confession.

" 12. He boldly affirmed to the person of a Counsellour that for his part he would paye none of the leuie appointed by the statute for this yeare, vnlesse it wer gotten from him by force.

" Fully confessed by the prisonnour.

" 13. Being in company of diuers persons, the sayd Thomas Harriott, in a seditious and braueinge manner, deliuered these wordes, that if the people of the Ilands wer as they might be, they would not pay one iott of the fore-sayd leuies, but make the Company to doe it.

" Proued by oathe against the prisonnour.

" 14. He openly and in plaine tearmes sayd that Mr. Lewes, the minister, and a sworne counsellour besides, was a foole.

" Proued by oathe.

" 15. The sayd Mr. Lewes, being publickly preachinge the worde of God vnto the people out of the pullpitt in Southampton Tribe Churche, the said Harriott openly and aloud interrupted him, being in the exerciseinge of his diuine function, and told him he was out of his text.

" Confessed by the prisonnour.

" 16. Lastly, ther was produced (as effects and motions caused by these seditious speaches and rebellious behauiour of the sayd prisonnour) the secondinge of him by some of the common people, who had bin his auditors, and nowe groweing to shewe themselues his disciples, wher of some of them sticked not to saye openly that they would be of Harriotts side ; others wer heard to wish that they had more suche Harriotts ; and one Mallory, and Will Hardeinge, a black-smithe, with diuers others, went of purpose to a village called Port-royall to heare (as they sayd) how Harriott would hold up the two Captaines Stokes and Yates, being bothe of them sworne counsellours for the plantation.

"The full of which article was proued against the prisonnour by oathe, and some of the sayd seditious delinquents punished accordinge to their demerritts."

Herevpon, accordinge to these profes and confessions, a censure passed vpon him by the Gouernour and Counsell, sittinge publickly in Court, the which with a very vnusuall vnanimitie was as followeth :—

"That he, the sayd Thomas Harriott, their prisonner at the barre, being accused and conuicted of all the turbulent behauiour and seditious speeches conteyned in the articles aforesayd, should be conueyed mannacled quite through the maine vnto Southampton Tribe (wher he had acted the most part of his insolencyes and mutinys), ther to haue one of his eares nayled to a whippinge post (which was purposely to be erected and called Harriotts Post), soe to stande the space of halfe a houre, then to be brought back to the towne of St. Georges, and in the pillory ther to lose his other care; to paye a fine of one thousand poundes of tobacco to the vse of the Honorable Company, and to remaine a prisonnour in the gayle of St. Georges dureinge the sayd Companyes pleasure."

The which sentence was shortly after executed vpon him, only in pitty and commiseration the Gouernour spared him one of his eares, vpon his future good behauiour, haueing bin also very fauourably vsed in the takeing away only of a peece of the other. A fauour notwithstandinge noe waye deserued by the delinquent who euen in the instant of the triall of his cause, had in diuers perticulers carried himselfe with much insolence, as amongst others an arrogant and impertinent exception takeinge against diuers of the Counsell, as not to be allowed for his competent judges, by reason (forsoothe) that one of them, in his examinations of him should tell him that he had made a fayre step to the gallowes; that another had sayd, vpon his demandinge to haue bayle, that it was not safe to allow bayle to a mutiner; that a third (vz.) Mr. Lewes the Minister, had in his prayer desired God to conuerte the mutinous and rebellious speritts of the Islands, or to cutt them of, and the like.[1]

Not long before this it was that the Gouernour made one Mr. John Yates (an ancient planter and a sworne Counsellour for thes Ilandes) the Captaine of Southampton Fort by Commission; who thereby also became obliged and tied to an attendance vpon that fort, and to a sufficient manneinge of it, with his owne people vpon all soudaine occasions and alarmes; as likewise to the entertainement of a resident gunner ther vpon his owne peculier charge, in consideration whereof he had graunted out vnto him (with a prouisoe notwithstandinge and reference to the Companyes approbation) the keepeinge of the ferry at Burnt-point; and for which (it being euery way to be sufficiently mainteyned by himselfe also (he was only to receiue the beneuolence and free gift of the people, the inhabitants of the Maine, and not otherwise,...

And here it was the will of God to take out of this world the writer of this History, hee intendinge a farther progresse in it, butt as I haue heard from the last mentioned Gouerners mouth the Company of Aduenturers in England, accordinge to theire wonted cauallinge manner with the precedinge Gouerners, played fast and loose with him as with the rest, and though hee stayed his full tyme att the Somer Islands and tooke much care and paines not only in orderinge the strengtheninge of the cheife forts, planteinge of necessarys and doeinge what possibly could be done in the infancy of this plantation, butt alsoe in establishinge honest and conuenient lawes for the good of the place, yett he returned with verry little proffitt or thancks more from that vngratefull Company then those which were before him.

[1] No record has been found of the assizes held between June 1620 and March 1626. The trial of Thomas Harriott seems to have occurred in 1622, at which date therefore this History breaks off.

FINIS.

A RELIC OF SIR GEORGE SOMERS.

The object represented below, on a scale of ½, is the mass of meteoric iron employed by Admiral Sir George Somers or Sommers, cir. A.D. 1600, for magnetizing his compass needles, see Fuller's worthies of Devon.

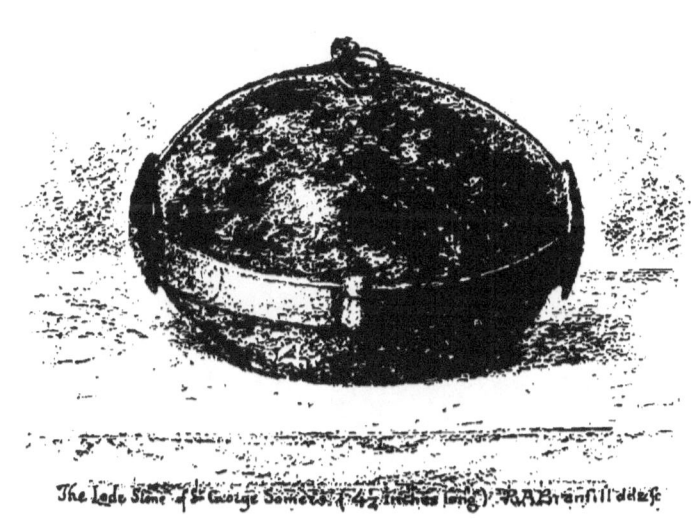

The Lode Stone of Sr George Somers (4½ inches long) R.A.Brenfill delt.

From the original in possession of Miss Bellamy Plymouth

APPENDIX.

I.

ON THE SITE OF THE PLACE OF INTERMENT OF THE HEART OF SIR GEORGE SOMERS.—*See* p. 175..

GOVERNOR SIR JOHN HOPE, by deed dated 14th July 1726, grants unto Samuel Smith of the town of St. George's, gentleman,

" All that lott, piece, or parcel of land, situate, lying, and being in the town of St. George's, containing from north to south-westward forty-one feet of assize or thereabouts (be it more or less); from north to south-eastward, fifty-four feet of assize or thereabouts (be it more or less); from east to south-westward, sixty-four feet of assize or thereabouts (be it more or less); and from east to northward, sixty-three feet of assize or thereabouts (be it more or less). Bounding on the west on the Governor's garden, south on the street or path, east on the lott now in possession of Peter Le Conte, and on the north by the Governor's said garden .."
—*Grants*, No. 9, *p.* 208.

Samuel Smith, by his last will, dated 25th March 1729, devises as follows :—

". . . Item, I give, devise, and bequeath unto my granddaughter Susanna Smith[1] aforesaid all that my lott of

---

[1] Susanna Smith (to whom the lot was devised in tail) married Wright Westcott, and the lot descended to Wright Westcott (his son) of Norfolk, Virginia, who barred the entail and sold it to Thomas Western

land in St. George's aforesaid (to be passed after the decease of my said wife, or sooner, if she my said wife pleases) adjoyning to the comon pound, and opposite to the tomb of Sir George Sommers (as in the grant thereof is set forth), unto her the said Susanna Smith, etc., etc."—*Wills*, p. 234.

Hence, it is evident that in 1729 the traditionary site of the tomb of Sir G. Somers was well known, that it was in or near the Governor's garden, north of Mr. Smith's property, and near the common pound.

Now we find at this day in what remains of the Governor's garden an altar tomb bearing the inscription :—

"CHARLOTTE HOPE
POSUIT
JOHANNES HOPE
PRÆFECTUS
24 DECEM. 1726."

It was, evidently, thought unnecessary at the time to say why she placed it; and if, as I presume, her object was only to mark in a more worthy manner a spot already notorious, the omission is sufficiently accounted for thus. Samuel Smith refers to it in his will three years later as a familiar object. The same spot was in 1819 still the reputed burial place of the "heart and entrails" of Sir George Somers, and as such, was opened in search of them by Admiral Sir David Milne, who, however, found nothing except fragments of a glass vessel or bottle, the character of which is not recorded.

(Commander R.N.), afterwards Admiral Thomas Western, whose family now owns it.
From a deed of 1805, I find that at that date what was formerly the "Pound Lot" was called "Peter Burchall's". This lot was next westward of the premises now occupied by Lane as stables, etc. It was the lot leased by Burchall to Western in 1795.

In 1795, the lot opposite this reputed tomb was leased by Peter Burchall to Thomas Western, and probably a plot of it drawn, which, however, has not been found.

In 1831, the same lot was surveyed and a plot drawn by Dan. R. Prudden, Surveyor-General, who inserted opposite the north-east angle of it, or opposite the north-west angle of the adjoining lot, which is known to have been formerly Colonel Samuel Smith's, a rectangle, with the words, "Tomb of Sir Geo. Summers", agreeing very well with the indications in Samuel Smith's will already quoted. This original drawing is in the secretary's office, but a copy of it is in the possession of Mr. Swainson, owner of the adjoining lot to the west, and in the copy the rectangle is moved about thirty feet to the west, and the words added, "Tomb of Sir G. Summers". "Hic situs corpus G. S. 1600." The Latin is wrong and the date wrong, and on what authority the place was changed, or the "Hic situs" inserted, is not known. It may have been put in from memory after the copy was taken, and accidentally set at the wrong corner. There are other slight deviations from the original in this copy, especially in the notations; and it is significant of the little attention paid to accuracy, that York Street is called Kent Street in both. The pound is inserted in Prudden's plot, who adds: "See the lease from Burchall to Western, dated 28th Nov. 1795, when the pound was included with the lot by Mr. Trott's survey."

There must have been many elderly men living in St. George's in 1726 who could remember Richard Norwood. He was doubtless concerned in the erection of the original monument, and survived until 1675. It is hardly conceivable that tradition could err within one lifetime so far as to fix upon a wrong site for an object of so great local interest; and I conceive, therefore, that the spot now marked by the commemorative inscription in the text (p. 175) is as well authenticated as the case requires. It is of the greater interest, because the precise site of the interment of his actual remains at Whitchurch, in Dorsetshire, cannot be identified, and his monumental inscription has disappeared in restorations of the church.

II.

THE FIRST GENERALL ASSEMBLIE, HELD ATT ST. GEORGES IN THE SOMMER ILANDES, BY INSTRUCTIONS FROM ENGLAND, BEGUNN THE FIRST DAYE OF AUGUST, IN THE YEARE OF OUR LORD 1620, CAPTAINE NATHANYELL BUTLER BEING GOVERNOUR, AND IN THE FIRST YEARE OF HIS GOVERMENT. —*See* p. 192.

The Forme and Composicion of the Generall Assemblie.

The Persons.

The Gouernour.

The Counsell.

The Bayliffes of the tribes.

Two sufficient Burgesses out of euery tribe to be chosen by voices.

A Secretary, to whome all bills are to be presented, and he to read them in the Assemblie, and to be sworne.

A Clercke to recorde the Actes; to be sworne.

The Order appointed by the Governor.

The first day, after a sermon in the morning, the burgesses, the secretarie, and the clercke are to be sworne.

And the whole company to be called ouer by the secretarye, and so to take theire places in the house, the Counsell sitting next the Gouernour, and the rest as they come.

This done, the Gouernour breiflie declareth the order, the *scope*[1] and benefitt of the Assembly, giueing instructions and *Advise*.[1] And soe the Assemblie riseth for that day, for

---

[1] See p. 195. The words in the MS. are here illegible.

they sitt only in the morninges, the afternoones being bestowed either in consultation with the Gouernour in his private house, or vpon some perticuler committees, to frame busines agaiust the next morninge.

Att the next meeting of the Assembly, the secretary reads distinctlie suche bills as be propounded, which being once read, whosoeuer wills riseth up, and speaketh either with it or against it.

In which accompt this order is to be observed.

He that entendeth to speake is to stand vp (vnless it be the Gouernour) bareheaded, wherby it is discerned that he has a meaninge to speake.

If more stand vp then one, he that is iudged to arise first is first heard.

Euerie man is to direct his speeche to the secretarie, and to be hard out without interrvption.

He that hath once spoken to a bill, thoughe he be presently answered and confuted, may not reply that daye, so that none may speake twice to one bill in one day, and this is to avoide ouermuche disputes and mispending of time. In speaking against any mans speeche, the party spoken against is not persoually to be named, to auoid heate of contention and the giueing of distastes.

Noe revileing or nipping wordes are to be vsed vpon any occasion whatsoeuer.

All bills are to be read three seuerall daies once (and but once): they come to the concludinge of them by voices, that so in the meane tyme they may aduisedlie be examyned, and euery man have space to deliberate, and soe accept or reiect them when they are putt to voices.

After a bill is read three seuerall daies, and sufficiently disputed vpon, the secretary is to demaunde whither it shalbe putt to voices or noe. The which being graunted, the said secretarie is to hold vp the bill in his hand, and to saie—as many as will haue this bill to passe for a lawe, lett him saie soe. If the crie *yea* be found apparently greater then the crie *noe*, the bill is enacted for a lawe; if on the contrary, it is dashed.

If it be a dowbt which crie is the greater, the secretary is to saie thus—as many as allow the bill, stand vp on your feete, and you that refuse it sitt still. And soe bothe the numbers being counted, the most carrie itt.

And in this manner all bills are to be decided during the whole tyme of the Assemblie.

Vpon the last daie of the Assembly, all the Acts that haue passed are to be read.

Which being donne, the Gouernour dismisseth the Assembly, concluding with some short speeche, as he findeth occasion.

All the acts being afterward digested into a convenient method, are to be sent into England to receiue their ratification by the Company there, in suche manner as by his Maiesties letters pattents is lymitted and appointed. And in the interim, the Gouernour here by Order of Court, ther is awthorised to putt in execution all the said Actes and Constitutions whatsoeuer, as he shall finde meete, prouided that the same be not repugnant to the lawes of England.

Note, that any man whatsoeuer, although he be none of the present Assembly, maie yett lawfully proferr a bill to the Secretarie durcing any session of any Assembly, prouided that it be for the benefitt of the publique, and be modestlie and cyvillie composed and required.

The Office of the Secretarie belonginge to the Generall Assemblye.

The first day of the Assemblie, the Gouernour haueing taken his place in the Howse, and the Company being come together, the Secretary is to present himself to the Gouernour to receiue his oathe.

Being sworne, he is to stand by his place, and then to call ouer all the Company by their names and titles they holde in the Assemblie, who are to present themselues vnto him as they are called, and soe receiuinge theire oathes from him, to retire to their places.

This action being performed, he is to read the forme and order appointed to be obserued in the holding of the Assemblie.

He is also to receiue all bills that shalbe deliuered vnto him during the whole tyme of the Assemblie, the which he is to cause the Clerke appointed and sworne for that purpose to engrosse into a booke.

All those bills, as occasion shall serue, he is distinctlie to read word for word with an audible voyce before the Assemblie. He is to obserue dilligentlie that all bills be openlie·read thre severall daies before they be putt to the question, and so to passe by voyces.

A bill being read thre severall daies, and sufficiently debated of, he is to holde it vpp in his hand, and reading the title of the bill, he is to demaunde whither it shalbe putt to the question or nott.

Being putt to the question, he is dilligentlie to observe whether by most voices it be allowed and enacted for a lawe or contrariwise ; and accordingly he is to recorde itt. Att the breaking vp of the Assemblie, he is to read ouer the titles of all such actes as during the whole tyme of *session* haue by the Assemblie bene enacted and confirmed. And lastlie, he is to dispose and construe all thesaide actes and statute lawes into a convenient and sutable forme and methode, that so they may be sent into England vnto the Company there to receiue theire confirmation, and in the interim to be putt in execution here by the Gouernour as he shall finde cause and occasion.

The Oath of the Secretarie to the Generall Assemblie.

You shall receive all suche bills as shalbe delivered and offred vnto you to be presented vnto this Assemblie. You shall accordinglie, as opportunitie shall serve, distinctly, word for word and with an audible voyce, reade them in the Assemblie; you shall dilligently observe and take especiall care that all bills be openly read three seuerall dayes before they be putt to the question, or come to be decyded by the plurality of voices; you shall heedfully and faithfullie take accompt of all suche bills as by most voyces shalbe passed and ennacted for lawes; you shall conceale the secretts of the House, and neither directly nor indirectly reveale or discourse them to any person whatsoeuer not being a member of this Assemblie. All this you shall sweare to performe and keepe to your vttermost powre and abillity, so helpe you God.

The Oath of the Clerke of the Assemblie.

You shall dilligentlie, exactly, truely, and faithfullie, as nere as possiblie you may, engrosse all suche bills as shalbe deliuered unto you for that purpose by the secretary; you shall assist and aide him in all suche imployments and affaires as (belonginge to this present Assemblie) he shall haue occasion to vse your service; you shall not reueale any busines or affaires handled or determyned by this Assemblie within your hearing or knowledge. This you shall sweare, performe, observe, and keepe to your vttmost, so help you God.

The which bills being found fitt, and becomeinge the cares of the House, and being such as this Assembly may take notice of.

The Oath of a Burgesse of the Generall Assemblie.

Being to be a member of this generall Assemblie, you shall sweare to vse and ymploy your best endevour as a furtherance thervnto. All suche proposicions as shalbe by you or by your meanes offred vnto the consideration and discussinge therof shalbe especially entended and levelled at a generall welfare: you shall not be lead by any partiall affection or respect of private interest or gaine to oppose or hinder the establishinge or ennactinge of any lawe ameing at the reformacion of any dissorder and abuse. In all suche actions as you shall practise and contrive duringe your whole time of assistance in this service, you shall strive to discharge a good conscience in all equity and integrity; you shall by all meanes conceale the secrets of the Howse, and not impart or discover, either by word, writinge, or any other meanes, to any one, not being of the present Assemblie, the passage and carriage of any affaire or busines that shalbe treated of and disputed dureinge the tyme of the whole sittinge and continuance of the saide Assemblie. And this and euerie parte therof you shall promise and sweare to keepe and performe to your vttermost powre and abillitie, so help you God.[1]

III.

HISTORICAL DOCUMENTS ANNEXED TO THE SLOANE MS., 750.

I. *The Voyage of the " Garland",* 1619.

Wee, the Gouernour and Counsell for the Sommer Islands, do giue certificat vnder our hands that vpon the thirtieth of

[1] For fuller information regarding the progress of self-government in the Colony, *see* a paper by the editor on the "Constitutional History of the Bermudas", in the *Archæologia*, vol. xlvii.

October 1619 the ship called the *Garland,* Wm. Wye, master, arriued here in the harbour of the Kings-Castle, haueing hadd a long and tedious voiag from England to these parts. And brought hither diuers passingers safe and well, with certen goods consigned to these Ilands, of which passingers sixe are said to haue died by the waie and two in the harbour. And of which goods, notwithstanding the clamour of losse and damage by diuers passingers, he and his company affirmeth to haue all sett ashore as farre as he or they knowe, having taken noe further charg vpon them but the conduction of the shipp only. As also that he brought in the said shipp diuers passingers bound for Virginia, wherof at sea died fowre, Captaine Whitney, their principall Commander, dieing here on shore at St. George. After which arriuall, he haueing staied twenty daies here in harbour before his shipp could be vnladed, by reason of the scarcity of boats and the tediousnes of the wether, althoughe he had all the assistance that possible could be given him from vs, there arose, the 19th of November in this place, a verie sore and tedious storme, in which storme the foresaid shipp was likly to haue perished, with all suche men and goods as were then in her. And by reason of whiche storme, the Master, for the saftie of the said shipp, was constrained to cutt ouer board the maine mast of the said shipp, being muche damnified in his cables, by whiche distres, not being able to performe his voiag to Virginia without his said mast.

II. *The " Garland's" Return to England without Orders.*

A Commission graunted to Wm. Wye, Master of the good shipp called the *Garland,* for the gouernment of the said shipp passengers and seamen, during his voyag from the Sommer Ilands into England.

To all to whome these presents shall comme to be seeno

or heard, I the Gouernour and Principall Comaunder now resident in the Sommer Ilands, sendeth greeting, whereas the Gouernours and Companie of the Cittie of London for the Plantacion of the said Ilands, by vertue of the Kings Maiesties Letters Pattents vnto them graunted, hathe giuen to me the said Gouernour, as appeareth by Commission under their seale, full charge and authoritie to execute and performe within these Ilands all suche things as to the place and office of a Captaine and Commaunder appertaineth, as well in causes criminall as civill. Nowe knowe you, that I the said Governour having vppon speciall considerations, fraughted out the good shipp called the *Garland*, from these parts into England, with diuers parcells of goods of tobaccoe, and other comodities due to the said Companie : by vertue of the said Commission giuen to me from the said Companie, doe authorise and enable Wm. Wye to be maister and Comaunder of the said shipp and Companye during the said voyage ; willing and commaunding all persons whiche shalbe shipped in the said shippe for this voyage, to accept and obey him, as their lawfull Commaunder in this kind, during the time of the said voyage. And withall doe give charge and commaund to the said Wm. Wye to performe and execute all suche things, either for gouerment or direction, as to the said place of maister and Commaunder of a shipp shall appertaine and not otherwise, whoe for the breache and transgression therof shall give accompt to the said Honorable Companie, now resident in London, att his retorne to England. In witnes wherof, I the said Gouernour haue hervnto putt my hand and seale, etc., 15th January 1619.

III. *An Investigation ordered* 1620.

A Commission-graunted to Wm. Seymour and Seymour Wodward, gent., etc.

To all men to whome these presents shall comme great-

ing, etc., wheras by reason of the negligence and wastes of
the last yeare, the late blast of our corne, and the putting
vpon vs of manie verie ill provided new commers, we are
falen into somme distres of bread: soe that manie are
altogether destitute therof: And because it is especiallie
my charge and care in doeing justice to all sortes, to succour the poore and distressed: Being informed that there
are divers vncharitable persons among you, whoe haueing
an overplus of cotton, and more a great deale then will
serve them and their familye for their sober expences
vntill the next harvest, doe either hide it, expecting a
dearer markett hereafter, or doe sell it at suche vnreasonable rates as are altogether vnconscionable, and full of
oppression, theirby provoking God's wrathe against vs to
punishe vs further in our next cropp, since we make a
praie of the necessities of our poore brethren: For the
redress and remedie of these inconveniences, it is thought
fitt (according to the lawdable custom vsed in England in
the like cases), that there be a due searche made in all
cabbins throughout all these Ilands, and in all likely places,
where anie corne maie be hidd and layd vpp. And if there
shalbe found in anie of the said places anie quantitie of
graine, more than shalbe judged fitt and requisitt for the
convenient sustenence vntill the next harvest, of the family
wherin suche corne shalbe found (a reasonable rate being
allowed for their purpose), that then the surplusage and
overplus shalbe sould to suche poore people as are knowne
(by all likelihoodes) to stand in greatest wants and necessities: And that att such prices as by honest men appointed for that purpose (whereof the bailiff of the tribe is
to be alwaies one), shalbe thought fitt and reasonable.
The payment being to be made presentlie, if the parties
haue wherewithall; or els at the farthest at the next
croppe; and for the faithfull and dilligent execution of the
premisses, I haue, and doe by these presents authorise,

constitute and appoint Wm. Seymour, my seiaut maior, deputie bailiff of Saudes tribe, and Seymour Wodward, the bailiff of the collony and steward of my house, to be Commissioners in this busines. Straightlie chardging and commaunding all bailiffes and other officers whatsoeuer, being resident within these Ilands, not onelie to acknowledg and reccine them accordinglie, but also to giue and afford all possible assistance for their better effecting of this service. Given vnder my hand at St. Georges the 4th daie of Marche 1619-20.

IV. A particular Commission graunted to Lewes Hughes, John Yaites, John Perenchieff and Jarvis Inglesbic, sworne Counsellors of Estate.

To all men to whome these presents shall comme greeting. There haveing bene diuers and sondrie persons sommoned and called before me the Gouvernour and the whole bodie of the Councell, to make their personall answers concerning certaine defamatorie and seditious sclaunders tending to the contempt of authoritie by the abuse of the Gouvernours person, the whiche said persons haveing bene vrged according to the statute, in that case provided, either to produce theer authors, or to be held soe themselves: and so to receive their censures accordinglie, they haue all of them performed thus muche, so that for the time it resteth upon the person of Miles Kendall, a sworne Councellor, and the bailiff of Sands tribe; but the said Miles Kendall being att that present soe visitted with Gods hands by sickness, as that he could not with the rest (according to sommons orderly given him), make his personall appearaunce to answer for himself. These are therefore to commaund and authorise thaforenamed Lewes Hughes, John Yaites, John Perenchieff, and Jarvis Inglesby, Counsellor as aforesaid, to make their personall repaire to the said Miles Kendall att the place where he is now resident, and there to confer togethor, and examyn him about the said particulers, and so to retorne how and vppon whome, he shall any waie disburthen himself hereof. Assuredly hopeing, that he will bothe consider duely of the respects in this faire course carryed vnto him, and also shew a readie willingnes, according to the dutie of the place he holds, to give a free passage to the execution of that justice, whiche a cryme of soe highe a nature requires.

Given att St. Georges the 8th of June 1620.

IV.

ABOUT PANIQUE FEARES SEIZEINGE VPON AN ARMY.
Probably by Captain John Smith. Sloane MS., 750.

It hath bin founde the generall practise of all able generalls in thoes panique feares which haue often befalne armies neuer to hazarde a battell before they hadd recouered and assured the speritts of their men: and this they commonly practised by one of thes two waies or by bothe. By makeinge of speches or by a strounge entrenchinge the terrified army in some place of advantage not farre from their enemie: and from thence by smale skirmiges of some selected men to lett the rest find (litle by litle) that neither their enemies wer inuincible nor more valient themselues, but that by the conduction of their cheifes and their obedience to their discipline, they might be broken.

Thus did Cæsar in his warre with Ariouistus,[2] who being lodged betwixt him and his victualls, whiche incited the feare, Cæsar herevpon marched with his whole army and fortified in an aduantagious place, about two miles distant from the enemies camp, ye which withall fauoured ye *carriage* of his prouisions of victualls vnto him, employinge one thirde of his army in the worck whilst the other two stoode

[2] Cæsar, *B. G.*, i, 31.

in battell, to repulse Ariouistus if he should attempt to hinder his fortifications: this being done, he left two legions lodged within thes entrenchments, and brought back all the rest of his army into his old Camp: and the morrow after presented himselfe in battell betweene bothe the Campes: but soe as that Ariouistus issueinge out vpon him, was by Cæsars best men, who wer ordered purposely to recciue him, soe entertained as he was gladd to retire with the worst: whervpon Cæsar finding the courage of his soldiers herby recouered, brought out all his army, and marchinge to the very retrenchments of his enemies Camp prouoked him to the combatt, fought with him and defeated him.

For mine owne part, I find noe cause to doubt, but that if our first discoverers vpon the severall partes in the West Indies, hadd bin but as heedfull and wise to maintaine those Indians in theis kindes of panique feares which they hadd of our men and armes at ye first fight, as Cæsar was to diseugage his soldiers from them, wee might to this daye have wrought more amongst them by the beateinge of a drumme than now wee can by the fireinge of a canon.

GLOSSARY OF UNUSUAL OR OBSOLETE WORDS AND EXPRESSIONS.

Alongst, 132, *along*
Appayd, 134, *paid*
Arrant, 253, *term of depreciation*
Articlers, 262-3, *drawers up of articles*
Barrettors, 186, *slanderers*
Be-painted, 196, *A. S. prefix*
Bœuf, 155, *beef*
Brabble, 23, *a dispute*
Branglinge, 234, *contentious*
Burgoisses, 193-4, *burgesses*
Cædar, 2, 91, 109, 173, etc., *cedar*
Cape merchant. *See* Index
Capitulations, 153, *stipulations*
Censure, 38, 254, *sentence*
Cloyed, 230, *choked*
Condeinge, 11, *conning,* a nautical term[1]
Coneycatching, 184, *cheating. Pigeoning*
Corps du garde, 237-8, *guardroom*
Delicate hopes, 264, *fond imaginations*
Embote, 53, *embark*
Endammage, 259, *A. S. prefix*
Fashionable, 39, *well fashioned*
Fiddle upon, 47, *prey vpon*
Galamafry, 288, *a confusion*
Gaster, 51, *frighten*
Geason, 232, *of inferior quality*

Go through stick, 71, "*go through thick and thin*"
Heraught, 72, *herald*
Houte, Howete, 41, 51, *hoot*
Ingenio, 206, 210, 291, *engine*
Loqueut, 242, *talkative*
Matachin, 19. *See* note in l. c.
Moores, 243, *negroes*
Opposite, 268, *opponent*
Panele, 226, *a kind of coarse sugar*
Portage, 16, *carriage of a thing*
Prolefull, 159, *prolific*
Provisoe upon the By, 206, *an incidental condition*
Pursuivant, 27, *officer of justice in pursuit*
Respectfully, 255, *respectively*
Saluted to the shoe, 74, *a profound salute*
Scoggin's dole, 59 (unknown)
Shent, 232, *shorn of, mulcted*
Skirmage, 229, *skirmish*
Snib, 129, 249, *snub?*
To take in snuff, 257, *to take in dudgeon*
Twang, 52, 263, *cabal or party*

---

[1] To Cond or Cun (*pronounced* cunning) vox nautica exp. Gubernatorem docere quomodo temonem dirigat. *Manwayring* in Dictionario Naut. deflectit à Lat. *conducere.* Mallem ab A.S. *cunnan,* scire, noscere, etc.— Skinner, *Etymologicon Linguæ Anglicanæ,* MDCLXXI.

INDEX.

Accidents in gunnery, 150
Acts of 1620, list of, 199
Adulteration denounced, 185
Alarms, false, 31, 93, 236
——— orders providing for, 280
Amazon River, 34
Ambergrece, 18, 21, 22, 27, 28, 30, 160
——————— its value, 164, 218, 273
Apprentices imported, 189, 205
——————— sale of, 273
Aqua vitæ, 67, 134, 137-8, 281-3
Argoll, Captain, 132, 211
Armada, the Spanish, 60
Armament in 1618, 107
Artillery. *See* Guns
Assembly the first, 188-90, 216, 292
———— its constitution, 193, 308
———— its difficulties, 203, *n*.
———— its rules and officers, 198
———— room erected for, 232
Assistants to Governor, 60
Assizes, 77, 78, 87, 89, 139, 156, 176, 187, 228, 233, 279, 286
——— charge to, 177
——— mode of conducting them, 176
——— when held, 201
Auditors, appointed by the Virginia Company, 128
Azores, 85

Bahamas, 85
Bailiffs or baylies, 77, 140, 154, 193, 287, 289
——— all fined, 228
——— petition Butler, 167
Baker, a pirate, 251, 257
Ballot, practise of, 131
Barker, Judge, 79
Barnstaple, ship of, 189, 216, 272, 276
Barrett, engineer, 35
Barrettors, common slanderers, 186
Bartlett, surveyor, 29, 36, 37, 39
Bedford, Countess of, 106
——— tribe, 106
Beer exported, 264
——— recovered from a wreck, 188
Bermuda, description of, 1, 2
——————— discovery, 9
——————— a locality in London, 45 *n*.

Bermuda Company, 128
Billetting of mariners, 266
Birds, enumeration of, 3
——— remark on the flight of, 3
——— abundance of, 13
Bishop, appeal to, 112
Boat escapes attempted, 13, 113
Boat voyage to Ireland, 79, 182
Boundaries Act, 202
Brazil, 85
Breakers, Mill's, 225
Bridges, 201, 228, 232
Brother Islands, 102
Bunbury, Mr. E. H., 9 *n*
Burgesses chosen, 188, 193
——————— their duties, 198, 313
Burning alive for petty treason, 180
——— in the hand, 187, 233, 287
——— of King's Castle, 151
Butler, James, 243
Butler, Nathaniel, Governor, 120-2
——— how elected, 131, 132
——— arrives, 148, 290
——— his first proclamations, 160
——— his first dispatch, 162
——— letter to the bailiffs, 168
——— acts as judge, 176
——— charge to the grand jury, 177, 187
——— speech to the Assembly, 194
——— reply to the Company, 215
——— erects a new residence, 231
——— charges against him, 249
——— his defence, 253
——— quits the island, 293

Cabins of palmetto leaves, 23
Caca-roache, 6
Cahows, 3, 41, 87
Canary Islands, 47
Cannibalism, case of, 65
Cape merchant, 69, 75, 97, 184, 210, 267, 272, 277
Carter, Christopher, 14, 16, 99, 249, 273
Carvel, Caravel, 93, 97
Cassada, Cassava, 238, 285
Castle, the King's, 35, 77, 87, 170, 200, 215

Y

Caswell, Mr. R., 211, 213
Cats, wild, 5, 92
Cattle sent from England, 42, 85, 124
—— difficulties with, 223, 260
Cavendish, Lord, 106, 160
Caves, allusion to them, 71
Cedar, exported, 80, 84
Chance medley, definition of, 181
Charge, Butler's, 187
Charles Fort, 107, 238
Children pressed, 205, 286
Church, erection of, 26, 137, 142, 161
—— assemblies held in, 192, 216
—— of England, 112, 153, 178
—— endowment of, 124
—— liturgy unpopular, 171
—— State services, 273
Churchwardens, 229, 283
Civic feasting, example of, 247
Clergy, benefit of, 90, 187, 233
—— demand for, 293, 294, 297
—— dissensions of, 57
—— opposition to the Governor, 24, 49, 50, 54, 61, 91, 112
——. *See* Ministers
Clerk of the Store, 58
Cockroaches, etymology of name, 6
Coin, its scarcity, 227
Commission, the Governor's, 75, 134, 148, 152
Common Prayer, use insisted on, 112
Communion Cup, presentation of, 211, 221
Company, The Virginia, 17, 26, 28, 39
—— business ill-conducted, 296
—— confiscates goods, 98
—— factions in it, 120, 122, 128, 130
—— general letters of, 209, 226
—— policy, its selfishness, 240
Conformity expected, 112
—— not secured, 171
Conies, 5
Coney Catching, 184
Cooper's Island, 39, 41, 273
Corn, Act for setting, 202
—— means of preserving, 281
—— supply to forts, 134, 201
—— want of, 210
—— (wheat), a failure, 3
Corporal chastisement, 79, 110, 111
Corruption of Officers, 141
Council, contempt of, 299
Counsellors of tribes, 281, 289
Crayford, shipmaster, 139
Criminal offences, list of, 181
Crowther-Crowder, 251, 257
Cudgel, its employment, 79, 110, 111, 261
Cuffe tobacco, 184
Cunningham Fort, 21

Dale, Sir Thomas, his orders, 77
Danby, 137, 139, 249
David's Island, 282
Davis, sea captain, 21, 23, 27
Deane, Paul, 90, 294
Defamation, extent of, 186
Defence arrangements, 52, 237
—— insufficiency of, 296
Delawne, 261
Delbridge, J., free trader, 27, 189, 216, 225, 272
Desertions, attempted, 113
Devils, Demonios, Isle of, 10
Devonshire Redoubt, 167, 215
—— —— Tribe, 106
Dice, use of, 252, 260
Discovery of Bermuda, 9
Division or dividend of tobacco, 207, 212
Drunkenness, prevalence of, 48, 59, 62, 67, 138, 185, 227
Dutch carpenter, 163, 250, 254
—— cruisers, 165, 166, 189, 212, 214, 220, 257
—— wreck, 146, 163, 164
Dutton, J., Bailiff, 148, 250, 255, 295

Ears, cutting off of, 140, 302
East India Company, 130
Egg, birds, 4
Elfrey, D., sea-rover, 33, 47, 132
Exchange, bills of, 210, 219
Execution of John Wood, 78, 89
—— —— of Paul Deane, 90, 294
—— —— of John Yates, 114
—— —— of one man, 187, 188
—— —— of two men, 287
Exercises, martial, 188, 229
Expenses, public, how met, 106

Famines or great scarcities, 33, 34, 40, 41, 159
Farrars, J. *See* Ferrars
Faucett, the widow, 30
Felgate, R., Captain, 35, 151, 155, 165, 299
Fencing, Act relating to, 202
Ferrars, Mr. John, 252, 262
Ferry at Burnt Point, 229
Fidicena tibicen, scissors grinder, 6
Figs, abundance of, 3, 84, 85
Fires, accidental, 150, 167
Fire resorted to, 91
Fish, abundance of, 6, 41, 43
—— primitive way of catching, 43
Fisher, Captain Edward, 33, 34
Flemish wreck, 68
Fluellen, a settler, 254

INDEX.   323

Flying fish, 65
Forced levies, 90
Forged letter imposes on D. Tucker, 119
Fortifications, 23, 29, 35, 39, 87, 161, 167, 169, 215
——— ——— list of, 107
Freedom of trade required, 240, 297
Freight on tobacco, 159, 209, 217
French Protestant Liturgy adopted, 172
French rovers, 47, 83, 86
Fresh water discovered, 282
Frigates, trading with W. Indies, 47, 70, 93, 144, 164

Gabriell or Gabry, N., 99, 100, 211
Gates, Sir Thomas, 14
General land, 106
General letters, 207, 269
Generality, a phrase for free men, 204, 212
Geneva Liturgy, 172
Glebe lands, 124
Gaol fever, 205
Goats, 5, 252, 260
Godwin, W., 79
Governor, how paid, 122, 125
——— ——— receives gifts, 146, 257
——— ——— spoke in assembly covered, 197
——— ——— Act relating to, 202
——— ——— addresses the Spanish ambassador, 275
——— ——— his guard, 176, 273, 283
——— ——— his progresses, 238
Grand jury, the first, 177
Grapes, their failure, 217
Great men's letters, 123
Grievances of the colonists, 241, 291, 293, 294, 296
Grove, Provost Marshall, 137, 141, 249
Guernsey and Jersey, Liturgy, of, 171, 172
Gunpowder plot, 273
——— ——— supply of, 32, 268
——— ——— waste of, 212, 220
Guns, recovered from wrecks, 26, 163, 237, 286, 289, 290, 291
Gurnet's Head, 26, 28, 29, 31, 32, 35, 170

Halbardiers, 176, 273
Halver, tenant on shares, 228
Hambleton, Marquis of, 106
Handicraftsmen bound to work, 229
Harbouring pirates, 212
Harcourt, R., 34, *n.*
Harriot, T., his sedition, 298, 299, 302
Hardships of settlers, 220, 297, 303
Hardinge, W., 301

Harvests, two yearly, 8, 159
Hats, wearing, a sign of dignity, 299
Healthfulness of climate, 8
Hearns or Herons, protection of, 233
Herrera, his history, 9
Hellicott, mariner, 97
High treason defined, 179
Highways Act, 201
Hilliard, Andrew, his sufferings at sea, 63
Hind, polygamist, 249
Hogs, wild, 5, 10, 13
———, Acts relating to, 230
Hog money, 76
Hope, Sir John, 305
Hostile projects against the settlement, 169
Hughes, Rev. Lewis, 49, 58, 60, 72, 81, 91, 111, 143, 152, 243, 245, 291, 301, 317
——— a Welshman, 57
——— boldness of, 50, 54, 112
——— quarrels with Tucker, 111
——— departs for England, 225
——— returns, 268
Hurricanes, or great gales, 60, 92, 156, 161

Immigrants. *See* Passengers
Indian corn, 3
Indian slave, the first imported, 84
Indictment, bills of, 178
Indigo, 3
Inglesbie, Jarvis, 317
Intemperance, its prevalence, 59, 138, 185
Interruption of preachers, 113, 301
Intrigues to get rid of D. Tucker, 118
Ireland Island, 105, 124
Irish fight, 229
Italian language, use of, 165

Jerusalem compared with Bermuda, 1
Johnson, Alderman, 131, 243
Joynes, Rev. R., 272
Justices of the peace, 289

Katherine's Fort, 35, 236
Keath, Rev. G., 24, 49, 56, 57, 73
——— a Scot, 57
——— his audacity, 24
Kendall, Edwin, 21, 22, 23, 27, 242
Kendall, Miles, 44, 121, 299
——— acting Governor, 122
——— intrigues to continue, 134
——— his riotous living, 159
——— superseded by Butler, 149, 152
——— goes to England, 225

Kendall, supported by Sir E. Sandys, 242, 248
—— returns to Bermuda, 269
Killock, a boat anchor, 64
"Kings", the three so-called, 17, 20
King's Castle, 35, 77, 87, 170, 200, 215
Kirby, a pirate, 144, 242, 246, 278
—— his death, 279
Land to the N.W., indications of, 3
Lang, Rev., 142, 212, 221
Law of England claimed, 297
Laws must be confirmed by the Company, 297
Lead, scarcity of, 290
Letters to the Company, 293
Lewes, Mr. *See* Hughes
Lignum vitæ, trade in, 84
Limestone sent to Virginia, 285
Liquor, great consumption of, 227
Liquors, supply of, 58
—— illicit traffic in, 226
Liturgy of Guernsey and Jersey, 171
Llewellin, Roger, 211
Loblolly, a porridge, 48, 66, 135
Lords, arbitrament of the, 124, 132, 211

Machiavel, a term of reproach, 55
Magazine ships, 110, 163, 189, 203, 242
Maine, The, a geographical expression, 67, 72, 77, 101, 136, 151, 237
Mallory, a settler, 301
Mangrove, bark for tanning, 98
Mansfield, John, 44, 52
—— Sir Robert, 106, 160
Manslaughter defined, 181
Matachin, or Matachina, 19
May, Henry, his shipwreck, 10
Meal, supplies of, 33, 44, 132
Melons, growth of, 3
Mellinge, Mr. T., 247, 249
Milford Lane, Strand, 45, *n.*
Mill's breakers, 225
Minister, arrival of one, 142, 242
—— trial of one, 54
—— house built for, 87
—— *See* Clergy
Misprision of treason defined, 180
Moore, Mr. R., first Governor, 17, 19, 20, 45, 60, 136
—— severe treatment by the Company, 39, 103
Moores, negroes so called, 243
Mount, the first, 28, 107, 137, 161
—— the second, 173, 204, 225
—— Keeper, 236
Mulberry sen. *Conocarpus,* 2, 3, 30
—— proper. *Morus,* 218

Murderers (a class of guns), 147, 289, 290
Musk melons, 3
Musquitoes, 6
Musters of all able to bear arms, 188

Needham, a settler, 252, 260
Negro slaves, imported, 84, 99, 144, 146, 211
—— —— dispute about, 242
—— —— owned by the Company, 219
Newfoundland, attempt to escape to, 19
—— —— trade with, 140
Newgate supplies emigrants, 204
Newport, Captain, 11
North, John, 211
—— Nathaniel, 211
Norwood, R., 77, 104
—— his alleged corruption, 104
—— his survey, 105, 106

Officers of the forts, 77
Olives, wild, 2, 3
Oranges and lemons, 3
Ordnance. *See* Guns
Ottwell, Provost Marshall, 252, 261
Overplus, The, its origin, 104, 106
—— appropriation of it, 132, 211
—— Tucker's house on it, 109, 111, 156
Overseers, annual, 288, 289
Oyeros, Oyez ! a cry, 176
Oysters, pearl, 291

Paget's Fort, 24, 26, 39, 88, 144, 231, 236, 239, 241
—— tribe, 106
Palmetto berries eaten, 64
—— cabbage, 33
—— houses, 23, 182
Panele, a coarse sugar, 226
Panique fears, essay on, 318
Parsnips grown, 3
Passengers, arrivals of, 17, 27, 28, 30, 35, 36, 142, 159, 189, 204, 225, 267, 268, 271
—— wretched stamp of some, 286
Pauper children, neglect of, 296
Payne, ——, a settler, 260
Paynter or Painter, S., 295
Pearl fishing, 291
Pembroke Fort, 39, 273
—— tribe, 106
Penal servitude, 294
Peniston's Fort, 23, 241
—— Island, 23
Perinchief, John, 317
Perjury denounced, 183

INDEX.   325

Perspective, glass, 164
Petition to the six Governors, 48
Petty juries, 176
Petty treason defined, 179
Philpot Lane, London, 128
Piety, example of, 32
Pigeon-house, a small redoubt, 241
Pillory, use of, 187-302
Pinuplicoe, Pimlico, 4
Pineapples, 3, 84, 98
Pinnaces, employment of, 36 37, 41
Piracy, acts of, 34, 37, 47, 85, 93, 98, 134, 144, 159, 212
—— danger of the Island becoming a centre of, 196, 209, 213
—— ill defined nature of, 214
Pirates, their ambiguous status, 48, 94, 96, 98, 214, 221, 242
Plague, suspicions of, 205
Plantains, abundance of, 3
Plants, enumeration of, 2, 3
Pocahontas and her companions, 271, 272
Poison, ivy, 2
Pollard, Mr., his trial, 99, 101, 103, 115, 117
Pomegranates, 3
Population, 30, 76, 227, 294
Port Royal, 42, 65, 81, 301
Portugals, 9, 47, 85, 86, 265
Potatoes, *Batatas*, 5
—— *Solanum*, 30, 285
Poultry, domestic, 5, 135, 285
Powell, a pirate, 85, 93, 95, 97, 102, 165, 239, 251, 257
Prayer-book objected to, 112, 171
Preachers, supply of, 211
Premunire threatened, 300
Presentments, 186, 229
Pressing of men, 286
Prices complained of, 295
Prickle pears, 2
Proclamations, 160, 166
Progresses, the Governor's, 67, 156, 237
Provisioning of forts, 201
Provisions seized, 160
—— obtained from a Dutch ship, 166
Provost Marshall, 35, 137
Puitt, Henry, 79
Pulpit, abuses of the, 24, 50

Radishes, grown, 3
Rats, the plague of, 5, 34, 90, 102, 132, 186
—— their sudden disappearance, 91
Readers, their duties, 283
Recusants not endured, 153
Reefs, their danger, 8, 265, 276

Registration of births, etc., 283
Reprieves at the gallows, 114, 140, 279
Reptiles, unknown, 6
Rhodes, climate compared with, 9
Riche, Geo., trial of, 101, 103 114, 117
—— a kinsman of the Earl of Warwick, 99
—— Mount, 174
—— Sir Nathaniel, 243
Roberts, ——, a planter, 211
Rosa solis (a liquor), 67, 138
Rules of the Virginia Company, 116

Sabbath observance, 249, 253
Sack (the wine), 138, 212, 220
St. George's, 19, 23, 28, 29, 33, 76
St. Katherine's Fort, 35, 236
Saker, piece of ordnance, 48, 241, 278, 286, 289, 290, 291
Salutes dispensed with by James I, 212
—— to Governors, 152, 154, 220
Sandys, Sir Edwin, 120, 131, 242, 247
—— elected Treasurer, 128, 130, 132, n.
—— his intemperance, 248
—— George (his brother), 120, 122
—— tribe, 42, 106, 265
Saunders, R., 79
Savage Islands, 38, 78, 85, 93, 132
Scandalum magnatum, case of, 301
Scarcity of provisions, 41, 166
"Scissors' grinder", 6
Scoggin's Dole, 59
Scot, ——, a planter, 261
Scoutin, Peter, a Dutch skipper, 145, 166
Sea-venture flats, 107, 290
Secretary, functions and fees of, 193, 219
Settlers, their complaints. *See* Grievances
Seymour, William, 315
Shark fishing, 237
Shares of land, 36, 77, 103, 104
Shingles, use of, 111
Shipping, *The Blessing*, 34, 115, 116, 123, 132 ; *Carwell*, 97 ; *Diana*, 110, 114 ; *Edwin*, 36, 37, 41, 43, 58, 69, 70, 71, 78, 84 ; *Elizabeth*, 27, 30 ; *Garland*, 155, 156, 163, 167, 185, 209, 313 ; *George*, 70, 72, 225, 246 ; *Gillyflower*, 125, 138, 140 ; *Hopewell*, 85, 86, 93, 95 ; *James*, 268 ; *Joseph*, 203, 216 ; *Margaret*, 36 ; *Martha*, 28, 29, 30 ; *Neptune*, 88, 92, 96, 97, 101 ; *Plough*, 17, 19, 26 ; *Rose*, 34, n.; *Seaflower*, 142 ; *Sea Venture*, 11, 26, 290 ; *Star*, 35 ; *Thomas*, 36,

INDEX.

43, 77; *Treasurer*, 132, 133, 140, 147, 156, 162, 250, 256; *Warwick*, 148, 151, 155, 156, 167, 188, 209, 237, 296; *Welcome*, 44, 45, 55; *Anon* (Delbridge's ship), 189, 216, 272, 276; Spanish prize, 33, 34
Shipwreck of H May, 10
—————— of Sir Geo. Somers, 11
——————— *See* Wrecks
Sickness on shipboard, 155, 204, 216, 265, 268
Sidesmen, their duty, 283
Silk culture, 30, 218
Silk spiders, 6
Simplicity, example of, 68
Six Governors, their appointment, 44, 47
Skirmishing, a mode of defence enjoined, 229
Slavery, penal, 295
Slaves. *See* Negroes
Smith, George, 213
—————— Captain John, 48, 57
—————— Sir Thomas, 20, 46, 82, 106, 116, 243
—————— frauds attributed to, 128, 129
Smith's Island, 20, 23
—————— Fort, 136, 144, 231, 239
Soil of the islands, 2
Somers, Sir George, his shipwreck, 11
—————————— his death, 15
—————————— stone, 15, 174, 305
—————————— commemorative inscription, 174
—————————— landing-place, 109
Somer's seat, *now* Somerset, 15, 42, 80, 87
Southampton, Earl of, 247
—————— Fort, 87, 161, 163, 215, 279
—————— tribe, 66, 106
Southwell, Captain, 120, 123, 128, 131
Spaniard's pillage of, condemned, 212
—————— wrecked, sent away, 274
Spanish treasure, 10
—————— hostility, 27, 276
—————— supposed attack, 31, 36
—————— wreck, 265
Stairs, public landing, 289
Stokes, Captain, 77
Storms, remarkable, 64, 92
Strappadoe, applications of, 57
Submerged rocks, indications of, to N.W., 266
Sugar cultivation, 3, 90, 206, 207, 210, 212, 217, 224, 230, 291
—————— soil not suited for, 217
—————— loaves, a handsome gift, 212, 220
—————— refiner sent out, 221

Sundial taken for navigation, 81

Tanning, attempts at, 98
Thomond, Earl of, his reception of runaways, 83
Three Kings of Bermuda, 18
Tobacco, 3, 29, 41, 110
—————— burning of, 224
—————— dividend of, 207, 208, 212, 214, 295
—————— export of, 224, 225
—————— freight of, 157, 209
—————— frauds in, 184
—————— how to be grown, 233
—————— office of triers, 238
—————— precautions taken, 222, 234
—————— proclamations concerning, 234
—————— quality of, 114, 167, 206, 234
—————— revenue paid in, 202, 219
—————— storm destroys, 267
Torches prohibited, 229
Tortoises. *See* Turtle
Torture, application of, 62, 63
Tower, —, Marshall, 35
Treasure, reports of, 10, 68
Treasurer, the disabled, 163
—————— fitted for freight, 157
Tribes, how laid out, 77, 105, 160
Triumviri, or Three Kings, 17
Trunk whale, 89
Tucker, Daniel, 63, 69, 70, 72, 85, 108
—————— his grant of land, 103, 106, 124
—————— his house at the Overplus, 109, 111, 114
—————— his fortifications, 107, 136
—————— leaves Bermuda, 122, 123
—————— intrigues at home, 131, 206, 211, 221, 247
Tucker, Mr., 69, 116
Tucker's town, 104
Turkeys, mention of, 135, 287
Turtle, Act for preservation of, 203

United provinces of Holland, 165, 209
Unnatural crimes, 183, 287

Vagabondage restrained, 202
Vine culture, 3, 76, 210, 212, 217
Virgin Islands, 78, 85, 132
Virginia, Somers reaches, 14
—————— commodities sent to, 277, 284, 285
Virginia Company, 11, 17, 128
—————— factions in, 116, 122, 127, 242
Virginian Constitution taken as a model, 75, 77
—————— maidens, attendants of Pocahontas, 271, 284

Walker, Robert, 102
Walters, Robert, 14
Ward, John, 213
Warnam, W., 257
Warwick, Earl of, his cattle, 85
—— his negroes, 211, 242
—— Sir E. Sandys, his enemy, 242, 247
—— Fort, 29, 62, 231
—— tribe, 106, 168
Warwick, wreck of the, 156
Water melons, 3
West Indies, trade with, 78, 84
Whale fishing, 88, 92, 256, 285
Whipper, a degrading office, 182
Whipping, a common punishment, 89, 182, 187, 233
Wild fowl, protection of, 233
—— hogs, 5, 10, 13
—— man of the woods, 43
Williams, Robert, 249, 252, 261
Wives assigned for sale, 271, 273
Wood, John, trial of, 78, 79
Wood, Ensign, his plots, 119, 134, 135

Wood killed by an accident, 147
Woodall, —, a settler, 251, 257
Woodward, Seymour, 151, 283, 315
Worsnam, Sir J., 131
Wreck, anonymous, 291
—— a Dutch, 145, 163
—— of the *Sea Venture*, 11, 290
—— of a Spanish ship, 9, 265, 278, 289, 291
—— of the *Warwick*, 156, 290
—— escape from, 276, 299
—— not complete if there are live creatures on board, 275
Wrecking practised, 146, 266
Wrongs pretended to have been committed by Butler, 249
Wyatt, Sir Thomas, letter to, 277
Wye, Capt. W., 313, 314

Yardley, Sir George, offerings to, 277, 278
Yates, Captain J., 134, 250, 255, 300, 303, 317
—— John, executed, 114, *n*.

www.ingramcontent.com/pod-product-compliance
Lightning Source LLC
Chambersburg PA
CBHW032351230426
43672CB00007B/669